Readings in
Applied Microeconomics

Readings in
Applied Microeconomics

edited by
LESLIE WAGNER
and
NIKOS BALTAZZIS

at The Open University

THE CLARENDON PRESS   OXFORD
IN ASSOCIATION WITH
THE OPEN UNIVERSITY PRESS
1973

Oxford University Press, Ely House, London W.1

GLASGOW NEW YORK TORONTO MELBOURNE WELLINGTON
CAPE TOWN IBADAN NAIROBI DAR ES SALAAM LUSAKA ADDIS ABABA
DELHI BOMBAY CALCUTTA MADRAS KARACHI LAHORE DACCA
KUALA LUMPUR SINGAPORE HONG KONG TOKYO

CASEBOUND ISBN 0 19 877046 1
PAPERBACK ISBN 0 19 877047 2

SELECTION AND EDITORIAL MATERIAL
COPYRIGHT © THE OPEN UNIVERSITY 1973

*All rights reserved. No part of this publication may
be reproduced, stored in a retrieval system, or transmitted
in any form or by any means, electronic, mechanical, photocopying,
recording, or otherwise, without the written permission of the
Publisher.*

PRINTED IN GREAT BRITAIN
BY RICHARD CLAY (THE CHAUCER PRESS) LTD
BUNGAY, SUFFOLK

Editors' Note

This book is the result of a collective effort and has developed out of the planning and preparation of a course at the Open University designed for second-level students of the social sciences. The joint editors wish to express their appreciation to the other members of the Course Team who have contributed in the preparation of the course in Microeconomics and this Reader:

Phil Batten	Ken Penney
F. S. Brooman	Andrew Pollard
R. Cookson	Pete Thomas
Frank Knox	Grahame F. Thompson
P. J. O'Leary	

Particular thanks are due to Phil Batten, Andrew Pollard, and Grahame Thompson. We jointly feel that a special mention of the assistance we have received from Pete Thomas in preparing the manuscript for publication will still understate his contribution, for we owe a great deal to his perseverance and patience during the time it took to prepare the book.

L. W.
N. B.

The Open University

Contents

Introduction

The past few years have seen a spate of books consisting of readings in economics. The field of microeconomics has been particularly well served. Therefore anyone proposing to add another collection of readings to the list ought to state clearly why such a collection is thought necessary. This can best be done by explaining how this reader evolved.

In planning the second-level course in Microeconomics at the Open University, the Course Team was faced with a number of problems relating to its objectives. From the very beginning it was felt that quite apart from presenting in rigorous terms the analytical tools of Microeconomic Theory, the relevance of these, their empirical verification, and their use in the consideration of everyday problems facing the community ought to be emphasized.

The Course Team was therefore faced with the problems of bringing together theory and practice. To establish that esoteric intellectual constructions are relevant to the analysis of empirical problems is not a simple task, especially when such constructs and the concepts behind them have to be developed virtually from scratch. But to attempt the exercise within the sixteen units available for a half-credit course at the Open University has been known to give rise to nightmares.

Nevertheless, a structure evolved and it was thought that the main emphasis on the applications of theory ought to come in the last part of the course. Here a selection of contemporary problems would be discussed using tools and methods developed in the earlier parts of the course. One of the partners in the relationship would have to precede the other. The second's belated entrance would be made more interesting, and we hope more appealing, after the audience had endured the exhaustive rigours of the first's performance. Glimpses of the second partner were, however, to be allowed not only to sustain the first's monologue, but to heighten expectations as to the thrill of the later dialogue. Thus, wherever possible, unit authors turned to the real world for their examples. Indeed the course itself opens with a comparative presentation of the two main allocative and distributional systems.

It is self-evident that if one is to teach students how to use the tools of analysis one needs to use examples. At the early stages such examples can be made up and the number of points to be emphasized can be restricted at will. Ideally one would wish to guide the student gently in his efforts to swim from shallow to deeper waters. It was in their attempts to steer such a course that the Course Team faced problems which led to the genesis of this reader. Although difficulties arise when a set book is to be chosen for a course, which together with the units provide the main reading material for students, such difficulties seem minor compared to those of finding suitable empirical material of a particular level and rigour, which would not make undue demand on the students' mathematical and statistical expertise. Within the course, mathematical as well as statistical elements are introduced and used in the discussion of, among others, demand determination and cost estimation, as well as in the formulation and resolution of optimization problems. There is, however, a limit to what can be included in a microeconomic course without imparting a particular bias to it.

Starting from the assumption that our students would have had little or no experience in manipulating estimating equations or deriving least-squares coefficients, and firmly bearing in mind that many students are deterred, if not actually frightened away, by too much technicality, at best losing the wood for the trees, the Course Team decided to gather such articles as would meet the students' requirements through their clarity and limited technicality. Thus, one objective was to aim for an intermediate level which would run parallel to that of the course. Another objective was to minimize the problems that might arise through the use of works based on non-British data. Nevertheless, cases arose when it was felt that on balance, foreign publications ought not to be excluded and this has resulted in the inclusion of, for example, the article by W. J. Baumol and W. E. Oates in Part IV. A further objective was to ensure that the empirical material was as up to date as possible. So the justification for this reader is that it deals with recent empirical and applied material relating mainly to British experience. As such we feel that it fills a gap in the literature currently available.

The contents of this book have been structured so as to take account of the pattern of the course in which it will be used. It is therefore divided into four parts. The first part, Planning and Prices, is composed of four readings. These include a review of the merits and disadvantages of a centrally planned and a decentralized economic system, the description of some of the problems faced by a particular market, housing, in both systems, and a discussion of the hypothesis of convergence of the systems. The second part contains five readings. The first two articles examine the problem of the existence and measurement of economies of scale in industrial production. The remaining three readings cover the area of supply price determination, analysing and documenting the different hypotheses put forward by the theory of the firm. In the third part the empirical determination of demand in three distinct markets, those of tobacco, herring and cars, is introduced by a chapter from a well-known textbook and concluded with an article on second-hand goods markets. Finally Part IV covers a variety of topics which come under the general heading of contemporary problems. Cost–benefit analysis and its application to the problems of slums as well as those of choosing a site for a new airport are the topics of three articles. Two readings deal with the problems of traffic congestion and the last one considers the likely effects of violent changes and disturbances on the resource allocation system. The use of the price system to tackle problems created by the existence of externalities is the subject of another reading in this part.

When, after some preliminary searches, it became clear that no other British publication existed covering the ground at the level of sophistication this reader has been chosen to do, the interests of the general student of microeconomics, who is preoccupied with the use of theory in empirical work, were added to the objective function of the Course Team involved in the preparation of the book. The result is a collection of articles and parts of books which could form part of the basis for an integrated course in microeconomics at second-year undergraduate level. This book, of course, suffers from the same disadvantages that all collections of readings are subject to, namely the variation in style and level of its component parts. It is, nevertheless, hoped that these parts will appear to have a common set of elements in their approach and methodology even though each one is concerned with a different particular problem of micro-economics.

PART I
Planning and Prices

Introduction to Part I

In what circumstances would central planning be superior to a decentralized system? Could the infusion of planning techniques improve the efficiency of the market economy in allocating resources? Is central planning always preferable? Or only in some situations? These fundamental questions are discussed by Richardson in the first reading. He points to a problem, common to all economies, of developing a system of information capable of accurately transmitting knowledge about scarcity, techniques, wants, and so forth. One problem of the centrally planned economy is that drawing up a plan which achieves an efficient allocation requires more knowledge than it is possible to collect. Even in the unlikely event of this being achieved, creating an integrated plan in which all the parts perfectly balance is an administrative impossibility, at least at the moment. And, for different reasons, an economy relying on the price mechanism is unlikely to achieve an optimum allocation of resources, for prices are imperfect knowledge carriers.

Richardson goes on to discuss situations in which a degree of decentralization would improve the efficiency of a centrally planned economy; and follows by considering the possible beneficial effects that the introduction of planning would have in a hitherto decentralized system. On the one hand, he sees the major benefits of decentralization as flexibility to change in consumer demand, sensitivity to the need for continual product improvement, and the downward pressure exerted by competition on profits and costs. Even so, firms may still benefit from planning. This will be true in the obvious cases where some firms are heavily dependent on each other; but this observation will hold for most firms if planning is interpreted as the systematic prediction of demand and supply. This, however, will only be possible when an individual firm has attracted a large enough clientele, as this alone makes prediction statistically feasible. But, if continuous product development is less important and the good in question homogeneous, then the advantages of decentralization—even with 'piecemeal planning'—may well be outweighed by the benefits of central planning.

This eclectic approach is consolidated by the second and third readings, which offer an illustration of how two countries—the Soviet Union and the United Kingdom—have respectively operated their versions of central planning and free market with regard to housing. Despite different ways of running their housing industries, a number of interesting similarities spring to mind. In both countries the central and local authorities have played a considerable role, particularly in the last twenty-five years. The U.K., for instance, re-acted to the Second World War by making the aspirations of the general public for better housing a primary political objective for all parties. The Soviet Union, though, had to wait until the post Stalin liberalization before significant changes in political attitudes were possible, and the wants of consumers accorded a more important position when drawing up state plans. But by the late 1950s, however, cheap housing had come to be considered as a cardinal political rule in both countries.

The measures taken by both governments were in some ways very similar. Both resorted to rent controls, though they were, of course, more rigid in the Soviet Union. In the private-housing sector of the U.K. (which has no Soviet equivalent), the government has taken measures which in effect have subsidized purchasers. And each state tried hard to boost the production of houses; but in neither country was the housing industry entirely under government control. They have, moreover, faced common difficulties: the supply of housing must at any time remain very inelastic; and World War II merely aggravated a situation in which housing requirements exceeded total supply. The need to expand construction quickly meant huge investments in materials, labour and land, which were not easily available in countries committed to full employment and the consequent pressure on all inputs. If all this was not enough, in both countries there has been a steady rise in costs throughout the post-war period.

What have been the results of these policies? The readings point to the increasing cost of housing to the consumer and lower standards in building and maintenance. In the U.K. market for private houses prices have rocketed and at the same time the government policy of subsidizing purchasers has come under attack. And what is visible in the house purchase market in this country reveals itself, though less obviously, in the market for rented accommodation, despite its semi-controlled status. In the U.S.S.R. the effort to provide low-cost accommodation has been associated with a fall in building and maintenance standards. Soviet housing costs rise and the gap between rents and costs widens each year. The dilemma facing the Soviet authorities is simple: either further subsidization is accepted or rents are allowed to rise. In a slightly modified way, this is the situation in the United Kingdom.

The final reading discusses the interesting debate of 'convergence'. Bornstein attempts to establish a theoretical basis by drawing on positive theories (Rostow's theory of economic development for instance), and on normative theories, based either on sociological evidence, or on Tinbergen's notion of the ideal economic system. Convergence, therefore, becomes a matter of a narrowing of the differences between economic systems. As for evidence, Bornstein turns to the post-war economic developments in the market and centrally planned economies. In the U.K., for instance, a greater role is now played by the state than hitherto; production in the privately-owned sector of the economy has become increasingly concentrated; and, furthermore, ownership has become separated from control, with concomitant changes in decision-making motivation. All of these have been subjected to a great deal of attention from economists. In contrast, therefore, the short period since the introduction by Eastern European countries and the U.S.S.R. of significant changes in their economies excludes the benefits of hindsight. And so, like all Western scholars, Bornstein has been limited to an outline of the intentions of these countries and any early changes effected or rejected. You should bear in mind that aims and objectives are often more ambitious than achievement, and the case for and against convergence appreciably altered.

1

Planning Versus Competition

by G. B. Richardson

SCOPE AND METHOD

What are the proper roles, in economic organization, of planning and of competition? In what circumstances should economic activities be fitted together deliberately through a coherent set of instructions given by a central authority? And when should this co-ordination be left to the spontaneous interaction of independent, decentralized decisions? Is planning essentially an alternative to competition or can it be employed, in an indicative form, not to replace but somehow to illuminate, guide and thereby improve the operation of market forces? These questions, it need hardly be said, admit of no definite answer, objectively valid irrespective of time and place. Nevertheless, they are real questions of obvious practical importance, so that it is worth while trying to find some answers to them, however partial and provisional these may be.

I wish to make only two preliminary observations, one about scope, the other about method. The scope of this paper is very wide. But its subject is competition versus planning, not capitalism versus socialism; the questions which I raised at the outset pose themselves in countries which have no private property in the means of production but seek to decentralize decision-taking. In so far as method is concerned, I seek justification in terms of what Sir Roy Harrod has called, rather grandly, the need for Continuing Conceptual Refurbishment. I try to take a fresh look at the first principles. Progress

From *Soviet Studies*, vol. xxii, No. 3 (Jan. 1971), pp. 433–47. Reprinted by permission of the author and the editor of *Soviet Studies*.

in economics does not depend only upon rigorous analysis, observation and measurement; it requires also that effort of imagination that enables us partially to escape from conventional categories of thought. Being realistic is not merely a question of testing hypotheses, important though this is; it also requires sustained and strenuous effort to consider whether our inherited stock of theoretical constructions do not distort our vision of the plain facts of economic life.

THE TASK OF ECONOMIC ORGANIZATION

Let us begin at the beginning and ask what it is that we want competition or planning to accomplish. The answer might be that their function is to secure an efficient allocation of resources. To say this, however, although obviously correct, may be misleading. For we normally concentrate, in economic theory, on the pure logic of resource allocation and, in order to exhibit this logic clearly, we assume that both ends and means are given. Thus we assume, in the so-called theory of consumers' behaviour, that income, prices and tastes are given and concern ourselves exclusively with the logic of choice. And when we turn to the economy as a whole and seek to establish conditions for efficient allocation in Pareto's sense, we follow the same procedure; we adopt the vantage point of someone standing outside the system with full knowledge of all the relevant preferences, resources and productive techniques. This approach is justified in that it enables us to focus our attention on the pure principles of economizing; but it is important, when we turn to consider the working of economic organization, to keep well in mind the obvious fact that in reality no one is provided with a bird's-eye view. Allocative decisions are in fact taken, and in the nature of things have to be taken, on the basis of individual beliefs and opinions, usually uncertain and sometimes contradictory. It is not merely that our knowledge is probabilistic in character; the point is that it is fragmented, in the form of imperfectly consistent estimates held by different people. The function of economic organization is therefore to make the best use of this knowledge, and, in appraising the relative effectiveness of different systems, we have to think in terms not only of allocative logic but of search and discovery.

Let us suppose that a body of men land on a desert island on which, in a variety of places, buried treasure is to be found. If the men have with them a map showing the location of treasure throughout the island, then a plan of campaign can readily be drawn up. The appropriate organization is that of central planning, each man being given a particular job to do. Of course there will be problems of incentives, of distribution and so on, but the propriety of centralized decision-taking can scarcely be in doubt. But let us now suppose that there is no map, or at least no map in existence that can be presumed accurate. Each man may have bits and pieces of information that he considers relative to the location of the treasure, but no more. There is now room for choice between alternative forms of organization. The centralized solution would be to invite the men to pool their information and opinions and endeavour therefrom to construct a map of the most likely location of the treasure; a plan of campaign could then be drawn up and jobs allocated. The purely decentralized solution would be to allow each man to go forth and dig where he liked. Now these alternative approaches differ in two ways. Under central planning, the activities of different men will be co-ordinated by means of a set of integrated instructions which, ideally, will produce an optimum pattern of search—or allocation of resources—with respect to the evidence and opinion embodied in the map. Under *laissez-faire*, on the other hand, such co-ordination as does take place will be the unintended result of each man taking account of what the others are doing; if, for example, men start to crowd in one corner of the island, then some will no doubt be induced to seek their fortunes in other areas where, if the evidence of treasure is less strong, the competition is weaker. Clearly, therefore, planning and competition represent alternative techniques of co-ordination; less obvious, perhaps, is that they differ also in the way in which they make use of knowledge. Under central planning, evidence and opinion will be consolidated in order to construct the map on which the programme of search is to be based. Under *laissez-faire*, however, each and every opinion will affect the pattern of search provided that whoever holds it is in possession of a pick and shovel. Now it does not seem to me possible, unless the circumstances are further specified, to say whether the consolidation of knowledge will improve the pattern of search; it is easy to see that something will be gained, as bits of the jigsaw are fitted together, but easy to see also that something may be lost if heterodox opinions are sacrificed in the name of consistency, and new findings, if they appear to threaten the presumptions of the

plan, are quietly put aside. All that one can say at this stage is that
the relative merits of planning and competition are not solely a
matter of the way in which they co-ordinate interrelated activities;
they depend also on whether, in a particular set of circumstances, it
is desirable to endeavour to weld a variety of estimates and opinions
into some kind of coherent whole.

I hope that the relevance of this naïve analogy is reasonably clear.
In normative economics, when considering how best to adapt means
to ends, we assume that we have knowledge of the available resources, opportunities and objectives in order to concentrate on the
logic of the problem. In positive economics, on the other hand,
when we come to consider how particular systems would work, this
assumption has to be abandoned. Maps are not provided; economic
organization has to find some way of constructing maps or of doing
without them. In a centrally planned system, the authorities take
steps to prepare a map; after discussions with the subordinate bodies
in the hierarchy, with the various industrial commissions or their
equivalents, they specify a feasible and desired future composition
of output and then proceed to give appropriate instructions designed
to ensure that it is produced. Consistency is thereby produced not
necessarily, of course, with resources, technical possibilities and needs
as they objectively exist, but with one central agreed or imposed conception of what these are. In practice, of course, planning systems
will differ as to the detail in which the future pattern of output is
set down, but the essence of the matter is that resources are allocated
according to some central view of objectives and opportunities built
up through some organized consolidation of the information in the
hands of the central and subordinate bodies.

In competitive systems, firms do what they like in pursuit of
profit and a large part of economic analysis is devoted to discussing
whether this will cause the right things to be produced in the right
amounts. The price mechanism is supposed to do the trick; if too
much of a good is produced, the price will sink below costs; if too
little, it will remain above them; in either event the profit motive,
combined with free mobility and competition, should bring the
required adjustment. For the flawless operation of this mechanism—
subject to qualifications about externalities, etc.—most economists
put forward an institutional blue-print, perfect competition, while
acknowledging with regret that scale economies may make it
impossible to secure its full realization in practice. Now I have

maintained elsewhere that perfect competition, even if realizable, could never do what is claimed of it.[1] The essence of the matter can be put quite briefly, but there is no room here for the full supporting argument. Under perfect competition, it would be quite impossible for any firm to know how much of a good to produce. According to the usual story, entrepreneurs are guided by prices; each of them sets an output that equates the price of the good he sells to its marginal cost. Now it is clear that current prices cannot be the appropriate signals; they reflect the appropriateness of past output decisions but are not directly relevant to decisions about what to produce for the future. Presumably, therefore, firms are supposed to equate marginal costs to future prices. But how then is a producer able to predict future prices, depending as they do both on the demands of consumers and on the supply plans of all his competitors? This the textbooks do not tell us; the most we are likely to be told is that producers are assumed to know what the relevant future prices are. But a little reflection suffices to show that even this is not enough to ensure that firms know what to do and that, as a result of their actions, the equilibrium configuration of output is obtained. For let us imagine that the system is out of equilibrium but that the true equilibrium prices are somehow announced to all producers as from on high. How would the possession of this information enable the individual firm to know which goods to produce, or cease producing, and in what quantities? If the future price of a good were known to be greater than the current cost of making it, then a profit opportunity may be said to exist; but if there is an unlimited number of firms equally able and ready to respond to the opportunity no individual firm will know whether to do so. A profit opportunity which is available equally for everyone is in fact available to no one at all.

My own view, therefore, is that there would be no tendency under conditions of perfect competition for the equilibrium associated with it ever to be attained. My fear is that the brief argumentation just provided will not persuade anyone who has not already accepted this view now to accept it. In any case a large number of economists —perhaps even an increasing number—continue to maintain (even

---

[1] See my *Information and Investment* (London, 1960), chs. 1 and 2. The same matter is dealt with, though less fully, in my article 'Equilibrium, Expectations and Information', *Economic Journal*, vol. lxix (1959), pp. 223–37.

although unable to prove) that perfect competition would produce the outputs and prices associated with its so-called equilibrium position. But it is particularly interesting to note that the founding fathers of the doctrine—or at least Walras and Edgeworth—had their doubts; they were aware of the informational deficiencies of perfect competition and sought to offer some remedy. Both suggested hypothetical systems of recontracting designed to ensure that the plans of producers and consumers were welded into a consistent set. Offers to supply a particular good were made, it will be recalled, first on a provisional basis, and did not become firm commitments until, after repeated revisions, plans to buy were seen to be consistent with plans to produce and sell. We shall consider later the way in which these proposals prefigure the organized dialogues of indicative planning. The question now before us is whether such a network of forward contracts, quite apart from administrative cost and complexity, does in fact provide a theoretical answer to the problem of co-ordination that the price mechanism, in perfect competition, cannot by itself resolve. I maintain that it does not. The obstacle to creating a complete and consistent network of contracts, in the last analysis, is simply the imperfection of our knowledge. Consumers do not wish to contract for their future purchases because they cannot foretell what their future needs and opportunities will be; and producers do not generally wish to commit themselves to forward purchases of inputs because they cannot predict the productive possibilities that will be open to them. By supposing that the network of contracts could ever be complete and closed, we assume away that essential imperfection of knowledge with which economic organization has somehow to cope.

HOW COMPETITIVE SYSTEMS WORK

But where do we go from here? I have rejected the traditional model of the working of a decentralized economic system, perfect competition; the introduction of a complementary apparatus of forward contracts, I have further argued, merely evades the problems created by the imperfection of knowledge. But free enterprise systems, as even their keenest critics would admit, do in fact work, at least imperfectly; central planning might work better, but one could not maintain that we have chaos without it. Let us therefore endeavour to set out how the market system does work, for until this is clear we are not likely to be able to judge how far, and in what ways, central planning can usefully supplement or replace it.

If we are to explain how the economic world goes round—at least, the capitalist world—we have, I believe, to attend to three circumstances. First, there takes place within it a great deal of what, for want of a better term, I shall call piecemeal planning. Secondly, much reliance is put on the fact that aggregates are often more predictable than are, on average, their several components. And thirdly there have evolved market structures and codes of business behaviour which facilitate foresight and thereby permit enterprise planning. We shall now deal with each of these circumstances in turn.

(a) *Piecemeal Planning*

Walras taught us, in his general equilibrium analysis, that all economic activities are interdependent; but, although this interdependence is universal, some activities are more interdependent than others. Consider the relationship between intermediate and final output. General-purpose inputs, such as steel and fork-lift trucks, will normally be bought on a market; the individual user will not choose to place contracts much in advance of his future requirements, and the individual seller will hope to secure some stability and predictability in the demand for his output by having a number of different accounts on his books. But in the case of specific-purpose inputs bought by only one firm or very few firms, other arrangements will generally prevail. Piecemeal planning will generally be the best means of dealing with close complementarity, both quantitative and qualitative, between output plans. It has to secure quantitative co-ordination, in the sense of making the rate of output of a final good appropriate to the rate of output of the required inputs; thus refining capacity has to be in balance with crude oil supplies. It has also to secure qualitative co-ordination where, for example, the development of a nylon polymer has to be hand in hand with the development of the processes used to spin it. Joint production planning and joint product development can be secured by a variety of techniques ranging from loose inter-company understanding to full vertical integration. A highly informal but highly effective form of piecemeal planning is conducted by Marks and

Spencers. Although it concerns itself with the product development, the output and even the investment decisions of its suppliers, yet its relationship with them is based merely on mutual trust and good-will. The operations of a major international oil company provide an example of extensive and highly developed piecemeal planning through vertical integration. The plain fact is that so-called market economies do not rely entirely on market mechanisms; their structure permits, and has in fact been adapted to permit, a great deal of piecemeal planning. It is in terms of the need for such planning, rather than in terms of conventional scale economies, that much industrial morphology has to be interpreted.

(b) The Law of Large Numbers

But, if planning is all around us, it is far from complete. A great bulk of output, final and intermediate, is, as we say, for the market. Producers of intermediate goods commonly deal with a large number of buyers and the producers of consumer goods almost always do. In such cases, refuge from uncertainty is sought not in planning but in what has been called the unstrict law of large numbers. Brick manufacturers do not try to forecast the demand for bricks by adding up the several demands that the many builders and contractors with which they deal say are likely to put upon them. They study the trends in aggregates. They rely on the cancelling out of random elements to which the demands of individual customers are subject. Of course, we should not rush to the conclusion that for a firm of a given size the larger the number of its independent accounts the better. In the first place, the gain from grouping does not rise in proportion to the number of accounts grouped but—if sampling theory can be followed in this context—to the square root of their number. And, secondly, the firm's forecasts will generally be part synthetic, part analytical; they will supplement the projection of aggregate trends with particular information about the likely demands of particular customers or groups of customers and the larger the number of accounts the greater the cost of acquiring this information is likely to be.

In her critique of French planning Mrs. Lutz[2] puts great stress on this unstrict law of large numbers and refers to a German school of writers who make it the corner-stone of their account of how fore-

[2] Vera Lutz, *Central Planning for the Market Economy* (London, 1969).

sight and co-ordination is made possible in market economies. Certainly the principle seems to me important, but I do not think that it can bear the full weight of explanation. It is certainly true that the aggregation of the component demands for a particular product makes for predictability, but if this is to result in predictability in the demand for the output of particular firms, then the structure of the markets in which they are operating has to be appropriate. Here, it seems to me, is the third essential requirement for the working of decentralized systems; market structure and business behaviour must be such as permit firms to plan current output and investment decisions; they must facilitate enterprise planning. Perhaps this too, like much else I have said, may seem obvious and certainly ought to be. In fact, however, the point is almost completely ignored in almost all the literature, and I have had very little success in drawing attention to it.

(c) *Market Structures*

Let us suppose that we are asked not to explain how markets work but to design them. We may imagine that we have been invited to advise the government of an East European economy, currently organized by detailed central direction, on how best to introduce some decentralized decision-taking. Let us suppose that we are concerned with an industry (producing a homogeneous commodity) in which enterprises are to be given freedom of decision with respect both to current output and to investment. We are asked to design an appropriate market structure and prescribe the rules to which the enterprises are to be made subject. Those who really believed in this theory of perfect competition might recommend along these lines; set up as many independent enterprises as the relevant scale economies permit, give them equal access to finance, instruct them to seek maximum profits and forbid them to limit the competition in any way. If this recipe were adopted, its proponents would urge, we would get as close as possible to the ideal self-regulating system with prices constantly varying to ensure the optimal adjustment of supply to demand. Were these recommendations to be accepted, then the enterprise managers would, I fear, be in despair. Even if they could form a capable estimate of the likely total demand for the product, they would have no idea how much they each and individually ought to plan to produce. We must hope, therefore, that these recommendations would be rejected.

But what then ought we to recommend? We could of course suggest that the authorities divide up the market between the several enterprises according to geographical area or some stated percentage share. This, at any rate, unlike the previous recommendation, could give to each enterprise something they could usefully try to predict; and the success or failure of their individual predictions would be made manifest. But most of the merits of decentralization would be lost; neither costs nor profits would be subject to competitive pressures, and it would be absurd not to arrange for the accidental surpluses that might develop in some part of the market to be used to offset scarcities in others. Let us then consider a further set of recommendations which, for ease of exposition, I shall put in somewhat simple-minded form. Let the price of the homogeneous commodity be fixed on the basis of some estimate of normal unit costs. Allot customers between the several enterprises in such a way that each of them has a regular supplier from whom he is normally obliged to buy. But lay it down that, should a buyer find his regular supplier unable to meet his full demands, then he will be transferred, in some pre-arranged fashion, to an enterprise with additional supply available.

How would these arrangements work? First we note that each supplier has now something he can aim at. His first job is to predict the demand from his regular clientele and plan to meet it. He can do this without the fear that, if other suppliers over-produce, he will no longer have a profitable outlet for his goods. Secondly, we should note that each supplier has a strong incentive not to underestimate his regular demand, for, if he does so, he will lose custom on a quasi-permanent basis to those who have the capacity to meet demands in excess of those from their regular customers. Thirdly, suppliers have an incentive not to overestimate demand, for, if they do so, they themselves will bear the losses occasioned by excess capacity. And finally, suppliers have an incentive to consider whether their rivals are likely to have underestimated demand, for, if this is so, there is an opportunity to wrest custom from them.

A market of this type, it seems to me, would have clear advantages over the perfectly competitive, flexible-price type of market that often represents the textbook ideal. Not only does it facilitate foresight; it ensures that errors of forecasting are borne by those who make them. In a flexible-price system, the sins of the few may be borne by the many; for over-investment, by causing a collapse of prices, will penalize all suppliers.

It is not difficult to discern the strong family resemblance between these recommended arrangements and competitive markets that actually exist in the manufacturing sector of free enterprise economies. These markets, to use the Hicksian terminology, are normally of the fix-price rather than the flexible-price variety; they are so usually because of oligopoly, sometimes because of inter-firm agreements, sometimes because of governmental controls. Firms do generally have regular clienteles, either because of transport costs, or product differentiation, or goodwill or for some other reason. If they cannot meet the demand of the regular customers, they lose them. If they install too much capacity, they suffer loss, but prices do not normally fall to the level of marginal costs. Of course, there is the danger, which engages the exclusive and almost obsessional attention of many economists, that prices may be kept too high in relation to unit costs. Inter-firm rivalry or the threat of entry may, and I am inclined to believe usually do, prevent this; but, if they do not, the public authorities can intervene.

But let us return to our hypothetical East European economy. The task given to us was that of designing a framework for workable competition in the supply of a homogeneous product. But it is natural to ask whether, in this context, the gains from decentralized decision-taking are really worth while. It is true that we have introduced competition in forecasting, but it is arguable that a central bureau, by collating all the available evidence, might make a better forecast than could any individual enterprise. Might it not therefore be better to maintain centralized control, fix an industry output target and give to the enterprises individual output targets derived from it? After all, it would still be possible to stimulate competition in cost reduction simply by fixing a uniform price and rewarding enterprises with the highest profits.

It seems to me that, so long as we take the case of a homogeneous product, or near-homogeneous product, the argument for decentralization is not strong. I for one would not wish to denationalize the coal mines. It is when we turn to the general case of product differentiation and, more especially, of continuous product development, that the merits of competition, of decentralized forecasting and investment decisions, come into their own. So long as there is uncertainty merely with regard to the future total demand for a homogeneous product then it seems not unreasonable to pool all the individual opinions and distil some kind of average view there-from; central planning, in other words, may be appropriate. But, where there exists uncertainty in its more general form, I can see little merit and much danger in endeavouring to agree or impose some central view about what lines of development, in product or process, ought to be pursued or about what product varieties will best meet the needs of consumers. In considering how we might design a workable market structure, I took the case of a homo-geneous product, for it is in that context that the forecasting problem, created by the interdependence of individual producers' plans, presents itself most sharply. I wished to show how it was possible to reconcile competition with the requirements for informed output planning even in this extreme case. But our imaginary East European reformers might have been better advised not to select homogeneous product markets as the first place in which to introduce decentra-lized decision-taking. For not only do product differentiation and development make it more important to have competition, they make it possible to dispense with the special hypothetical arrange-ments according to which customers were allotted among suppliers. Provided that we have short-run price stability, as indeed we generally do in manufacturing business, then firms will generally be able to proceed from estimates of the total demand for their product class to estimates of the sales which they themselves will be able to make; but they will be obliged to recognize, in this general case, that they may lose custom not only if they are unable to supply but also if they cannot offer a price product combination as attractive as that offered by rivals.[3]

I set out, in this section of the paper, to say something about the way in which market economies cope with the problem of allocat-ing resources under conditions of imperfect competition. Of course, this summary account is quite inadequate; nothing has been said, for example, about prices, but then their role in promoting efficient allocation is well known. My aim was to make these points; first, that critical interdependencies both quantitative and qualitative

---

[3] How strange it is that economists have often set up, as a paradigm of decentral-ized decision-taking, the hypothetical system—perfect competition—in which not only the workability but also the advantages of decentralization would be most in doubt.

are dealt with by private, piecemeal planning; secondly, that in the absence of such deliberate co-ordination enterprise planning and prediction depends very largely on what has been called the unstrict law of large numbers; thirdly, that an essential condition for this prediction and planning is the existence of market structures and codes of business behaviour different from those to which economists usually give their warmest approval; and, fourthly, that the merits of competition are strongest where products are heterogeneous and subject to constant development.

INDICATIVE PLANNING

It is perfectly apparent, from the preceding discussion, that planning and competition are in one sense compatible; they can and do co-exist peaceably, on the basis of a division of labour, within the same economy. But I maintained at the outset, nevertheless, that planning and competition were essentially alternative ways of organizing economic activity with different roles to play. For the remainder of this paper I wish to consider whether there is a kind of planning, indicative planning, which can be adopted in conjunction with competition to co-ordinate the same set of economic activities. Can indicative planning be used, not to replace decentralized decision-taking, but to make it better informed?

Indicative planning, as practised in France and Britain, is a procedure by which the government works out, after consultation with private industry, a set of more or less disaggregated output targets for the various commodity groups within the national product. These targets are said to be consistent and usually, in some sense or other, to be agreed; they do not correspond, however, to binding obligations imposed on individual firms. What can be said in the light of the analysis of this paper, about the logic and utility of these arrangements?

In terms of our analogy of the treasure hunt, indicative planning would correspond to an arrangement which brought the men together to compose a map but then left them free to seek their fortunes as they each saw fit. On the face of it, this would not appear to be a very effective procedure, for the searchers would have neither much incentive to disclose their true opinions about the location of the treasure nor any clear indication, once the map was constructed, of what they each and individually ought to do. Nevertheless, this combination of centralized forecasting and decentralized decision has sometimes been represented as the peculiar virtue of the system; the copious French literature on the subject abounds with references to the way in which indicative planning illuminates but does not dictate enterprise decisions, often moving on to references about the reconciliation of order with freedom, harmony with diversity, organization with initiative and so on and so forth, in a manner that seems to belie the reputation of the French language for clear and precise expression.

I recall reading that the origins of indicative planning might be sought in the work of Quesnay, whose Tableau Economique represents the earliest attempt in the field; be that as it may, it seems to me that, in so far as the logic of the process is concerned, Walras is the true forerunner. The process of consultation by which a set of consistent interrelated output plans is said to be built up under indicative planning reminds us forcibly of the hypothetical system of re-contracting, which both Walras and Edgeworth said could, theoretically, provide a direct route to equilibrium. If indicative planning is taken to be such a process, then the objections made against the Walrasian conception apply here also. Given that knowledge is imperfect, admitting of both uncertainty and difference of opinion, then individual expectations and plans cannot thus be knitted together into one single consistent set. It may indeed be that the remote origins of indicative planning, based as it is on a supposed concensus, ought to be sought not in Walras, nor even in Quesnay, but in Rousseau's influential if obscure notion of the General Will.

But perhaps the analogy with re-contracting should not be pushed thus far. In the first place, the output targets in the plan are not associated with contracts to buy or to deliver; they represent some agreed expectation about what future outputs are likely to be. Secondly, the disaggregation in the plan is not carried through right down to output targets for each individual firm's product lines; the figures relate to the outputs of branches or industries usually large and highly diversified. Given these qualifications, the logic of indicative planning is less easily assailed, if only, I fear, because it becomes more difficult to discover what it is.

The target output figures set out in the plan are normally obtained by a combination of two methods. One method is to estimate the future rate of growth of the national product and proceed from there to deduce the rate of growth of the component elements. Let us call

this the analytical approach. The other method is to call for estimated output figures from industries; sometimes the firms or
associations approached are asked to give two estimates, one corresponding to what they themselves expect to happen, the other to
what they think would be appropriate to the particular rate of
growth of output postulated in the plan. Let us call this the synthetic
approach.

On the face of it, one might not wish to put much faith in industry output figures reached by the analytic method, if only for the
reason that this method proceeds from what is more predictable,
namely aggregates, to what is less predictable, namely components
thereof. In so far as the larger sub-aggregates are concerned, such
as consumption, investment, government expenditure and so on,
the procedure makes some sense, if only because these totals are
subject to governmental policy influence. But when we come to deduce industry outputs, far less the output of particular products, the
approach becomes highly questionable. One reads not uncommonly
that rates of output growth for individual products could be deduced from the rate of growth of national product, provided one
could calculate the appropriate income elasticities of demand. If
one conceives these in terms of the relationship between changes in
aggregate output and particular outputs as manifested at the end
of the planning period, *ex post*, then of course the statement is
tautologous; but if income elasticities are taken to refer to the change
in the demand for an individual product consequent on a certain
change in national income other things being equal, then of course
the statement is not true. Income changes represent only one of the
many factors which influence the demand for particular products
or product groups; they often appear more important than they are
simply because we are working in terms of models which abstract
from the elements of changing requirements, changing products,
changing processes and costs and so on.

But let us wave aside these difficulties and suppose that industry
output forecasts are produced and that, for the sake of argument,
each and every firm becomes convinced that they are correct. What
then? I cannot believe that an accurate forecast of the output of,
say, the mechanical engineering industry, in the classification
featured in the British Plan of 1965, would have been of much use
to an individual manufacturer of compressors, or diesel engines, or
cranes, or pumps. No doubt forecasts would be somewhat more use-

ful if they were further disaggregated, but even a forecast for cranes as such would not much help the individual manufacturer to esti-mate the demand for his particular type of dockyard crane, or steel-works crane, or moving overhead crane, diesel-powered crane, small electric crane and so on. And there is the further crucial point that, the more detailed the disaggregation, the less credible the analytic procedure becomes.

But forecasts, it may be said, are also synthetic. In general, moreover, they are agreed with the industries concerned. This latter claim, in my own experience, does not amount to much. The large firms or trade associations consulted are usually prepared to agree to a very wide range of industry output forecasts, not merely be-cause they wish to please, but simply because the relationship between the likely size of the future output of their own product and the size of the so-called industry output figure is so very tenu-ous. The remedy then lies, it may be urged, in further and further disaggregation, down, if necessary, to the level of the outputs of each individual firm. But here we go out by the door through which we came. If indicative planning is taken to mean the knitting to-gether of each and every output plan, then it does indeed come close to the Walrasian conception of a complete network of forward con-tracts. It presumes a consensus that simply does not exist, for no amount of organized dialogue, it seems to me, can hope to weld the expectations of each and every entrepreneur into a consistent plan.

If this analysis is correct, then there exists no coherent logical basis even in a closed economy for indicative planning; whether the process yields indirect benefits, such as creating confidence and in-ducing managements to look ahead, is a matter I do not propose to discuss. My own view is that the government should not attempt to set detailed output targets in the manner of the French and British plans, but there is good reason why it should endeavour to estimate the growth of total output and to influence the way in which it divides between investment, exports, government expenditure and the like. And I believe that the publication of its opinions and intentions on these matters will be of some use to some firms. It is evident, more-over, that governments will be much concerned with piecemeal planning; they will engage in it directly within the public sector or in partnership with the private sector and they may wish to supervise or even to stimulate the arrangements made by private firms. For many it seems natural that all the islands of piecemeal planning should gradually come together, that the sea of market relations should recede and that which was an archipelago become a continent. I believe that this is a mistaken view. My argument has been that there are sub-sets of economic activities so rigidly related that it is desirable to plan their co-ordination on the basis of some consensus of expectation and belief. Equally, there are wider areas within which the interdependence of individual activities is much looser; decentralized decision-taking, co-ordinated through the market, is here appropriate. Rather than endeavour to impose a consensus, it is better to let individual decisions be taken on the basis of a variety of opinions as to what an uncertain future may hold in store.

2

Housing—Supply and Demand

by R. L. Harrington

There is an old canard about a man who claimed to have taught his parrot to be an economist. When pressed, the man admitted that all he had done was to teach the bird to repeat the words supply and demand, but he thought that that was good enough. He may have underestimated the difficulties facing the student of economics, but he certainly showed that he knew what the subject was about. Economics is concerned with supply and demand and the the early chapters in all textbooks are devoted to these fundamental concepts, an understanding of which is necessary to all subsequent work. Now almost everyone knows that if supply increases then, other things being equal, price will fall, and that if demand increases then, other things being equal, price will rise. These propositions have become common knowledge and, in consequence, are often assumed to be trivial. But nothing could be further from the truth. As I shall seek to show, it is the persistent ignoring of the elementary economics of supply and demand that is largely responsible for the problems and difficulties of the market for housing.

Although many of the problems go back a long way, it will be sufficient for present purposes to concentrate on the post-war period. The housing market may be regarded as being composed of three distinct, but interrelated, sub-markets; the market for owner-occupied housing, the market for private rental accommodation, and the market for council housing. I shall concentrate mainly on the market for owner-occupied housing.

From *National Westminster Bank Quarterly Review*, May 1972. Reprinted by permission of the author and the National Westminster Bank Ltd.

At the end of the last war the United Kingdom had a severe shortage of accommodation of all kinds. Such a shortage was not new; but enemy action plus normal wastage during six years in which there had been virtually no new construction had greatly worsened the problem. The number of separate families considerably exceeded the number of houses. The 1951 census showed that more than five years after the war was over the number of 'households' still exceeded the number of occupied dwellings by more than a million. The difficulties were increased by rising aspirations. The war, like other wars before it, had brought about an upsurge of radical feeling motivated by a desire to 'build a land fit for heroes to live in'. Along with the demand for social security and free medicine had come the feeling that the nation should be better housed.

Whilst such sentiments were laudable, their translation into reality could not be easy. If the number of houses is less than the number of families then it is a matter of arithmetic that not every family can have its own house; some must share, or live in temporary accommodation, or accept accommodation which would normally be considered intolerable. Nor was the post-war problem of shortage one which would disappear quickly. Houses are long-lasting assets and newly built houses are likely to be only a small proportion of the existing stock. When one allows for the fact that some new construction is necessary to replace old houses being demolished or otherwise becoming uninhabitable, and that some is necessary just to keep up with a continually rising population, it is apparent that the making good of any sizeable shortage of housing will require a long time. Even a large increase in the number of new houses becoming available may make only a small impact of the total stock of houses in the short term.

To show more precisely the relationship between new housing and the stock of existing houses I will take an example. In 1955 the estimated stock of dwellings in the United Kingdom was roughly fifteen million. The annual construction of new houses during the late 1950s was roughly 300,000 which after allowance for slum clearance and other losses produced a net increase in the housing stock of a little over 200,000 houses, a rate of increase of close on 1·33 per cent per annum. Had the rate of new construction been increased by 50,000 houses per annum—a sizeable increase for the building industry—this would only have raised the rate of increase of the housing stock to 1·66 per cent per annum, that is to say, by

0·33 per cent. Such an increase in the rate of new construction would have increased the total stock at the end of five years by less than 2 per cent above what it would otherwise have been. At the end of ten years the increase in the number of houses due to the expanded rate of new construction would have been less than 3 per cent.

To put this in the language of economics, one would say that the supply of housing is inelastic. In the short run the supply is fixed, in the long run it changes only slowly. Changes in price will not, therefore, have much effect on supply.

It was inevitable that the United Kingdom should have a shortage of houses for many years after the war. What would have been a sensible response to this situation on the part of the authorities? If they had been content to leave things to the market, that is to say, to the free play of the forces of supply and demand, the price of housing (both rental price and purchase price) would have risen to a point where many people would have been unable to acquire the amount of accommodation considered to be socially desirable. It is, after all, the role of price to ration the available supply. Thus, whilst there would have remained a housing shortage, in the sense that the stock of houses could not have provided everyone with housing of some arbitrarily determined standard, there would have been no scarcity in the economic sense. Effective demand, backed by purchasing power, would not have exceeded supply. A policy of allowing market forces to raise prices so as to choke off excess demand might appear, and at the time probably did appear to many, to be callous. Was it right that people should be denied adequate housing just because they could not afford to pay? Such a reaction, though natural enough, reveals a confusion of thought. Whilst from the standpoint of one individual person it is true that he cannot get all the housing he desires because he cannot afford it, from the standpoint of the community as a whole this is not the reason why, at any moment, some have to go without. The reason is one of available supply, or, as put above, one of arithmetic. There are not enough houses for every family to have one. The fact that some people were living in poor conditions would in no way have been the result of prices being high. Rather, prices would have been high because, at any lower price, the available supplies would have been insufficient to meet the effective demand.

Given a shortage of housing, a policy of allowing market forces to reflect this scarcity, that is a policy whereby housing became dear, has one important advantage—it encourages people to economize on accommodation. Some people with spare rooms let them and some people living in large houses move to smaller ones, and so on.

There were good reasons why housing should have been dear after the last war: there are good reasons why it should be dear now. Nothing is to be gained by making cheap a commodity, demand for which is already likely to exceed supply. This is, however, what happened; and the consequences, almost wholly bad, are very much with us today. Perpetuating this fallacy, successive post-war British governments have acted on the principle that because good housing is socially desirable it ought to be cheap so that everyone can afford it. The fact that there was simply not enough to go round was not allowed to disturb this cosy but essentially foolish idea.

In the market for private rented accommodation, action to make housing cheap took the form of rent controls. These controls did not increase the available supply of accommodation; in fact they actually decreased it. By denying landlords a reasonable return on their capital they provided a disincentive to the maintenance in good condition of privately rented housing, with the result that many houses fell into disrepair and became slums long before they need have done. Rent controls were quite arbitrary in their effect: rich and poor tenants were subsidized alike, rich and poor landlords were penalized alike. These measures were devoid of both equity and of common sense, but once established they produced a situation in which their abolition would mean hardship for some. As a consequence, they have lasted a long time. Only recently, in the White Paper, *Fair Deal for Housing*, have the Government announced plans for important changes in rents for both private and council-house tenants.

The folly of prolonged rent control is now well known; less well known is the effect that kindred policies have had on the market for owner-occupied housing and how this market, in its turn, has been heavily subsidized. Rent controls resulted in excess demand and this was diverted into the uncontrolled sector of the market, the sector in which houses were bought and sold. The natural consequence was that the price of owner-occupied houses rose. Again, rising prices were not the *cause* of some people being unable to buy houses; rather they were the *consequence* of there being not enough houses for all who wished to do so. There was no good reason for subsidizing owner-occupiers. However, massive subsidies have been given throughout the post-war period. These have been less explicit than the subsidies inherent in low rents to private and to council-house tenants and, in some cases, have arisen less intentionally. Nevertheless, it is the case that the demand for houses to own has been continually bolstered by subsidies, and still is.

First, there is the subsidy resulting from artificially low rates of interest throughout much of the post-war period. Initially, the government avowedly sought very low rates of interest, but in the 1950s and 1960s the policy switched to one of moderating the prevailing rise in rates. Although nominal interest rates reached record levels in the late 1960s, real rates of interest were still low, due to the persistence of inflation. Inflation benefits borrowers of money in that they repay loans in money of depreciated value. A person who borrows £100 for a year at a nominal rate of interest of 5 per cent will repay £105 at the end of the year. If during the year there is a rate of inflation of 5 per cent then the £105 repaid is worth in real terms no more than the £100 borrowed; and the real rate of interest is zero. If the rate of inflation exceeds the nominal rate of interest, then the real rate of interest will be negative.

When prices are expected to rise, nominal rates of interest will tend to move upward in defence of real rates. It is this which largely explains the high nominal rates experienced during the 1960s in Britain and elsewhere. Real rates of interest have been low throughout most of the post-war period.

THE REAL COST OF MORTGAGE BORROWING

In relation to borrowing for house-purchase, the activities of the building societies are of prime importance. Building societies, almost alone among financial intermediaries lending to the private sector, have had little government interference in their affairs in the period with which we are concerned. In addition they have had favourable tax arrangements which, together with the absence of government controls, have enabled them to compete effectively for deposits whilst still lending at relatively low rates of interest. Furthermore, and this is another important element in the subsidy to owner-occupying, interest payments on mortgage loans have been tax-deductible throughout the post-war period. The net cost of a mortgage has always been considerably below that suggested by gross interest payments.

Tax relief is allowed on nominal interest payments and as we have seen, in an age of inflation, the nominal rate of interest is in excess of the real rate. The results can be surprising, as an example will show. Assume a person who pays income-tax at the standard rate (currently, approximately 30 per cent of earned income) and whose interest on a mortgage is at a rate of 8 per cent per annum. If there is a rate of inflation of 5 per cent per annum, the net real rate of interest, representing the real cost of the loan to the borrower, is calculated as follows:

Nominal rate of interest	8·00%
Less rate of inflation	5·00%
Equals real rate of interest	3·00%
Less tax relief at 30% of 8%	2·40%
Equals net real rate of interest	0·60%

In other words, the real interest cost per £1,000 of mortgage loan to a standard-rate income-tax payer in a time of inflation at a rate of 5 per cent would be £6 per annum. Moreover, it is appropriate to point out that mortgage interest payments can be offset against surtax as well as income-tax. The greater the marginal rate of tax paid by a person the less the net cost of a mortgage to him. A reduced nominal rate of interest, a higher rate of inflation and a higher marginal tax rate will reduce the real interest cost of a mortgage and may even make it negative. Table I gives the relevant rate of interest faced by mortgagors for the years 1949–69. It will be seen that this has been low throughout the period. In the 1950s, for six years out of ten it was even negative.

The consequences of cheap money for housing are not hard to predict. The cheaper the borrowing by mortgage the more stimulated the demand. Mortgage repayments are usually the main cost in home ownership, especially since the abolition of Schedule A taxation in 1963. It can be argued that this abolition was a major error; it was definitely a move in the wrong direction, and it is worth pausing awhile to understand why. A person who owns a house may either occupy it himself or let it to someone else. If he owns a house whose rental value is £500 per annum, and lets it, he will gain £500 per annum, but tax, if he pays at the standard rate, will

TABLE 1

Nominal and Real Rates of Interest on Housing Loans, 1949–1969

	Average rate of interest received by building societies on mortgage lending (1) %	Effective standard rate of income-tax on earned income (2) %	Net rate of interest (3) %	Rate of inflation (4) %	Net real rate of interest (5) %
1949	4·20	35	2·73	1·8	0·93
1950	4·17	35	2·71	4·0	−1·29
1951	4·19	37	2·64	8·2	−5·56
1952	4·32	37	2·72	6·1	−3·38
1953	4·55	35	2·96	2·6	0·36
1954	4·58	35	2·98	2·9	0·08
1955	4·66	32	3·17	4·9	−1·73
1956	5·32	32	3·62	5·1	−1·48
1957	5·98	32	4·07	4·3	−0·23
1958	6·13	32	4·17	3·7	0·47
1959	5·98	30	4·19	1·8	2·39
1960	5·89	30	4·12	2·5	1·62
1961	6·28	30	4·40	3·3	1·10
1962	6·61	30	4·63	2·9	1·73
1963	6·27	30	4·39	2·5	1·89
1964	6·16	30	4·31	3·3	1·01
1965	6·63	32	4·51	3·8	0·71
1966	6·95	32	4·73	3·6	1·13
1967	7·20	32	4·90	3·3	1·60
1968	7·46	32	5·07	3·2	1·87
1969	8·07	32	5·49	5·8	−0·31

Sources: Columns (1) and (2) *Annual Abstract of Statistics.* Column (4) C.S.O., *National Income and Expenditure.*

cost him just less than £200 (we are now dealing with unearned income). If, on the other hand, he chooses to occupy the property himself, he will gain income in kind, that is, income in the form of housing services, worth £500 per annum, and on this he will pay no tax.

Income in kind is just as important as income in money, and it is irrational that the latter should be taxed whilst the former is not.

Consider two people each of whom earns £2,000 a year. One owns a house worth £5,000; the other owns no property. Their standards of living are clearly different, yet the tax system treats them both alike. As long as tax is levied only on money income and not on income in kind there will be an incentive to maximize the latter at the expense of the former. Owning and occupying a house is one of the main ways in which this can be done today.

This argument might appear to lead to the conclusion that a general tax on wealth is desirable because all other durables also yield income in kind. However, most consumer durables are subject to purchase tax. Thus a tax is already imposed on their acquisition if not on the flow of imputed income that they provide. Housing is the glaring exception; it is the most important durable good that most people acquire, but its acquisition and the services that it provides are alike untaxed. Indeed, its acquisition is subsidized in various ways and the higher the tax bracket that a purchaser is in, the greater the subsidy he receives.

Faced with a continuous rise in the prices of houses for owner-occupation the authorities have generally followed a course similar to that in respect of rented accommodation: they have sought to subsidize demand on the grounds that this was the way to increase the number of people who could afford to buy their own houses. In fact, the number of people able to buy a house is limited by the number of houses available; and the continued favourable treatment of building societies, the abolition of Schedule A taxation, the introduction of option mortgage schemes and attempts to get the building societies to keep their rates of interest low have no influence on the supply of houses in the short run, and probably not in the long run either.

It may be objected that high prices for houses will stimulate new construction. This may be so. If it is, then the least one can say is that it is a costly way of increasing supply. But it is equally possible that high prices will not stimulate new building. This would be the case if the rising prices being paid by purchasers of new houses accrued largely or entirely to landowners and not to construction companies. Frequent press reports of soaring land values, and the financial difficulties of many small building firms, suggest that this may very well be what is happening. If it is thought desirable for the authorities to increase the rate of house-building, then there are surely better ways of doing this than by wholesale subsidies to demand. It might well be that if there were no such subsidies there would be less need to worry about current increases in supply; that is to say, the attempts at improving the housing situation may have made it worse.

But if buyers are subsidized as long as prices are high, why worry? Even if the process appears silly do we not get back to an equilibrium whereby what is lost on the swings is gained on the roundabouts? If the eccentric British public prefers to obtain mortgages at very low rates of interest and then pay very high prices for houses, does this matter? The answer is that it matters very much.

It was shown above how the combination of tax relief on interest payments and a high rate of inflation could reduce the real interest cost of a mortgage to a very small amount. These calculations implicitly assumed that houses were only maintaining their values in real terms, that is to say that house prices were rising at about the same rate as the general price level. The house-owner still gains from inflation because the real value of his liability (a mortgage) is reduced whilst the real value of his asset (a house) remains constant. But it is unrealistic to assume that houses merely maintain their value; for most of the post-war period house prices have been rising faster than prices generally and this means that house-owners have made real capital gains. When such gains are taken into account, it appears that buying a house is, in the long run, a profitable investment. Much of today's rising demand for more and better accommodation, usually ascribed to increasing affluence, may very well be an investment demand for housing with more and more people coming to see ownership of bricks and mortar as one of the best means of building up capital. The so-called demand for space in part results from the cost of space being little or nothing.

The provision of housing consumes many scarce resources. It is clearly uneconomic that resources which are costly to the community should be made costless to the individual. In an age when there is much talk of the dangers of over-population, and concern is expressed about the urbanization of the countryside, it cannot be good sense to subsidize people to consume space. Space is valuable, and the buildings which are created on it are costly. Economic sense requires that those who wish to use valuable resources should, in general, be obliged to pay a price at least equal to the opportunity-cost of these resources.

INTER-TEMPORAL REDISTRIBUTION OF CONSUMPTION

Besides artificially increasing the demand for housing, current policy ensures a redistribution of consumption which is also wholly undesirable. Consumption is so redistributed for each house-owner over his lifetime that he is made poorer when younger and wealthier when older. The need for more money to be lent by the building societies and for low interest rates is often defended as being necessary to help young married couples to buy their own houses. In fact, these young married couples are the people who suffer most from the consequences of the policies supposedly designed to aid them.

Throughout this article I have continually asserted that, in current circumstances, the cost of a mortgage in real terms is very low or even negative. This is doubtless perplexing to those who are currently repaying a mortgage and to whom the repayments seem onerous. An example may show what the real cost of house-owning is. Suppose a man with a mortgage of £4,000 whose annual payments are £360, the breakdown of which, between interest and repayment of principal, is not of immediate importance. If inflation is occurring, then the annual payments will be worth progressively less in real terms: the real value of the £360 per annum will be gradually diminished.

For example, if prices were to rise steadily by 8 per cent each year over a period of thirty years the real value of £360 would at the end of the period be less than one-tenth of what it was at the beginning. If inflation were at the lower rate of 5 per cent per year the real value of £360 would fall by the end of the period to the equivalent of £83, that is, less than one-quarter of the original worth. And even if inflation were at the relatively modest annual rate of 3 per cent a year the real worth of £360 would, over thirty years, fall to the equivalent of £148. Meanwhile, no doubt the mortgagor's money income will be increased periodically and thus the cost of his mortgage as a proportion of his income will fall.

It may be that, because of inflation and competition for deposits, building society interest rates will rise. There has been a trend towards higher interest rates on mortgage borrowing in the postwar period. This would constitute a partial offset to the picture conveyed above, but no more than that. On the other hand, the figures given in the example are about right; that is to say, if there is a new mortgage loan of £4,000 then in current conditions, £360 would be approximately right as a figure for gross annual payments. The net-of-tax annual cost of a £4,000 mortgage would be below £360.

The main lesson to be learned from this is that a mortgage costs more in its early years. The young couple aged twenty-four who have just bought a house will, in all probability, find the payments a strain. Their forty-five-year-old neighbours, who live in a house of equivalent value but bought fifteen years ago, are by now making payments of very small value. Since the nominal rate of interest will be higher, due to inflation, than it otherwise would have been, it is apparent that inflation causes every mortgagor to redistribute consumption over time; he is worse off when young and better off when older than he otherwise would have been.

This is not the end of the matter, however. It is necessary to ask what these payments, the real values of which diminish with time, really represent. If house prices are rising in real terms, then to measure the cost of housing one must offset against interest payments on capital the appreciation of that capital. If the general price level is rising by 5 per cent per annum, while house prices are rising by 10 per cent per annum, that is, the value of houses is rising in real terms over and above the appreciation due to the fall in the value of money, each year's capital gain will be larger than the previous year's.

The position of the mortgagor may be seen by looking at his gains as compared with his payments in different years. On the assumptions made above, and assuming also that tax is paid at the standard rate (rounded to 30 per cent), this is what will have happened by the end of the first year:

he will have paid out:	£360

and he will have gained: increase in value of house	400
reduction in debt	40
tax saving (30% of £320)	96
	£536

The mortgagor has lived in the house for nothing and made a profit (unrealized) of £176.

By the tenth year, the outstanding debt is reduced and the interest charged is correspondingly less. Consequently, the propor-

tion of the £360 payment applied to debt reduction is greater. The
capital gain on the house is very much higher.

In the tenth year he will pay out: £360

and will gain: increase in value of house   945
                reduction in debt   80
                tax saving (30% of £280)   84
                                                                      ——————
                                                                     £1,109

This means that during the tenth year the owner, in addition to
living in the house for the year, becomes better off by almost £750.

The pounds in question will, of course, be worth less than the
pounds borrowed in the first place, and the sum of £750 will be
worth only about £460 in terms of the earlier money values. But,
then, the £360 annual payment is correspondingly less onerous
and is the equivalent of only £220 in the first place.

Thus in the (not unrealistic) example, far from it costing anything to own a house, the occupier was making a large and growing
profit from his house-ownership. The payments made to the building society may be viewed more as saving than as an actual cost,
in that they can be recouped (with gains) by selling the house.
However, since such payments must be made, they would best be
described as forced saving.

Although this forced saving can be recovered by selling the house,
it is still undesirable. One cannot be continually on the move and,
in any case, selling one house and buying another costs money.
Until the house is sold all of the payments to the building society
have to be financed somehow. These payments, as we have seen,
are highest (in real terms) in the early years of a mortgage. This is
why the first house purchase is so difficult.

In short, under present circumstances, housing is a good investment for most people. Its real cost is low and, in consequence,
demand is high and real property values are rising. The process
can snowball: rising real property values create new demands which,
in turn, push up property values still further. People who already
own property obviously stand to gain, but people trying to buy
houses for the first time are finding things more and more difficult.
Policies designed to help young married couples to buy their own
houses have, in fact, made things much harder for them.

CONCLUSION

To sum up, the market for housing is, like all markets, subject to the forces of supply and demand. To say this is not to say that the authorities must never intervene but, rather, that any intervention must take account of the forces of supply and demand and not just ignore them. The failure to do this is the real failure of post-war housing policy.

The market for housing has been, and is, characterized by inelastic supply in the short run. In the long run, elasticity may not be much greater. All forms of assistance to demand may then be expected to achieve little other than a rise in the price of houses. In as far as rising prices become the accepted order of things (and therefore the expected order of things) they create an investment demand for housing and encourage more and more people to consume more and more housing resources. This, in turn, reacts back on prices: there is a snowball effect. If at any time some people are unable to obtain such housing standards as are currently considered socially desirable this is not because they cannot afford it—though this is how it appears to the individual—it is because supply is not sufficient to provide such standards for all, not, that is, without some form of physical limitation on the maximum amount of housing that the wealthie can consume. Subsidies to demand will be at best ineffectual, at worst counter-productive.

If a situation could be brought about in which demand was no longer artificially stimulated, we should probably find that existing supply was adequate and the housing problem would be no more. But even if we cannot be sure of this, we can be sure of one thing: without a greater appreciation on the part of the authorities of fundamental economic principles of supply and demand, the housing problem will never be solved.

3

The Problems of Soviet Housing : A Survey
by David Cattell

Nothing has changed the landscape or the lives of the Soviet citizenry more than the doubling of the urban housing fund since the death of Stalin. The average housing space available per person is still below the minimum health standard of nine square metres set by the Soviet regime in the 1920s and probably a majority of families are still sharing apartments, even in new housing. In Leningrad, for example, between 1959 and 1964, of the 570,000 families receiving accommodations only 60 per cent received separate apartments. Among couples 50 per cent received their own apartment and single adults only 20 per cent.[1] Nevertheless, if the present efforts are continued, the goal is in sight. Moscow, the most advanced Soviet city, plans to eliminate all communal apartments by 1980, and for the whole Soviet Union it is planned that on the average the sanitary norm should be achieved by that same date.[2]

But beyond the physical changes brought about and to be brought about by an increase in housing space, what other developments have accompanied and resulted from this housing boom and how fundamental to the system are they? What is the role of urban governments in this process? Has the new housing helped to alleviate the growing social problems in Soviet cities and made social controls easier?

From *Jahrbuch der Wirtschaft Osteuropas*, vol. iii (1972), pp. 231–48. Reprinted by permission of the author and Günter Olzog Verlag.

[1] *Stroitelstvo i arkhitektura Leningrada*, No. 2, (1967) p. 25.
[2] *Ogonick*, 21 Dec. 1968, pp. 1–3 in *Current Abstracts of the Soviet Press*, I, no. 10, p. 12.

In the first decades of the Soviet regime city governments together with local party organizations acquired considerable autonomy. They were largely left to their own devices to provide for the daily needs of the population because the central authorities were too busy with industrial plans and had few resources to disperse to cities. At most Moscow allocated some civil construction funds mostly to the new cities. What controls it did impose were primarily restrictive. Local revenues including taxes were strictly limited and designated centrally. Prices for utilities and most services to consumers were determined in Moscow and set close to the actual cost providing little profit for cities. In the area of housing the restrictions worked a particular hardship. On the one hand, the city had to guarantee a minimum amount of space to each of its *bona fide* citizens and could not deprive them of this space except by court order and only for extreme cause. On the other hand, the established rent schedules were set low enough so that no worker as part of the great socialist state would have to pay more than 10 per cent of his salary for rent (in fact by 1960 it averaged much less than 5 per cent) and so that local officials could not use non-payment of rent as an excuse to remove citizens from their space. Even under Stalin the income from rents was insufficient in most cases to cover current costs. The slow inflation of the rouble over the years has reduced the real income from rents even further. From 1937 only partial adjustments were ever made in the rent schedules covering mainly new housing. It is small wonder that cities were able to do little on their own to improve and expand housing. But with the Five-Year Plans and the rapid expansion of the urban population beginning in the 1930s new housing was absolutely essential. Reluctant to allocate central funds, the leadership turned to the profits and material resources of industry to find construction funds for new housing construction. This gave industry a major stake in housing. By the 1950s industry and related organs controlled about two-thirds of urban state-owned housing and in many cities, especially those which were rapidly expanding, local governments were almost entirely squeezed out of the housing field. Many industries not only controlled their own housing but also their own communal services.

In spite of the severe restrictions placed on local governments by Stalin and their lack of resources, many cities did a remarkable job in organizing services for their citizens. The way in which local leaders after World War II rapidly organized and reconstructed their cities with a minimum of help from Moscow was proof of their capability. But all the efforts were unequal to the growing crisis in housing. Cities were falling more and more behind.

Beginning with Malenkov and continuing through the present regime the Soviet leadership shifted priorities to include as a major goal the improvement of consumer services and bringing housing up to the health standard of nine square metres of housing space per person with modern conveniences.[3] In Soviet terms this meant the end of autonomy for local governments and industry and bringing housing construction and controls into the central domain. It meant building enough new urban housing to triple the amount already existing and investing billions of roubles in the next decades. The Stalinist *ad hoc* approach to housing construction depending on industry and local governments to construct housing from excess and scrounged resources was unequal to the task. Thus after thirty years of 'perfecting' the organizational and planning genius of the Soviet Union, it was applied to a whole new sector of the economy, housing, beginning in the 1950s.

Construction was taken out of local hands and consolidated into large city or regional *glavki* under union-republic direction. Basic construction units were increasingly combined into giant trusts and *kombinats*. The basic allocation of funds, materials, labour, etc., was done from Moscow by the State Committee on Construction (*Gosstroi*) and Gosplan. Although this creation of giant industries to produce large quantities closely fits the traditional mode, nevertheless, the reorganization was not as simple as originally assumed and took a decade to accomplish. Partially it was disrupted by the 1957 reforms. By the 1960s the reorganization had been achieved and the capacity of new construction more than doubled. The average yearly production of new urban housing went from an average of

[3] In measuring 'housing space' in the Soviet Union, account is traditionally taken of only living area allocated to the individual. It excludes kitchens, bathrooms, closets, and all corridors whether for general use or not. Such a measure was realistic when kitchens, bathrooms, and other facilities were largely shared. In most new housing, however, individual facilities are today provided for each family and many Soviet writers argued that statistics should no longer be kept on the basis of housing or living space. They felt housing statistics should be measured exclusively in 'general usable space' in each building, and, in fact, increasingly authors and statistical abstracts use this method of measurement. In this paper both 'general usable space' and 'housing space' are used and identified. Housing space represents approximately 65–70 per cent of general usable space.

about 30 million square metres of general usable housing space in
the early 1950s to an average of 80 million in the early 1960s. To
achieve these output goals was not merely a matter of concentration
and centralization, costs had to come down if the Soviet Union
was going to have enough capital for its other commitments as well
as housing. Cutting cost was first of all handled as a technical problem by means of (1) improved designs, (2) reducing standards of hall
space, ceiling heights, safety factors, etc., (3) mechanization and
(4) mass production techniques particularly in the form of pre-
fabricated housing. These changes and improvements cut costs in
roubles, material, labour and time by 25–50 per cent (for example,
see Table 1). The second approach was to improve planning. The
key reform here was to make the city government the fundamental

TABLE I

*1961–62 evaluation of different types of housing construction mostly in
Kiev*

	Brick	Large Block Prefab	Panel Prefab
Cement per square metre of housing space—kilos	280	262	160
Steel per square metre of housing space—kilos	39	44	26
Labour per square metre of housing space—workdays	5·2	3·4	2·45
Cost per square metre of housing space—roubles	148·7	126·6	115·2
Time to construct—months	11–12	8–9	5–5½
Percentage of prefab products in construction	50	74	90 plus
Cost of each panel—roubles	—	15·25	6·12

Sources: Sh. M. Ginzburg, *Ekonomika krupnopanelnovo domostroeniia* (Moscow,
1965), pp. 6–7, and G. N. Gerasimov, *Deiatelnost partinikh organizatsii v
zhilishchnom stroitelstve posle XX cezda KPSS*, p. 9.

planning body. This permitted comparative costing in supplying
services and engineering so that for the first time the regime had
some meaningful comparative figures to provide for the most
optimum placement, height and size of housing units in respect to
cost.

The shift to local level planning initiated as an economy measure has also significantly increased the authority of local government. Making the city the co-ordinator of construction has given it for the first time some power over its own development in relation to its goals and general plans. This increased role for cities, however, was not immediate. Although Khrushchev's 1957 reform was initially intended to strengthen the participation and influence of the city in this and other fields, in fact the role and authority of local government for the years of the reform were reduced, a price Khrushchev seemed to have had to pay for achieving other parts of his reform. Industry continued to dominate the planning and control of new housing. For example local soviet participation in the construction of new housing declined in this period:

    1960   14·6 million square metres of general usable space
    1961   12·4 million square metres of general usable space
    1962   10·7 million square metres of general usable space[4]

It was not until after Khrushchev's ouster that cities began to attain the position originally intended.

It was not only the 1957 reforms which had kept the cities from playing their intended role but also the lack of long-range plans to spell out goals and authority. Although the Soviet regime has always considered itself the father of planning and although there had been much talk in the 1920s and early 1930s about the model cities of the future in the Soviet Union, little in the way of long-range city planning had been accomplished. By the 1950s only a few large cities like Leningrad and Moscow had developed fairly complete development plans. At best the other cities were only in the initial stages of drafting development plans. Then in the early 1950s when it was decided all cities should have plans there were not enough qualified personnel to deal with more than a few cities at a time and each plan took several years to complete. Furthermore, even when passed into law, the plans still could not be enforced against the powerful ministries. Finally, changing assumptions of the Soviet leaders about future development made many plans obsolete, as for example, the on and off again decisions as to whether to produce automobiles for mass consumption and the need to plan roadways and garages accordingly and whether to try new measures to restrict the growth of large cities. As a result, in large part long-range

---

[4] *Ekonomika zhilishchno-kommunalnovo khoziaistva* (Moscow, 1965), p. 54.

planning did not exist or was ineffective in influencing the first wave
of the housing boom.

Even though general plans were still not approved for the majority
of Soviet cities by the early 1960s the participation of cities in short-
range planning did not have to wait. With the reversal of the 1957
reforms, which occurred early for construction in 1962, local integrated planning for housing became possible. The key link was the
expanding authority of the chief architect of the city. He is the chief
agent of the Committee on Construction and the ministries of civil
construction. To help him a co-ordinating committee on construction of local authorities in government, industry and the party is
appointed in each city. Although the chief architect is primarily
responsible to his superiors at the republic level, he is also part of
the local government as a member of the executive committee of
the city soviet and, at least theoretically, is responsible to the local
soviet. It might be possible for him to ignore this dual subordination
as his colleagues in the departments of education and finance, also
attached to the local executive committee, have done; but in the
chief architect's case there are good reasons for him not to ignore his
relations with the city officials. It is from the city he must get the
numerous services from sewers to consumer outlets to supply the new
housing developments. The political strength of the local party and
government officials are also useful to him in lobbying Moscow for
a bigger share of the housing funds and materials and to pressure
the local construction *glavki* and their subordinates to live up to their
contracts. Thus cultivating local officials is essential for the chief
architect to get his job done, and as a result has brought most local
governments closely into the planning and construction process.

Over the last fifteen years the power of the chief architect and his
expanding office have become considerable. All new housing, regardless for whom it is built, is planned in detail and contracted
through his office, and it remains under his close supervision until
it is finally turned over to its 'owners'. Although his control over
industrial construction is much less, he has the final word at least
locally as to where a new plant is to be placed and the design of its
façade. Thus the chief architect's role in housing has made him a
major agent of the central government and the powerful co-ordinator of all construction at the local level. Interestingly, an important
qualification of the chief architect is that he must be trained pro-
fessionally. He cannot be just another government or party bureau-

crat; his status and legitimacy is primarily determined by his professional attainment—not typical of top administrators in the Soviet civilian bureaucracy.

From the aggregate statistics and the published reports the reorganization of construction can be considered highly successful. A look at the miles of new housing in Moscow and other large cities seems to confirm the assertion. But, in fact, this is only part of the picture. There are two major deficiencies in the construction system hidden in the statistics and propaganda: the unequal development of housing construction and the poor quality of much of the output. (Neither of these shortcomings, of course, is unique to housing.) It is true that large cities like Moscow, Leningrad and Kiev have done remarkably well expanding their capacities and fulfilling their goals, but the small and medium cities have developed much slower and rarely fulfil their goals.

Construction problems are compounded for the smaller cities. To begin with there are not enough graduate architects and engineers to fill all the positions open for chief architects and their staff, so the smaller cities tend to lose out. For example, in the case of the Perm Oblast, there were places for thirty-three chief architects but of those holding the posts only five had diplomas in architecture. In Bashkirs, of those holding sixty-three posts only two had diplomas.[5] Similarly there are shortages of skilled construction workers. For example, of the one million new workers in civil construction added from 1955 to 1961 less than half were trained construction workers.[6] Again it has primarily been the small city construction trusts which suffer because the skilled workers are attracted to large cities and heavy industry which pays better. Furthermore, small cities initially had only a few small construction trusts on which to build large organizations capable of producing thousands of square metres of new housing. Even when the construction units were concentrated over large areas the capacity of the new regional glavki was unimpressive. Consequently some glavki found it difficult, if not impossible, to create the large complex kombinats to

[5] Arkhitektura SSSR, No. 6 (1966), p. 1. In the U.S.S.R. in about 1960 there were only 64 architects per million of population compared to 364 in England, 240 in Sweden, 130 in the United States, 312 in Bulgaria, 100 in Czechoslovakia, 129 in Poland and 154 in Hungary. (B. R. Rubanenko, Arkhitekturno-planirovochnie resheniia domov v sovremennom stroitelstve (Moscow, 1960), p. 19.)

[6] V. L. Kobalevskii i dr., Ekonomika i organizatsiia gorodskovo khoziaistva (Moscow, 1964), p. 149.

build prefab housing. Yet it is the prefab construction which has been primarily responsible for reducing cost, time and materials, and raising quality. As a result this new method of construction has been slow to develop outside the large cities (see Table 2). By 1964 the Caucasian republics of Azerbijan, Georgia and Armenia had only built a total of 875,000 square metres of panelled apartments in the whole area.[7] Panel prefabs accounted for only 8·5 per cent in Belorussia, 11 per cent of Uzbekistan and 8 per cent in the Ukraine in 1964.[8] In the R.S.F.S.R., 138 enterprises outside Moscow and Leningrad were projected to build 10·3 million square metres in 1966 but in fact built only 8·8 million square metres or 85·4 per cent.[9] It often happens also that cities without strong chief architect offices manned by qualified personnel and without efficient construction trusts are those with weak city governments and in which the enterprises control and operate housing to their own liking. Thus the housing boom has benefited primarily the large cities both in improving their living conditions and strengthening local government, while the changes in provincial cities has been slow. It is not surprising, therefore, that Moscow and Leningrad is still growing in spite of various efforts by the leadership to stop their growth and a decline of their birth rates.

TABLE 2

Percentage of Large Panel Construction in New Urban Housing in the Public Sector

	U.S.S.R. %	Moscow %
1960	3·5	9·2
1962	15·2	47·2
1964	25·0	51·0
1966	31·5	55·0

Source: *Zhilishchnoe stroitelstvo*, No. 11 (1967), p. 15.

The problem of the poor quality of construction is general throughout the Soviet Union, but it also is more acute in the smaller cities. The issues of every architecture and construction journal

[7] *Zhilishchnoe stroitelstvo*, No. 4 (1964), p. 10.
[8] *Ekonomika stroitelstva*, No. 1 (1965), p. 34.
[9] V. T. Robotov, *Finansirovanie i kreditovanie zhilishchnovo stroitelstva* (Moscow, 1967), p. 139.

laments the lack of quality. Although mechanization and factory-prefabricated panels have markedly improved quality over the large block buildings and traditional brick construction, the final product still has a hastily assembled look. More important, within a couple of years the façades begin to crumble and cracks open between the panels. Even by Soviet quality standards, which are not high, as much as 60 per cent of new housing is defective, and usually the defect is so basic there is no remedy.[10] In Moscow, 43 per cent of new housing was defective in 1963 and 65 per cent in 1964.[11] In Leningrad in 1965, 65 per cent of the housing barely met minimum standards of quality, and to bring the deficient up to the minimum 42,147 additional work-days had to be expended. This was, however, an improvement over 1965 when it required 51,504 additional work-days.[12] Soviet planners estimate that often as much as 30 per cent of the labour in construction is expended on repairs to bring the housing up to minimum requirements.[13]

The major causes of poor quality are (1) the excessive, almost exclusive, emphasis on production and cost, and (2) the disinterest and rapid turnover of the often poorly trained construction workers. Although the number of construction workers had more than doubled from 1950 to 1965 less than half were trained workers. In order to remedy the lack of skilled labour force, in February 1968 the Central Committee and the U.S.S.R. Council of Ministers passed a resolution on improving the conditions and training of construction workers. Some two million skilled workers were ordered to be added to construction of all kinds from 1968 to 1970 including 834,000 trained in vocational and technical schools. Even in cities like Leningrad the turnover of construction workers has been as high as 30 per cent a year and studies have shown that trusts with large turnover produce housing of inferior quality.[14] Skilled workers have been attracted to the higher-paying jobs in heavy industry. The regime took a major step to slow down turnover at the beginning of 1969 by raising the wages of construction workers on an average of 25 per cent, and workers in construction materials on an

---

[10] *Stroitelstvo i arkhitektura Leningrada*, No. 7 (1964), p. 15.

[11] *Arkhitektura SSSR*, No. 7 (1965), p. 5.

[12] *Stroitelstvo i arkhitektura Leningrada*, No. 7 (1966), p. 2.

[13] *Zhilishchnoe stroitelstvo*, No. 5 (1967), p. 29.

[14] *Voprosi proizvoditelnost ... truda ... v ... sebestoimosto ... v ... zhilishchnom stroitelstve* (Leningrad, 1962), p. 15.

average of 23 per cent. This may be the most significant step yet taken by the Soviet Union to improve quality and shows the genuine seriousness of the regime in trying to solve this crucial problem.

It was part of the rationale of the reorganization of housing initiated by Krushchev to follow the same pattern for the allocation and management of housing as for construction. The overall standards would be set in Moscow and the operational level would be concentrated in local governments. Industry was to be removed completely from the housing field. Khrushchev, however, abandoned entirely this part of the scheme and, in fact, during his regime enterprises became even more dominant in the field than before. Thus, for example, by removing local industry from the control of local governments, he reduced their income and their means to maintain housing. Brezhnev and Kosygin, however, have renewed Khrushchev's original ideas in this area; but thus far, the changes have been slow. The first city to take over housing from industry in 1965 was Leningrad which was already strong in housing and had a long-standing strong city government. Then came Moscow, followed gradually by other cities. The programme as a whole is running into many obstacles. In urban centres, where the housing problem remains acute, enterprises have resisted giving up their housing because it is so crucial in their recruiting of labour. More important, there does not seem to be unanimous support for these reforms, at least among economic planners. The profits and particularly the excess profits of industry are still considered a major source of housing capital, and better housing is still an important part of the workers' incentive system. It received new emphasis in the economic reforms in 1965. Thus, at least in cities where labour incentives are considered crucial and housing is short or inferior, industries will continue to play a major role and, if not control housing directly, will continue to dominate the allocation of new housing space.

The reorganization of construction was relatively simple compared to bringing housing management under some kind of central control. Although structurally the reform offered no problem and followed traditional schemes of hierarchical control, the efforts to find formulas and standards of control to cover the infinite variety of housing situations in Soviet cities has proved fruitless thus far. As a result the converse solution to the problem is becoming more attractive, that is, to go back to Stalinism and make it a local responsibility with Moscow assuming only the most general type of control. The leadership in fact is experimenting along these lines as indicated by the amount of authority over housing it has given to Moscow and Leningrad. It is, however, caught between the very uneven and poor performance of small and medium-sized cities in housing maintenance and its commitment to better housing for all. Consequently as rational as autonomy may seem and work in some cities, the leadership cannot abandon its efforts to find formulae enforceable from Moscow.

Turning over housing to city governments on the one hand greatly advances their political stature and makes possible for the first time rational planning of urban affairs. On the other hand, it is a mixed blessing. If cities are not to have new sources of income and authority, they cannot hope to handle the management of the vast housing fund. In fact the maintenance of this fund is rapidly becoming a major problem approaching a crisis. The weakest link in the whole housing system is maintaining housing at some acceptable standard. The condition of much of urban housing according to even Soviet reports is poor, little better than slums. The first difficulty is financial. The amount of rent collected falls far short of expenses and increasingly so. The various Soviet studies of the problem are all unanimous that housing rents cover at best little more than half of the expenditures currently made to keep up housing and only at a level which even the Soviets deplore (see, for example, Table 3). Whether from tradition or lack of sufficient resources the central government has consistently resisted supplying adequate subsidies. Thus local governments are forced to find other funds, all too scarce at this level. Desperate to get around this overwhelming burden, cities often reduce maintenance to a bare minimum, providing housing with little more than protection from the elements. Other repairs and improvements are left to the responsibility of the tenants. But with the growing priority of consumer comforts it is doubtful that these minimal levels will suffice. Under these circumstances it is not surprising that some local governments do not want to take over housing particularly when those enterprises with the most dilapidated housing are the ones first willing to transfer their housing. Nevertheless, if we are to believe Soviet calculations, in the long run the turning over of housing to local governments will be more efficient than to industries. They can

TABLE 3

*1962 Expenses and Income for Housing Maintenance in roubles per square metre of usable space**

	Local Soviets	Enterprises
Expenditures:		
Administration	0·23 rouble	0·32
Maintenance personnel	0·49	0·36
Maintenance	0·33	0·52
Current repairs	0·76	0·82
Other	0·03	0·21
	1·84	2·23
Capital repairs	1·91	2·03
	3·75	4·26
Income:		
Apartment rent	1·49	1·52
Rent of non-living space	0·75	0·22
Other	0·38	0·27
	2·62	2·01
Loss:	1·13	2·25

Source: B. M. Kolotilkin, *Dolgovechnost zhilikh zdanii* (Moscow, 1965), pp. 102–103.

* Includes 85 per cent of state living fund of local soviets and enterprises.

organize housing into larger, more efficient blocks and provide closer supervision.

The second major difficulty of the maintenance problem is that the higher cost of maintenance is not just confined to the old pre-revolutionary and pre-World War II housing, but the millions of new square metres of housing space are also a burden. Theoretically maintenance on new housing should be much less for the first ten to twenty years but in fact this has not been the case for Soviet housing. There are several reasons for this. The modern services of new apartments compared to the pre-revolutionary and Stalinist structures are much greater. For example, each family is now supplied with its own kitchen and bath, and many modern apartments have elevators and gardens which significantly add to maintenance costs, particularly Soviet elevators which frequently break down. Most important, however, has been the general low quality of new construction and the high repair costs from the beginning. It has been an almost universal complaint. One study of 609 apartment buildings in the 1960s showed that 64 per cent needed roof repairs in four years, 90 per cent in eight years, and all in ten years, although the roofs were supposed to last thirty years. Another investigation in Leningrad in the same article reported that one series of new apartments after three or four years needed a capital repair expenditure of 9·9–14·2 roubles per square metre of housing space.[15] The result was that the money spent on current and capital repairs throughout the U.S.S.R. in the 1960s was almost 40 per cent of that invested in new housing.[16] In the case of the largest republic, R.S.F.S.R., expenditures by repair construction organizations went from 338 million roubles in 1960 to 940 million in 1968 and is expected to reach 2–2·5 billion roubles by 1975.[17] In the same eight years capital investment in new housing increased only slightly. Furthermore, the figures for the future would seem to be unrealistic because they assume a constant standard of repair; and if the leadership's pledge to provide modern accommodations for the population is to be taken seriously, current standards of repair and modernization are quite insufficient. Thus the capital repair budget may soon reach that of new housing of 6–7 billion roubles a year.

The growing financial burden of housing clearly cannot be solved by urban governments from their current resources. Several possible courses are open to solve the problem. More profits from local industry and from republic and all-Union enterprises in the area could be assigned to local governments. Some steps have been taken in this direction. For example, local governments have been allowed to retain a larger percentage of the profits of local industry. In 1966 local government retained 20·2 per cent of 667,400,000 roubles, and 38·7 per cent in 1968 or 924,000,000 roubles.[18] The central government could also allocate more tax revenues or increase substantially its subsidization of local governments; but this, of course, would cut into other programmes. But the long run financial solution would seem to depend on a new realistic rent schedule. There has been some discussion of this solution and some important changes have

---

[15] *Arkhitektura SSSR*, No. 6 (1968), p. 22.
[16] B. M. Kolotilkin, *Dolgovechnost zhilikh zdanii* (Moscow, 1965). p. 110.
[17] *Zhilishchnoe i kommunalnoe khoziaistvo*, No. 2 (1969), p. 21.
[18] *Finansi SSSR*, No. 1 (1969), pp. 33–48 in *Current Abstracts of the Soviet Press*, II, No. 1, p. 6.

been made in the accounting and planning of costs, such as establishing a value for land and co-ordinating service costs, thus making it possible to establish a realistic rent schedule. Furthermore, the recent increases in personal income and the raising of minimum wages again to 70 roubles would seem to provide an adequate base to raise rents and keep them well within the capacity of all workers to pay. Only some exceptions might still have to be made for pensioners.

Equally important to the financial issue is the problem of how to organize and plan for maintenance. The traditional Soviet solutions of centralization and standardization do not work for housing repair and maintenance. Even the more recent panacea of mechanization has only a very limited application and requires major investments. It is primarily the shortage and lack of skilled manpower which undermines any attempt to raise standards from whatever level. For example, it was estimated in 1965 that there was a need for 1·5–2·0 times the number of workers then employed in current housing repairs.[19] One reason is that as far as prestige and wages, housing maintenance and repair personnel are at the bottom in every category. The salary of workers in current housing repairs in 1962 was 43–63 roubles per month at a time when the minimum wages for urban workers was 40 roubles per month.[20] The low level of skills is exemplified by a study in Moscow in 1963 where among 2,000 technical inspectors in housing management and repairs only 450 (23 per cent) had higher or middle education and 1,200 had worked as inspectors less than five years.[21] Thus housing maintenance and repair work is inadequate and of poor quality— undermining the leadership's decision to improve significantly living standards. One study in 1958–9 found 76 per cent of the repairs in a sample of 20 buildings in Leningrad substandard.[22]

Under Stalin housing committees and bureaus had become important instruments of social organization as well as managers of housing maintenance. Although the primary means of organizing

[19] *Ekonomika zhilishchnovo khoziaistva: seminar* (Moscow, 1962), p. 47.

[20] N. M. Emelianov, *Organizatsiia zarobotnii plati v zhilishchno-kommunalnom khoziaistve* (Moscow, 1963), p. 40.

[21] *Gorodskoe khoziaistvo Moskvi*, No. 8 (1964), p. 29.

[22] *Ekspluatatsiiai kapitalnii remont zhilikh zdanii* (Moscow and Leningrad, 1962), p. 32.

and mobilizing the population has been through places of work, the day-to-day activities of the citizenry have been organized and controlled through the housing machinery. In both cases supervision is by the party, but it is secondary to its production efforts, and as a result the primary task falls on the local government and trade union officials. The activities associated with residence include, in addition to minor housing regulations, sports, recreation, some youth activities, adult education, infant and child care, pensioner activities, meting out discipline for minor infractions and hooliganism, fire prevention, tree-planting, etc. These regular activities are organized into committees subordinate to the housing bureau and its housing committee. Furthermore, if a new propaganda effort is needed or volunteers are wanted to plant trees, patrol streets, clean up streets and parks, etc., it is the task of the housing bureau and its committees to recruit and supervise. The various cultural-mass activities of the housing bureau committee are financed from 1–2 per cent of the rents collected and up to 5 per cent of the rent collected for the non-living space. Thus the housing bureau has over the years become a basic focal point for Soviet society. Most of the housing bureaus were formed rather haphazardly in the 1920s and 1930s and varied from bureaus controlling a few thousand square metres of housing up to 70,000–80,000 square metres. The individual bureaus were subordinate to the local government, industry, etc., depending on who allocated and controlled the housing. Theoretically their activities were co-ordinated by the local government, but only today is this actually becoming true as local governments are taking over all housing. Housing bureaus have also theoretically been subordinate to their local housing committee elected from the community. In fact the bureaus have directed and continue to direct the activities of the housing committee.

The administrative inefficiency of the small bureaus and the desire for 'scientifically' planned community units has brought about a gradual consolidation of the bureaus so that on the average each housing bureau and committee supervises an urban community of about 25,000 square metres in smaller cities to 70,000 square metres in large cities. In drafting long-range master plans for urban areas after World War II the architects, engineers and geographers came up with the *micro-rayon* as the scientific basic urban community. Each *micro-rayon* has its own basic services such as a cafeteria, general produce store, minor repair units, laundry, club rooms, recreational areas, etc., and all are supervised by the housing bureau. The housing spreads from the centre core of services with a radius of 400–700 metres. This scheme of *micro-rayons* was the basis on which all new urban housing was built in the 1950s and 1960s. By the end of the 1960s, however, the concept of the *micro-rayon* was being challenged. By this time it was becoming clear that the Soviet Union was not going to escape all the problems of urbanization associated with the West as had been promised. Neither the *micro-rayons* and the social control structure developed around its housing bureau nor the doubling of urban housing was going to solve the problems of growing alienation, hooliganism, crime and congestion.

It was not only the growing crime statistics, never published but frequently alluded to, but the re-introduction by the 1960s of sociology and the expansion, however crude, of survey research which made clear the high level of alienation and the failure to integrate the population socially into *micro-rayons*. It was found that a large portion of those living in a district spent the major portion of their working, leisure and shopping time outside the *micro-rayon*. Furthermore, most personal relationships were found to be with relatives or friends in the same social strata formed at places of work or school and as often out of the district as within. Finally from the largely unsuccessful mass experiment with volunteer public organs organized by the community under Khrushchev it was realized that a large portion of the population worked as hard to keep out of participating in local community activities as those who actively volunteered. Although the lack of close neighbourhood communities is a common feature of most industrial cities, the nature of the Soviet problem is unique because of the stratification of Soviet cities and the Soviet emphasis on collective action (*kollektivnost*).

From the time of the revolution equality in the Soviet Union was never more than a myth and nowhere was this more true than in the allocation of housing space. Under Stalin inequality increased with the growing shortage of housing and by the special housing allotments provided various categories of workers, high-ranking professionals and politicians. But while the space allocated per individual varied greatly, there was not the marked segregation between rich and poor urban districts. The method of allocating the scarce space in the 1930s and 1940s tended to mix the high and low together in the same apartment buildings with some exceptions. Thus, except for the summer villas of the well-to-do, there are not distinct rich and poor areas. However, the current housing boom has begun to threaten this homogeneity and make the contrast between rich and poor apparent as well as real. The major culprit is co-operative housing. As currently organized only families earning 200 roubles or more a month are likely to be able to qualify to join co-operatives. Thus mostly the middle and upper income groups tend to predominate in co-operatives.[23] This discriminatory quality of co-operatives seems to be one reason the regime has kept them to less than 10 per cent of the total of new housing and mixed them with buildings of public housing.

Even though the integrative character of Soviet urban housing has helped to reduce tensions, it has intensified the authoritarian structure and made it difficult to develop spontaneous urban communities. It was expected and the population accepted that the party and government élite living in each community should manage and control the community. Thus the elected members to the various soviets and government officials living in a district are responsible for supervising and taking an activist role in all local activities. The same is true for party members. The rank-and-file party mem-

---

[23] It has been estimated that the typical payments of shareholder per month are:

Payment of loan	11·43
Interest	0·86
Maintenance cost	4·57
	16·86 roubles
Gas and electricity	5·56
	22·42 roubles

Status of shareholders in building co-operatives in the U.S.S.R. in percentage in 1964:

	%
Workers	23·7
Engineers and technicians	20·3
Medical workers	9·3
Office employees and military	10·3
Teachers	9·4
Workers in science and arts	9·8
Pensioners	6·3
Workers in retain services	2·3

Source: Iu. Ia. Dankova, *Zhilishchno-stroitelnaia kooperatsiia SSSR* (Moscow 1965), pp. 8, 12.

bers are especially assigned this task. As a result it is the practice that the local party, government élite or their representative are elected to the position of house leader in each apartment building and to the housing committee of the *micro-rayon*. As a mechanism of control this hierarchical community system has worked well. By supplementing this basic control structure with activist organizations such as the auxiliary militia (*druzhnii*) and comradely courts the regime has managed to maintain order for the most part. A major difficulty of the system, however, is that it places responsibility on the élite already overburdened. They tend to see their local community activities as their least important task and tend to neglect them. At the same time the system undermines any collective action at the mass level. Furthermore, the housing boom with its million of new individual family apartments makes it possible for Soviet families to retreat even further from collective community activities. Although Soviet planners are increasingly recognizing some of these problems, few solutions have been offered. The old Bolshevik economist, Stanislav G. Strumilin, proposed going back to one of the earliest and revolutionary ideas of the first days of the regime, the commune type apartment building, *domkommuna*. His ideas received quite a bit of publicity in 1960 and a few architects drew up plans for this type of housing. Only a few, however, have been constructed and primarily they have been for unmarried adults.

Space has not permitted a discussion of all the various ramifications of the housing boom on Soviet society but the three problems discussed: the creation of a mammoth housing construction industry, the attempts to develop an acceptable and efficient system of housing maintenance, and the search for viable urban communities do cover the over-all scope of the problems and the Soviet response, and suggest some general conclusions. First and foremost the analyst cannot help but be impressed by the size and the serious commitment of the regime to solving the housing crisis. The momentum for new housing construction has built up for fifteen years without any major slow-ups. The impact on the major cities has been overwhelming and is slowly spreading to the smaller cities. And in 1965 mass production of new housing was promised the peasantry. Although the regime initially saw new housing construction as primarily a task for Moscow, increasingly city governments have been brought first into the planning and more recently into the supervision and control over new housing. A major impetus has been the gradual recognition that centralization has completely failed in respect to housing maintenance and repairs. The problem of preventing old and new housing from deteriorating into vast slums and raising the quality of housing still remains to be solved. Even the cost of keeping standards at a minimum level is mushrooming. Although Moscow continues to decree solutions and establish more standards, the regime no longer seems to expect to find the solution in this way. Increasingly it is at the level of urban government that the leadership is experimenting and taking a second look at Stalin's policies of local autonomy. The real question is whether the present leadership will go beyond Stalin and give cities the resources, authority and prestige to tackle the problem. Thus far, what they have given is preciously small in relation to the problems facing metropolitan centres. It is also clear that doubling and even tripling the urban housing fund will also not solve the social problems of urbanization. Increased alienation and the isolation of the family and lack of community cannot be willed away by the perfectly engineered urban district. The traditional authoritarian structure of communal relations still keeps order and thus far the Soviet Union has escaped the anarchy and violence of so many urban communities of both the non-socialist and socialist world but the pressures are building up. The rapid expansion of new housing seems to be only buying time.

4

East European Economic Reforms and the Convergence of Economic Systems
by Morris Bornstein

Economic reforms in Eastern Europe (including the U.S.S.R.) during the 1960s have often been interpreted as lending support to the proposition that Eastern and Western economic systems are 'converging'. The purpose of this paper is to analyse carefully the convergence hypothesis and to examine the recent East European economic reforms in the light of this analysis.

The concept of 'convergence' comes from biology and anthropology. In biology, it refers to 'the development or possession of similar characteristics by animals or plants of different groups due to similarity in habits or environment (as the resemblance in form of body of the whales and fishes)', while in anthropology it applies to 'the independent apparently accidental development of similarities between separate cultures'.[1] Thus, the thrust is similar evolution of nominally different organisms in response to common forces.

From *Jahrbuch der Wirtschaft Osteuropas*, vol. ii (1971), pp. 247–66. Reprinted by permission of the author and Günter Olzog Verlag. This paper is based on research supported by grants from The University of Michigan Comparative Economics Program and Center for Russian and East European Studies, whose assistance is gratefully acknowledged. I also wish to thank the Hoover Institution, Stanford University, for the use of its research facilities.

[1] *Webster's New Third International Dictionary* (1967), p. 498. The use of the term and the debate over its meaning and applicability in anthropology go back to the beginning of the century, while it was used even earlier in biology. Cf. A. A. Goldenweiser, 'The Principle of Limited Possibilities in the Development of Culture', *Journal of American Folklore*, vol. xxvi, No. 101 (July–Sept., 1913), pp. 259–90.

In this paper, the 'convergence hypothesis' refers to the proposition that the 'capitalist regulated market economies' (CRMEs) of the 'West' (including Western Europe, North America, and Japan) and the 'socialist centrally planned economies' (SCPEs) of Eastern Europe and the U.S.S.R. are becoming more alike, as each group adopts features found in the other. This formulation of the hypothesis does not imply a 'meeting' of the two types of economic systems in a third—merely that the difference between them is being narrowed. Also it does not assume imitative borrowing by one system of features of the other; rather, it suggests that changes occur as each system adapts to its circumstances. Finally, it permits increasing divergence within groups, as some economies in each group move faster in the convergence process than others in the same group.

'Convergence' in this sense is quite distinct from 'coexistence'. The latter refers to the absence of military and perhaps political (though not ideological) conflict between countries or blocs with different socio-economic systems. There is ample historical evidence that countries with different economic systems can coexist peacefully while countries with similar economic systems can experience severe conflicts. Thus, there is no clear link between the convergence of economic systems and the diminution of international conflict. The Soviet concept of 'competitive coexistence' involves 'peaceful competition' in such respects as economic growth, economic stability, and living standards. It assumes that a comparative evaluation of the performance of the SCPEs and CRMEs will show the superiority of 'socialism' over 'capitalism' and eventually lead to the adoption of Soviet-style socialism in the West. It is thus not a convergence hypothesis as defined above, because it postulates change in only one direction, rather than mutual convergence. Therefore, like unidirectional Western theories, it posits 'submergence' rather than 'convergence'.[2]

Section I of this paper analyses the theoretical foundations of the convergence hypothesis. The next section examines the empirical evidence for the convergence of Western and Eastern economic systems, with special emphasis on recent East European economic

---

[2] Zbigniew Brzezinski and Samuel P. Huntington, *Political Power: USA/USSR* (New York: Viking Press, 1964), p. 419. These issues are also discussed in Hans Mayrzedt and Helmut Romé (eds.), *Koexistenz zwischen Ost und West: Konflikt, Kooperation, Konvergenz* (Vienna: Europa Verlag, 1967), esp. pp. 19–79.

reforms. Section III presents some conclusions. Within this framework, I do not attempt either an exhaustive listing or summary of the literature on convergence, or a detailed treatment of economic reforms in the individual East European countries. Rather, the aim is to assess the extent to which East European economic reforms tend to support the convergence hypothesis.

I. THEORETICAL FOUNDATIONS

The theoretical foundations of the convergence hypothesis include both positive and normative theories of convergence. The former argues essentially that convergence has been observed historically and may be expected in the future. The latter asserts that it is the *desirable* direction for the evolution of the CRMEs and the SCPEs.

Positive Theories

The origin of positive theories of convergence is largely in the economic history of industrialization and in sociological studies of modernization.

The first strand is exemplified by Rostow's stages of economic development.[3] He asserts that the economic transformation of societies proceeds through five stages. (1) In the *traditional* society, there is a ceiling on the attainable level of *per capita* output, because modern science and technology are not applied. (2) The *preconditions for take-off* are developed when science and technology are applied to new production functions in both agriculture and industry; economic progress becomes a conscious goal; entrepreneurship develops; and an effective centralized national state emerges. (3) During the *take-off*, the obstacles to steady growth are overcome by the forces for economic progress, and self-sustaining growth develops: the rate of investment rises, new industries expand, new techniques spread, and the economic, political, and social structure changes to support steady growth. (4) In the *drive to maturity*, modern technology is extended over the whole front of economic activity, new industries develop, import substitution occurs, and the economy achieves the technical and entrepreneurial skills to produce whatever it wishes. (5) In the stage of *high mass-consumption*, durable

[3] W. W. Rostow, *The Stages of Economic Growth* (Cambridge: Cambridge University Press, 1960).

consumer goods and services become important sectors, and the
'welfare state' emerges.

Rostow argues that advanced economies have followed, and developing economies may be expected to follow, this basic path of
economic development regardless of differences in economic
systems, which are relevant only in so far as they affect the timing
and speed and certain special features of national experience. The
result is similarity among nations in technology, level and composition of GNP, and other structural features, despite differences
in economic systems. Thus, he concludes that the modernization of
the Russian economy in the twentieth century was somewhat
different but on the whole not unique. 'Its domestic imperatives and
external ambitions have produced a version of the common growth
experience, abnormally centred in heavy industry and military
potential.'[4]

Starting from the assumption of a basically similar pattern of
technological evolution, sociological theories of convergence hold
that industrializing societies change in a common direction towards
increasing occupational differentiation; the mobilization of the
tradition-bound into markets, bureaucracies, and other institutions;
an increase in state power; and the development of similar integrative mechanisms.[5] Similarities in these respects develop as a
result of the limited possibilities of adapting to large-scale industrialism, even though there may be differences among countries in
the length of time for the process of adaptation or in the process of
industrialization itself.

The tendency towards a 'common industrial society' has been
explained by Kerr, Dunlop, Harbison and Myers as follows:[6]
Technology is a unifying force because at a given time there may be
several possible economic combinations or social arrangements but
only one best technology. The same technology calls for much the
same occupational structure, which in turn becomes the class
structure. Thus, social arrangements will be more similar from one

---

[4] Ibid, p. 104.

[5] The sociological literature on convergence is summarized and evaluated in
Ian Weinberg, 'The Problem of the Convergence of Industrial Societies: A Critical
Look at the State of a Theory', *Comparative Studies in Society and History*, vol. xi, No. 1
(Jan. 1969), pp. 1–15.

[6] Clark Kerr, John T. Dunlop, Frederick H. Harbison and Charles A. Myers,
Industrialism and Industrial Man (Cambridge, Mass.: Harvard University Press,
1960), pp. 282–96.

society to another when they are more closely tied to technology, more diverse the farther they are removed from technology. This is visible in the management of large-scale industry, which is run in different types of economies by professional managers separated from both ownership and political power but constrained by market forces, state planning, or both, and guided by a similar web of rules.[7]

In this industrial society, the state plays a dominant role in determining the general rate of growth and level of economic activity, providing public services, fixing the distribution of power in society and settling conflicts among power groups, and setting rules for the interaction between organizations and the behaviour of members within organizations. But despite large-scale organization, extreme centralization is not feasible; some decentralization of decision-making is necessary, especially in the production of consumer goods and services, for reasons of efficiency and initiative. Thus, industrial society is 'realistic', rejecting unworkable alternatives and seeking successful practical compromises. As a result, the force of ideology— an obstacle to convergence—fades.

A careful formulation of the 'common industrial society' argues merely that different societies tend towards similarity in these respects; it does not assert that they become identical. '. . . due allowance must be made for a looseness of fit between different elements of the social system', because 'the diffusion of technology, as with the diffusion of political models, passes through a cultural filter', and the consequences for social organization are not uniform.[8] The result is 'pluralistic industrialism' with many common features, rather than a single identical pattern.

It is interesting to compare this conception with the Marxist view. They are similar in that both hold that technology determines

---

[7] 'The managers, whether private or public, will be professionals, technically trained and carefully selected for their tasks. They will be bureaucratic managers, if private, and managerial bureaucrats, if public; each responding to the rules and the technical requirements of the job. The distinction between the private and the public manager will decrease just as the distinction between the private and the public enterprise; distinction among managers will be more according to the size, the product and the nature of their enterprise. The controlled market and the controlled budget will bring more nearly the same pressures on the managers. The private enterprise, however, will usually have more freedom of action than the public enterprise; but the middle class and the middle bureaucracy will look much alike.' Ibid., pp. 291–2.

[8] Weinberg, op cit., pp. 10, 14.

the 'relations of production' and together with it constitutes the substructure which determines the superstructure of society (social relations and culture), and hence one should expect societies using the same technology to become similar in other essential features. Also, like Rostow's, the Marxist analysis envisions successive stages of development—but these are feudalism, capitalism, socialism, and eventually communism. They also differ in regard to how much economic factors dominate over social, political, and cultural factors.[9] Further, because the Marxist interpretation postulates that socialism will succeed capitalism, it excludes the mutual convergence of the two systems. If, in contrast, in terms of Hegelian dialectics, one regarded capitalism as thesis and socialism as antithesis, then their synthesis would represent a 'convergence' incorporating features of each, plus perhaps features not found in either.[10] This position is close to the normative approach to convergence.

Normative Theories

The normative theory of convergence stems from the attempt to apply welfare economics to the design of economic systems. It has been formulated by Tinbergen in considering the choice of the 'optimum regime'.[11] His approach is to define the 'best' economic system and show that existing systems deviating from it should move towards it.

In trying to determine the optimum regime, one takes as *given data* the physical and psychological characteristics of the society considered, including (1) physical data like production functions and resources; (2) psychological data like the preferences of consuming units, usually expressed in terms of their utility functions; and (3) the social welfare function by which the society's rulers are guided. The *unknowns* to be found are (1) the institutions which best fit and (2) the appropriate numerical values for the instruments to be used —both to be chosen so as to maximize the given social welfare function. In regard to this problem, Tinbergen examines six main

[9] For Rostow's view of the differences, see Rostow, op. cit., pp. 148–56.

[10] Stanislav Andreski, *Elements of Comparative Sociology* (London: Weidenfeld and Nicholson, 1964), p. 343. (Also published, with identical pagination, as *The Uses of Comparative Sociology* (Berkeley: University of California Press, 1965).)

[11] Jan Tinbergen, 'The Theory of the Optimum Regime', in his *Selected Papers* (Amsterdam: North-Holland Publishing Co., 1959), pp. 264–304.

types of choices to be made among institutions and instruments, reaching the following conclusions:

1. *Size of the Public Sector and Nature of the Tax System.* The normal activities of government include internal and external security, stabilization, and providing the legal framework for private activity. In addition, the public sector's production activities should include (*a*) those with important external effects and (*b*) those with increasing returns, because neither would be operated properly according to private profit criteria. The former group comprises education and health as well as energy, transportation and the like. The latter criterion applies also to the same activities and in addition to a number of heavy industries. The precise frontier between the public sector and the private sector should depend on the specific circumstances, including the types of industry in a country, the organization of public enterprises, and the level of efficiency in public and private enterprises. However, under almost all circumstances, small-scale activities such as agriculture and retail trade more appropriately fall in the private sector, sometimes through co-operative arrangements. As is well known, in principle neither income-taxes nor general indirect taxes are compatible with the optimum conditions of welfare economics, but income transfers through 'lump-sum' payments are hard to carry out in practice. Thus, income-taxes, specific indirect taxes on goods deemed harmful and subsidies on goods deemed desirable, and perhaps taxes on wealth are likely to be used.

2. *Degree of Centralization in Public Sector.* There is an *a priori* argument in favour of decentralization from central to intermediate and lower agencies, because it promises more freedom, less friction and lower costs. However, this argument should be overruled where decentralized administration leads to incorrect decisions because of external effects not considered by the authority making the decisions. Each instrument of policy has a certain action radius, which specifies which agency should exercise the instrument. Decentralized administration is also inefficient if there are economies of scale requiring larger optimal units. Thus, one may conclude that questions of purely local interest, like local energy supply and transportation, should be left to local authorities. Nevertheless, although decisions are to be made locally, higher bodies may establish criteria or general rules for these decisions. Economic policy generally, on the other hand, must be conducted in a rather centralized way. And

where big agglomerations (like large corporations and cartels) exist, their actions influence others so much that they should be subject to an even more centralized authority; that is, big enterprise requires control by even bigger government.

3. *Decentralization in Production, by Size of Enterprise and Location.* The optimum size as determined by the minimum cost of production is preferred, but it depends partly on the costs of transporting the product to consumers and thus on population density.

4. *Markets and Prices.* There is a presumption in favour of free competitive markets, but different types or degrees of state regulation may be required because of externalities, increasing returns, instability, extreme shortages, etc. However, both monopoly prices and price discrimination among buyers should be rejected.

5. *Social Insurance System.* Coverage should include unemployment. illness, accidents, death of breadwinner and old age, but the treatment of family allowances is not so clear. The level of benefits for unemployment should provide security but not tempt to inactivity; 80 per cent of wages seems to be the upper limit. Financing can come from the contributions of workers, employers and the state. The first two are similar, as both are paid by the employer and borne by the worker. The higher they are, the more they act as a tax on the employment of labour and thus can serve as a tool of anticyclical policy. But the greater the public contribution, the larger the possibilities for redistribution of income. The choice between administration of the system by public or private bodies depends partly on their relative efficiency.

6. *Social Control through Production Councils.* Co-determination by workers, or their representatives, in the production process satisfies psychological needs but may conflict with efficiency. Satisfactory reconciliation will depend on the cultural tradition of the specific country.

Thus, welfare economics can offer only some general criteria for the choice of the optimum regime. Even if one assumes a particular social welfare function, the optimum regime will still depend on various structural data of the society considered, and the optimum regime for one country need not be the same for another. However, despite this variation, one can hypothesize that the optimum regime will not be some form of extreme, characterized by complete absence of either the public or the private sector; complete centralization or decentralization in production and exchange; complete equalization of income; or a single-tax system. The reason is simply that the choice of the optimum regime in these respects depends on the nature of industries or social groups, and these would not be uniform across an economy or society. Thus, in each country there will be some cases where more or less centralization is desirable—e.g. where external effects or increasing returns are more or less important. Therefore, the optimum regime will not be one-sided, and a one-sided regime will not as a rule be optimum.

Accordingly, an economic system tending toward one extreme is suspect. As economists persuade (themselves and) politicians of the direction and extent of deviation from the optimum, the economic system will be modified in the direction of the optimum regime. If the Eastern SCPEs and the Western CRMEs deviate from the optimum on different sides, the respective changes in each will lead them to converge towards the optimum. To what extent does the empirical evidence support this prediction?

II. EMPIRICAL EVIDENCE

Empirical arguments in favour of the convergence hypothesis point to various changes in the CRMEs which make them more similar to the SCPEs, and to changes in the SCPEs which make them more like the CRMEs. In this section, the former developments will be examined first briefly. Then the changes in the SCPEs represented by the East European economic reforms will be analysed more closely.

Changes in the CRMEs

Various changes relevant to the convergence hypothesis have occurred in both the private sector and the public sector since the 1930s.[12]

The private sector has experienced a tendency towards increasing concentration, as it seeks to take advantage of economies of scale in

[12] For more detailed treatment than is possible here, see, for example, Andrew Shonfield, *Modern Capitalism: The Changing Balance of Public and Private Power* (New York: Oxford University Press, 1965); E. S. Kirschen *et al.*, *Economic Policy in Our Time*, 3 vols. (Chicago: Rand McNally, 1964); Bert G. Hickman (ed.), *Quantitative Planning of Economic Policy* (Washington D.C.: Brookings Institution, 1965); and Geoffrey Denton, Murray Forsyth and Malcolm MacLennan, *Economic Planning and Policies in Britain, France and Germany* (London: Allen & Unwin, 1968).

production, distribution and research and development, as well as to secure the benefits of greater market power in finance and pricing. The growth of enterprise has been accompanied by the separation of ownership from control, which is effectively exercised by an autonomous managerial staff—what Galbraith calls the 'techno-structure'. Its aim is not profit maximization as much as sufficient profit to assure the security and growth of the organization. It attempts through advertising and other sales techniques to create, mould and control consumer tastes. Because it wants large and stable demand for technically sophisticated products, it develops close links with government agencies procuring complex industrial systems, such as those for military and space programmes. As a result, there are various similarities in organization, planning and pricing in the industrial sector in the CRMEs and SCPEs.[13] Even the pressures for decentralization are similar in the two cases—leading to reforms in Eastern Europe which to some extent parallel the division of large Western corporations into autonomous units with separate accounting ('profit centres') which trade with each other and with outside enterprises, in order to stimulate competition and initiative and provide standards for measuring managerial performance.

Greater public ownership of the means of production in the CRMEs is sometimes cited to support the convergence hypothesis. Usually reference is made to the nationalization of key industries (coal, iron and steel, railways, energy) after World War II in various West European countries, particularly France, Italy, and Great Britain. However, for the CRMEs as a group, public ownership is limited and does not appear to be increasing significantly.

---

[13] John Kenneth Galbraith, *The New Industrial State* (Boston: Houghton Mifflin Company, 1967), esp. pp. 389–92. Superficially, this may resemble Burnham's earlier (1941) theory of the 'managerial revolution'. However, Burnham predicted that—in both West and East—managers (defined to include those engaged in controlling physical production, but excluding those concerned with purchasing, sales, and finance) would become the ruling class in society, running the economy through their control of the state, which would own all of the major instruments of production. Cf. James Burnham, *The Managerial Revolution* (New York: John Day Co., 1941), esp. pp. 71–2, 80–4, 219–21. Instead, in both West and East, managers have become *part* of the ruling élite, rather than the élite itself; although ideologies and economic systems differ, the professional managers perform basically similar roles.

More important evidence in favour of convergence may be found in growing state intervention in the economy. It is now widely agreed in the CRMEs that the government's role in the economy should include not only (1) formulation and enforcement of 'rules of the game' for the private sector, but also (2) provision of 'public goods' such as defence, education and health; (3) production through state enterprise and/or regulation of private enterprise in activities characterized by externalities, indivisibilities and increasing returns, such as electric power and transportation; (4) stabilization of output, employment and prices; (5) reduction of inequality in the distribution of income and wealth, through taxes, transfer payments of various types (unemployment compensation, health insurance, old-age pensions, family allowances), and the provision of free or subsidized services (such as libraries and parks); and (6) economic planning for long-term growth. Although variously called, sometimes for ideological reasons, 'indicative planning' in the CRMEs attempts to set feasible medium-term targets for GNP, employment, income distribution, foreign trade, regional development, etc., and to implement them partly by the 'information effect' on the plans of business firms and partly by using the usual instruments of economic policy, such as credit, taxes, price regulation, and the like.

Changes in the SCPEs

Two striking but isolated changes occurred in the 1950s. In 1953 Yugoslavia moved from close imitation of the Soviet model of highly centralized administrative planning to a decentralized economy in which worker-managed enterprises pursue profits in a market environment regulated by various, mostly indirect instruments of state intervention. Second, in Poland agriculture was de-collectivized in 1956. However, these developments were not copied in other East European countries, for a variety of political and economic reasons.

Not until the early 1960s was there a general movement in Eastern Europe towards a somewhat different pattern of reform. We shall consider in turn the principal reasons for reform, the main sources of resistance to reform, the chief features of reform blue prints, and the actual implementation of reforms in the area.

Reasons for Reforms. By the early 1960s, there was growing recognition in Eastern Europe of the need to shift from a more centralized economic system in the 'extensive' phase of economic development to a less centralized system in the 'intensive' phase. In the first phase, the chief aims of 'economic construction' were to change the structure of the economy drastically and rapidly—to industrialize, to urbanize, to adjust to changes in territory as a result of World War II, to develop backward regions. The methods were socialization of the means of production, a sharp increase in the rate of investment, rapid expansion of the industrial labour force and revision of the income distribution. In the 'intensive' phase, the emphasis is no longer on rapid structural change, but rather on smaller, marginal changes in the composition of output, technology, etc. With a slowdown in the rate of growth of the labour force, capital-deepening rather than capital-widening is stressed. In the consumer goods sector, there has been a shift from a sellers' market towards a buyers' market for many goods, as a result of the rise in living standards and the availability of stocks.

Thus, the economic system must be altered to deal with the new problems of the 'intensive' phase. More decisions must be made at lower levels and on technical-economic rather than political grounds. In turn, these decentralized decisions must be guided by more rational prices and more appropriate performance indicators. Increasing discrimination and buyer resistance by consumers require greater responsiveness of production to demand. The coercion and ideological appeals used to mobilize resources in the extensive phase are replaced by more emphasis on incentives. Finally, in the intensive phase, foreign trade and international specialization acquire new importance, as a means to obtain economies of scale beyond the capacity of the domestic market, as a source of competition to discipline highly concentrated domestic industry, and as a source of innovation in products and technology.

Although these problems were perceived by some economists in the 1950s, it was not until the 1960s that the shortcomings of the traditional system were understood by political leaders in various East European countries, after they recognized the deteriorating performance of the economy in declining growth rates of national income and industrial production, rising capital–output ratios, unsaleable surpluses of consumer (and sometimes export) goods, and other economic indicators.

Discussion of the need for reform and of specific reform proposals was aided by political destalinization after 1956, which permitted freer discussion of new ideas in the economic sphere and the inflow of information from abroad. The latter brought both greater awareness of economic growth and living standards in Western Europe, and greater understanding of the operation of regulated market economies, in contrast to the 'anarchic' capitalist economies depicted in orthodox Marxist writings. What was previously regarded as a question of principle, e.g. central determination of enterprise production plans, became a matter of technique. Similarly, economists in the Communist countries were permitted to use techniques—such as mathematical programming and econometrics—previously condemned as 'bourgeois'. Both many economic problems and possible methods of solving them were depoliticized. As a result, it became possible to propose 'mixed' economic models combining central macroeconomic planning using sophisticated mathematical tools with greater reliance on market forces for microeconomic decisions.

Finally, there was a 'bandwagon' effect. The publication of the Liberman debates in the U.S.S.R. beginning in 1962 was taken in Eastern Europe as a signal that some reforms could be considered acceptable to the Soviet leadership. It then became permissible to propose reforms elsewhere, and advocates of reform in one East European country could point to developments in another to legitimate their own proposals.

Resistance to Reforms. The political leadership was slow to recognize the need for change and the form it should take. It was reluctant to believe that the system itself, rather than the incompetence of individual officials, was responsible. Also, in some cases, deficiencies in the statistical system failed to disclose the facts and causes of declining economic performance. In addition, reform was opposed on ideological grounds: reliance on the market was inconceivable in a socialist planned economy, because socialism was more than simply public ownership of the (principal) means of production; it required central planning of investment, output, prices, and distribution; capital and land charges, production for profit, and emphasis on material incentives were incompatible with socialism.

Reforms were also opposed on more pragmatic grounds. (1) Some feared reform would mean loss of central (Party) control over the main directions of economic development. While central planning could assure the priority development of sectors important to the national welfare, decentralized decision-making by autonomous enterprises in response to market forces could lead to the shift of resources from investment and military programmes to consumption, including 'frivolous' consumption. (2) Because centrally planned economies typically operate under conditions of repressed inflation and administrative allocation (rather than price rationing) of many goods, a shift towards the market would inevitably mean open inflation—which would in turn affect the distribution of income and cause or aggravate balance of payments problems. (3) At the same time, unemployment might occur as enterprises shifted to a profitability criterion and subsidies were curtailed or abandoned. (4) Adjustments in the foreign sector might be especially painful, because the liberalization of foreign trade would expose the weak competitive position of many producers. (5) Finally, some opponents simply could not believe that a 'mixed' system combined centralized planning of some aspects with decentralized enterprise decisions on others was feasible; they considered them alternative approaches which could not be fitted together harmoniously.

Reforms were also opposed on more personal grounds by various interest groups. The Party apparatus and ministerial and financial bureaucracy believed that devolution of more authority to enterprises and decision-making in the light of market forces would diminish their power. Although reforms would enhance the authority of enterprise management, not all managers were enthusiastic about them. Some who were successful under the old system did not look forward to the challenge to become independent, cost-conscious, innovation-minded entrepreneurs selling products in a competitive buyers' market. Workers, in turn, were concerned about the impact on their real incomes of changes in wages and prices under the reform, and about loss of jobs as a result of the curtailment of unprofitable production.

Finally, economic reforms were resisted on the ground that liberalization in the economic sphere might spread, threatening the paramount role of the Communist Party in national life. Freer discussion of alternatives in the economic sphere might lead to demands for open discussion of literary, cultural, and even political issues. Economic reforms imply some diffusion of power, first to enterprise management but subsequently to the population through reliance on the market for guidance on the composition of at least part of national output. It was feared that professionals in other fields might also seek greater autonomy. As the events in Czechoslovakia showed, these were not idle fears.

Main Features of Reforms. The struggle between pro-reform and anti-reform forces produced different reform models or blue prints in the various East European countries. It is beyond the scope of this paper to consider each country separately in detail.[14] However, some of the chief features of the reforms common to several, if not all, of the countries can be noted, briefly.

One common feature is a somewhat greater role for market forces. The aim is to adapt production more closely to demand, through the greater use of financial indicators such as sales, profits, or profitability (usually in relation to capital) to evaluate enterprise performance—instead of gross or net output or cost reduction. In turn, managerial incentive schemes have been revised to relate bonuses to the new indicators, and managerial and worker bonuses are to be paid from profits. 'Economic effectiveness' and *khozraschet* are to be stressed, and subsidies reduced. Greater use is to be made of indirect financial 'levers' such as prices, taxes, and credit, in

[14] Surveys of the reforms in the various countries include Karl C. Thalheim and Hans-Hermann Höhmann (eds.), *Wirtschaftsreformen in Osteuropa* (Köln: Verlag Wissenschaft und Politik, 1968), and United Nations, Economic Commission for Europe, *The European Economy in 1968 (Economic Survey of Europe in 1968)* (Geneva: 1969), ch. II, sec. 2. Financial features are analysed in Gregory Grossman (ed.) *Money and Plan: Financial Aspects of East European Economic Reforms* (Berkeley: University of California Press, 1968). The Soviet reform is discussed in Eugene Zaleski, *Planning Reforms in the Soviet Union, 1962–1966* (Chapel Hill, N. C.: University of North Carolina Press, 1967); George R. Feiwel, *The Soviet Quest for Economic Efficiency* (New York: Frederick A. Praeger, Inc., 1967); and Michael Ellman, *Economic Reform in the Soviet Union* (London: Political and Economic Planning, 1969). The Czech reform is examined in K. Paul Hensel *et al.*, *Die sozialistische Marktwirtschaft in der Tschechoslowakei* (Stuttgart: Gustav Fischer Verlag, 1968); George R. Feiwel, *New Economic Patterns in Czechoslovakia* (New York: Frederick A. Praeger, Inc., 1969); and Oldřich Kýn, 'The Rise and Fall of Economic Reform in Czechoslovakia', *American Economic Review*, vol. lx, No. 2 (May 1970). On the Hungarian reform, see István Friss (ed.), *Reform of the Economic Mechanism in Hungary* (Budapest; Akadémiai Kiadó, 1969), and Richard D. Portes, 'Economic Reforms in Hungary', *American Economic Review*, vol. lx, No. 2 (May, 1970). Soviet accounts of the East European reforms include R. N. Evstigneev, *Ekonomicheskie reformy v evropeiskikh stranakh sotsializma (Economic Reforms in the European Socialist Countries)* (Moscow: Politizdat, 1968); and Akademia Nauk S.S.S.R., Institut ekonomiki mirovoi sotsialisticheskoi sistemy (U.S.S.R. Academy of Sciences, Institute of Economics of the World Socialist System), *Planirovanie i upravlenie narodym khoziaistvom v sotsialisticheskikh stranakh (Planning and Administration of the Economy in Socialist Countries)* (Moscow: Mysl', 1969).

place of detailed output targets and input authorizations and central administration of supplies. In turn, enterprises are to receive greater autonomy in preparing and executing plans, as the number of enterprise targets fixed by higher authorities is reduced; at the extreme (in Hungary), enterprises receive no plans from above. Administrative rationing of producer goods is to be replaced at least in part by wholesale trade through direct contacts between enterprises and their suppliers and customers.

However, in some countries devolution of authority to enterprises is limited by the creation of 'associations' (or 'directorates' or 'centrals') which, depending upon the country, control the activities of their member-enterprises in some or all of the following respects: production plans, assignment of customers, pricing, allocation of investment and research and development. The powers and behaviour of the association thus determine the extent to which 'decentralization' to the enterprise and the market can in fact occur.

In regard to investment, a greater share of total financing is to come from self-finance of enterprises (from depreciation allowances and retained earnings) as well as from repayable bank credits, rather than from free budget grants. Enterprises are supposed to have more authority over investment projects, but all major investments will still be decided and chiefly financed centrally, and the availability of materials, equipment, and labour will determine the extent to which enterprise and bank funds can be used for decentralized investments.

Reform of producer goods prices from the traditional system of cost-plus non-scarcity prices is obviously essential to any decentralization, in order to provide appropriate signals for decentralized decision-making in a market framework. In this respect, most of the reforms are deficient. In the U.S.S.R. and East Germany, for example, the new prices include capital charges and eliminate or reduce losses and subsidies, but they are not scarcity prices which would permit the abolition of administrative rationing of producer goods. However, both the Hungarian reform and the Czech model aim at a partial shift towards more flexible prices approaching market-clearing levels, through the creation of a three-category price system including centrally set 'fixed' prices, 'controlled' prices set by enterprises within limits specified by the central authorities, and 'free' prices set by enterprises in response to market conditions.

Finally, in foreign trade, only in Hungary are enterprises to have significantly greater autonomy in making export and import decisions and establishing direct contacts with foreign firms, although such powers for associations are envisioned in the Bulgarian, Romanian, East German and Czech reforms.

Not only the reform blue prints but also the actual implementation of reforms—in terms of extent, timing and speed—varies by country, as a result of the continuing struggle between pro- and anti-reform forces. Once a reform model is formally approved by the Communist Party, opponents can no longer object openly. But while accepting the approved 'principles', they can attempt to block, delay or dilute the detailed application of these principles—stressing the need for caution and phased experimentation, and urging the reversal of measures which prove 'unsuccessful' or unpopular. Polish, Czech, and most recently Bulgarian experience shows that there may be a large gap between reform blue prints and subsequent changes in the economy.

A detailed country-by-country account of the status of reforms is beyond the scope of this paper. However, Table 1 attempts to summarize the situation at the beginning of 1970 in various countries of the area. It excludes Yugoslavia, where a radically different economic system had already been established in the early 1950s, as well as Albania, which has not joined in economic reforms. The classifications in the Table necessarily simplify both the complex nature of the reforms and the considerable variation among countries. Assessment of the extent to which there has been 'significant' change is inevitably partly a matter of subjective judgement. Also, the situation in each country is in flux, and further advances or retreats may occur between the completion of this paper and the time it meets the reader's eye. Nevertheless, the Table is useful to show how reforms differ by country and how reforms have been reversed in various cases.

At one extreme is the Hungarian reform, involving a basic change from a command economy towards a socialist market economy. At the other are the limited reforms, essentially seeking improvements within the framework of the old system, in the U.S.S.R., Poland and Romania. Bulgaria and East Germany may occupy an intermediate position. The Czech reform model was in many respects similar to the Hungarian, but many key features have now been suspended or eliminated. Some retrenchment has also occurred in

TABLE I

Main Features of Economic Reforms in Eastern Europe

Feature	Hungary	Czechoslovakia	Bulgaria	East Germany	Poland	Romania	U.S.S.R.
1. Substantial increase in enterprise autonomy	x	(x)	(x)				
2. Primary performance indicator(s)							
(a) Sales					x		x
(b) Profits	x			x	x		x
(c) Profitability					x		x
(d) Value added (wages and profits)		x	x				
3. Industrial associations	(x*)	x	x	x*	x*	x	
4. Price reforms							
(a) Centralized calculation on traditional cost-plus lines	x	x	x	x			x
(b) Introduction of capital charges	x	x	x	x	x		x
(c) Greater role for decentralized price-setting in response to market forces	x	(x)					
5. Shift towards financing investment via credit and self-finance, instead of budget grants	x	x	x	x	x	x	x
6. Use of profits taxes to regulate behaviour of firms	x	x	x				
7. Greater role for enterprises or associations in conduct of foreign trade	x	(x)	(x)	x		x	
8. Introduction of workers' management		(x)					
9. Decollectivization of agriculture					x*		

Key:

Blank space = No significant change from traditional soviet-type command economy model.

   x   = Change adopted after 1965.

   x*   = Change adopted before 1965.

  (x)   = Change adopted was subsequently curtailed or eliminated.

Bulgaria since the beginning of 1969. Thus, reforms in Eastern Europe are quite uneven in character and speed, and a genuine transformation of the economic system is evident only in Hungary.

III. CONCLUSIONS

On theoretical grounds, it is reasonable to expect that differences between economic systems will narrow over time. Positive theories of convergence observe that industrial nations use similar technology and therefore develop organizational arrangements for the management of industry and the regulation of the economy which are broadly similar—subject to cultural and other constraints. The normative theory argues that, although the 'optimum regime' will vary among countries according to structural characteristics and the prevailing social welfare function, it will most likely lie between extremes in respect to the arrangements for ownership, production and distribution. Thus, countries seeking to improve their economic systems are likely to move toward 'mixed' or compromise solutions concerning the size and role of the public sector, centralization in decision-making, the use of markets, and social welfare programmes and other measures to affect the distribution of income and wealth.

The empirical evidence suggests much less of a case for convergence than that perceived by enthusiastic heralds of convergence like Pitrim A. Sorokin. In brief, Sorokin asserts that the U.S.S.R. and the United States will converge to a single 'integral type' of society intermediate between their present orders and incorporating the best features of each without the defects of either. He reaches this optimistic conclusion because he believes the two countries are now more similar than is generally realized, and are becoming still more alike, in twelve different spheres: natural sciences and technology, social sciences and humanities, philosophy, ethics and criminal law, education, sport and recreation, fine arts, religion, family and marriage, the economic system, social relationships and the political system.[15] The evidence hardly supports such a conclusion.

[15] Sorokin's views were first presented in his wartime book, *Russia and the United States* (1st edn.: New York: E. P. Dutton and Co., 1944; 2nd edn.: London: Stevens & Sons, 1950). A concise statement appears in his 'Mutual Convergence of the United States and the U.S.S.R. to the Mixed Sociocultural Type', *International Journal of Comparative Sociology*, vol. i, No. 2 (Sept. 1960), pp. 143–76; reprinted in his *The Basic Trends of Our Times* (New Haven, Conn.: College and

On the other hand, there is more evidence for convergence than is conceded by Soviet writers on the subject, who argue as follows: Comparisons of technology and industrial structure of Western and Eastern economies miss the central point: ownership of the means of production and the resulting social relations. Partial nationalization in the West can hardly be considered 'socialization' of the means of production. While state intervention in the economy may be increasing, its aim is to help the monopolistic bourgeoisie maintain and increase profits; hence its class character is quite different from that of the socialist state which guides the economy for the benefit of society as a whole. Capitalist economic 'programming' is not comparable to socialist 'planning'; through public ownership, the latter can co-ordinate the entire economy, while the former is only partial, indicative and imperfect. Also, it is a mistake to regard the changes in East European economies—such as greater independence for enterprises and greater use of financial 'levers'— as 'decentralization' which weakens the role of the state. Economic reforms in Eastern Europe do not reduce the role of planning; instead, they improve and strengthen planning. Therefore, although in the Western capitalist economies the scientific-technical revolution makes the scale of production greater and thus in a sense increases its collective character, and the role of the state in the economy grows and elements of planning are introduced, these are merely steps towards the transformation of capitalist economies into socialist economies. On the other hand, there is no evidence for fundamental changes in the socialist economies. Hence, instead of mutual convergence there will be only unidirectional progress from capitalism to socialism, as envisioned by Marxist theory.[16]

University Press, 1964), pp. 78–159. His position is trenchantly criticized by Alex Inkeles, 'Russia and the United States: A Problem in Comparative Sociology', in Philip J. Allen (ed.), *Pitrim A. Sorokin in Review* (Durham, N. C.: Duke University Press, 1963), pp. 225–46.

[16] E. Bregel, 'Teoriia konvergentsii dvukh ekonomicheskikh sistem' ('The Theory of the Convergence of the Two Economic Systems'), *Mirovaia ekonomika i mezhdunarodnye otnosheniia*, No. 1 (1968), pp. 15–28; V. Golosov, 'Kontseptsii 'konvergentsii'—orudie antikommunizma' ('Ideas of "Convergence"—Instrument of Anti-Communism'), *Nauchnye doklady vysshei shkoly, Ekonomicheskie nauki* No. 3, 1969, pp. 88–93; V. Cherpakov, 'Teoriia konvergentsii i deistvitel'nost'' ('The Theory of Convergence and Reality'), *Voprosy ekonomiki*, No. 2, 1968, pp. 87–96; and G. P. Davidiuk, *Kritika teorii 'edinogo industrial'nogo obshchestva'* (*Criticism of the Theory of 'The Common Industrial Society'*) (Minsk: Nauka i tekhnika, 1968).

A dispassionate evaluation of the evidence suggests that the true situation lies between these extreme views. There clearly is some empirical support for the convergence hypothesis in the changes which have occurred in the Western CRMEs and in the Eastern SCPEs in the last decade. But the evidence indicates that this process is limited, slow and irregular. As far as the East European reforms—the focus of this paper—are concerned, an analysis of developments during the 1960s shows strong pressures for reform, resistance to reform on political and economic grounds, the adoption of modest compromise reforms in most countries, and uneven implementation of the reform blue prints. The divergence of the Hungarian reform (and the now suspended Czech reform) from the rest of Eastern Europe is much more conspicuous than any general movement in the area away from the traditional system of centralized administrative planning and control.

While there is some evidence for convergence, the differences between the Western CRMEs and the Eastern SCPEs are still very important, and will not be narrowed easily. Although greater similarity in organizational forms and instruments of economic policy may be observed in the CRMEs and SCPEs as both try to combine planning and the market, fundamental differences are likely to persist in ownership arrangements, methods of resource allocation and principles of income distribution. These differences are rooted in the political–social environment in which an economic system operates. This environment determines the distribution of power in society, the nature and relative importance of collective and individual preferences, and the trade-offs between economic efficiency and other aspects of social welfare, as evaluated by the prevailing preferences.[17]

[17] My conclusion therefore is less affirmative and more qualified than Tinbergen's, for example. For the most recent statement of his position, see H. Linnemann, J. P. Pronk and J. Tinbergen, 'Convergence of Economic Systems in East and West', in Emile Benoit (ed.), *Disarmament and World Economic Interdependence* (Oslo: Universitetsforlaget; New York: Columbia University Press, 1967), pp. 246–60.

PART II

Production and Supply

Introduction to Part II

The area of production, particularly 'costs of production', is a very fertile one for empirical studies. Data on costs are available in firms' internal accounts and through engineering information, and firms have often been ready to allow economists to see this information and to use it. Moreover, with a little manipulation the data can be related to cost concepts, such as fixed, variable, average and marginal, that are found in economic theory.

A major concern of cost studies is to relate changes in costs to changes in output levels, to study the effect of changes in scale, and to establish the existence or otherwise of economies of scale. The most comprehensive study of economies of scale in British industry was undertaken by research workers at the Department of Applied Economics at Cambridge University in the 1960s. Aubrey Silberston's paper summarizes both the theoretical basis of economies of scale and the results of the Cambridge research. It provides the most up-to-date information on economies of scale in U.K. industry.

Economies of scale are important in their impact on the structure of industry. Silberston indicates this through his various Tables and Pratten's paper shows the detailed implications for the motor industry. Pratten was the author of the final report on the Cambridge research and the paper is taken from a chapter of his book. Its value lies in showing the detailed study and research required to establish the quantitative existence of economies of scale.

The theory of the firm is a more difficult area for empirical study.

The concepts provided by the theory, such as profit maximization and marginal cost pricing, are much less amenable to empirical testing. The data are often not available in the form required and even if they are, firms are inclined to regard them as part of their commercial secrets. The drawbacks in asking firms what they do, or think they do, are well known.

The different methods of empirical research in this field are well illustrated by the chosen readings. The paper by Hague reports on research carried out by members of the Centre for Business Research at the Manchester Business School. The research consisted of in-depth investigation and interview of pricing policies in 13 companies. It required 4 researchers working for 6 years to compile the study.

The part reproduced here relates to the objectives of firms. This must be the basis for any theory on pricing behaviour and the traditional assumption of profit maximization has been under attack for some time. Given the nature of this attack it is perhaps surprising to record that Hague found that '5 out of the 13 firms studied were anxious to maximize profits'. Hague points out, however, that some of these firms were also anxious to achieve other objectives, such as minimizing redundancies, which might conflict with this objective. Hague's main point arising from this is that firms pursue a multiplicity of objectives and therefore satisficing objectives may be more appropriate than maximization.

The paper by Skinner illustrates an alternative empirical approach. Skinner attempts to test the pricing policies of a number of firms, mainly small and medium, in the Merseyside and North Wales area. He uses the questionnaire method and indicates his awareness of the difficulties of this type of investigation. His report draws attention to one of the criticisms often made of cost-plus pricing theories. While businessmen may argue that they use a mark-up or some form of cost-plus pricing, their other answers indicate that they allow for changing market conditions so that an element of marginality enters into their pricing decision, even if it is only the mark-up which is varied.

Finally Townsend's paper is included because it deals with an area of important public policy interest—the benefits and disadvantages of oligopoly structure. There are a number of aggregative studies relating structure to performance but Townsend provides a study of a particular industry in a British context which is a little more rare. The evidence he provides is by no means conclusive. He concludes that as far as petrol distribution is concerned an oligopoly structure has probably meant lower prices than might have occurred in a more competitive structure.

5

Economies of Scale in Theory and Practice[1]

by Aubrey Silberston

I. GENERAL CONSIDERATIONS

This article concentrates on a comparatively narrow subject—
technical economies of scale for plants and firms. It discusses the
sources of these economies and gives quantitative estimates for a
number of specific industries. For the most part it deals with static
economies of scale of the classic type. I refer later to dynamic factors,
such as learning and the growth of firms, and also say something about practical implications, but this is not my main concern. My excuse for dealing with so comparatively narrow a subject,
at a time when these problems are being discussed with reference to
an ever wider range of factors, is that the relationships I wish to
talk about are at the heart of most present-day discussions, but are
not, in my view, always analysed with sufficient care. Nor are
quantitative estimates usually given, other than by reference to
those made by Bain.[2] For the estimates given here I rely on the
work of my colleague Cliff Pratten—work with which I was associated for several years.

Classic economies of scale relate to the effect on average cost of

From *Economic Journal*, Special Issue in honour of E. A. G. Robinson, March
1972, pp. 369–91. Reprinted by permission of the author and the Royal Economic
Society.

[1] I am grateful to A. B. Atkinson, K. D. George, R. C. O. Matthews, C. F.
Pratten and M. F. G. Scott, whose comments and suggestions have been extremely
helpful.

[2] J. S. Bain, *Barriers to New Competition* (Cambridge, Mass.: Harvard University
Press, 1956).

production of different rates of output, per unit of time, of a given commodity, when all possible adaptations have been carried out to make production at each scale as efficient as possible. This is the long run average cost curve of the firm, or the 'scale curve' as it is more usefully called. The scale curve has a date on it, so to speak, because it assumes a given state of technical knowledge, but it is timeless, in the sense that it shows the potentially lowest costs of producing at any scale at a given moment of time. A high scale of output may require a different technique from a low scale, but this technique is known, and is not adopted at small scales simply because it is not an economical technique at those scales. The scale curve is therefore reversible—the fact that certain techniques are used in a large plant does not affect the techniques to be adopted in a small plant, even if, in this timeless world, the large plant is built 'first', in some sense.

The scale curve is drawn on the assumption of given factor prices: factors are assumed to be in perfectly elastic supply, so that their prices are not affected by scale. This introduction of factor prices makes it clear that at each scale the least-cost combination of factors is sought, so that the particular 'blue print' chosen at any scale depends *inter alia* on factor price ratios. This establishes the important point that 'technical' economies of scale are not purely technical. A scale curve applicable to one economy, with a given set of factor prices, may be different from that applicable to another economy, with a different set of factor prices.

It is assumed that, at any point on the scale curve resources are used efficiently—not only has the least-cost combination of factors been chosen, but there is no slack, or 'X-inefficiency', as Leibenstein[3] would call it. In other words, we are on the production frontier.

It is implicit in what has been said that any given plant is conceived of as being built *ab initio* to produce at a particular scale. At that scale, the short-run and long-run cost curves of the firm will be tangential. At any moment there is a particular plant in existence, and this plant may be used more or less intensively, its average costs tracing out the short-run cost curve of the firm.

We assume, for the moment, that we are dealing with a single-product, single-plant firm, so that 'plant' and 'firm' are synonymous. This assumption will be relaxed shortly.

[3] H. Leibenstein, 'Allocative Efficiency vs. "x Efficiency"', *American Economic Review*, June 1966.

Some difficulty is caused by the notion of 'average' costs of production. Since we are dealing with long-run concepts it is assumed that costs include the cost of capital equipment and buildings, including some minimum rate of return—the 'market' rate of interest perhaps. The normal commercial way of dealing with capital costs is of course to assume some length of life, and then to work out a depreciation charge per annum. To this needs to be added an annual charge for interest. When these sums are divided by the capacity of the plant, average capital costs per unit of output are arrived at.

In a static world, capital is constant over time. In the absence of rising prices the method of calculating average capital costs just described would be the theoretically correct one. If prices rose, capital (and depreciation) would have to be valued at current prices. In a non-static world, however, both capital and output change over time: one is no longer dealing with classic economies of scale in the narrowest sense. When one broadens the concept— as one has to, to give it some relevance to actuality—to take account of a stream of costs which may vary over time,[4] it is necessary to discount future streams of costs in order to be able to compare present values. The obvious way of doing this is to calculate, for a number of hypothetical plants of different scale, the present discounted value of future variable costs, plus future expenditure on maintenance, etc. To this must be added the initial costs of capital, research and development, etc. Economies of scale will be present if the total present value, so calculated, divided by the assumed output capacity for each plant, is lower the larger the scale of plant. This is equivalent to saying, when account is taken of the future, that average costs are lower at larger scales of output.[5]

One last factor to be mentioned here is that of vertical integration or 'depth' of production. Every product is manufactured in a number of succeeding stages. The depth of production in any particular plant is partly a function of the history of the plant, and partly of technical and economic considerations. When calculating average costs at different scales for our single homogeneous commodity, it is clearly necessary for comparability to assume the same depth of production in plants of all scales. It should not be forgotten,

---

[4] The need to do this will become clearer when we discuss 'dimensions' of scale in Section II below.

[5] In practice, it did not prove possible in the work discussed below to calculate average costs in this way, and more conventional methods had to be used.

however, that the ideal depth of production may itself be a function of scale: the larger the scale, the greater may be the desirable degree of depth. But the opposite is also a possibility—for example when vertical disintegration brings about economies as an industry grows in scale. In empirical studies, this question of the depth of production raises considerable problems, and has to be borne constantly in mind.

II. THE DIMENSIONS OF SCALE

It was said earlier that economies of scale relate to the effect on average costs of production of different rates of output, per unit of time, of a given commodity. But this is too simple a way of analysing scale economies. As soon as one considers the problem further, or attempts to do empirical work, one realizes that the answer to the question 'scale of what?' is not simply 'scale of output per unit of time'. Scale has many *dimensions*, as it is convenient to call them. This point was first brought home to me when George Maxcy and I were studying the economics of vehicle production.[6] We found that car bodies of a given style were often intended to remain in production for several years, and engines for even longer. In so far as there were initial costs that varied little with the length of production run, the cost of these per unit varied primarily with the total number of car bodies or engines produced and not with annual output.[7] It was not good enough therefore to think only of economies of scale per unit of time—it was necessary to treat time itself as part of the story, and to consider total production over time.

It could be argued that an output of X per annum for Y years is the equivalent of an output of XY per annum for one year. But it does not follow that an output of X per annum for Y years would necessarily be produced in the same manner as an output of XY in one year. The higher the rate of output per day or per week, the more scope there is likely to be for mechanized processes which would be uneconomical at smaller rates of output. Hence we have to consider at least two dimensions of scale economies: the rate of output of

[6] G. Maxcy and A. Silberston, *The Motor Industry*, Cambridge Studies in Industry (London: Allen and Unwin, 1959).

[7] Alchian emphasizes the difference between rate and quantity of output (A. Alchian, 'Costs and Outputs', in *The Allocation of Economic Resources, Essays in Honor of B. F. Haley* (Stanford University Press, 1959)). This is the same point.

a product at a particular period of time, and the period of time for which the product is produced.

Further dimensions of scale need to be considered if we are to understand fully how scale economies may arise. For this purpose we need to drop the assumption that firms produce only one product and own only one plant.

In practice, virtually all firms produce several products. This may be for technical reasons, as in the case of true joint production, or simply for cost or market reasons. In the latter case there may or may not be some technical connection between the way different products are made. For example, a firm processing raw rubber may go on to manufacture tyres and inflatable rafts. The earlier stages of the production process may be common for both products, so that a technical link exists. Alternatively, a firm producing beer and skittles may find no technical link in manufacture, although there may be a marketing link at the end of the production process.

When several products are made, or several processes carried out, in one plant it will probably be easier to exploit technical links in manufacture than when products are made in widely separated plants. This will apply vertically as well as horizontally, so that depth of production will be important. With a many-plant firm or industry, the main source of technical economies may come from specialization between plants, perhaps at different stages of the production process.[8]

Thus each of the two dimensions referred to above relates to a number of different interrelated products. And each of these dimensions may be considered in relation to either the plant or the firm or the industry (or even the whole economy).

One way of analysing these various dimensions of scale is to distinguish three main aspects. The average cost of producing a product (or a group of similar products) can be regarded as a function of all three of these (they have been numbered for convenience).

D.1 Time periods
D.2 Products
D.3 Units

[8] Where this occurs it is not obvious why the separate plants need necessarily be under common ownership. It may be the case, however, that certain common fixed or semi-fixed costs may usefully be spread over a large number of plants. Or possibly close control over operations in several plants may bring economies, for example when the output of one plant is used as the raw material of another.

A subdivision of these three principal dimensions of scale may be helpful for a fuller understanding of them.

D.1 *Time Periods*
(*a*) Life of plant and equipment
(*b*) Life of (each) product

D.2 *Products*
(*a*) Total output over time (of each product) [including output profile over time]
(*b*) Output per unit of time (of each product)
(*c*) Standardization between products

D.3 *Units*
(*a*) Plants
(*b*) Firms
(*c*) Industries

D.1 (*a*) relates to plant and equipment which is not specific to a particular product and D.1 (*b*) to the time period over which a product is produced. Other things equal, longer life reduces costs per unit of output. The rate of discount must clearly be considered in this context (and in D.2 (*a*) also) since output at different points in time is at issue.

D.2 (*a*) relates to the savings from spreading initial costs over the output of a product, and D.2 (*b*) to the possibilities for mechanization, etc., that come from high output per unit of time. D.2 (*c*) is relevant to the savings in design and capital costs that may be obtained from producing similar products, especially if the same equipment can be used for them. Marketing economies may also apply when a group of similar products is made.

D.3 (*a*) relates to the savings that may arise from increases in the scale of plants, e.g. savings in administration. The degree of depth or vertical integration is also relevant here, since it affects the possibilities for technical linkage within the plant. D.3 (*b*) relates to savings that may arise from the size of the firm, e.g. in administration, research, etc., and also from specialization between plants. D.3 (*c*) is relevant to the external economies that may arise from the size of the industry as a whole, e.g. from vertical disintegration.

These dimensions of scale have implications for diseconomies as well as for economies. The less standardization there is between products, for example, the smaller the technical possibilities of gaining advantages from scale, and the more complicated the problems of management. Similar considerations apply to the multiple activities of firms. Industries too may suffer as well as gain from scale in that external diseconomies as well as external economies may arise.

III. THE SOURCES OF ECONOMIES OF SCALE

In his discussion of the optimum firm Robinson[9] distinguishes a number of sources of economies of scale—the division of labour, the integration of processes, vertical disintegration, the economy of the large machine, the balance of processes and the economies of massed reserves. Pratten and Dean[10] give a similar breakdown—indivisibilities, the economies of increased dimensions, the economies of specialization, the economies of massed resources, superior organization of production and the learning effect.[11]

This way of classifying the sources of scale has the virtue of clarity, in that it enables the reasons why economies may arise with scale to be readily understood. But it has the disadvantage that it does not bring out clearly the way in which economies are related to the various dimensions of scale. With this in mind, I have tried to reclassify the sources of economies of scale, in an attempt to bring out more clearly than hitherto the contributions made by the various factors. My suggested classification is given below, followed by a brief note on each item. For convenience the various categories have again been given numbers.

Sources of Economies of Scale

A. Which affect capital costs (per unit)
   A.1 Initial fixed costs
   A.2 Working capital

[9] E. A. G. Robinson, *The Structure of Competitive Industry*, Cambridge Economic Handbooks (Nisbet, Cambridge University Press, 1931).

[10] C. F. Pratten and R. M. Dean, *The Economies of Large-Scale Production in British Industry*, Department of Applied Economics Occasional Papers, No. 3 (Cambridge University Press, 1965).

[11] My present view is that the learning effect is best treated as a quasi-dynamic factor, not included in the classic notion of economies of scale: this is discussed below.

B. Which affect operating costs (per unit)
 B.1 Specialization of labour
 B.2 Vertical linking economies

C. Which affect both capital and operating costs (per unit)
 C.1 Increased size
 C.2 Specialization of plant

A.1 *Initial Fixed Costs*

Some costs may be constant whatever the scale of output of a product, e.g. design costs or research and development costs. The larger the total output over time, the lower will be these costs per unit.

A.2 *Working Capital*

The use of massed resources leads to economies in stocks. Stock economies may also result if larger output per unit of time allows flow production to replace batch production.

B.1 *Specialization of Labour*

Greater specialization of labour will be possible if scale per unit of time increases, thus reducing operating costs per unit. Operating costs per unit may also be reduced if flow production replaces batch production, because idle time may be less.

B.2 *Vertical Linking Economies*

At large scales of output per unit of time it may be possible to link successive stages of production without sacrificing economies at each stage. Economies may arise as a result of linkage, e.g. saving of fuel (as in the manufacture of iron and steel) and saving of transport costs (when weight-losing materials are used at one or more stages of production).

C.1 *Increased Size*

With increased size of plant, capital costs may not go up proportionately with scale. The amount of initial outlay on research and development or selling expenses may behave in a similar way: it may rise, but not proportionately. *Operating* costs per unit of output may fall because the costs of operating a plant may not rise proportionately with its size, and hence with its output.

C.2 *Specialization of Plant*

As output per unit of time (and also total output over time) increases, more specialized plant and equipment may become economical, i.e. the sum of capital and operating costs per unit of output may fall. At the scale where a more specialized technique becomes profitable, capital costs per unit are likely to be higher with the more specialized technique than with less specialized technique, and operating costs to be lower.[12] At higher scales of output, capital costs as well as operating costs per unit may be lower with more specialized techniques.

It will be seen that the *sources* of economies of scale have been put in terms of economies arising within a plant, while the *dimensions* of scale were discussed with reference to firms and industries, as well as to plants. This is not inconsistent. All the economies connected with the various dimensions or scale arise from savings in capital or operating costs, of the types listed under categories A, B and C above. Although these sources of economy may apply beyond the plant, therefore, their nature remains essentially the same.

IV. MEASURING ECONOMIES OF SCALE

I do not intend to discuss here the various alternative methods of measuring potential economies of scale. This has been done by Pratten and Dean[13] and by Pratten in his recent book.[14] In the work at the Cambridge Department of Applied Economics we adopted an 'engineering' approach, relying largely on estimates given to us by those in the appropriate industry, but also cross-checking with any published work that we could find.[15] The discussion of dimen-

---

[12] More specialized techniques are likely to be more mechanized than less specialized techniques. They are not adopted at small scales of output because their low operating costs per unit are more than offset by high capital costs per unit, arising from the fact that their capacity cannot be fully utilized.

[13] *Economies of Large-scale Production.*

[14] C. F. Pratten, *Economies of Scale in Manufacturing Industries*, Department of Applied Economics Occasional Papers, No. 28 (Cambridge University Press, 1971).

[15] Bain, *Barriers*, also used the engineering approach, as did J. Haldi and D. Whitcomb, 'Economies of Scale in Industrial Plants', *Journal of Political Economy* (Aug. 1967), in a valuable study.

sions of scale above brings out very clearly the danger of relying, for estimates of any accuracy, on aggregative methods of estimating economies. For example, the use of time series on industry costs and output is not only likely to throw together products which are scarcely comparable, but also to ignore altogether the question of dimensions of scale. When one constructs engineering estimates, on the other hand, one must necessarily examine carefully the appropriate dimensions of scale for each product.

The range of technical processes considered is of especial importance in engineering studies, since the problem of balance will affect the scale at which average costs reach their minimum. If some operations have a large minimum optimum scale, while others have a small minimum optimum, a plant in which both operations are carried out must duplicate the latter operation if balance at minimum cost is to be achieved. The minimum optimum scale gives the lowest cost of producing a given product, therefore, when that product is subject to a specified range of operations. With a larger range of operations the minimum optimum may be raised, but it cannot be lowered, because one of the existing operations dictates the present minimum optimum, i.e. acts as the lowest common multiple.

We have talked so far of the economies of scale for producing an individual product, even when a range of products is produced. In practice, it may be inconceivable that one product only could be produced. For example, a factory could not reasonably concentrate on the production of black shoes for men, of one size, in size 9 only. It must produce a range of sizes and, almost certainly, a range of styles. In cases such as this it is necessary to measure the economies of scale for producing a *group* of products—a group that is assumed to remain unchanged with scale, and to be reasonably homogeneous, in that individual products use similar materials and production methods, and cater for similar markets.

V. THE IMPORTANCE OF ECONOMIES OF SCALE

To assess the importance of economies of scale one needs first to construct a hypothetical scale curve for a given product or group of products. Most of the evidence suggests that such a curve will be *L*-shaped—i.e. will fall at first and then become horizontal. The point at which the curve becomes horizontal is the minimum optimum or efficient scale (*m.e.s.*). It represents a given rate of output per unit of time, although in constructing the curve such dimensions of scale as total output over time will have had to be taken into account.

If one now asks whether or not economies of scale are 'important' for the product concerned, there are various ways of answering this question. One is to estimate how much *capital* would be needed to build an *m.e.s.* plant. If the sum needed were large in relation to the internal or external resources of any one firm in an economy under study, then in some meaningful sense the economies of scale could be said to be important: a plant of *m.e.s.* would cost so much to build that this would constitute a serious barrier to entry into the industry.

An implicit assumption here is that average costs at *m.e.s.* are appreciably lower than at smaller scales. If this were not so, the *m.e.s.* would be of no great interest, since at smaller scales no serious cost penalty would be incurred. One way of gauging this is to ask what increase in average costs would occur at, say, half the *m.e.s.* If the increase were over 10 per cent one might perhaps conclude that economies of scale were important, but if it were under 5 per cent one might regard the *m.e.s.* as of little significance.

Another factor that must be considered is whether one is dealing with gross or net output. Bought-in raw materials, etc., may constitute a large proportion of total costs. If material prices do not change with quantity bought, average costs will not be much reduced at large scales of output, even when there are considerable economies in processing the bought-in materials. It is therefore necessary to look at economies of scale for *value-added* as well as at economies of scale for *gross output*, especially because it is economies for value-added which are likely to be of the greatest relevance to the height of entry barriers into any particular industry.

So far we have considered the importance of what might be called 'absolute' scale, i.e. whether the minimum optimum scale is absolutely large in the sense that a plant of this scale would cost a great deal of money to erect and equip. But for many purposes it is more interesting to consider the importance of 'relative' scale, i.e. whether a plant of minimum optimum scale would supply some appreciable proportion of the market in which it operates. This is of interest from the point of view of efficiency and of industrial structure. If the market is too small to contain even one plant of the minimum optimum scale, then it follows that any plant set up to produce for that market cannot be as efficient as it is possible to be, because its scale will be too small. If the market is big enough to hold a number of optimum scale plants, then efficient scale will be possible. But if the number of efficient plants that a market can hold is small, a problem of industrial structure may arise, since economies of scale will not be compatible with an industry containing more than a small number of firms. In other words, if one wants efficient scale, the price one has to pay may be oligopoly, or even monopoly.

It will be clear from this why it is desirable to look at relative scale as well as at absolute scale. But the use of a relative measure of scale implies that economies of scale which are small from the point of view of a large market may be great from the point of view of a small one. If a plant representing only 1 per cent of the United States market in a particular industry is large enough to gain all possible economies of scale, one would not consider scale economies to be important in *that* market. But it may be that, for technical and economic reasons, a similar plant would have to be built in a much smaller market, if the lowest possible costs were to be achieved there. A plant which represents only 1 per cent of the United States market might, however, represent a very significant share of the Australian market or the Nigerian market. It follows that whether economies of scale are 'important' or not will be a function of the size of the market, as well as of the capital required to build a plant of optimum scale. And even the capital aspect has its relative component, since what is a great deal of capital for a small country may not be much for a large one. Large countries are obviously much better placed than small countries, therefore, to take advantage of the economies of scale.

There is one important proviso to be made about this conclusion. The market for the products of an industry may not be coterminous with the boundaries of the country in which it operates: the Swiss watch industry is perhaps the best-known example of this. The 'market' for Swiss watches is not Switzerland alone but the whole world. To determine whether economies of scale are important in relation to a market, therefore, one must consider the home plus the export market: the latter may be as large as the former, and possibly even larger. The size of the export market is not given, however. It depends, among other things, on success in product design and in marketing, as well as on low costs of production. But this applies to the home market also. The potential home market for a product may be large, but it may be satisfied by imports. Thus, whether a firm can find a market large enough to take the output of a plant of minimum optimum scale will be a function of its success as a competitor as well as of the size of some given market.

The extent to which export markets can be found, or imported goods can be held off, will depend partly on rates of tariff and on costs of transport. The lower these are, the less clearly defined will be the market open to a firm, and the higher they are, the more clearly defined. If transport costs are high in relation to economies of scale, the possibility arises of separate markets *within* a country, in the sense that competition between regional markets may be weak. This is particularly likely to occur in a country as large as the United States.

Another type of sub-market may arise for a product. If, for example, one takes the market for synthetic fibres in the United Kingdom, then the market for one fibre only, say nylon, will be smaller than this. But here again the question of competitive success enters into the story, because nylon's share of the market depends, among other things, on the success with which it is marketed in relation to terylene and other synthetic fibres.

When we ask whether economies of scale are important, therefore, we need to relate the minimum optimum scale to the scale of the relevant market; but the relevant market is not something which we can take as given. It is affected by the competitive performance of the firms concerned, and one element only in that performance will be the economies of scale they have managed to obtain. The more steeply the scale curve falls, however, the greater will be the opportunity for economies of scale, and the greater the impetus for firms to seek markets which transcend regional and national boundaries.

VI. EMPIRICAL ESTIMATES OF SCALE ECONOMIES

I have listed elsewhere[16] some of the findings of research into economies of scale. For the present purpose I confine myself to the empirical results of my colleague Cliff Pratten, of the Department of

[16] A. Silberston, 'The Relationship between Size and Efficiency', in *Changes in the Industrial Structure of the U.K.*, Papers read at the Society of Business Economists Conference at King's College, Cambridge, Apr. 1970, and published by the Society.

Applied Economics at Cambridge. These are summarized in Table 30.1 of his *Economies of Scale in Manufacturing Industries*, which includes estimates of both absolute and relative economies of scale. Table 1 reproduces Pratten's key Table, somewhat rearranged and omitting some products for which information is incomplete. These estimates have been made on assumptions regarding dimensions of scale which differ according to each product, and Pratten's book must be consulted by anyone wishing to understand the basis of each estimate. It will be noticed that twenty-five industries only are included, and there are thus necessarily many omissions. It is probably true, however, that a substantial proportion of those products with significant[17] technical economies of scale are included. To that extent, therefore, the Table perhaps gives an impression that economies of scale are more important, taking British manufacturing industry as a whole, than is the case on the average.

Column (2) of Table 1 gives estimates of the *m.e.s.* in terms of physical output, e.g. 2 million tons per annum of Portland cement, rather than in terms of the capital cost of a plant of this scale. It can be seen fairly readily that the *m.e.s.* estimates for most of the products listed imply capital costs running into millions of pounds.[18] Among products for which capital costs are on the relatively low side, however, are individual dyes, bread, iron foundry castings, machine tools, cotton textiles, books and plastic products. At the other extreme are products like steel and aircraft, although in the latter case initial research and design costs are of especial importance.

Table 1 shows the importance of economies of scale in two other ways—it shows the increase of costs of production per unit at 50 per cent of *m.e.s.*, and it gives *m.e.s.* as a percentage of the United Kingdom market (including the export market) and of any important sub-market.[19] It also shows some important sources of economies of scale, in terms of the categories that I analysed earlier. Pratten discusses these sources fully in his detailed treatment: his categories are somewhat different from mine, but there are close similarities. The position is too complex to be summarized satisfactorily, and my attempt to do so should not be taken as more than broadly indicative.

---

[17] The meaning of 'significant' in the present context is explored further below.

[18] Unfortunately it was not possible on this occasion to make detailed estimates of capital costs.

[19] See footnote † of Table 1.

TABLE I

Estimates of Economies of Scale

(1)	(2)	(3) % increase in costs per unit at 50% m.e.s. (over costs at m.e.s.)		(4) m.e.s. as % of:		(5)
Product, etc.	m.e.s. (physical output)*	(a) Total costs	(b) Value added	(a) U.K. market in 1969	(b) Sub-market†	Important sources of economies of scale‡
1. *Oil* general purpose refinery	10 million tons p.a.	5	27	10	40 (regional mkt.)	C.1, C.2
2. *Chemicals*						
(a) ethylene plant	300,000 tons p.a.	9	30	25	100 (regional mkt.)	C.1, C.2
(b) sulphuric acid	1 million tons p.a.	1	19	30	100 (regional mkt.)	C.1, C.2
(c) plant—individual dye	(large)	22	44	100	—	A.1, C.1
3. *Synthetic Fibres*						
(a) polymer plant	80,000 tons p.a.	5	23	33	66 (nylon)	C.1
(b) plant for filament yarn extrusion	40,000 tons p.a.	7	11	16	33 (nylon)	C.1, C.2
4. *Beer*—brewery	At least 1 million barrels p.a.	9	55	3	6 (regional mkt.)	C.1
5. *Bread*—bakery	Throughput of 30 sacks of flour per hour	15	30	1	33 (city with 1 million population)	C.1, C.2
6. *Detergents*—plant	70,000 tons p.a.	2.5	20	20	—	C.1
7. *Cement*—Portland cement works	2 million tons p.a.	9	17	10	40 (regional mkt.)	C.1
8. *Bricks*—works making non-Fletton bricks	25 million bricks p.a.	25	30	0.5	5 (regional mkt.)	B.1, C.1

		5–10	12–17			
9. *Steel*						
(a) Steel production—blast furnace and L.D. route	9 million tons p.a.	5–10	12–17	33	—	B.2, C.1
(b) Works making wide strip and other rolled products	4 million tons p.a.	8	13	80	—	C.1
10. *Iron foundry*						
(a) Making cylinder blocks	50,000 tons p.a.	10	15	1	30 (car cylinder blocks)	A.1
(b) Making small engineering castings	10,000 tons p.a.	5	10	0·2	—	A.1
11. *Cars*						
(a) One model and its variants	500,000 cars p.a.	6	10	25	50 (cars of 1,200 cc)	A.1, C.2
(b) A range of models	1 million cars p.a.	6	13	50	—	A.1, C.2
12. *Aircraft*—one type of aircraft	>50 aircraft	>20	>25	>100	—	A.1
13. *Bicycles*—a range of models	<100,000 p.a.	(small)	(small)	10	—	A.1, C.2
14. *Machine tools*						
(a) one type	(varies with type)	5 (varies with range)	10 (varies with range)	>100	—	B.1
(b) factories	300 employees	>4	>10	0·5	—	B.1
15. *Diesel engines*—models in range 1–100 h.p.	100,000 units p.a.	>4	>10	>10	100 (individual size)	A.1, C.2
16. *Turbo generators* one design	4 p.a.	5	10	100	—	A.1, B.1
17. *Electric motors* range of models (1–100 h.p.)	£10 million p.a. (1969 prices)	15	20	60	—	A.1, C.2
18. *Domestic Electrical Appliances* range 10 appliances	500,000 p.a.	8	12	20	50 (refrigerators or washing machines)	A.1, C.2
19. *Electronic capital goods*						
(a) one product (e.g. computer or radar equipment)	1,000 units p.a.	8	13	100	—	A.1, B.1
(b) range of products	£200 million p.a.	10	16	100	(much higher for individual product)	A.1, B.1
20. *Cotton textiles*						
(a) spinning mills	60,000 spindles }	(small for mills, but high for individual products)		2		A.2, B.1
(b) weaving mills	1,000 looms }					A.2, B.1

TABLE I—*continued*

(1)	(2)	(3) % increase in costs per unit at 50% m.e.s. (over costs at m.e.s.)		(4) m.e.s. as % of:		(5)
Product, etc.	m.e.s. (physical output)	(a) Total costs	(b) Value added	(a) U.K. market in 1969	(b) Sub-market†	Important sources of economies of scale‡
21. *Warp knitting*	100 knitting machines	(small)	(small)	3	(much higher for indiv. products)	A.2, B.1
22. *Footwear factories*	300,000 pairs p.a.	2	5	0·2	(much higher for indiv. groups of products)	C.2
23. *Newspapers*	(circulation equiv. to highest reached in U.K. i.e. popular Sunday paper)	20	40	30	100 (one class of newspaper)	A.1, C.1
24. *Books*						
(a) one title	10,000 copies	36	50	100 (hard-backs)	—	A.1
(b) firms	(small)	(small)	(small)	2	—	B.1, C.1
25. *Plastic products*						
(a) one product	(large)	(large)	(large)	100	—	A.1
(b) firms making range of products	(small)	(small)	(small)	1	—	B.1, C.2

* m.e.s. = Minimum Efficient Scale = Minimum Optimum Scale.
† Where applicable, i.e. regional market for trades where transport costs are important, and markets for important individual products for trades making a range of products.
‡ See Section III of the text for definition of A.1, C.1, etc. The sources quoted in Column (5) are not of course meant to be exclusive. Other sources of economies of scale apply in virtually every case.
Source: Based on Table 30.1, Pratten, *Economies of Scale in Manufacturing Industries* (1971).

Table 2 rearranges the material in Table 1 to show individual industries in descending importance of the market share represented by their *m.e.s.* It splits up some of the industries shown in Table 1, e.g. chemicals, into individual products, but where appropriate plants rather than products have been taken. The choice was necessarily somewhat arbitrary. It was made according to whether individual products (including groups of related products), or the entire output of a plant, seemed to be the more important from the point of view of market substitutability. Additional factors were the extent to which there are technical links in manufacture between the various products made in a plant, and the degree of flexibility in product-mix.

The 'market' in Column (2) is usually the total United Kingdom (home and export) market, but in some cases it was more appropriate to take a sub-market: this radically alters the picture for some products. Another thing done in Table 2 is to show the increase in costs at 50 per cent of *m.e.s.* in terms of value added only, and to omit the figure for total costs. As will be seen from Table 1, the differences between the two figures may be large, but the value-added figure seems the more appropriate to consider in looking at the economies of scale open to the maker of a particular product. The total cost figures are important also, however, because they reflect the importance of raw material costs. Where there are low increases in total costs at 50 per cent of *m.e.s.* but high increases in value added (as in the case of oil refineries or sulphuric-acid plants) it follows that, however efficient large-scale production may be, it may be more important for competitive success to buy raw materials or components cheaply than to manufacture at the most efficient scale.

The order in which industries are listed in Table 2 gives some indication of the importance of relative scale for particular products in the United Kingdom market. But for the importance of scale to be fully brought out, the figures for *m.e.s.* in Column (2) need to be supplemented by those for the increase in costs at 50 per cent of *m.e.s.* In the case of machine tools, for example, the *m.e.s.* may be greater than the entire British market for a particular type, but the penalty for producing at half the optimum scale is only 10 per cent on value added. It does not necessarily place a manufacturer at a great disadvantage, therefore, if his output of a particular machine tool is well below the *m.e.s.* In the case of (nylon) polymer manu-

TABLE 2

*m.e.s. as % of U.K. market—in relation to % increase in value
added at 50% m.e.s.*

	(1)	(2)	(3)	(4)
	Product, etc.*	m.e.s. as % of market	% increase in value added at 50% m.e.s.	Scale factor (n)‡
12.	Aircraft	>100	>25	0·68
15.	Diesel engines . . .	>100	>10	0·86
14a.	Machine tools . . .	>100	10	0·86
23.	Newspapers . . .	100	40	0·51
2c.	Dyes	100	44	0·47
16.	Turbo-generators . .	100	10	0·86
19a.	Computers, etc. . .	100	13	0·82
9b.	Steel rolling—plant . .	80	13	0·82
3a.	Polymer manufacture .	66	23	0·70
17.	Electric motors . .	60	20	0·74
11b.	Cars	50	13	0·82
18.	Refrigerators, etc. . .	50	12	0·84
1.	Oil refineries—plant . .	40	27	0·66
7.	Cement—plant† . .	40	17	0·77
9a.	Bulk steel production—plant.	33	12–17	0·80
5.	Bread—plant† . .	33	30	0·62
3b.	Polymer extrusion—plant .	33	11	0·85
2b.	Sulphuric acid—plant .	30	19	0·75
10a.	Cylinder blocks—plant.	30	15	0·80
2a.	Ethylene—plant . .	25	30	0·62
6.	Detergents—plant .	20	20	0·74
13.	Bicycles	10	(small)	—
4.	Beer—plant† . .	6	55	0·37
8.	Bricks—plant† . .	5	30	0·62
21.	Warp knitting—plant .	3	(small)	—
20.	Cotton textiles—plant .	2	(small)	—
24b.	Books printing—plant .	2	(small)	—
25b.	Plastics—plant . .	1	(small)	—
10b.	Engineering castings—plant .	0·2	10	0·86
22.	Footwear—plant . .	0·2	5	0·93
			Mean	0·73
			Median	0·76

* Unless a plant is specified, 'product' refers to one type, model or range
of models.   † Serving regional sub-market.

‡ The scale factor is the value of n in the equation $C = aX^n$

(C = Total Value Added, a = Constant, X = Scale (of physical output).)

facture, on the other hand, the increase in value added at 50 per cent *m.e.s.* is 23 per cent. Even though the *m.e.s.* is 66 per cent rather than 100 per cent of the United Kingdom market, it could be argued that, in some meaningful sense, economies of scale in nylon polymer manufacture are no less important than in machine tool manufacture.

It is interesting to consider whether some method can be found for combining our two main indicators—*m.e.s.* as a percentage of the market, and the percentage increase in value added at 50 per cent of *m.e.s.* One possibility[20] is to calculate the proportion of *m.e.s.* at which value added would be, say, 10 per cent higher than at the *m.e.s.* itself. To help us do this, it is useful first to calculate the 'scale factor' implicit in our figures, especially as this is of considerable interest in its own right.

Using the figures in Column (3) of Table 2 for the increase in value added at 50 per cent *m.e.s.*, one can calculate the scale factor *n* in the following equation

$$C = aX^n$$

C = Total costs
a = Constant
X = Scale of physical output
n = Scale factor

This is done in Column (4) of Table 2. It will be seen that the mean value for *n* is 0·73 and the median 0·76. This is a good deal higher than is suggested by the 0·6 rule.[21] Ethylene and bread plants come nearest to this figure, but in general the increases in value added at 50 per cent *m.e.s.* in Table 2 are too low to achieve it. It should be remembered, however, that we are dealing with the range of the scale curve from 50 per cent to 100 per cent *m.e.s.* (and with only two points in the range). Over this range, one would expect the curve to fall more slowly than over lower ranges of output, where the value of the scale factor might well be smaller than over the 50–100 per cent range.[22] In addition, the 0·6 rule is applied

[20] Suggested to me by A. B. Atkinson.
[21] This 'rule' is derived from technical considerations, particularly relating to increased size of plant. It is frequently quoted in the technical literature.
[22] A log-linear equation such as $C = aX^n$ does of course imply a greater slope for the scale curve at small scales than at large. There is reason to believe, however, that the slope of the scale curve may often be greater towards the left-hand side

generally to the capital costs of individual items of plant rather than to value added. It is interesting that in Haldi and Whitcomb[23] we find that the median scale factor is about 0·62 for items of industrial equipment, 0·73 for the construction costs of plants as a whole, and 0·73 also for operating costs. Their data are said to cover a wide range of scales, so that lower scale factors than in Table 2 might be expected. This is in fact what we find, when we remember that Haldi and Whitcomb's 'operating costs' include raw materials costs. It is evident from our Table 1 that increases in *total* costs[24] when going from 100 to 50 per cent of *m.e.s.* are much less than increases in value added. The scale factors would be a good deal higher for total costs, therefore, than for value added alone, and almost certainly higher than Haldi and Whitcomb's figures.

We can now estimate the proportion of *m.e.s.* at which value added would be 10 per cent higher than at *m.e.s.* This can be done by finding the appropriate value of X in the equation $C = aX^n$, using the values for n given in Column (4) of Table 2. The results are given in Column (2) of Table 3, expressed as a percentage of *m.e.s.*, while in Column (3) of Table 3 they are expressed as a percentage of the market. Products, etc., have been listed in Table 3 in descending order of magnitude of the figures in Column (3). The listing in Table 3 can therefore be said to indicate some sort of ranking by 'importance' of economies of scale for different industries, etc., in the British economy. Although only a sample of products and industries has been covered, the results are clearly of interest. They do not on the whole contain any great surprises—everyone would expect to find aircraft, newspapers and computers, for example, in the top ten—but the high position of dyes and the low position of beer and bricks are less to be expected, especially when, in the case of the last two, regional sub-markets have been taken.

The ranking in Table 3 takes no account of the sums required, for initial capital and other costs, to manufacture each product or group

than is implied by the values of n calculated here for the range 50–100 per cent of *m.e.s.*

[23] *Journal of Political Economy*, Aug. 1967.

[24] Total costs are the nearest category in Table 1 to Haldi and Whitcomb's operating cost figures, although our total costs include capital costs as well as raw material costs.

of products at the indicated scale. If these sums were estimated, considerable differences would be clearly found. It is obviously easier, for example, to enter the dye 'industry' at the indicated scale than to enter the aircraft industry. A relatively high figure in Column (3) of Table 3 implies that, from the point of view of economies of scale, there should in the United Kingdom be only one 'plant', or a very

TABLE 3

Scale at which value added per unit is 10% higher than at m.e.s.

(1)	(2)	(3)
Product, etc.	Indicated scale expressed as % of m.e.s.*	Indicated scale expressed as % of market†
2c. Dyes	84	84
23. Newspapers	82	82
12. Aircraft	74	74
19a. Computers, etc.	59	59
15. Diesel engines	51	51
14a. Machine tools	51	51
16. Turbo-generators	51	51
3a. Polymer manufacture	73	49
9b. Steel rolling	59	47
17. Electric motors	69	41
1. Oil refineries	76	30
11b. Cars	59	30
18. Refrigerators, etc.	55	28
5. Bread	78	26
7. Cement	66	26
9a. Bulk steel production	62	21
2b. Sulphuric acid	68	20
2a. Ethylene	78	20
10a. Cylinder blocks	62	19
3b. Polymer extrusion	53	18
6. Detergents	69	14
4. Beer	86	5
8. Bricks	78	4
10b. Engineering castings	51	0·1
22. Footwear	26	0·05

* Calculated by using the equation $C = aX^n$ (*v.* Table 2, footnote 3), taking the values of n in Column (3) of Table 2.

† Table 3, Column (2) *times* Table 2, Column (2).

small number of plants. If, however, the necessary capital and other initial costs are not high, there will be a tendency for the actual number of plants to exceed this number, because of the comparative ease of entry into the industry. Where capital and other entry costs are high, on the other hand, there will be less possibility of entry, and thus fewer obstacles to achieving economies of scale.

In most industries with relatively high 'indicated scales' (as shown in Column (3) of Table 3), there are high entry costs also. This reduces the possibility of entry, but it also increases the chances of monopoly or oligopoly, which have their own dangers. Economies of scale in such industries can be said to be especially 'significant' in that they give rise to especially serious problems. High initial costs may, on the one hand, make it difficult for economies of scale to be grasped, especially in small countries (where the size of the market presents additional difficulties). The absence of keen competitive conditions may, on the other hand, make it difficult to eliminate firms when an industry finds itself, for historical reasons, with too many plants for the indicated scale to be readily achieved by any one firm. Nationalization is one way of dealing with this last problem—as in the case of the British steel industry—although it reduces competition, at least within one country. An expansion in the size of the market can in theory deal with all the problems, since this makes it possible for high entry costs and high 'indicated scales' to be reconciled with a reasonable degree of competition. Greater competition in industries of this sort may not necessarily follow from an increase in the size of the market, however, as experience in the European Economic Community makes clear.

Relatively high 'indicated scales' and low entry costs seem to me to give rise to less serious problems. In industries of this sort, the population of firms may well be changing rapidly, but at any moment of time it is possible that an appreciable proportion of the industry's output will be produced at somewhere near the indicated scale. In any event, there are not in Table 3 many examples of this type of industry (dyes is the outstanding exception), so this is probably not a common situation.

In the light of this discussion, and of the figures given in Table 3, I feel it necessary to modify the view that I have previously expressed (op. cit., p. 63) that 'most industries . . . have a fairly small technical optimum in relation to the size of the U.K. market'. There are a good many industries in Table 3 for which this is not true, if 'indicated scale' in Column (3) is taken as a measure. In addition, several industries not in Table 3 can probably be found with high indicated scales. It seems to me now, however, more important to consider industries with 'significant' economies of scale in the sense in which I have used the term here—i.e. industries with a combination of high indicated scales in relation to the market and high initial capital and other costs. Table 3 is, I believe, weighted quite heavily in favour of these particular industries. If this is so, it is probably fair to conclude that there are comparatively few industries which have 'significant' economies of scale in this sense—in relation always, of course, to the size of the United Kingdom market.

VII. OMISSIONS

The estimates that have just been given relate to technical economies of scale. They take account, where appropriate, of heavy capital costs incurred in initial research and development, and to that extent relate to research economies also. But they do not deal completely with research economies, since they do not consider the relationship between scale, research 'output' and economies in research costs per unit of output. I have summarized briefly elsewhere some of the evidence on this (op. cit., pp. 64–5), and reach the conclusion that it supports the case for firms of large size but not for giant size, at least in relation to the United States market.

The estimates given above take no account of economies (and diseconomies) in management, marketing and finance, to name the chief omissions. The evidence on these is not very satisfactory. On the one hand, the managerial factor may sometimes favour small scale, both for plants and firms. On the other hand, marketing and finance may usually favour large scale. On balance, the estimates of technical economies of scale given above perhaps underestimate rather than overestimate the importance of economies of scale, when all relevant economies and diseconomies have been taken into account, including those open to firms as well as to individual plants. In relation to other types of economies, however, such scanty evidence as there is suggests that technical economies will often be dominant.

Nothing has yet been said about 'learning' effects. These are the economies that arise through time as greater familiarity with an operation accrues. They have been discussed especially in connection with the production of new types of aircraft, but they occur very generally in industry. These learning effects can, of course, be important in practice, although they may tail off after a new process has been in operation, or a new product manufactured, for two or three years. They can be reduced in importance by initial expenditure on training, etc. and in this way may give rise to economies of an A.1 type. But they are not an economy of scale in the sense that they lead to a saving of resources which is directly associated with production on a large scale per unit of time. They are connected with production *over* time, and are thus dependent on a long period of production. In a sense, therefore, they are connected with total output over time, but the economies derived from them tail off, and are thus different in nature from those usually associated with this dimension of scale.

VIII. ECONOMIES OF OVER-ALL SIZE AND ECONOMIES OF GROWTH

There are a number of other factors connected with the size of firms which are thought to have a bearing on the efficiency and competitive ability of large firms. While some of these may be important in practice, I do not think it right to class them as economies of scale, as that term is generally understood. What I have in mind here are what can be called 'economies of over-all size' and 'economies of growth'.

Economies of over-all size are those advantages open to large firms in addition to those derived from economies of scale. Financial economies are perhaps the most obvious example. In general, it is easier and cheaper for a large firm to raise money. This will be so, even if the output of the firm comes from an agglomeration of plants making widely differing products, with few plants large enough to benefit fully from technical economies of scale. This financial advantage comes about because large firms are simply better known than small firms and also are able to spread their risks more widely. None of this necessarily guarantees that large firms will in the end be more successful than small firms. Singh and Whittington,[25] for example, found no relationship between profitability and size. Other things being equal, large size is likely to help firms to

[25] A. Singh and G. Whittington, *Growth, Profitability and Valuation*, Department of Applied Economics Occasional Papers. No. 7 (Cambridge University Press, 1968).

raise money, but their profitability will be a far more important factor.

The spreading of risks may obviously benefit an individual firm, since one part of the business may do well when another part is earning low profits for reasons particular to itself. Also some products may be at a very early or late stage in their life-cycles, earning comparatively small profits (or none at all with project in the research stage), while others may be at the peak of their profitability. Risk-bearing economies can therefore certainly be regarded as one of the advantages of large size. Whether they can also be said to be economies of scale is another matter. The crucial question here is whether resources are saved or not. It is of course possible to think of resource-saving derived from the spreading of production among several products. This might occur, for example, when labour employed in one line can readily be transferred to another line when the first line is depressed. Unemployment or under-employment are thus avoided, extra training costs may be small, and resources are more fully employed than would otherwise be the case. To the extent that this happens, therefore, one can say that a true economy of scale has been achieved. In general, however, it seems unlikely that most risk-bearing economies will be of this resource-saving nature.

Perhaps the most obvious advantage of over-all size is that derived from the market power that flows from it. This monopoly element —which may be connected more closely with the over-all size of a firm than with the scale of its purchases or sales of individual commodities—may lead to savings in the buying costs of raw materials and components.[26] It may also lead to more profitable or more sheltered conditions in the product market. But monopoly advantages derive largely from a transfer of profits from small to large firms, or risks from large to small firms, and are not therefore true economies of scale.

Economies of growth have been much discussed in recent years. Edith Penrose has defined them as 'the internal economies available to an individual firm which make expansion profitable in particular directions'.[27] When defined in this way, they are derived from the unique collection of productive services available to a

---

[26] i.e. savings additional to those derived from large-scale purchases which reduce the real costs of suppliers.

[27] E. T. Penrose, *The Theory of the Growth of the Firm* (Oxford: Basil Blackwell, 1959), p. 99.

particular firm and the exploitation of the opportunities open to that firm. They are not necessarily connected with the size of the firm, and once grasped might 'disappear' in the sense that they could be hived off into a separate firm without loss of efficiency. This is not, however, the only context in which the economies of growth have been discussed. Attention has been concentrated on the fact that a growing firm will be investing heavily: this is likely to encourage invention and innovation, because continuous thought will necessarily have to be given to the best way of carrying out the capital investment programme. Growth is also likely to create a good climate in a firm, giving widespread promotion opportunities, and helping morale and recruitment.

Large size and growth may both bring advantages to the individual firm, therefore. While some of these advantages may benefit one firm at the expense of other firms, some will also benefit society generally, for example by encouraging innovation. Some of these benefits to society could reasonably be called economies of scale, in the sense that a saving of resources is associated with large scale. But they are different in their nature from the technical economies of scale on which we have largely concentrated.

IX. PRACTICAL IMPLICATIONS

This article has been concerned, as was said at the beginning, with a narrow, though much discussed, range of problems. It has dealt primarily with technical economies of scale, and the quantitative estimates that have been given refer to these. It has been seen that, of the thirty or so products for which empirical estimates have been given, a good many can be said to have appreciable economies of scale, in relation to the size of the United Kingdom market. The sample of products investigated is almost certainly biased towards those which are likely to have 'significant' economies of scale, in the sense discussed in Section VI, and is therefore not fully representative. But the results show, nevertheless, that in a number of British industries the relevant market may not permit output at the minimum optimum scale at all, or may only permit output at this scale from a comparatively small number of firms. In cases such as this, a widening of the present market would obviously enable optimum scales to be achieved in the long run more readily than at present.

But care is needed before this conclusion is used to draw policy conclusions for British industry or for the British economy generally. It has already been pointed out that, where raw materials or components are a large element in total costs, savings in buying costs may be more important for achieving low costs than the processing of these materials in a plant of the minimum efficient scale. Another important proviso concerns the varying X-efficiencies of different firms. The fact that the scale curve is drawn on the assumption that X-inefficiency does not exist has little to do with the real-world situation. It is well known that in practice the efficiency of firms in given circumstances varies widely. This is especially so if efficiency is taken in its broadest sense, to include such factors as success in product design and marketing; and it helps to explain why many small firms do better than large rivals who are better placed to take advantage of economies of scale.

Another consideration is that large firms, although potentially well placed to take advantage of economies of scale, may not in fact do so. It may be that they do not seek sufficient standardization in their products to allow them to benefit fully from scale, or their market situation may not permit them to do this. It may also be that they own a large number of small plants, few of which are able to gain the advantages of scale, and which cannot be replaced quickly; or that, even if they have large plants, these plants have been built over a long period of time, and are far from perfectly adapted to their present scale of output. For all these reasons, large firms may fail to grasp the economies of scale which are theoretically open to them—partly because the period of adjustment required may be such a long one—and smaller, better adapted, firms may in fact be more efficient.

Technical progress is another factor that has to be taken into account. A large plant which has been built up over a period of years may contain machines and equipment of many different vintages. A new small plant, equipped with the latest techniques and producing a standardized product, may have substantially lower costs.

In practice, therefore, conclusions about the comparative efficiency of existing firms of different scale, or even of plants of different scale, cannot be drawn simply from what we know about the economies of scale that are theoretically possible under ideal conditions. Similar considerations apply to *a priori* comparisons between the efficiency of firms operating in markets of different sizes, for example in the United States, the Soviet Union, or the European Common Market, as compared with the United Kingdom market. Little can be said on this subject without a detailed examination of particular firms and particular market situations.[28]

It is dangerous to push this type of argument too far, however. While it may be true that great differences in efficiency exist in practice, it is also true that the potential existence of economies of scale is bound to exert pressure on firms to grasp these advantages. Even if nobody has yet done so, somebody will do it tomorrow, especially in industries where technical economies of scale are of great importance. At the moment, British industry is probably fairly well placed as regards one particular dimension of scale, i.e. size of firm, in comparison with most of its competitors, other than those in the United States. I have argued elsewhere, when talking of the over-all size of firms, that—'U.K. firms are thus very much in the big league compared with those in any country other than the United States. So, if in this respect we are inefficiently small, it follows that almost everybody else is inefficiently small also' (op. cit., p. 68). Good fighting stuff, but a little complacent in tone perhaps even at the time, especially as it took no account of specialization within firms and of the age of capital equipment. But in any event it is almost certainly becoming less true daily, as firms in countries like Japan not only grow rapidly in over-all size, but also take much fuller advantage than we of technical economies of scale.

[28] Such an examination is at present being carried out at the Department of Applied Economics, Cambridge, by T. A. J. Cockerill, in collaboration with myself, but the problems, both of data collection and of interpretation are, not surprisingly, proving to be formidable.

6

Economies of Scale in the Motor Industry
by C. F. Pratten

I. GENERAL INTRODUCTION

(a) *Structure of the Industry*

The British motor industry consists of firms producing cars, commercial vehicles, tractors and components and accessories for these. This paper is concerned principally with the manufacture of cars and commercial vehicles, especially the former.

The industry produces nearly two million cars and half a million commercial vehicles annually. Peak production of cars was achieved in 1964, while 1964 and 1969 were peak years for commercial vehicle production. In 1969, some 45 per cent of car production was exported and 39 per cent of commercial vehicle production. Imports have been rising, especially of cars. In 1969 they represented about 10 per cent of new registrations of cars.

Four firms dominate the industry. They are British Leyland and three subsidiaries of United States manufacturers—Vauxhall (General Motors), Ford and Chrysler (formerly Rootes). In 1969 these firms accounted for over 99 per cent of the cars produced and some 98 per cent of the commercial vehicles. There are several independent manufacturers of high quality and sports cars and heavy commercial vehicles, but their total output is very small. British Leyland's share of car production in 1969 was over 48 per cent while that of Ford was nearly 30 per cent. British Leyland

From *Economies of Scale in Manufacturing Industry* (Cambridge University Press, 1971), pp. 132–49. Reprinted by permission of the author and the publishers.

accounted for 40 per cent of commercial vehicle production in 1969, as against 27 per cent for Ford and 24 per cent for Vauxhall.

As a consequence of its development by mergers, British Leyland's production facilities are fragmented. In all it has sixty manufacturing centres spread throughout the U.K. It assembles cars at seven separate sites in the U.K., but assembly of the cars it produces in large quantities is concentrated at two sites. The three other major companies each has two main production centres, one in each case being in a development area.

(b) *Processes of Production and Sources of Economies of Scale*

The main processes of production performed by motor manufacturers are the casting and forging of components such as engine blocks, the machining of components for engines, gear-boxes etc., the production of bodies by pressing operations and the assembly of sub-assemblies into the final products. The four main U.K. motor manufacturers all press bodies, make engines and assemble cars and commercial vehicles but the extent to which they make castings, forgings and other components varies.

Processes of this sort can give rise to considerable economies of scale. The manufacture of car bodies, for example, is particularly subject to initial fixed costs economies, while the machining of components gives much scope for economies through specialization of plant. Casting is less important as an area for economies of scale, as is assembly. Both can, however, benefit from initial fixed cost economies, together with economies in working capital and specialization of labour.

(c) *The Dimensions of Scale*

The two main dimensions of scale for the motor industry are the output of particular models and the over-all capacity of firms. The latter gives rise to economies in selling and in research and development. Besides the output of individual models and the capacity of firms, the output of a range of models which incorporate common components, the capacity of individual plants and the extent of vertical integration are other important dimensions of scale affecting costs of production.

TABLE 1
Profile of the Motor Industry

	Production of cars, taxis and chassis with engines*		Total motor industry†				
	1963	% of all manufacturing industry	1963	% of all manufacturing industry	1968	% of all manufacturing industry	1968 as % of 1963
Number of employees ('000)	149·0	1·9	444·9	5·6	466·2	5·8	105
Sales (£m)	1038·3	3·7	2059·6	7·4	2770·7	7·0	135
Net output (£m)	327·1	3·0	736·6	6·8	995·7	6·2	135
Capital expenditure (£m)	49	4·8	88	8·6	—	—	—

Concentration

Concentration ratio for the 5 largest firms in 1963

Cars   91·5%
Commercial vehicles   84·1%

Size of Establishment and enterprises (1963)

	Establishments		Enterprises	
Number of employees	Number	% of employees	Number	% of employees
Less than 100	905	5	762	5
100–999	254	18	160	11
1,000–3,999	70	29	28	11
4,000–7,499	18	22	6	8
7,500 and over	8	26	10	65
	1255	100	966	100

* Firms with more than 25 employees, only.
† Motor vehicle manufacturing, including the production of cars, commercial vehicles, tractors and certain parts for vehicles.

II. THE STRUCTURE OF COSTS

The following breakdown of the cost of sales to outside buyers, including sales of spare parts, for the Vauxhall Motor Co. is typical for the industry: materials and services 61 per cent; wages, salaries, etc. 25 per cent; special tools and depreciation 9 per cent; tax, interest and profit 6 per cent.[1] Fixed capital overheads have increased as a percentage of total costs in recent years. This trend reflects heavy investment by the companies in highly mechanized techniques, and increased vertical integration. Operation below full capacity, because of low demand and strikes, has also increased the burden of fixed costs.

A feature of the cost structure is the rather high proportion of bought-out materials and services. Although the extent of this has been reduced by the increased vertical integration in the industry, materials, components and services bought out still represent about 60 per cent of sales for U.K. manufacturers. Selling costs (included in the breakdown of costs for Vauxhalls given above under both services bought out and wages and salaries) are a relatively small proportion of total costs for this industry. The main item on the selling side is publicity, including advertising, which accounts for around 2 per cent of sales turnover. The costs of warranties and of transport are other significant items of costs, but the latter is usually paid for separately by buyers of new cars.

III. INITIAL COSTS

The total output of particular models is clearly an important factor determining costs because of the initial tooling costs, particularly for body pressings. There are other substantial initial costs for models, including the costs of design, the building of prototypes and the disruption caused by the introduction of a new model. The suppliers of special components for models incur similar costs. There is some difficulty in specifying the initial costs for cars because:

(1) the costs depend on the extent of variation from other models in a firm's range. Firms use the same basic engine for a number of models and may be able to use the same components (though in practice designers even within the same

[1] Vauxhall Motors Limited, *Operating Review* (1968).

firm often select different components for different models of a similar size).

(2) firms frequently publish figures purporting to give the capital cost of introducing new models, but it is often difficult to distinguish the cost of introducing a new model *per se*, from the costs of expanding (or replacing) capacity which would otherwise have been incurred.

(3) there are economies of scale for introducing new models. If a firm introduces new models frequently, it can build up a team of designers, make use of ideas for styling in a number of models, learn by experience and so on.

(a) *Body Costs*

We deal first with body costs because the body is the most distinctive feature of models, and because tooling costs for bodies account for a substantial part of total tooling costs. An American estimate published in 1965 gave the minimum tooling costs for a new steel body as £2–2·5m.[2] Two U.K. companies have suggested that the tooling costs of a new body would be much higher. One of these firms, for example, has estimated tooling costs for a new car body to be about £3m, with a further £¾m for a shooting brake or van (£1 million for both) based on the same model. This gives a total of £4m, and is based on the assumption that costs are tightly controlled. It was estimated that the figure of £4m could be reduced by about £½m if a short run were expected.[3] Also a firm may reduce costs by tailoring the new design to make use of tooling for a previous model.

In practice a firm may introduce several variations of a model, e.g., 2- and 4-door versions, and designers may indulge in relatively expensive tooling: thus in the event body tooling costs may well exceed £5m for a model aimed at a substantial share of the market.

Table 2 shows some estimates made by a motor company of the

---

[2] R. S. Morrison, 'F. R. P. Stalks the Car Body Field', *S.A.E.*, 2 April 1965. This figure should probably be increased to £3m–£4m to allow for subsequent price rises.

[3] Where a short run of a model is expected some savings in tool costs can be made by using fewer, though larger, body pressings. But if this policy is used the buyer's maintenance costs are increased because damage to a large panel is less easily dealt with than that to a small one.

effects of increasing the output of a model on the costs of steel bodies. The main economies are achieved by spreading tooling costs,[4] but there are also economies in the use of materials and labour which are allowed for in the main part of the Table and are also shown separately in the last two columns of the Table.

TABLE 2

Index of Costs for Body Shells

Annual output ('000)	Index of body costs			Unit material costs	Unit operating labour costs
	Expected life of basic model				
	2 years	5 years	10 years	(2-year life)	(2-year life)
25	100	78	70	100	100
50	86	70	66	100	97
250	64	58	57	97	90
500	57	56	55	96·5	80
1000	56	55	54	96	80

The costs include tooling, materials, labour, depreciation and other works overheads, and are for the production of body shells, i.e. they include the cost of assembling panels. For the purpose of making these estimates, it is assumed that the total output of the factory at which the body is made is not affected by the output of this model. No allowance is made for interest on capital.

The Table illustrates an important feature of initial costs. These can be spread either by making many units during a short period, or by extending a model run over a longer period of time. The figures indicate that an output of a million units, whether spread over two years (500,000 per annum) or five years (200,000 per annum), is required to achieve the main economies of scale for body production costs: costs which represent about 15 per cent of the ex-factory costs of cars produced in large quantities (see below).

The spreading of body costs by high rates of production per annum or over runs of long duration are not, of course, equally

[4] The main cause of wear on body tooling is the number of times the dies are placed in the presses rather than the number of bodies which are stamped. A substantial proportion of tooling would still be usable after an output of a million units, if spread over five years, but the cost of repairing tooling would increase.

attractive options: for example, the retention of an unchanged body for an extended period may involve marketing problems. These are discussed below.

(b) *Engines and Other Parts*

Engines are changed less often than bodies, and much machinery for manufacturing engine blocks can be adapted for the production of different engines. However, if a radically new engine is to be introduced, new machine tools and transfer equipment are usually acquired for its manufacture. Similarly new tools and equipment may be required for other parts, depending on whether existing components are used or new ones introduced.

(c) *Total Initial Costs*

We now consider total initial costs for models. For the purpose of illustrating the effect of spreading initial costs we have assumed that:

(1) the life of the model is 4 years[5]
(2) the capacity of the engine is 1,500 cc
(3) the body is a new one
(4) extra presses and factory space are not required.[6]

Given these assumptions, the initial costs would be of the order shown:

Output over 4 years	200,000	1,000,000
If a new basic engine is not required:		
Total initial costs (incl. development, tooling and disruption costs)	£m 8–12	12–18
Initial costs per car	£ 40–60	12–18
If a new basic engine is required:		
Total initial costs	£m 11–16	16–26
Initial costs per car	£ 55–80	16–26

[5] In the past, U.K. manufacturers have changed their leading models at intervals of more than 4 years.

[6] If presses and additional factory space are required, this will add greatly to the capital expenditure for the new models.

The main initial costs are for design, testing and tooling. By synchronizing a change-over of models with the annual holidays, a firm might aim to limit the loss of output to the equivalent of two weeks' production of the model, costing perhaps £1m for a production rate of 100,000 cars a year, and £2·5m for a rate of 250,000 a year. However the loss of production equivalent to six weeks' output is not unknown.

A range of costs is shown for each rate of output because initial costs of models vary between companies. They are also affected by the policy of a company. For example, if a company wishes to increase its share of the market by introducing a completely new model, it may have to spend more on initial costs to make a more appealing model. The initial costs for an output of a million units are shown to be 50 per cent more than those for an output of 200,000 units. This increase occurs because the range of variants produced may increase with output, progressively more tooling has to be duplicated as the rate of output is increased, and disruption costs are approximately proportional to scale.

The estimates of initial costs given so far do not include initial costs borne by suppliers. These are substantial for many components. In some cases motor manufacturers pay separately for initial costs e.g. dies; in others they are included in the price per unit paid by the motor manufacturer for components.

An offsetting source of economies for initial costs is that when a new model is designed and new tooling has to be bought, advantage can be taken of technical progress in new and improved materials and techniques to reduce the costs of the new model. For example, if metals with improved qualities have been introduced, it may be possible to reduce the weight of materials used or substitute different materials. Any savings are of course proportional to output. If similar changes were made for existing models, this might necessitate changes of tooling.

IV. PRODUCTION COSTS[7]

(a) *A Single Basic Model* (*with variations*)

As a part of the description of initial costs, estimates of production costs for pressing operations were given in Table 2. The main pro-

[7] For the estimates given in this section, it is assumed that production is concentrated in one complex.

duction processes not dealt with so far are casting, the machining and assembly of components such as engines and gear-boxes, and assembly.

1. *Castings and forgings.* The most detailed analysis of the technical economies of scale for the U.K. motor industry previously carried out was by Maxcy and Silberston.[8] For castings they estimated that an output of 100,000 cars a year was sufficient to enable a manufacturer to avoid any serious competitive handicap. The production of castings was discussed in the previous chapter. The information we give there suggests that economies for outputs substantially greater than those suggested by the earlier study may now exist. Economies of scale for forgings which are more important than castings in terms of costs are similar to those for castings.

2. *Engines and transmission equipment.* The following estimates of the capital and operating costs for new lines to machine engine blocks were obtained from a U.K. motor company.[9] It is assumed that the life of the engine would be about ten years.

Annual capacity (thousands)	25	100	250	500	1,000
Capital cost £m	0·65	1·5	2·25	4·5	9·0
Index Numbers of Costs per Engine					
Capital charges	173	100	60	60	60
Operating costs	129	100	80	80	80
Operating costs and capital charges	155	100	64	64	64

The estimates indicate large economies of scale up to an output of 250,000 units a year, but economies exhausted at that level of output. However, there is an important qualification to this assessment; machinery has to be duplicated for outputs above about 250,000 units a year,[10] and for outputs above this level there is an increase in costs until sufficient output is again reached to fully utilize the

---

[8] George Maxcy and Aubrey Silberston, *The Motor Industry* (London: Allen & Unwin, 1959).

[9] Two recently introduced techniques which increase the flexibility of engine lines and/or reduce the economies of scale for engine production are the machining of engines with a varying number of cylinders on the same equipment, and the use of shell moulding techniques to make more accurate castings which, it is claimed, reduce the machining required.

[10] The maximum capacity of a single line depends on the number of shifts worked and other factors.

duplicate plant. Also it is important to note that in practice firms generally have separate lines for different basic engines, so these economies relate to the output of each type of engine rather than a firm's total output of engines.

The economies of scale for the assembly of engines are proportionately smaller than for machining engine blocks. A comparison of assembly costs for vehicle diesel engines showed labour costs between 20 per cent and 25 per cent lower for engines made at a rate of 100,000 a year compared with an engine made at a rate of 2,500 a year.

Detailed estimates of costs for transmission equipment were not obtained, but the picture is broadly similar to that for engines. There are large economies of scale up to outputs of about 400,000 units a year for a single model, and above this output lines have to be duplicated.

3. *Assembly*. For assembly Maxcy and Silberston again give a figure of 100,000 cars a year for the output required to enable a firm to use the most efficient techniques of assembly. The main development which has taken place since the Maxcy–Silberston study is the introduction of more automated tools for assembly. The following figures represent recent estimates of the effects of capacity on labour requirements for assembly.

Annual Output (thousand cars)	60	125	300[11]
Index of labour requirements	125	100	90

A U.K. manufacturer provided the following estimates of labour and capital costs for assembly lines:

	15	30	60	80
Capacity of line per hour				
Output per year assuming two shifts (thousands)	55	110	220	294
Labour costs per unit (Index)	125	100	90	88
Capital costs per unit (Index)	130	100	82	72

For rates of output above 80 cars per hour it was suggested that the efficiency of a single line would be affected by the increasing speed at which the track would have to move. However, higher rates of output are achieved in the U.S. where lines with a capacity of more than 120 cars an hour have been built. But it is worth noting that

[11] From Eurofinance. *The Automobile Industry of Western Europe 1965–1970.*

for one of the leading European producers the maximum rate of production per hour on assembly lines is only 16 units.[12]

A U.K. manufacturer also estimated that the effects of putting a mix of models on its existing line reduced capacity by about 8 per cent. If a firm operated a line for a single model, it could redesign parts of the line and increase capacity. For some operations it would be economic to substitute capital for labour and this process of substitution applies generally not to assembly alone. The economies of scale for assembly operations will be seen from this to be proportionately small, as is the case with the assembly of engines. Assembly operations are relatively labour-intensive. For U.K. car manufacturers, assembly operations including the assembly of engines, account for some 45 per cent of total direct labour costs.

4. *Bought-out materials and components.* Costs of materials and components are the largest group of costs for car production. For many items, e.g. steel, tyres and much electrical equipment, the reductions in unit price paid for outputs of more than 25,000 units a year of a model are small. This is because the total industry output of standardized products is large. For other items including castings, forgings and electrical components special to a model, there would be economies of scale attributable to spreading the costs of dies and the use of more efficient techniques for outputs above 100,000 units a year. For all materials and components there would also be some economies of scale for suppliers' overhead costs, and for many items there would be economies for transport costs. Another source of economies as requirements increase is that firms can benefit by buying from a number of suppliers. One firm commented that 'for a volume of 25,000 (of a model per year), we would only use one source of supply, for a volume of 100,000 to 500,000 we may use two or three sources of supply. By bringing in competition, there is usually a price advantage. This could be as much as 10 per cent.'

5. *Production overheads.* For outputs much above about 250,000 units of a model, the economies of scale for direct production costs are relatively small, as the engine transmission, painting (which we have not dealt with separately above) and assembly lines have to

---

[12] Other estimates of maximum output per line per hour for this manufacturer were machining engine blocks and transmissions 64 per hour, assembling engines 33 and painting 32.

be duplicated.[13] It is difficult to determine the effect on production overhead costs for power, purchasing departments, general management, the provision of other services etc. at higher levels of output. Important economies certainly exist for some of these costs and we have allowed for some economies for these costs in the following summary of the economies of scale for producing one model in varying quantities. Also large firms may spend more on buying, testing and research and this may reduce the costs of materials etc. An important item of overhead costs is for warranties; these can amount to 3 per cent, or more, of costs.[14]

6. *Summary of the economies of scale for the production of one basic model.* Table 3 shows our estimates of costs for a firm producing a single model at varying levels of output at one site. The costs are based on U.K. prices in 1968. It is assumed that the firm makes only one model and that its total output changes with the output of the model. Costs are based on those for firms using a mix of vintages of plant which has been built up over time, i.e. it is not assumed that the firm is using entirely new plant. If all new plant were assumed to be used, this would increase the economies of scale, because capital charges for which economies of scale are proportionately greater than average would be increased relative to other costs.

The estimates indicate that the largest economies of scale are achieved over the range 100,000 to 250,000 units. It is assumed that the engine and assembly lines would be duplicated for outputs of 500,000 units and that there would be four lines for an output of a million units. The economies in operating costs for outputs above 250,000 units are attributable to pressing operations, the production of components, operating a number of lines in parallel and for overheads. In practice a firm with an output of a million units of one model could operate three engine, transmission, painting and assembly lines, and possibly only two lines. If so the economies would be

[13] There are of course discontinuities, i.e. for outputs of 400,000 units of a range of models, two lines would be required for engines and assembly, but not transmissions, and unit costs for some operations would be higher than for outputs of 250,000 units. The experience of one company was that it was only for rates of output of 250,000 units a year, or more, that a satisfactory paint plant to meet their standards of quality could be installed.

[14] If the quality of control declines at higher scales of output because it becomes proportionately more difficult to control production at high rates of output, the cost of warranties will be a source of diseconomies of scale.

TABLE 3

Illustrative Estimates of Costs and Scale for the Production of One Basic Model and its Variants *

Output (thousands a year)	100	250	500	1,000
Initial costs for model £m	15	20	28	38
	Costs per Vehicle £			
Initial costs	38	20	14	10
Materials and components bought out†	265	250	240	235
Labour (direct and indirect)	102	90	86	83
Capital charges for fixed and working capital	60	53	50	48
Total ex-works costs	465	413	390	376
Index	100	89	84	81

* A production run of 4 years is assumed, and the basic model is assumed to be in the range 1,000–1,200 cc.

† The estimates of economies for material and component purchases which we obtained from firms varied. Some estimates suggested that these economies would be smaller than those shown and others that the economies would be greater. It is assumed that the total output of suppliers is not affected by the purchases of the firm considered.

Source: The estimates in this Table and in Table 4 are based on the data given above and our discussions with firms in the industry.

larger—equivalent to another £10 per car over the range 250,000 to 1 million units a year.

(a) *A Range of Models*

The main source of higher costs for a firm making a range of basic models, and the same total output as a firm making a single model, would be the higher level of initial costs although other costs would also be raised.[15] Our tentative estimates of costs for a firm making a range of three basic models are shown in Table 4. It is assumed that one model is made in greater quantity than the other two. For example, that at an output of 250,000 units a year, the

[15] Higher stocks of spare parts at the factory and at distributors is another important source of higher costs, and the need for capital to finance these stocks may present problems apart from the cost of finance.

firm makes 150,000 units of a model of about 1,300 cc, 50,000 units of a model of about 1,000 cc and 50,000 units of a model of about 1,800 cc (for each model there would be body and engine variants). The proportional division of output at each scale is assumed to be the same.[16] The economies of scale are greater for the models produced in smaller quantities as economies, in proportional terms, decline as scale increases (see Table 3).

It was also assumed, for the purpose of preparing this Table, that models have a life of four years. In the past, U.K. companies have changed their models at longer intervals than four years, but as an offset to this, British Leyland in particular has many more than three basic models in production, the rate at which models are changed seems likely to speed up in the future.

TABLE 4

Illustrative Estimates of Costs and Scale for a Range of Models (consisting of three basic bodies with variants, and five basic engines) *

Output (thousands a year)	100	250	500	1,000	2,000
Initial costs for model £m	40	50	60	80	110
		Costs per vehicle £			
Initial costs	100	50	30	20	14
Materials and components bought out	290	270	255	247	240
Labour (direct and indirect)	120	100	92	87	84
Capital charges for fixed and working capital	75	65	58	53	48
Total ex-works costs	585	485	435	407	386
Index of average costs	100	83	74	70	66
Index of marginal costs		72	65	66	62

* Costs have been 'standardized' to be comparable with those in Table 3. If the range of models included large and sophisticated models this would, of course, raise average costs per unit, but we have ignored this factor.

The estimates shown in Table 4 suggest substantial economies of scale for the production of cars if the range of models does not increase with scale. There are however a number of important factors

[16] If it were assumed that the output of models made in relatively small quantities increased more than proportionately with scale the economies would be greater.

which have not been allowed for when preparing these estimates which tend to increase the economies of scale.

(a) Large firms are able to spread the costs of introducing new techniques and of improving the supply of materials over a larger output. This gives them a greater incentive to incur expenditure on innovation.

(b) Since large firms can increase their capacity by relatively large absolute amounts, they have greater opportunities for introducing new plant of the optimum size and of fully utilizing it quickly.

(c) Costs per unit for new plant are likely to be lower for large firms, since they can spread the costs of designing plant over more plant. They are also likely to have greater knowledge of the equipment etc. available.

(d) Large increases in vehicle output lead to substantial increases in output for material and component suppliers. These can then achieve economies of scale in excess of the reductions in material and component costs shown in Table 4.

V. COMMERCIAL VEHICLES

Separate estimates of the economies of scale for commercial vehicle production have not been obtained. However, most light commercial vehicles are variants of cars, the bodies are relatively simple, and they are not subject to as rapid evolution as cars. Also engines and chassis are usually common to both light commercial vehicles and cars.[17] The main scale effects of producing light commercial vehicles for a car manufacturer are to obtain:

(a) the benefits of spreading the special initial costs of commercial vehicles. (The number of each model of light commercial vehicle produced is much smaller than that of car models. This offsets the fact that the special initial costs are much smaller.)

(b) the economies of scale for common components by increasing total output of these components.

[17] It is also interesting to note that companies buy out many diesel engines. A number of manufacturers use the same diesels made by specialist manufacturers. In this way economies of scale for engine manufacture are gained.

For heavy commercial vehicle production, we should expect there
to be economies of scale for the production of components and
engines, and the assembly of chassis. When comparing economies of
scale for cars and commercial vehicles there are two conflicting
forces. The annual output of commercial vehicles is relatively small
and, as the economies of scale diminish at the margin as scale is
increased, we should expect large economies of scale for commercial
vehicle production. On the other hand, the relatively high cost of
material inputs tends to damp down the economies of scale. A leading
U.K. manufacturer estimated that direct labour costs for a sixteen-
ton truck were only 3 per cent of total factory costs, as compared
with more than 8 per cent for a car. There are generally relatively
small economies of scale for material costs, which are proportionately
more important for commercial vehicles.

VI. FACTORIES

Estimates of the effects of fragmentation of production facilities in
different factories were not obtained. If individual factories are so
small that operations for individual models have to be duplicated
at a number of sites, this will clearly increase production costs. In
the past, fragmentation in the U.K. has resulted in vertical disintegration of production, and the separation of the manufacture of
different models, rather than in the duplication of facilities for
producing the same model. The main costs of vertical disintegration are the extra costs of transport and loss of flexibility. Extra
transport costs are serious if bodies and/or chassis have to be moved.
Moving car bodies over short distances, of, say, 30 miles may cost
as much as £2 a body.[18] As regards loss of flexibility, if production
is concentrated, redundancy created by new investment can be
handled by reallocation of work, and space no longer required for
one operation can be used for another operation. Where production
facilities are geographically separated, however, flexibility is reduced. The division of production between a great many sites may
also involve loss of control and management problems, especially if
labour relations are indifferent and/or good management is scarce.

[18] This estimate is for transport costs alone. In addition there are costs for loading and unloading, for damage caused by transporting the bodies and for loss of
control. Also if the extra costs are added to the price then purchase tax and dealer's
margins further increase the effect on the final price.

Although it is difficult to quantify the effects of fragmentation of production facilities, these may be important.

An important dimension of scale is the operation of plants in a number of countries. When overseas plants are first set up they are usually assembly plants, and are built to get within tariff barriers or to reduce costs of transport. In time, local operations often expand vertically and local supplies are obtained. The economies achieved by adding overseas plants are that:

(1) during the early years, the demand from the overseas plant may enable the company to operate its U.K. plant at a higher rate of capacity utilization than it would otherwise achieve (for this to apply it has to be assumed that the overseas market could not be supplied entirely from U.K. production. The importance of this effect is probably exaggerated in practice because firms underestimate the extent to which some markets can be supplied from the U.K., and the speed with which vertical integration will in fact take place at the overseas plant).

(2) an increase in output enables economies to be achieved, e.g.
   (a) technical economies for the production of components or models which are centralized. For example, although British Leyland makes a range of models at its Australian plant, it exports sports cars to Australia from the U.K. Ford is using engines made in the U.K. for cars assembled in the U.S., and is planning to centralize the production of automatic gear-boxes for its European plants.
   (b) where the plants duplicate production facilities, there are economies for design work and some overheads.

A point worth noting about overseas plants for a study of the economies of scale, is that U.K. firms have usually had a smaller share of the markets in which their overseas plants operate than of the U.K. market. The overseas markets themselves are expanding, and the economies of scale to be obtained by merging overseas operations have therefore become proportionately larger in relation to their U.K. operations.

VII. FIRMS

The production economies of scale for manufacturing cars on a large scale have been described above. In this section we outline the advantages of vertical integration for a firm, and the effect of scale on the non-technical factors determining the success of firms of different sizes.

(a) *Vertical Integration*

The main advantages of vertical integration for firms in this industry are:

(1) increased control over production
(2) improved flexibility for planning
(3) the ability to take a view of the total effect of its decisions.

These factors are important in an industry which is subject to cyclical variations in demand. Also, it is supplied by industries themselves subject to substantial economies of scale, whose costs are very sensitive to levels of capacity utilization, e.g. sheet steel producers. Where vertical disintegration involves body and chassis production, as it did in the past for B.M.C., there could be serious differences between the interests of the assembler and of other firms involved in vehicle production. Now an over-all view is taken, so pressure to fill capacity by exporting etc. is greater, thus tending to increase capacity utilization and hence efficiency.

(b) *The Non-Technical Forces*

C. E. Edwards[19] analysed the non-technical forces affecting the competitiveness of American manufacturers. He showed that the major manufacturers had important advantages, apart from the technical economies of scale, and that for obtaining these advantages the total output of a firm was more important than the output of particular models. These advantages are now discussed.

1. *Distribution costs*. Distribution costs, including transport costs, form a larger proportion of costs for U.S. motor manufacturers in

[19] C. E. Edwards, 'Dynamics of the U.S. Automobile Industry' (COLUMBIA, 1965).

their home market than for U.K. producers with their more concentrated market. In the U.S., the three largest firms operate a
number of widely scattered assembly plants and this has given them
an important cost advantage compared to the smaller 'independent'
companies who have to transport finished products. Similar advantages can be obtained by large-scale British manufacturers in
export markets which in 1969 accounted for 45 per cent of car production. There are also substantial economies of scale for supplying
overseas markets in large quantities. The following estimates illustrate these economies.

Number of cars sent from U.K. to Canada per year			
(thousands)	5	10	60
Index of transport costs per car[20]	100	85	70

2. *Marketing.* One of the marketing advantages enjoyed by the
three leading American car manufacturers, to which Edwards
draws attention, is the spreading of advertising expenses. (Expenditure on advertising accounted for about $\frac{1}{2}$ per cent of U.K. manufacturers' sales in 1963.) Another advantage claimed was the confidence of consumers in the products of the leading manufacturers.
This is particularly important for products such as cars which form
a substantial item in family budgets, people are less likely to be ready
to take a risk. Also, a small-scale manufacturer is not in a good
position to spread the risks involved in style changes. A large-scale
manufacturer can adopt a number of styles simultaneously, and can
afford to change an unsuccessful style comparatively rapidly.

An important marketing factor is the maintenance of an adequate
dealer network. Edwards found that there are economies of scale
which are partly attributable to advertising at this level of marketing.
There are also economies for supplying spare parts and trained
service engineers. Edwards estimated that in the U.S. a market of
400,000 units per year is required to achieve an efficient dealer
network unless franchises can be duplicated. The need for widespread points of sale and service facilities are part of the explanation.[21] A final marketing scale advantage is that success may breed

---

[20] Unit costs for transporting 5,000 cars a year would be about £40.

[21] One difference between the marketing of cars and tractors on the one hand
and heavy commercial vehicles on the other, applies to the provision of servicing
facilities. Commercial vehicles travel much greater distances in such markets as

further success in marketing. A firm with a large share of the market tends to set the style, and the fact that its cars sell in large quantities is itself an advertisement. On the other hand, if people like a distinctive car, this tends to give small firms an advantage.

Marketing costs are related to the output of models as well as the total output of firms. Particularly when introducing a model, firms advertise a model rather than their range. A firm with a large share of a market has an advantage when introducing a new model because it is likely to have more and better distribution outlets. Other things being equal, it will therefore win a larger share of the market for its new models.

Another important factor affecting the success of firms is that exported mass-produced cars generally sell at lower ex-factory prices than cars sold on the home market. A relatively small firm might thus offset some of its scale disadvantage by sticking to the home market, although this has not been buoyant in recent years. In practice, the percentage of cars exported by the leading companies is approximately the same, but a higher proportion of B.M.C.'s exports are special models which it does not sell overseas at lower ex-works prices. It therefore sells a relatively smaller proportion of mass-produced cars in export markets than other major manufacturers, and thus benefits as far as export discounts are concerned.

3. *Research and development.* Another advantage of large-scale producers is the ability to spread the costs of research and development (apart from the costs of developing new models), although these costs have represented a very small percentage of the turnover of the independent U.K. groups in recent years. Subsidiaries of U.S. companies have an advantage in being able to take advantage of research and development work carried out by their parents. They can also make use of their parent's experience of investing in new techniques and more capital-intensive techniques.

4. *Labour relations.* A recent study[22] of labour relations in the motor industry has suggested that there is not a consistent relationship

---

the U.S.A., and the E.E.C., and it is necessary to build up comprehensive servicing facilities if the vehicles are to be sold in any part of the market. Cars and tractors can be marketed in parts of these markets with less complete coverage of servicing facilities.

[22] H. A. Turner, G. Clack and G. Roberts, *Labour Relations in the Motor Industry* (London: Allen & Unwin, 1967).

between the size of the firms and the quality of their labour relations. The authors found that there were considerable variations among both the large and the small companies in this industry. But the number of firms compared was inevitably very small: too small to support firm conclusions about the effects of size. Also the study was principally concerned with strikes and the causes of strikes, rather than the incidence of restrictive practice among labour.

VII. THE SURVIVAL OF SMALLER SCALE FIRMS

Companies manufacturing cars on a relatively small scale can reduce the disadvantages of high tooling costs by concentrating on a limited range of models, preferably for types of cars for which the over-all market is limited, so that they have a substantial share of the specialist market. Jaguar and Rover (now a part of British Leyland), Rolls-Royce, Volvo and American Motors all operate in such markets. This policy is likely to be more effective if the size of engine required for the specialist product is outside the range of those mass-produced by the large-scale motor manufacturers. A higher price can then be charged for a non-competing article. When independent, the Rover Co., and particularly Jaguar, achieved returns on capital comparable to, or better than, the leading car manufacturers by this type of specialization.

Another way in which a relatively small firm may be able to reduce initial costs is by keeping the same basic model in production for a long time by attracting customers with conservative tastes, or buyers who are not fashion conscious. Alternatively, it might accurately foresee trends in design and be the first to produce new designs, thereby achieving longer runs. Or a company with a small share of the market may not aim to attract customers who frequently change their model of car every time they buy a new car. A company with a large share of the market needs to attract repeatedly customers who may change their car every year but do not wish to buy the same basic model year after year.

Another way in which a firm with a relatively small output may be able to reduce its costs is by buying out a higher proportion of its product. For example, it may buy out engines and/or bodies and thereby obtain the advantages of scale enjoyed by its suppliers.

A marketing strategy of producing for special markets is not limited to the smaller firms. British Leyland in particular has inherited this policy. The 'Mini' is smaller than any cars produced by Ford or Vauxhall, and British Leyland also produces a wide range of sports and quality cars. There are two possible disadvantages of this strategy. Production of special types of car might affect the efficiency of producing other cars in large quantities. Even with delegation, it may not be possible for a firm to be expert in a wide range of sub-markets. Other difficulties may be created; for example, piece-rate negotiations may be complicated if, measured in terms of units produced per employee, productivity varies greatly between employees because of the wide differences in types of model and their scale of output. Also it may be difficult to achieve different standards of quality, and reputation for quality, within one organization. The other problem concerning this strategy is that it might become increasingly difficult to find new niches in the market.

It is worth considering very briefly the sources of economies of scale when firms such as Rover and Jaguar merge with larger firms. If, as is usually the case, production facilities are not rationalized, economies for production costs are limited; the main sources would be for some common components and for material costs. If the company taken over produces products outside the range of the firm which acquired it, economies may be limited even if production is concentrated, because separate lines may have to be set up for engines, transmissions and assembly. However, there may be some economies for distribution and a larger enterprise may be able to supply more finance to its subsidiaries than they could raise if independent.

IX. CONCLUSIONS

We have attempted to estimate technical economies of scale for this industry, and have found that these are considerable. We did not attempt to quantify non-technical economies of scale, but our discussion of these suggests that, if anything, they add to the over-all advantages of scale in the industry, particularly because of marketing economies. Our conclusions on technical economies can be summarized as in Table 5.

The estimates make clear that there are substantial economies which U.K. firms cannot exploit because of their size. Even when production for both home and export markets is considered, this is still true: total U.K. car output was only 1·7 million in 1969. In the case of subsidiaries of U.S. companies, there is scope for reductions in costs by international integration of their activities, although tariff and other barriers inhibit this. In the case of British Leyland, there is also some scope for integration with overseas operations, but again there are barriers in the way of this.

TABLE 5

Summary of Minimal Efficient Scale (m.e.s.) for Cars

A firm making	Annual output* (000's)	% of U.K. market	Percentage increase in average total costs at 50% of m.e.s.	Percentage increase in average value added at 50% of m.e.s.
One model and its variants	500	50†	6	10
A range of three basic models	1,000	100	6	13
Size of works	No estimate made			

* A life of four years is assumed for models. The estimates of economies for the production of one model are based on those for a firm making only one model. If a firm made a range of models the economies would be smaller. On the other hand the assumptions are based on conservative assumptions about the number of engine and assembly lines used.

† The output is related to U.K. output of models in the range 1,000 cc to 1,300 cc.

For commercial vehicles, the smaller scale of production makes the achievement of scale economies even more difficult, but integration of car and van models is helpful here.

The possibility of achieving a scale somewhere nearer the *m.e.s.* in the U.K. rests mainly on an expansion of home and export markets. Firms themselves can make a contribution by reducing model variety and by keeping particular models in production over a long period of years. This is how the small manufacturers have to behave, although they are helped by being able to buy standardized components at relatively low prices. Unfortunately for the larger manufacturers, keener international competition in recent years has increased pressure for greater model variety and shorter model life. Success in introducing new models may, indeed, now be of much greater value to a firm than the reduction in costs that longer model runs can bring.

With the market completely dominated by three U.S. subsidiaries and one British firm, the scope for further rationalization by mergers among companies operating in the U.K. seems to be very limited. Pressure for rationalization within firms, in spite of market forces to the contrary, is the main hope for further economies of scale, together of course with a general expansion of the market. More remote possibilities are some form of merger between British Leyland and another European (or Japanese) firm to take advantage of the scope for spreading initial costs for models and using common components, and a merger between Chrysler U.K. and another manufacturer.

7

Pricing in Business
by D. C. Hague

I. THE FIRM'S OBJECTIVES

Introduction

Business objectives are a vast subject, not least because they are important for every conceivable kind of business activity. No manager, at any level in any firm, can do his job without having some sort of objective. But discussion of objectives can, and often does, create a tremendous amount of confusion. Most people in business are reasonably clear as to what an objective is, but one is less sure how far firms define objectives precisely and pursue them consistently. Moreover, the confusion of terminology is undeniable. Words like aims, aspiration levels, goals, objectives, plans and targets are sometimes used as synonymous with each other and sometimes not.

The word 'objectives' is a good one because it covers the whole field and is widely accepted. There is no point in adding further confusion by trying to introduce a new term. We shall therefore use the word 'objectives' to describe the whole range of firms' plans, intentions and wishes. In this section, we discuss some of the general characteristics of business objectives in the firms we studied. In Section II, we shall look at the objectives which these firms pursued in pricing. In Section III, we shall draw some conclusions about objectives.

From *Pricing in Business* (George Allen & Unwin, 1971), pp. 45–94. Reprinted by permission of the publishers. This volume is now available in a paperback edition.

Non-Operational Objectives

An important distinction must be made at the beginning of any
study of objectives. This is between operational and non-operational
objectives. The simplest and most traditional of all statements of
objectives is probably that 'We are in business to make money'.
Alternatively, a firm may say: 'We are in business to make motor
cars', or 'to sell transport'. Similarly, a firm may set itself the objective of striving for product or process innovation, of serving the
community, or merely of perpetuating itself. Statements like this are
very vague indeed. They describe objectives which are 'non-
operational'. They do not say, or even imply, exactly what action
the firm should take to achieve them. At any moment, a number of
different courses of action will often be perfectly compatible with
each non-operational objective. Indeed, the reason why firms set
themselves non-operational objectives is often precisely this. No
specific action is prescribed for the manager responsible for day-to-
day activities. This vagueness enables individual managers in the
firm to work together with a sense of unity and of common purpose,
while none of them is committed to any precise action in any particular set of circumstances. Disputes over whether specific objectives are realistic or acceptable are avoided.

We found that all the firms we studied had some non-operational
objectives. Indeed, in two firms they were written down and cir-
culated to managers. In a few firms, what seemed to be operational
objectives were treated effectively as non-operational ones. Managers who had been set to earn a particular rate of return on capital
did not expect to be criticized by their supervisors if they did not
attain it.

Another kind of objective we found was one which laid down the
results the firm as a whole was expected to achieve in a general way.
It set out the levels of turnover, profit, etc. to be reached by the
whole firm but it did not explain in detail how any individual product, or department, was expected to contribute to those results.
Nor did it provide a plan of action for those responsible for individual
products. These objectives were again non-operational ones for
managers concerned with particular products, even though for the
whole firm they were less vague than the non-operational objectives
discussed in the previous paragraph. Indeed, they were often quite

precise. This second kind of non-operational objective is important because it helps to determine the atmosphere within which managers have to set and to achieve specific targets for individual products. All the firms we studied had non-operational objectives of the second kind, whether they were implicit or explicit, or worked out in more or less detail.

Operational Objectives

All the firms also had operational objectives. The distinguishing characteristics of operational objectives are:

1. They set specific tasks for the firm or for particular individuals or groups.
2. They enable the firm to discover whether or not these tasks have been performed.
3. They state clearly the way the firm will judge whether or not the tasks have been achieved, both in terms of what will be judged and how.
4. They set a time limit for carrying out each task.

It is because they are precise that operational objectives *are* operational.

If they are to achieve their targets, firms must have arrangements for stating at least their key objectives in operational terms and for comparing performance with these operational objectives. Only in this way can they discover how far their objectives have been achieved. Firms should go on to study any differences between results and objectives and take whatever remedial action is necessary to bring the two back into line. However, this leads us beyond objectives to control systems.

Some idea of the scope for disagreement over terminology where business objectives are being discussed was given in the introduction. It seems to us that such disagreement is the one thing to avoid. It does not much matter which words are used within a company to describe its objectives. What matters is that each word which *is* used should have a precise meaning for everyone who is expected to use it. We believe that, wherever possible, the firm should choose and define the terms it uses so as to emphasize the distinction between operational and non-operational objectives. It should ensure that its important objectives, at least, are stated in operational terms.

Optimizing and Satisficing

Two words are continually met with in business-school discussions of the way in which business decisions are taken. They are the words 'optimizing' and 'satisficing'.

'Optimizing' means, first, that the firm must set objectives, or criteria, by which performance in any activity is to be judged. Second, it means that the alternative courses of action open to the firm must be examined to see how well they meet these criteria. Third, the best, the optimal, alternative, must then be chosen.

Although there is a good deal of discussion of optimal decision-taking in the management literature, most of this is really concerned with the extreme case where an optimal result is defined as one which maximizes something—usually profit. Of course, the definition of optimizing given above means that an optimal solution to a problem need not require the firm to maximize anything. If the firm's objective is to earn a 15 per cent return on capital, and not to maximize profit, then an optimal decision in any situation will be one which allows the firm to earn 15 per cent on capital. Maximization is simply a special case of optimization, where an optimal solution requires alternative courses of action to be judged by how well they satisfy the criterion that the firm wishes to maximize a given variable, perhaps profit. Indeed, in the literature it is difficult to find examples of optimal decisions or decision techniques, where the objective is *not* to maximize or minimize some variable. The same was true of our firms.

However, we still have to suggest what firms which do not attempt to maximize profit are trying to do. One possibility is that they are still optimizing. We have seen that a firm which does not attempt to maximize profits may nevertheless still be trying to take optimal decisions. It may simply be setting out to earn a particular absolute amount, or percentage rate, of profit, but an amount less than the maximum one. It may still be taking whatever decisions will bring it as close as possible to earning that amount. If it does this, of course, then the fact that its objectives are less demanding than maximizing objectives will mean that more than one solution to a particular problem can be optimal. However, this is not very important in practice. Optimizing almost always means maximizing or minimizing.

In practice, too, as we shall see, even when firms attempt to maximize, they usually do so subject to various constraints. Prices may be set so as to maximize profits, subject to the constraint that the over-all level of employment in the firm must not be reduced significantly below the current level; or that the level of inventories must not be increased. We should perhaps emphasize that where individual managers or departments are setting prices (or indeed taking other decisions) they are bound to be doing so subject to such constraints. For the constraints within which individual departments operate will usually have been set for them at higher levels in the firm.

If firms do not seek to maximize profit, the likelihood is that they will not optimize at all but that they will 'satisfice'. Writers like Simon, and Cyert and March have spent a great deal of time emphasizing that firms often satisfice.[1] What we do not know is just how common 'satisficing' behaviour really is. When they 'satisfice', firms do not try to find that course of action which brings them as close as possible to a particular objective. Instead, they set minimum levels of performance in each of a number of different fields—say, a return of 10 per cent on capital employed, a market share of 25 per cent and production running at 90 per cent of existing capacity. These minimum levels of performance are often described as 'aspiration levels'.

Two things then usually seem to happen. First, the firm takes no non-routine decisions at all so long as the aspiration levels set for a product, department or indeed for the whole firm are being achieved. Only if the firm fails to earn the required rate of return on capital employed, or to reach the required market share, will special action be taken. So long as all aspiration levels are being met, it will seem unnecessary. The firm may or may not be exceeding the minimum level of achievement which it has set itself but, so long as it is not achieving less, managers will be content to leave things as they are. Second, if any aspiration level does cease to be met, the firm will then take some remedial action. In taking this action it will not seek to optimize anything. Those responsible for ensuring that a particular aspiration level is reached once more

[1] See, for example, R. M. Cyert and J. G. March, *A Behavioral Theory of the Firm* (Englewood Cliffs, N.J.: Prentice Hall, 1963), pp. 26–43.

will accept the first solution they find which they think will enable them to meet this aspiration level again—even if the solution is inferior to the optimal one. They will make no attempt to find a still better solution. Very often, the way of discovering a satisfactory solution to a problem will be to ask what was done on the last occasion that the problem arose. Provided what was done was successful last time, it will be done again.

Of course, aspiration levels will not necessarily remain unchanged. At the least, negative precedents seem to be accepted. Firms often seem to argue in this way. 'We earned 15 per cent on capital last year. We must therefore earn at least as much this year.' They say this, even when external conditions will make it harder to earn 15 per cent this year than last. Where external conditions give them more freedom, firms appear to raise aspiration levels over time; unfortunately our evidence does not allow us to say how this was done in our firms.

The fact that they do 'satisfice' in this way seems to explain most satisfactorily how firms can tolerate inconsistencies among their objectives. Cyert and March, in particular, argue that where a satisficing firm ceases to reach one of its aspiration levels it will proceed to search for a solution which will enable it to meet, or exceed, the aspiration level once again. They go on to argue that each of these decisions is taken in isolation—that such decisions are taken sequentially.[2] The firm usually finds it too difficult to make sure that a decision which is taken in order to ensure that a particular aspiration level is reached once again also allows it to continue to reach all its other aspiration levels. To make all such decisions completely consistent would usually be beyond the capabilities of human beings, even if the complexities of large organizations did not play their own part in preventing consistency.

Before leaving this section, we must define sub-optimal decisions. An optimal decision, we have seen, is one which comes as close as possible to achieving a particular objective. (Strictly, an optimal decision will be one which fits in with all the over-all objectives of the firm.) A sub-optimal decision is one which provides an optimal solution to a particular problem from the viewpoint of a particular department or manager, but which does not at the same time meet the firm's over-all objectives.

There are two main ways in which this can happen. First, the

[2] Op. cit., p. 35.

objectives of the individual department may differ from those of the firm. The sales department may seek to maximize the volume of sales, while the firm as a whole is seeking to maximize profit. In operating so as to maximize sales, the sales department is sub-optimizing. Whether it will be allowed to sub-optimize will depend on the way the firm is run. Second, sub-optimization can occur, even though an individual department really is trying to achieve the firm's over-all objectives. What may happen is that the department finds that it is too low down in the organization to have the information it needs to be able to optimize. It may then be forced to sub-optimize because it lacks information. For example, the sales department may not have enough information about what effect a change in the sales of particular products will have on the profits of the whole firm. So it may not be able to sell those quantities of products which would enable the whole firm to earn the optimal amount of profit, even though it is attempting to do so.

In our case studies, we did not find any clear examples of sub-optimal pricing decisions. We did find evidence in one firm (Alpha Ltd.) of sub-optimal thinking, though perhaps not of sub-optimal decision-taking. There is no reason to believe that the decisions that Alpha Ltd. actually took prevented the firm from achieving its over-all objectives. Yet the way that pricing and other marketing decisions were discussed in the marketing department suggests that this department was basing its discussions on different objectives from those of the Board. Alpha Ltd. itself doubts the correctness of our observations, but we still think we are right. We feel also that these differences of objective must have made it harder for Alpha Ltd. to take good pricing decisions, even if they did not actually prevent them being taken.

II. PRICING OBJECTIVES

Introduction

Here we consider the objectives that our firms pursued in setting prices. The most convenient way of doing this turns out to be to consider, first, profit objectives; second, market objectives; and, finally, other objectives.

How Profit Objectives Were Stated

All the firms we studied had one or more marketing and pricing objectives set in terms of profit. The following were the main ways in which profit objectives were stated.

Money profits. The first, simplest and most basic measure of profit was as an absolute sum of money. This measure was used by all firms. Having such a measure is a necessary part of the budgeting process, since budgets use the common measure of money to judge all of a firm's activities by a single standard. Calculating profit is a necessary—and legally required—part of the process by which a firm reports on its activities to its shareholders. Equally, it is a vital part of the firm's internal reporting process, though of course it would be unusual for the profit figures used by management to be calculated on exactly the same basis as those given to shareholders in the published accounts. Profit also represents one part of the flow within the company, and between it and the parent company (if any) or the shareholders.

Return on sales. Our firms always had figures which enabled them to calculate ratios of profit to sales. Absolute levels of both profit and sales turnover were budgeted. However, the return on sales was not a significant profit objective (or even indicator) in all our cases.

The Surgical Instrument Company did use the rate of profit on sales as one of its criteria for deciding whether to proceed with the development of the new scalpel, but it put more emphasis on return on capital employed. Dee Plastics calculated its gross margin as a percentage of selling price. Other firms using return on sales or turnover in this way included Alpha Ltd. and Wensum Engineering. Both Fourways Manufacturing and Heavy Technology made use of a similar concept: return as a margin on costs.

Return on capital. This measure of profitability was used by all firms. In principle, it is the most useful way of measuring profitability. Yet it is also among the most misleading.

Rates of return can be defined in several ways, but we must distinguish two. First, there is profit for the period in question, expressed as a percentage of the value of the assets used in earning that profit. Usually, this will be the value at which these assets stand in the balance sheet. We shall describe this rate of return as the rate of return on capital employed.

The second measure of rate of return on capital is used where a new asset is being acquired. More and more firms are calculating the DCF (discounted cash flow) return on such assets. This works out what return the investment is expected to yield over its life—assuming that the predictions of its earnings turn out to be correct. We shall have more to say about DCF returns later. For the moment, our concern is with return on capital employed.

The big problem in calculating the rate of return on capital employed lies in the difficulty of valuing capital assets correctly. Book value (namely, cost less depreciation) will be correct only if there is no inflation, and if the depreciation method used reflects exactly the rate at which the asset actually depreciates. Put this way, we can see that only by a miracle will the book value of an asset equal its actual value in a world where there is both inflation and technical change. Inflation makes the values of both new and existing assets appreciate; technical change makes them depreciate. Depreciation charges are usually best seen as a simple way of ensuring that, when plant has to be replaced, retained profits have been made available to allow for this.

However, it must be emphasized that these profits will not necessarily be available in a liquid form. Effective capital and cash budgeting will be needed for that.

To allow for inflation, more firms will need to do what some firms already do—undertake the regular revaluation of capital assets. This method will still not deal with the other important factor leading to changes in asset values—technical change. If technical improvements reduce the cost of new assets of a particular kind, then the value of existing assets will fall. In the contemporary world where prices rise steadily, though technology improves too, there is merit in using rates of return on the current values of assets to evaluate performance. The reason is that it emphasizes the fact that using book values often overstates rates of return on capital and so makes management's job too easy. This explains why managers frequently resist the revaluation of assets. In addition, revaluation does mean extra work, and careful cost/benefit evaluation is necessary to see how frequently it can economically be undertaken.

It follows, of course, that there are even bigger difficulties in the way of comparison of rates of return on capital employed between firms. Definitions of capital employed vary from firm to firm, as do accounting practices and depreciation conventions. Some firms revalue capital at intervals; others do not. However, useful information can be obtained from comparison of trends from year to year in the return on capital in any given firm, provided that the basis of calculation used remains constant.

Despite all these reservations, we must recognize that achieving a given rate of return on capital is a major objective for most firms. Firms borrow capital with which to trade. For the shareholder (or other lender) who provides that capital, it is the return on each pound invested that matters. Return on capital (measured as accurately as it is profitable to do) is therefore the most significant indicator of the profitability of the firm, even though knowing what rate of return is currently being earned will not necessarily enable the firm to know whether a better one is possible. So long as the firm measures return on capital employed consistently between departments, and uses it for internal comparisons only, there is no serious problem in using it.

It is perhaps worth pointing out that even if the firm is earning a high return on capital employed, as defined above, it may not necessarily be doing the best it can for its shareholders. A major problem in business finance is to ensure that the capital structure of the firm—especially the relationship between fixed-interest borrowing and the issuing of equity capital—is optimal. The ultimate aim of the firm must be to give a high (or maximum) rate of return to equity shareholders. Earning a high (or maximum) return on capital employed is only the first step in this larger process. However, it is an important first step.

In our study, the only firm which tried to calculate the return on capital employed for individual products and product lines was the Surgical Instrument Company. The DCF return on the capital employed in producing the scalpel was therefore one of the main criteria by which the project was evaluated, before the Board gave authority for it to be put on the market. In all the other firms we studied, return on capital was one extremely important criterion by which the over-all performance of the company was judged, but not the performance of individual products. A specific target rate of return was laid down for the whole firm at some stage in the long-term forecasting or short-term budgeting process. A number of firms judged their performance by looking at their rate of return on capital before tax. Wessex Timber Industries was one of them.

None of our firms appeared to take tax explicitly into account when pricing. Perhaps tax is not very important for pricing decisions so long as the rate of (pre-tax) return required from any product takes account of the level and structure of taxation in a general way and yields a big enough rate of return after tax. It is with investment decisions that the fact that the British system has provided investment and depreciation grants or allowances has made it essential to allow for tax explicitly.

The refusal of the twelve firms, apart from the Surgical Instrument Company, to calculate rates of return on capital for individual products was realistic. Many products were produced jointly with others—with raw materials, labour and plant devoted to making more than one product. For example, Basic Foods processed several foodstuffs from the same raw material on the same machines. Dee Plastics and Wessex Timber Industries produced wide ranges of similar items, of different sizes, on the same plant. In these three firms, no attempt to allocate either current or capital costs to individual products could have given very accurate results. Even for those firms and products where such a calculation would have been less difficult, it was not thought worthwhile.

Profit Objectives

We now go on to look in detail at the profit objectives pursued in the firm we studied. Five of the firms tried to maximize profit; they were: The Surgical Instrument Company, Dee Plastics, Heavy Technology, Medlock Engineering and Clean Engineering.

The Maximizers

The Surgical Instrument Company Ltd. The Surgical Instrument Company is the odd one out in this list. It was the only one of the five firms which set out to maximize profits that was not virtually compelled to do so either to meet the competitive pressures it faced in a depressed market or in order to reach the level of profit required from it by the parent firm. The Board of the parent firm did not set the Surgical Instrument Company a minimum rate of profit which it was expected to earn on each individual product. However, the parent Board did keep a careful check on the over-all return on capital earned by the Surgical Instrument Company. The latter therefore thought it best to take the trouble to work out the rate of return on capital for every product.

The attempt to maximize profits can be split into two distinct stages. In the first, capital was allocated to the production of disposable scalpels only after the Surgical Instrument Company had looked at the known alternative uses for this capital. The only way in which the parent Board could be persuaded to invest funds in a new project was for those concerned with it to show that it would yield a satisfactory rate of return on that investment. The Surgical Instrument Company was seeking a DCF return of at least 12 per cent to 15 per cent on its investment in any major products, but might accept a lower rate on less important ones. In this case, it was decided that beginning to produce scalpels was the best way of using the funds in question, taking into account all relevant alternatives and the opportunities and constraints for each alternative. The company sought the most profitable use for these assets—it maximized.

In the second stage, the scalpel was priced. In doing this, the marketing manager of the company was under pressure to set whatever price would maximize profit and this was thought likely, for the scalpel, to be a rather high one. He looked at the rate of return both on capital and on turnover. While the company realized that it was easier to reduce a high price than to raise one that had been initially set too low, it had only recently entered the scalpel market and faced a number of competing products. The prices of these products effectively gave the maximum price which could be charged for a new scalpel. If the Surgical Instrument Company had set a price higher than this, it could not reasonably have expected buyers to change from existing products to the new one. Its price was therefore set to maximize return, but taking into account the prices of competing scalpels.

Three of the remaining four firms which tried to maximize profits were operating in very difficult market conditions. They were Heavy Technology, Medlock Engineering and Clean Engineering.

Heavy Technology Ltd. In Heavy Technology, it was the general and sales managers who were responsible for setting pricing objectives fitting in with the company's philosophy. The firm had not defined its profit objectives precisely, though it was generally agreed in the firm that a rate of return of about 15 per cent was required on the funds put into any new investment. The firm was anxious to embody the latest scientific and technological developments in new products, in order to maintain its position as the most technically advanced firm in the industry. It also sought to maintain its market share and to earn sufficient profit to finance an intensive research and development programme. Profitability was thus treated as very important. Without it, research and development would have suffered. As a result, the company had in the past had to satisfy the parent Board that it was earning at least as much as in the previous year, and close to a 15 per cent return on capital employed. New capital was allocated by the Board on the basis of past achievement.

With the market depressed when we studied the firm, things had changed. It would have been unrealistic for the general and sales managers to continue to pursue the objective of earning a 15 per cent return on capital, since Heavy Technology had been forced to reduce its prices in order to obtain business. Holding or increasing its market share, and so maximizing profit (or minimizing loss), were now seen as the most important goals.

The complete set of the objectives which had been pursued by Heavy Technology at one time or another in pricing contracts was as follows:

(a) to earn a profit of about 15 per cent on capital for the company;
(b) to guarantee the company's survival;
(c) to keep its share of the market;
(d) to provide funds for research, development and product innovation; and
(e) to maintain a high level of employment, particularly for staff.

In the difficult market situation, objectives (a), (d) and even (e) had virtually been abandoned, in order to maintain profit and survive. A new profit objective—to minimize losses whilst increasing market share if possible—had been tacitly adopted. This was effectively profit maximization (loss minimization) but with the hope that it would still be possible to maintain the existing level of employment, especially among staff.

Medlock Engineering Ltd. The competitive position faced by Medlock Engineering was equally difficult. It was very hard in this case to discover operational pricing objectives for the product we studied which were different from the non-operational objectives of the whole firm, and which could give definite guidance to managers. In our study of Medlock we were concerned only with export markets. The (non-operational) objectives there were:

(a) to keep the factories working at a high level of activity;
(b) to provide an acceptable level of contribution to fixed costs and, if possible, profit;
(c) to obtain technical experience that could be of value in the home market in future.

These goals clearly do not represent precise, operational objectives, though they do emphasize the marginal character of export sales in Medlock Engineering. The notion of marginal pricing for such sales was well established.

Medlock Engineering normally set each of its departments to earn a return of 15 per cent on capital employed (at book values). However, it was accepted that it would often be difficult to earn this rate of profit in the export market. While the profit objective was not formally changed on export business, lower rates of return were in fact accepted by the Board. Many export sales were truly marginal, covering variable cost and little more. The objective was to choose the most profitable combination of sales open to the firm. At the time of our study, the emphasis was on using these export sales to minimize losses at a time when the home market was depressed. Given the capacity of the firm, it was hoped to keep employment at current levels, but had it been necessary to choose between lower profit and lower employment, employment would have been allowed to fall. The overriding aim was to minimize losses.

Clean Engineering Ltd. The other case where the market was so depressed that the firm was forced into trying to maximize its profits, was that of Clean Engineering. Here, again, it was not possible to distinguish clearly between operational and non-operational pricing objectives. The company's main pricing objective was to keep its existing (approximately 15 per cent) share of the market for water purification equipment at a time when there was intense competition for business, but when the size of the total market was increasing. Even if it had kept its market share, Clean Engineering would have found it hard to provide the Board with the required rate of profit. The Board ostensibly concentrated its attention on the rate of return on capital employed, requiring Clean Engineering to achieve between 15 per cent and 20 per cent. However, when we studied the firm, it was a matter of attempting to use all plant and equipment at tolerable profit (or loss) levels, knowing that the result would be a return of far less than 15 per cent. Indeed, prices were little above marginal cost. The desire to keep labour, plant and equipment in use was again an important factor, though the desire to maximize profit (minimize losses) was seen as paramount. Fortunately, though trade was bad, it was not quite bad enough to require a cut in employment.

Dee Plastics Ltd. The parent company of Dee Plastics Ltd. was essentially interested in receiving a given percentage rate of return on the capital that it had invested in the subsidiary. However, the parent company did not attempt to interfere in the running of Dee Plastics. It recognized that only the local management had the expertise needed in manufacturing and marketing venetian blind slats. Within Dee Plastics, the profit objective for each contract was to earn the 'normal' gross margin of about 25 per cent of the selling price, which was thought to be the optimal margin. This was a margin over prime costs, which were defined as raw materials, sundry direct process costs and carriage. The gross margin of about 25 per cent had to cover labour costs, overheads and profit. Higher prices could sometimes be obtained, and the gross margin on some contracts had been as high as 27 per cent.

On the other hand, we have seen that for larger orders Dee Plastics was prepared to accept lower margins. If one customer were to take all the output produced by working two shifts on one production line, the firm would be willing to accept a gross margin for all this business of between 15 per cent and 20 per cent. The lower unit contribution to profit was seen as worth having because a single set of negotiations was needed and a high level of sales guaranteed. Alternatively, if the whole output of a single shift on this one product line had already been sold, it would now have been possible to set a lower profit margin for the output of the second shift. A substantial level of sales would already have been guaranteed, and a substantial proportion of the firm's fixed costs covered, especially because there would have been no significant increase in overhead costs if two shifts were worked instead of one. Nevertheless, Dee was finding it impossible to provide as high a return on capital as the parent firm would have liked. Dee Plastics had little spare capacity, though thought was being given to the desirability of expanding it by putting down another production line in the existing factory, and by building another factory. Because there was this capacity constraint, Dee was a firm trying to maximize profits while accepting that it could not sell more than the output produced by the existing plant when working the two shifts.

The Satisficers

Alpha Ltd. The eight remaining firms were, quite simply, satisficers. First, there was Alpha Ltd. The operational objectives set for any product group within Alpha Ltd. have to be seen in the context of the company's objectives. Alpha Ltd.'s profit objective was 'to return a satisfactory reward on over-all company operations'. This non-operational objective had been made more precise when objectives were set for the product 'Alpha' itself; but some objectives, even for 'Alpha', remained non-operational. For example, the price of 'Alpha' was to be set by taking into account its total profit contribution to the product group and to the company. In this context, 'Alpha' was required to provide a 'satisfactory' margin of profit, after all costs had been met; but the size of a 'satisfactory' margin had not been defined.

On the other hand, 'Alpha' was set the task of providing a specific share of company profits, within the annual budgeting procedure. When the figure for profit in the budget was being set, the objective was a satisfactory, rather than the maximum possible, amount. At product-manager level, the basic strategic aim was to increase both 'Alpha's' market share and the total amount of 'Alpha' sold. There was an explicitly stated belief that, in the long run, the best guarantee of satisfactory profit would be for the market share held by 'Alpha' to be maintained. However, there was no attempt to quantify this relationship between profit and market share. While it was clearly thought to exist, no one could say exactly what it implied for individual, short-run marketing decisions. These were aimed mainly at achieving short-run market-share objectives. The conflicts, actual and potential, which lay behind the attempt to guarantee long-run profit by maintaining short-run market share will be looked at in more detail later.

Gamma Products Ltd. The second satisficer was Gamma. The objectives which Gamma pursued in pricing its battery for shavers were:

(a) to obtain a specified share of the battery market within a year;

(b) to sell x thousand Gamma shavers in the same period;

(c) to distribute Gamma's batteries and shavers through 75 per cent of the total number of electrical shops in the U.K. (which normally handled Gamma's products) and 75 per cent of barbers' shops (which handled a large proportion of shaver sales, but which had not previously sold Gamma's products).

These objectives were set after the firm had studied forecasts of the markets for batteries and shavers, in terms of both volume and value. The forecasts were made for each year of a five-year period, beginning with the year of Gamma's introduction, and were revised at fairly frequent intervals as experience was gained in the market.

A review of market forecasts undertaken a few months after the introduction of the Gamma shaver, led the firm to reduce its estimates of the total market demand for shaver batteries by about 20 per cent, while its forecast of the total demand for shavers was rather more than doubled. As a result, the sales-volume and market-share objectives for Gamma's batteries were both reduced, whilst those for shavers were both increased very considerably. The Board and the product managers of Gamma had always realized that the initial forecasts might well be wrong. They accepted them as a reasonable basis for planning because so little information was available. The targets based on them were accepted as achievable.

A similar series of estimated figures was prepared for the costs of Gamma batteries and shavers, and for the revenues and profits expected from them. Depending on the assumptions made, a wide range of possible annual profit figures was shown for each of the five years after the forecast was made. Profit was estimated in absolute amounts of money throughout. In the case of shavers, this was because there was no capital investment in shavers by Gamma Products; manufacture was contracted. The profit on turnover from Gamma shavers was small by the firm's normal standard, whatever assumptions were made. But, since the shaver had been developed in order to keep up Gamma's battery sales, the actual rate of profit was regarded, as comparatively unimportant so long as sales of batteries, and profits from them, increased.

Wensum Engineering Ltd. Wensum Engineering, too, would have liked to earn more than it was currently earning, in order to satisfy the parent Board. In practice, for various reasons, it arrived at a lower profit than it might have done. Wensum Engineering was originally asked by the parent firm to provide a return on capital employed of between 20 per cent and 25 per cent. Wensum explained that 'the broad aim is to obtain a given percentage return on investment rather than a particular market share for each product group'. However, Wensum's managing director felt that past performance, viewed rather cautiously, demonstrated that this rate of return on capital employed could not be reached. He was able to get the target rate of return reduced to a less ambitious one of 17 per cent. The parent firm had to allow for the fact that Wensum sold a significant proportion of its output to other members of its group on very favourable terms. There was a problem of transfer pricing here. This was to some extent a circular process, because the rates of return Wensum was asked to earn depended in part on the prices at which it was forced to transfer its products to other members of its own group. If the transfer price had been increased, the return on capital employed required of Wensum by its parent board would undoubtedly have been raised too. We studied Wensum's annual price review, which was carried out by a committee that did not include the managing director. Its members were the marketing manager, the accountant and the domestic sales manager. The export sales manager's position was ambiguous. Though nominally a member of the committee, he attended only part of the meeting. No specific instructions were given to the members of this committee. They already knew that the minimum goal was a return on turnover of 10 per cent to 12 per cent. It was explained to us that capital would be turned over 1·5 times, giving a return on capital employed of 15 per cent to 18 per cent. The parent firm required 17 per cent. However, in the price review meeting, the minimum return was taken as the required rate of return.

The managing director confirmed that he did not give any specific directive to the review meeting. He said, 'They know what we are trying to get.' As we shall see, things did not work out even as smoothly as this implies. The decisions taken in the meeting did not yield even the minimum rate of return on capital of 17 per cent. This may explain why, after the meeting, the domestic sales manager raised some prices on his own.

Fourways Manufacturing Ltd. Fourways Manufacturing expected each of its products to cover the general overheads which were regarded as being associated with its production, and to make an 'acceptable' contribution to profits as well. In addition to this non-operational objective, there was the operational objective that, for every group of similar products within each product line, there should be a standard percentage rate of recovery, or margin (expressed as gross invoice value less commission, labour cost and material cost). Individual products were expected to provide a margin of this size over an appropriate time period. This was either a year, or the expected life of the product, depending on the particular circumstances. The standard rate of recovery of overheads for each product was expressed both as an absolute sum of money and as a percentage of costs. From it was calculated a tentative price, which was then adjusted to take market conditions, including the prices of competing products, into account. In the case of the new product whose pricing we studied, the amount expected to be earned over and above commission, labour and material costs, was based on forecasts of several factors. These were the amount to be invested in the product, its launching and development expenses, its manufacturing costs and the expected levels of sales in the first years of its life. The forecasting and profitability exercise was repeated several times during the development of the product.

Basic Foods Ltd. In Basic Foods there was a close link between over-all company objectives and the specific objectives for the product studied. This was perhaps because the product accounted for a great deal of Basic Foods's turnover. Over-all objectives for the group of which Basic Foods was a member were set when the budget for the following five years was drawn up. (The budget for the first year was worked out in detail, whilst plans were drawn up for the remaining four years in whatever degree of detail was felt to be appropriate.) The group's over-all objectives were set in general terms by the executive board of the parent firm. This general plan provided an outline of intended future developments, which the subsidiaries of the group could use in drawing up their own one-year and five-year plans, tailoring them to meet their own specific objectives.

The objectives of Basic Foods were set by its own Board. They took account of the general, over-all objectives laid down by the executive board of the parent, of how far current performance was matching current objectives and of forecasts of those factors which were likely to affect Basic Foods's operations in the future. These objectives for the first year, and for all five years, were presented to the parent's executive board together with Basic Foods's capital budget for the first year. From this document and from discussion on it, detailed objectives were agreed for the first year of the five-year period for each of Basic Foods's products. When we studied Basic Foods, its underlying (non-operational) objective was 'to maintain adequate growth while maintaining profitability so far as this is possible'.

The capital budget outlined Basic Foods's plans for dealing with the main problems it anticipated meeting. It covered all aspects of marketing policy and gave Basic Foods's forecasts of sales volumes, sales value, costs, profit and return on capital employed as well as the internal rate of return expected on its total planned capital expenditure for the period. The capital budget represented a set of intentions based on a limited number of assumptions; from it were developed the annual plans and budgets for all Basic Foods's activities.

The company recognized that with a fluid competitive situation, like the one for the product we studied, the marketing and pricing decisions made by Basic Foods, or by any one of its competitors. were bound to have a substantial impact in the market in which they operated, and not least on market shares. As a result, it was accepted as likely that the budgeted figures for sales, profits, etc., would have to be changed. Pricing decisions were made to meet a combination of marketing (i.e. sales volume and market share) and financial (i.e. sales value and profit) objectives, given the over-all objective of maintaining growth and profitability.

Epsilon Ltd. Epsilon Ltd. seemed to be less concerned with its over-all profitability than was Basic Foods, although a target rate of profit on capital employed was set in advance and was aimed at over a period of five years by the whole company. How far any level of profitability either for the whole firm or for an individual product was regarded as satisfactory depended on the current market situation and on the Board's interpretation of the word 'satisfactory'. But what profit had been earned in the past seemed to have a significant influence in determining what was accepted in the present.

To understand the profit objectives for Epsilon, we must look in some detail at the objectives of Epsilon's marketing staff. The operation of launching 'Epsilon' on a national scale was to be carried out in two phases. First, there was to be a limited test-market period, during which 'Epsilon' would be introduced and (it was hoped) successfully established in two different regions. Then the sales coverage for 'Epsilon' was to be extended over the whole country. The two test-market regions were chosen to allow the firm to discover whether consumers in different geographical areas accepted 'Epsilon's' physical attributes and its performance, as well as to test alternative methods of sales promotion. This was to be done before the product could be introduced on a national scale.

Objectives were set for both stages of this operation. Epsilon Ltd. wished not merely to establish 'Epsilon' in the market, but to establish it as the leading brand in the more expensive part of the market. Specific targets were set for yearly periods up to five years ahead, covering both phases. They were set in terms of profit, sales volume and sales value, market share, the scale of distribution to retail outlets (and hence availability to customers) and the percentage of customers who had tried the product. It was also expected (and indeed intended) that not more than 30 per cent of 'Epsilon's' sales would be at the expense of the company's own similar products. Again, these objectives seem to have been satisficing ones.

Wessex Timber Industries Ltd. Turning now to Wessex Timber Industries, we find that its Board had set a pre-tax rate of return on capital employed which was to be achieved from sales of timber. The managers and salesmen of Wessex had to ensure that the budgeted output of timber would be sufficient to provide this level of profitability. However, as labour was the limiting factor for Wessex, its ability to work at high levels of output depended on heavy investment in plant and equipment. Consequently it was important to ensure that, as the scale of the firm's investment increased, it continued to earn an acceptable rate of return on capital employed. Ensuring that increased investment did not reduce the rate of return on capital lay at the heart of Wessex's management problems.

The firm's operational pricing objectives had to take account of two major requirements. Wessex was asked:

(a) to provide the return on capital of $12\frac{1}{2}$ per cent before tax required by the Board:

(b) to work as near to 100 per cent of capacity as possible.

In order to turn these general requirements into precise objectives, the management of Wessex Timber Industries Ltd. met quarterly to review past performance and to set budgets for the following quarter. Variances between budgeted and actual performance in the previous quarter were studied to see if they were likely to recur. For example, since the amount of labour that was available for employment was the main factor determining how much of Wessex's capacity could be used, it was particularly important that labour variances should be analysed, and taken into account if necessary, in setting the next quarter's budget.

From these discussions emerged a forecast of output in the next quarter, usually expressed in thousands of feet of processed timber, Since the Board required the $12\frac{1}{2}$ per cent before-tax rate of return on capital, the management had to ensure that selling the budgeted output of timber would achieve this target. The production manager forecast the effects of changes in costs in the coming period. These were incorporated into a build-up of expected costs for the quarter, for each type of timber processed. Cost per foot of timber ready for sale was calculated on the assumption that output targets would be achieved.

To calculate what price had to be charged to ensure that selling the budgeted output would provide the budgeted cost levels was then a simple matter. This price was the salesman's target; his job was to get the best price he could for any sale of timber, but he was given only the freedom of being allowed to charge prices within plus or minus 1 per cent of those shown in the company's price list. It follows from what has been said that if the salesman really did get the best price he could for any timber sold, then the firm could be regarded as maximizing profits rather than satisficing—given the supply of labour. However, our judgement is that if one considers the way in which the budget was set, the firm was probably satisficing rather than maximizing. We suspect, though we cannot prove, that salesmen might have obtained higher prices if greater pressure for profit had been put on them.

Universal Corporation. The final satisficing firm was Universal Corporation. Its objective, laid down by the parent Board, was to obtain a given return on capital employed over a five-year period. Precise rules were laid down for calculating the rate of return on capital employed, and these regulated all the Corporation's activities. Universal's objectives were defined in this way because of two interdependent factors. First, it had to rely considerably, but not completely, on internal funds to finance investment. It therefore had to earn profit margins big enough to service large amounts of capital expenditure. The second factor was that its plant took a long time to construct. The size of its plants and their complex technology meant that a number of years had to elapse before any newly planned plant could be put into operation. Because its pricing objectives were framed so as to ensure that it earned the required rate of return on capital, and to some extent because it was tradi- tional, Universal Corporation had set its prices on the basis of unit cost. The definition of this unit cost—and therefore of price—was being changed at the time of our study. The unit cost used had previously been average cost at predetermined volumes of output. Universal was now beginning to use marginal cost and was relating this to particular ranges of output.

The reasons for adopting a system of marginal cost pricing were complex, and the change was undertaken only after considerable discussion with the parent Board and with Universal's distributing agents. The objective in making the change was rather more clear cut. While charging prices related to marginal cost, the corporation aimed to cover its over-all expenses in the short run, i.e. in periods of up to a year. Over the longer run (say, one to five years ahead) Universal Corporation wanted to base prices on marginal cost in order to help its distributors to recognize likely future patterns of cost and so of demand. Since it would be easier for them to deduce such patterns from marginal rather than from average costs, mar- ginal cost pricing was intended to enable distributors to make better forecasts of their likely future demands for the products of the Corporation.

Profit Objectives Summarized

We may now sum up. All the firms we studied had profit objec- tives. In every case, the firm had an objective stated in terms of rate of return on capital. The difficulties in measuring capital were usually glossed over and it was usual for the rate of return to be set for the output of the whole firm or department rather than for an individual product. Only some of the firms treated rate of return on turnover as an operational objective in pricing, but all of them set a target profit, in budgets, as an absolute sum of money.

Five of the thirteen firms could be regarded as maximizers, but only one (Surgical Instrument Company) maximized profit as part of a freely chosen policy. Dee was forced to maximize because the Board of the parent firm was insisting on high (or increased) profits. The other three were seeking to earn as much as they could in markets where trade was depressed. The remaining firms were satisficers.

Market Objectives

Market objectives provide the firm with criteria by which it can judge its performance in each of its markets. The firms we studied concentrated on three measures: sales volume, sales value and market share. All of them had set specific, measurable market objectives for pricing, using at least one of these criteria.

The terminology used was not the same in every case; for example, 'sales volume' was used by Alpha Ltd.; 'output' by Wessex Timber Industries. Although, where there are stocks, output need not equal sales volume, in practice the two may come to the same thing. This was obviously true where goods were produced to meet specific orders, as in Wessex Timber and Clean Engineering. Output and sales could differ where goods were produced for stock. They did so in Epsilon Ltd., in Fourways and in Wensum.

Volume of sales. With the exception of Clean Engineering, all our firms set targets for the volume of sales to be achieved in specific (usually budget) periods. These targets were set in units of output, or in turnover, according to the product. In the case of Clean Engineering, which wanted to keep its 15 per cent share of the growing market for water purification equipment, estimates of market size were available. When sales volume was considered it was therefore as a derivative, rather than as a determinant, of the firm's desired share of a market of the estimated size.

Sales volume and capacity. In some cases, targets for sales volume depended upon production capacity. The clearest example of this was in Dee Plastics where, but for the constraint imposed by its limited production capacity, its marketing effort would have been devoted to increasing sales and taking market share from the dominant competitor. A major reason why extra capacity had not been installed was that it was not clear that the extra volume and market share could be obtained at an adequate profit. The case of Wessex Timber was similar, though here it was labour, not plant, that was the limiting factor. In Heavy Technology, the situation was slightly different. The main objective here was to maximize profit (minimize loss) but to hope that this would allow the firm to work near to full capacity in the highly competitive market situation that the company faced. The benefit that Heavy Technology would obtain from a particular contract was judged by the effect that obtaining it would have on the profit-and-loss position, but with an anxious eye on the proportion of capacity which would be at work. With Medlock Engineering, the situation was broadly similar. Export orders were judged by their 'contribution' to profit and by how far they would fill the gap between demand from British customers and total productive capacity. But the main objective was to maximize profit.

Sales value. Sales value, or turnover, objectives were normally set in terms of the firm's net receipts, though these were often hard to calculate. For instance, when Epsilon Ltd. calculated company revenue, it began from retail prices. Retail prices were notional, because there was no resale price maintenance for 'Epsilon'. The notional unit retail price was multiplied by estimated sales volume, and retail margins, trade discounts, etc. were then deducted. Similar calculations were made by the other consumer good manufacturers, although in the case of Basic Foods sales at below notional retail price were not so numerous as for Alpha Ltd., Gamma Ltd. and Epsilon Ltd.

The manufacturers of industrial goods, like The Surgical Instrument Company and Wensum Engineering, used similar concepts when setting their sales-value objectives. They began from ex-works selling prices and allowed for trade discounts. For Heavy Technology calculating turnover meant adding together the values of all individual contracts. A similar position existed in Medlock Engineering and Clean Engineering.

Market share. Market-share objectives were set by most firms, though the importance attached to them varied. They were most important to the consumer-good manufacturers. For Alpha Ltd., whose 'Alpha' was competing with 'Omega' for this particular consumer market, movements in market share were seen as the most significant indicators of success or failure. As a result, market-share objectives had a crucial place in budgeting for 'Alpha'. Market-share objectives were stated as a percentage of the total market both in terms of sales volume and value. Although the remaining consumer-goods manufacturers (Basic Foods, Gamma Products and Epsilon Ltd.) did not each compete with a single major competitor, they used similar measures of market share to judge market success. In the cases of Gamma Products and Epsilon Ltd., both of which were launching new consumer products, attention was concentrated on the market share which they wanted by the end of the launch period. This would be a major determinant of the product's success or failure.

Most of the industrial goods manufacturers did not regard market-share objectives as so important. However, Heavy Technology, Dee Plastics, Medlock Engineering and Clean Engineering all faced very keen competition. Keeping their positions in their respective markets had become extremely important. So, they had to pay a great deal of attention to market share.

Market share was a less important objective in pricing for the other firms. The Surgical Instrument Company, Wessex Timber Industries and Universal Corporation all had estimates of their current shares of their markets; they all planned on the basis of estimated, future market shares; all of them used these estimates to obtain an idea of how their products were faring on the market. Even so, the projections were far from critical for either marketing or pricing decisions. Medlock Engineering had set no objectives for its share of the world-wide market for its exported product. Although data was available about markets in a number of individual countries, there was no effort to determine what share of these markets the firm should try to obtain or to hold.

Scale of distribution. The scale on which the consumer goods we studied were distributed was an important criterion of marketing success for their manufacturers. The larger the number of retail outlets selling a product, the greater was the number of potential buyers. Accordingly, consumer-goods manufacturers often set objectives for the scale on which they wanted their products to be distributed, in a way that was not always appropriate to the manufacturers of industrial goods.

With Epsilon Ltd. and Gamma Products, which were launching new consumer goods, the objective in each case was set as the percentage of all possible retail outlets which were to be selling the product within one year. In test-markets, the objective was set for the limited area and for the period of the test-market only. Alpha Ltd. did not treat as an objective the percentage of shops it wanted to stock 'Alpha'. 'Alpha' was an established product, and the number of outlets through which it was available had largely been determined already. While its distribution pattern was measured and reported on, the struggle with 'Omega' was fought by other means.

In addition to its distribution objectives, Epsilon Ltd. had set objectives for the trial marketing of 'Epsilon'. The aim was that by the end of the test-market, or introductory period, 'Epsilon' would have been sampled by a given percentage of the available body of consumers. During this trial period, 'Epsilon' was to make use of various forms of sales promotion. It was believed that the scale of such trials was important in determining the rate at which customers would become aware of 'Epsilon'. Once they were aware of it, some of them would be likely to switch their custom from other brands, so increasing 'Epsilon's' chances of achieving its other objectives.

Market Objectives Summarized

We must now sum up again. So far as market objectives were concerned, all our firms set sales-volume and market-share objectives. In a few cases, the market share aimed at was somewhat influenced by the desire to sell enough output to keep employment at current levels.

Market-share objectives were of varying importance for our firms. They were more important for consumer-goods producers and for the four firms selling in difficult markets. The scale on which the product was available to consumers was an important objective for consumer-good manufacturers.

Other Objectives

A number of other objectives might be relevant to particular pricing decisions. Examples are: using capacity to the full (an objective distinguished from that of reaching a given sales volume); setting levels of output or inventory, or reducing variations in them; adjusting to particular aspects of national policy; and attempting to set or alter the public image of the firm.

In our studies, we found two major objectives of this kind. Clearly, our firms were concerned to ensure that their pricing decisions did not result in unacceptable levels of and/or variations in inventory. They were also keen that they should not be unnecessarily criticized either by the Prices and Incomes Board or by the Monopolies Commission. However, the two main 'other objectives' were those of keeping the percentage of capacity employed at a high level and ensuring that the firm kept in the forefront of technological development.

The objective of keeping capacity employed was a significant objective for Heavy Technology, Medlock Engineering and Clean Engineering. We have already discussed its relevance to their sales-volume objectives. They put more emphasis on maintaining profit than on maintaining employment, even though the desire to maintain employment could be justified on purely economic grounds. To lay off labour, if depression in the firms' markets was not going to last for very long, would be expensive in terms of redundancy payments, re-training costs and so on. The objective of keeping capacity occupied was more important in the case of Dee, where it was linked to its desire to take market share from its major competitor.

One or two of the firms making technically advanced products emphasized the need, sometimes, to take orders at low prices in order to gain experience needed to develop advanced products. Heavy Technology and Medlock Engineering were the firms which put most emphasis on this. Heavy Technology, in particular, took export orders for its larger products at low prices because the business gained gave excellent experience in designing and operating products bigger than the U.K. market would require for some years. This gave them a head-start over domestic competitors who had not done so.

III. SOME CONCLUSIONS ABOUT OBJECTIVES

The Importance of Profit

We begin this final section by looking at the profit objectives of the firms we studied to see what generalizations we can make about them. Our list of the 'classic' business objectives suggests that profit maximization is an important business aim. However, it appears from our case studies that this traditional idea of economists that firms are above all interested in maximizing profit is defective in several ways. This is not to say that there are no other reasons for attacking the economist's assumption of profit maximization. We do not pretend that ours is anything like a complete list of the possible criticisms of the idea of profit maximization; we can only say that these are the ones we found in our researches.

To ensure that this section is not misinterpreted, it must be stressed at once that we were rather surprised by the emphasis that our firms did put on profit. Over the past twenty or thirty years, it has become fashionable for economists to question their traditional assumptions, and to believe that few firms actually seek maximum profits. The reasons suggested for their failure to do so are that they hesitate to exploit their customers; that they fear that high profits in any line of activity will attract new entrants to it and so eliminate those profits; that high profits will lead to intervention by governments to reduce prices; and so on. Indeed, one had begun to wonder whether supposed philanthropists like doctors (especially American doctors) were the only remaining profit maximizers.

It therefore came as a salutary surprise to discover that five of the thirteen firms studied were anxious to maximize profits. It will be recalled that these firms were: The Surgical Instrument Company, Dee Plastics, Heavy Technology, Medlock Engineering and Clean Engineering. It is true, of course, that Heavy Technology, Medlock Engineering and Clean Engineering would have liked to maintain employment. Nevertheless, in seeking to maximize profits or minimize losses, they would have been prepared to see men laid off rather than abandon this attempt. Dee Plastics was being pressed hard to increase profits, by its parent firm, in a situation where it found it difficult to compete successfully with its much bigger rival.

Of course, there are various ways of increasing profit towards a maximum level, and changing price is only one of them. Others which a firm seeking to increase its profits should consider would include: cutting overhead costs, eliminating uneconomic customers or products, reducing inventories, reviewing purchasing policy, and so on. Nor should it be forgotten that even if a firm is using pricing policy to increase profit this does not mean that prices have to be put up. If demand for a product is sufficiently responsive to price cutting, profitability may be increased by cutting prices—not by raising them. The willingness to seek increased profits through price *cuts* is one element in the greater flexibility in pricing which we should like to see displayed by more firms, especially in Britain.

It is important to emphasize at once that this proves nothing about the objectives of British firms in general. What we are saying about profit maximization is true for only five of the firms we studied. What is more, there is one very important reason why we should not expect these five firms (or indeed our whole sample) to be typical ones. Six of the firms taking part in this survey (Dee Plastics, Heavy Technology, Medlock Engineering, Clean Engineering, Wensum and Fourways) were firms which were concerned about their over-all profitability. They included (somewhat oddly) two of the satis-ficers—Wensum and Fourways. Indeed, these six firms asked us to look at the products we studied partly because they hoped we might be able to suggest ways of making them more profitable and so increasing over-all profit. This being so, it is hardly surprising that a high proportion—five of our thirteen firms—should have sought to maximize profit. This is not to say that no other firms seek to maximize profit. Nor, indeed, can we say whether our satisficers, when pricing other products, sought bigger (or even maximum) profits. Our survey simply does not allow us to know. All we can do is to report the fact that five of the firms we studied were extremely anxious to earn higher profits from all their activities.

Nevertheless, we have already shown that this is not quite the whole story. While these firms were keen to earn high profits, they were also anxious to maintain employment and output. They seemed to hope that a change in price might help to improve profitability in a less painful or disruptive way than would any of the alternative courses of action that they could have followed to increase profits. If necessary, they would have reduced employment —but they hoped it would not be necessary.

So far as profitability is concerned, perhaps the best interpreta-tion is to say that three of the five firms seeking high profits (Heavy Technology, Clean Engineering and Medlock Engineering) were essentially satisficers. Perhaps Dee was too. These firms were re-acting in the way satisficers do react when one or more of their aspiration levels fails to be met. Here, the failure was to earn suffi-cient profit. The reaction was to concentrate on taking decisions to ensure that the firm could once again achieve this one objective (profit) by setting levels of price which, purely from a pricing point of view, were as close to profit-maximizing ones as the firm could make them. The aim was to maximize profit, and simultaneously to hope that if pricing policy led to maximum profit it would be possible to avoid significantly changing other aspiration levels— those for production, employment, inventory levels and so on—or indeed the extent to which these aspiration levels were being reached. The attraction of trying to use price alone to improve profitability was that, if the attempt succeeded, all the potentially painful adjustments required in order to do so would have to be made outside, not inside, the firm. Profit could be increased while the constraints represented by the other aspiration levels still held. The firm would increase its profits either at the expense of its competitors, if a cut in price took business from them; or at the expense of its customers, if a rise in price did not cause them to change to other suppliers.

We are therefore convinced that, in at least four of the cases where the firms studied would have liked to maximize profits, they were satisficers, and not maximizers, at heart. In easier conditions, we believe they would have left prices unchanged so long as the aspiration levels for profits were being met.

All this points to a very important conclusion. Pricing is one activity (some marketing and investment decisions may be others) where the main burden of adjustment can be imposed on persons or groups outside the firm. It falls upon expenditure by customers on the firm's products, or upon the market shares, sales receipts and profits of competitors, rather than on the firm's own levels of employment, production, inventories, etc. The reason why our firms behaved as they did seems to be that, when trade is difficult, it is both easier and more attractive to make adjustments at the expense of one's customers and competitors rather than of one's colleagues and employees. We believe that this explains why firms that are satisficers when taking decisions about production, inventories, employment, etc., may become maximizers when they set prices. They are forcing those outside the firm to bear the burden of change.

Even when firms do try to maximize profit through their pricing decisions, however, difficulties arise. What our studies did was to spell out some of the reasons why profit maximization is a nonoperational objective. The main reason is that firms rarely know as much as they would like to know about the relationship between the price of any one of their products and the amount of it which is bought. Because of this, even firms which do want to maximize profits cannot move, all at once, to a position where they earn them—subject, of course, to the constraints mentioned above about maintaining acceptable levels of employment, output, etc. We think that firms often attempt to move towards maximum profit in a series of steps.

The result is this. Unless the firm's market is an extremely stable one, and competitors' actions in that market rare or unimportant, profits are unlikely ever to be maximized, even in a firm that wants to maximize them. The firm will be trying, continually or at discrete intervals, to alter prices so as to move towards maximum profit, perhaps rather slowly. Yet the price for each product which would maximize those profits will also be changing all the time. Perhaps we may use the analogy of the children's game of Hunt the Thimble. Using the loudness of the music as an indicator of how close one is to the thimble, one is always trying to move closer to it, not farther away. The complication here is that, with pricing, the correct analogy is with a situation where the thimble is moving about for most, or all, of the time. In these circumstances, firms are unlikely ever to reach profit-maximizing positions, although they will always be tending towards them. One wonders whether a satisficing philosophy is spilling over here. Perhaps a firm increases its price by less than the profit-maximizing amount, partly because it has become accustomed to taking its other business decisions in ways that give less than optimal solutions. At the same time, of course, we must add that businessmen have had to become accustomed to taking decisions like these with less data than they would ideally like.

What we are saying is, first, that the biggest obstacle to taking pricing decisions so as to maximize profit is that profit maximization would require firms to know too much about the demand relationships for the products of their firms. Either information is unobtainable—like accurate predictions of future changes in the economy—or it can be obtained, but only at a price that would be greater than the value of the information. Second, a subsidiary obstacle is that profit maximization would also imply the need to keep achievement continuously in line with what maximization requires. Third, we are saying that if firms are used to satisficing, then, even if conditions become so difficult that they feel they must try to maximize, they may be timid in doing so. This leads to a fourth difficulty. Even if it knew how to do so, no firm would find it tolerable to be continually and minutely adjusting prices, output, inventories, marketing policy, etc. so as continually to maximize profits within a changing environment. One important reason for this is the sheer administrative inconvenience and cost of changing prices frequently.

To sum up, we have so far seen in this section that five of our firms were anxious to maximize profits. Given the unrepresentative nature of our sample, we cannot say how typical these firms are, but we suspect that four of them were satisficers rather than maximizers at heart.

The remaining firms were nearly all 'straightforward' satisficers, but the case of Wensum Engineering is interesting. Talking to managers in Wensum, it became clear that everyone would have been delighted, in principle, if the firm could have maximized profits, or at any rate have increased them substantially, provided that this could have been done without much disturbing the pattern of employment, output, etc. There would then have been congratulations from the parent firm. Yet Wensum has to be classified here as a satisficer, not a maximizer. The managing director set Wensum the target of a profit of 10 per cent to 12 per cent on turnover. Once set, this became, not a minimum to be exceeded if possible, but the profit at which the firm aimed.

Conflicts Between Objectives

Perhaps the most important conclusion which emerges from our analysis of pricing objectives is that in every firm these were multiple. While all firms pursued at least one profit objective, they all had some kind of sales-volume or market-share objective as well. Some firms also had more nebulous objectives, like remaining in the forefront of technological advance.

It is clearly not impossible for a firm to pursue a number of objectives simultaneously, though it is always more difficult than pursuing only one. Ideally, the firm could construct some kind of 'goal index'. It might, for example, decide that it wanted to maximize an index which gave a 50 per cent weight to an increase of 1 per cent in net profits: a 30 per cent weight to an increase of 1 per cent in market share; and a 20 per cent weight to an increase in employment of 100 men. It could then try to set prices on this basis. Hardly surprisingly, we did not find any firm doing so.

Another way of pursuing more than one objective at a time would be to use a ranking procedure. In practice, it is likely that this would mean deciding which was the most important objective, at any moment or in any set of circumstances, and then giving it absolute priority. Satisficing is simply a variant of this. Several aspiration

levels are set. If any one of them fails to be met, priority is given to
reaching it again. This is a simple type of ranking. One ranks the
objective which is not being met as coming first; the other objectives
are then for the time ranked as unimportant.

Of course, the fact that a firm seeks to pursue multiple objectives
does not necessarily mean that there will be conflicts between them.
If a firm knows that it will earn the maximum possible profit for the
following year if it has a 40 per cent share of the market, it can perfectly well pursue the objectives of maximizing profit and holding
a 40 per cent market share. However, things are very rarely as certain as this. The fact that a firm is trying to pursue multiple objectives must make it more difficult to specify these objectives precisely
than if it has only one. Even when the objectives can be specified,
it will be difficult for the firm to ensure that the ones it is pursuing
are always mutually consistent. Firms rarely have the knowledge
they need in order to pursue mutually consistent and multiple
objectives.

Our studies lead us to think that firms sometimes resolve this
problem by treating what appears to be an independent objective
as a constraint on another apparently independent objective.
For example, we have described five of our firms as profit maximizers. In fact, four of them were also anxious to keep existing
capacity and labour fully employed. If they really had treated the
employment constraint as absolute, they would have been maximizing profit (or minimizing loss) subject to the overriding constraint
that output was not to fall below the level required to keep men and
plant fully employed. One objective would have become a constraint
on another. What is more, the constraint (maintaining employment)
would have turned out to be a more important objective than what
had initially appeared to be the primary objective (maximizing
profit).

Conflicts between objectives—Alpha Ltd. In some other firms, something rather similar seemed to happen. For example, Alpha Ltd.
was seeking a particular absolute amount of profit, and was also
aiming at a particular market share. Any conflict between these
objectives was resolved through the budgeting procedures. Alpha
aimed to earn a certain absolute amount of profit and to hold at
least a certain market share, by the end of five years. If this given
market share had turned out to be compatible with the larger
money profit, or if the given money profit had turned out to be

compatible with a bigger market share, all would obviously be well. However, if either the market share or the money profit proved to be too low, at the desired level of the other objective, the conflict between the two objectives would need to be resolved. This would have been done by changing one (or both) objectives during Alpha Ltd.'s budgeting process in the way we shall consider later.

We did not observe Alpha Ltd. for long enough to see how far the two aims did prove to be compatible, but there was confidence among the firm's manager that there was no conflict between its profit and market-share objectives. This was not based on a knowledge that the particular level of profit and market share were demonstrably compatible. It was expressed in a conviction that maintaining or increasing market share in the short run was the best guarantee of adequate, even maximum, profit in the long run. We have no way of saying whether this belief was true, because we do not have the data one would need to prove it. Nor did anyone in Alpha Ltd. Yet the fear of conflict between profitability and market share was eliminated. Anyone who feared there was such a conflict convinced himself that it did not exist through the comforting rationalization, propagated by his colleagues, that the two were compatible.

Since there were those in Alpha Ltd. who found it hard to see how its two main objectives ever could be incompatible, we should perhaps emphasize that an increase in market share will not always lead to an increase in profit. Beyond some point, an increase in market share will have to be 'bought' so expensively, either by price cuts or by increased expenditure on sales promotion, that it will be accompanied by falling profit. Similarly, for example, a change in inventory control arrangements, intended to minimize costs of holding inventory by reducing stock levels, may have undesired effects elsewhere in the firm. For example, it may lead to shorter production runs and so to higher production costs. The objectives of simultaneously minimizing both inventory and production costs will then conflict.

In fact, Alpha Ltd. accepted the objective of achieving, at the end of five years, a certain market share and a given amount of profit. It then used its budgetary machinery to determine what its precise objectives were to be in any particular year. Like other firms, Alpha Ltd. was likely to find that some conflicts had to be eliminated during the budgeting process, but the problems raised by these conflicts could then be looked at in precise, numerical terms for specific periods of time.

Conflicts occurred in several of our firms between the aims of increasing short-run profits and of building up to the long-run volume of sales which they sought as an assurance of long-run profit. All of them were firms where competition was very keen in the sense that it was oligopolistic and far from impersonal. This kind of conflict was strong in the case of 'Alpha' because the total market for both 'Alpha' and 'Omega' was growing slowly. This slow growth restricted the duopolists largely to fighting each other to keep existing business and gave them little opportunity to attract new custom.

Conflicts between objectives—Basic Foods, Ltd. Basic Foods was another firm which faced a conflict between its objectives for profitability and market share. Basic Foods had decided that it wanted to remain among the two or three firms with the biggest shares of its market. The market was growing, but competition was increasing too, and it had lost its traditional role as market leader. Basic Foods was convinced that it could not afford to hold its own prices at the existing level if the trend of prices for products like its own continued to be downwards. If it did, then an internal memorandum suggested that the result would be 'a rapid and accelerating loss of market share which would soon reach the point where no further growth in volume could be involved'. It is not clear whether this was intended to imply that growth in sales volume was needed in order to maintain Basic Foods's profit or to keep up its level of employment and activity, or both.

Nevertheless, Basic Foods saw that if it tried to keep its existing market share by cutting prices, its profit would fall too far. A middle course was therefore chosen, but was not defined precisely. Basic Foods asked for its increased sales to be made at prices that were not 'totally unprofitable'. It set out to hold back the growth of the small firms in the market, without making quite such big price cuts as they did. It set out to match fully any reductions in the prices charged by the bigger firms. It also aimed to extract 'the maximum profit from the remaining business'.

Like Alpha Ltd., Basic Foods was trying to balance market-share objectives against profit objectives. In the way they were stated in the previous paragraph, Basic Foods's objectives were non-operational. For example, it is not clear how much profit it was ready to sacrifice in order to maintain market share. What is clear is that

Basic Foods, like Alpha Ltd., believed that too big a loss of short-run market shares, even if it protected short-run profit, would lead in the long run to a fall in market share that was too big to be acceptable. Basic Foods did not go on, as Alpha did, to argue that keeping short-run market share was the way of best guaranteeing long-run profit, but the underlying attitude was much the same.

As with Alpha Ltd., Basic Foods translated these vague objectives into specific budgets for profit, sales, etc. for the following year. It was at this stage that the conflict between market-share and profit objectives was resolved. Detailed budgets were worked out which set objectives that were thought to be compatible with each other. As it turned out, the problem of how far to cut prices in order to keep market share was resolved for Basic Foods by the other firms in the market. In particular, one big competitor cut its price and forced Basic Foods to follow. In other words, when finally forced to decide, Basic Foods chose to keep up its market share. It did this, not knowing for certain what the implications for profit would be, except that it was likely to fall. Even if the fall were substantial, Basic Foods felt that it had no choice but to follow its major competitor in cutting prices. This was seen as its only hope for survival.

Conflicts between objectives—other firms. In several of our cases, a conflict between profit and marketing objectives was more potential than actual. For example, the Surgical Instrument Company wanted a good profit, but found that the prices charged by its competitors put a clear upper limit on the price of its scalpel. Similarly, there was thought to be no serious conflict between profit and market objectives in Wensum Engineering, at least during the annual price review. The order budget for the next year had been completed before the price review we studied. When the order budget had been drawn up, no allowance had been made for the effects of price changes that might be made during the price review. It was assumed that any changes would be small, so that they would make no difference to the budgeted figure for sales volume in the next year. We were told that when the price review was completed, budgeted sales figures would be changed only for products whose prices had been altered by more than 5 per cent. Wensum rarely acknowledged an overt link between prices and sales, so that it equally saw no need to acknowledge conflicts between profit and market-share objectives.

An increase in profit caused by a price rise of 5 per cent does seem to imply no significant drop in sales. However, we remained suspicious when told by Wensum that sales of *all* its products were quite insensitive to price changes—even within this range of 5 per cent.

At the time of our study, profit was a more important objective for Wensum than sales volume or market share. Wensum seemed to us to be very much a 'satisficer' looking at objectives sequentially. Currently, it was the profit objective that was not being met, so that attention was being concentrated on increasing profits, without much attention being given to what might happen to volume or market share. However, it is only fair to say that Wensum had a fairly large number of competitors, each with a fairly small market share, so that it was not concerned about what happened to market shares in the way that Alpha Ltd. and Basic Foods were.

One firm where the process of budgeting really did seem to have carefully eliminated any element of conflict between objectives was Wessex Timber Industries. At their quarterly price-setting meetings, those who set prices in Wessex agreed the results for the previous quarter and compared them with the budget for that quarter. The budget output for the next quarter was set in the light of this analysis. The budgeted output, together with the level of costs anticipated in the next quarter, was used to determine the likely—and the budgeted—level of unit costs in that quarter. To obtain its list price, Wessex added to these costs an allowance which would ensure that the firm earned the desired return on capital of $12\frac{1}{2}$ per cent. Everything was consistent with everything else. No conflict was apparent between objectives. Any conflict between objectives and achievement that occurred during those three months could be analysed at the next quarterly pricing meeting and could be taken into account in building the next budget. However, the basic objective was to sell all the output which could be produced, with a labour force that was always smaller than Wessex would have liked, at the best level of prices that could be obtained. Given this shortage of labour, conflicts between objectives did not really exist.

Fourways Manufacturing also had a clearly expressed set of objectives that would be fully met if the firm achieved its budgeted level of sales at the list prices of its products. As the following figures indicate, with the product we studied, something was radically wrong with the budget

SALES OF PRODUCT

BUDGET		ACTUAL	
Year 1	*Year 2*	*Year 1*	*Year 2*
96	142	11	38

Fourways's sales forecasting for this product was obviously not good; this could scarcely have been disputed. But, in the short run, Fourways did not go on to alter the price of the product, or the budget, to remove the difference between the actual and budgeted levels of sales. Sales may well have been as low as this because the new model was paying for the deficiencies of its predecessors. An earlier product produced by Fourways Manufacturing had been very unreliable, and had earned the company a bad name. The new product was technically more satisfactory, but there were problems of reliability and performance. Even so, it seems more likely that the new product, which used a revolutionary technique, suffered because buyers thought that its price was very high rather than because of these previous failures. However, the budget remained unrealistic. Conflict here was clearly not within the objectives set, but between these objectives and reality.

Problems of Reconciling Conflicts Between Objectives.

Two major aspects of conflicts between objectives remain to be discussed. First, we need to see how successfully detailed figures worked out during budgeting removed conflicts between broad objectives. This seemed to be done most successfully in firms like Alpha, Ltd., Basic Foods, Wessex Timber and the Surgical Instrument Company. The vagueness of what were effectively non-operational objectives for the whole firm enabled everyone within the firm to accept them with little hesitation. The process of budgeting forced choices, especially between market share and profitability. So far as we can tell, the firm was setting aspiration levels rather than trying to maximize. So long as all the aspiration levels continued to be met, there was no difficulty. If one aspiration level failed to be met, a great deal of effort was devoted to ensuring that this particular objective was reached again. We have seen that price cutting by its rival forced Basic Foods to cut its own prices in order to maintain its market share, and that this was done even though it was by no means certain that profit would continue to be satisfactory at the lower price. We think that, faced with a similar choice, Alpha Ltd. would have set out to hold or maintain its market share as the best guarantee of long-run profit, even though this might have reduced short-run profit below the aspiration level. Market share was, or seemed to be, the main objective.

Our studies show that, if it is in a really difficult position, a firm is likely to concentrate on meeting the threatened aspiration level, almost irrespective of the effects on the others. In less difficult situations it seems that, at the very least, the figures in budgets are made consistent. The number of objectives seriously pursued by our firms was limited, certainly in any given period of time. The pursuit of only one objective was often felt to be enough of a problem for the firm to face at any given moment; difficulties arose when two were being simultaneously pursued. On at least some occasions, when these difficulties became too great, one objective was abandoned in favour of the other(s).

While the firm's budgetary procedures turn disputes over broad objectives into more limited arguments over the objectives of particular departments or products, the problem of setting detailed objectives through budgets is nevertheless a very complicated one. Indeed, once it resolves itself into a matter of which figures are to go into detailed budgets, conflict over objectives raises the second issue that we must discuss. This is that individual departments have their own objectives and will press to be allowed to pursue them. While this brings the possibility of sub-optimization, it may also make things easier rather than more difficult. Instead of strategic debates at Board level about, say, precisely how much profit is to be sacrificed for precisely how much extra sales volume or market share, one has disagreements between departmental managers over what is to happen. These are likely to be treated in a more routine way than would be possible at Board level, without the honour of any top manager becoming too much involved.

The result is that the issues that arise when basic objectives are being converted into budgets and targets are very detailed and technical. A lot of the acrimony which accompanies disputes over broad objectives at Board level is lost in a mass of detail. Conflicting interests and pressures seem less important. It also seems that the process of budgeting will often convert maximizing procedures into satisficing ones. Once enshrined in a budget, a profit or market-share figure is likely to become a floor one should not fall below rather than a minimum figure which is to be exceeded by as much as possible.

Conclusions

It is clear from this final section that, on objectives, our survey has reached very similar conclusions to those of Simon, and Cyert and March. Our firms rarely pursued a single objective. Objectives were almost always multiple. Because of this, there were often conflicts, if not contradictions, between objectives. Where these conflicts and contradictions became too difficult to deal with, our firms took one of two ways out. Either they concentrated on two objectives, or even one, at the expense of the others; or they pushed the resolution of conflict down into the detailed budgeting procedure. This often led in the end to the same result, with firms emphasizing one objective—if only for a time—to the exclusion of others. What is more important, once this kind of conflict was resolved through the budgeting process it became very difficult for us to see exactly how it was being dealt with, even though it also became more of a routine matter. We did not have the time or the resources needed to follow through the whole budgetary procedure in detail.

One should therefore not be surprised in pricing if conflicts between objectives occur, given the complexity of modern business, the number of people taking decisions and the intricacy of information and control systems. Conflicts between objectives are bound to arise. It may be hard to define, let alone reach, just that mixture of values for the firm's objectives which give the best, the optimum, result for the whole organization. Firms must also accept that many decisions will be taken which are best from the point of view only of a particular part of the firm; they must accept that a good deal of sub-optimization is inevitable. Yet, while carrying out our research, we found that businessmen were often trying to conceal conflicts between different objectives, as though feeling that they should be ashamed of them.

A number of recommendations flow from our findings. First, since firms may well be forced to sub-optimize, pricing decisions may have to be taken with a limited number of objectives in view. Pricing decisions may well mean sub-optimization. Not all the firm's objectives will be seen as relevant to a particular pricing decision. This is partly because to look at all of them would make the decision too complicated; it is partly because pricing decisions are often not being taken at the top of the firm. It is therefore important for those who take pricing decisions to be quite clear which objectives the firm sees as relevant to each pricing decision and how these objectives are to be related, or ranked. Perhaps it is easier with pricing decisions than with any other decisions for the firm to take optimal decisions. The effects of optimization are borne by those outside rather than inside the firm.

Second, pricing objectives should be clearly stated. Where it is sensible to do so, they should be stated in numerical or other precise terms. This makes both the pricing decisions, and the later control of operations and analysis of results, much easier. However, it is important not to over-emphasize numerical objectives. Firms must not concentrate too much on numbers. It is easy to do this. Numbers are the things one knows; qualitative, but nevertheless important elements in the problem, are therefore often given too little weight.

Third, contradictions between objectives which cannot be eliminated should be recognized and accepted. Some conflict between objectives is inevitable. There is no need for businessmen to be ashamed of these conflicts. They should bring them out into the open, acknowledge them and look carefully at their implications.

Fourth, it is not enough for top management alone to understand what the firm's objectives are and what is the relative importance of each of them. Continuing efforts should be made to ensure that all those at lower levels in the firm are fully informed about those objectives of the firm which are relevant to them in their own decisions.

To sum up—it is usually impossible or impracticable for the firm to devise a comprehensive set of objectives that is completely consistent. In pricing, the important thing is for those taking pricing decisions to isolate the objectives that are relevant to each individual decision. At the very least, they must understand how objectives are to be ranked in taking each decision and then give priority to the most important. At best, they should decide on a mutually consistent set of objectives for each decision.

* In connection with this study a Pricing checklist by Professor Hague has been produced which is available for sale from the Centre for Business Research, Manchester Business School, Booth St. W, Manchester M15 6PB.

8

The Determination of Selling Prices
by R. C. Skinner

INTRODUCTION

There seems to be little doubt that 'cost-plus' pricing is fairly widely used in British industry. About 80 per cent of the firms in the survey by Hall and Hitch[1] claimed to use it some or all of the time. In a survey recently carried out by me on Merseyside, 70 per cent of the respondents claimed to use it for some or all their products or services.[2] The prevalence of the method, however, is not at all easy to understand. This is quite apart from difficulties over profit maximization or marginal-cost pricing; probably few people nowadays would put forward these principles as realistic generalizations about the behaviour of firms, however useful they may (or may not) be in macroeconomics or welfare economics. It is not proposed to define cost-plus pricing at this stage; indeed, one of the main objects of the investigation reported here was to ascertain just what it does mean. As normally understood, cost-plus pricing has three obvious defects:

(a) It is difficult to believe that, as a general rule, sales volume can

From *Journal of Industrial Economics*, July 1970, pp. 201–17. Reprinted by permission of the author and Basil Blackwell, Publisher.

[1] R. L. Hall and C. J. Hitch, 'Price Theory and Business Behaviour', *Oxford Economic Papers*, No. 2 (May 1939). Reprinted in T. Wilson and P. W. S. Andrews (eds.), *Oxford Studies in the Price Mechanism* (Clarendon Press, Oxford, 1951).

[2] I am indebted to Mr. J. A. Banks, a distinguished sociologist, and Mr. W. T. Osborn an economic statistician, both of Liverpool University, for valuable advice on the design of the questionnaire used in the investigation.

be estimated independently of price. If, however, sales volume depends on price, unit costs[3] must also depend on price, and so the method involves a vicious circle in attempting to use cost as a basis for price-fixing.

(b) Sales volume will almost certainly depend on customers' willingness and ability to pay for a firm's products, and these factors are not likely to be unaffected by the prices charged.

(c) Sales volume will also be affected by the behaviour, particularly the prices, of a firm's competitors, relative, of course, to the firm's own behaviour. It is difficult to believe that, as a general rule, sales volume can be estimated without taking account of competition.

These three difficulties would seem to imply that a firm which uses cost-plus pricing could well end up with no sales and no profit at all, and that it is therefore not a rational method for a firm with any interest at all in its profit. I know from first-hand experience of firms which employ (or used to employ) cost-plus pricing in a quite extreme form. Anyone with experience in industry will know that they are firms which seem to pay remarkably little attention to the likely effects of their prices on demand and on competition, and are unaware of the extent to which unit costs are affected by different assumptions about sales volume. There is, however, little evidence to indicate whether or not ignoring competition and demand is common. There is, of course, empirical evidence, particularly the studies by Edwards, Pearce, Fog, Haynes and Lazer,[4] of firms which adjust their prices to take account of competition and demand, even if initially they may be arrived at on a cost-plus basis. Joel Dean[5] has even distinguished this as a separate pricing method, and named it 'variable or flexible mark-up pricing'. Given sufficient flexibility,

[3] As used here, 'unit costs' means average total cost per unit, not just average variable cost per unit.

[4] R. S. Edwards, 'The Pricing of Manufactured Products', *Economica*, vol. 19 (Aug. 1952); I. F. Pearce, 'A Study in Price Policy', ibid., vol. 23 (May 1956); B. Fog, *Industrial Pricing Policies* (North-Holland, Amsterdam, 1960); W. W. Haynes , *Pricing Decisions in Small Business* (Lexington, Ky.: University of Kentucky Press, 1962) (summarized in W. W. Haynes, 'Pricing Practices in Small Firms', *Southern Economic Journal*, vol. 30 (April 1964)) ; W. Lazer, 'Price Determination in the Western Canadian Garment Industry', *Journal of Industrial Economics*, vol. 5 (March 1957).

[5] J. Dean, *Managerial Economics* (Englewood Cliffs, N.J.: Prentice-Hall, 1951).

this would resolve the difficulties described above. It is not clear, however, how common flexible mark-up pricing is in Britain. The studies by Edwards and Pearce were very restricted in scope, and the firms involved may well not have been cost-plus pricers; after all, about 20 per cent of the Hall and Hitch[6] sample claimed not to use the method. The same criticism cannot be applied to the surveys by Fog, Haynes and Lazer, but these studies are somewhat lacking in quantitative data, and it may well be that what is true of Scandinavian and North American industry is not true of British industry.

The investigation reported in this paper is an outcome of the work of Haynes and Heflebower,[7] and attempted to discover just what cost-plus pricing means. To anticipate: the main conclusion is that, although 70 per cent of the respondents in the survey claim to use cost-plus pricing, great weight is given in fixing prices to competition and demand, although not quite as much weight as to a firm's own costs and profit. The investigation was also designed to establish what proportion of firms can be described as profit-maximizers; it was found that not more than half, and possibly much less, could be described in that way. This possibly helps to explain the popularity of cost-plus pricing: prices arrived at in this way can perhaps be interpreted as being in some sense more 'fair' than prices not based mainly on costs.[8] Information was also sought as to how 'progressive' firms are in their accounting methods, and whether large firms are more progressive than small: the firms in the survey proved to be progressive in some ways but not in others, and firms with 100 or more employees proved to be, on the whole, more progressive than smaller firms. Progressive accounting methods are relevant to cost-plus pricing, in order to ensure that firms can earn even a reasonable profit.

THE INVESTIGATION

The survey was carried out during the first half of 1968 by means of a postal questionnaire despatched to all members of the Merseyside

---

[6] See note 1 above.

[7] R. B. Heflebower, 'Full Costs, Cost Changes, and Prices', in National Bureau of Economic Research, *Business Concentration and Price Policy* (Princeton, N.J.: Princeton University Press, 1955).

[8] See Fog, pp. 112–14.

Chamber of Commerce. The difficulties of the questionnaire method are well known, the main one being that of formulating questions whose meanings are precise, but not so precise as to make the questions unintelligible. The difficulties cannot be entirely overcome by means of interviews, as no one is ever then quite sure just what questions have been asked: it is very difficult for an interviewer to avoid leading questions. Several methods were used to overcome the difficulties. A covering letter was sent with the questionnaire, explaining the purpose of the investigation, promising anonymity to those who desired it, and offering to send all respondents a summary of the results. The covering letter was printed on the headed notepaper of the Liverpool and District Branch of the Institute of Cost and Works Accountants, replies were requested to be sent to me at the University of Liverpool, and it was stated that the questionnaire had been despatched by the Merseyside Chamber of Commerce.[9]

The questions were expressed at reasonable length, partly in order to avoid ambiguity, and partly so that the answers could be as brief as possible. The suggested answers were mostly either ticks, or marks on a scale from 0 to 4. The second type of answer was to indicate the importance of each of a number of factors in pricing decisions, and follows the work of Professor Shackle.[10] The respondents were invited to give supplementary information where they felt that the simple answer indicated was not adequate, but few did so. The questionnaire ran to seven 12 in. by 8 in. pages; it comprised 32 questions, some of which were in two or three parts, so that there were, in effect, 51 questions, in all, calling for 83 items of information. However, some types of company (such as organizations providing services) were told that certain questions did not apply to them, and some respondents did not answer all the questions that did apply. On the other hand, some companies answered questions which were stated not to apply to them; these answers were accepted, as it was decided that the companies themselves were best able to judge what did or did not apply to them. Some care was

[9] The questionnaire, covering letter and summary of replies were produced at Liverpool University; they were printed and despatched by the Institute of Cost and Works Accountants, in a set of envelopes supplied by the Merseyside Chamber of Commerce.

[10] See G. L. S. Shackle, 'Business Men on Business Decisions', *Scottish Journal of Political Economy*, vol. 2 (Feb. 1955). The interpretations suggested for the marks were as follows: 4—vitally important; 3—very important; 2—fairly important; 1—slight importance; 0—no importance.

taken that the significance of *individual* questions was not too obvious, and some cross-checking questions were inserted: in analysing the replies, contradictory or ambiguous answers were treated as no answers. The respondents were asked if they would be prepared to amplify their answers in an interview, and of those who did so, telephone inquiries were made of a sample, partly in order to obtain clarification of ambiguous answers, and partly to ascertain how certain of the questions had been interpreted. The response rate was little more than 10 per cent, but this was probably not poor by British standards, in view of the length of the questionnaire and the low average size of the firms surveyed. The response was no doubt unrepresentative, but probably less so than any previous survey on the subject. Further details of the survey are given in Appendix A.

COST-PLUS PRICING

The questionnaire asked specifically whether or not the companies ever used cost-plus pricing, and whether they used it for pricing all products, for pricing new products only, for revising the prices of existing products (Question 12—those questions identified by their numbers here are reproduced in Appendix B). Seventy per cent of the respondents claimed to use cost-plus pricing. In practice, most pricing decisions are likely to be price revisions, and an idea derived from the work of Eitman[11] was that cost-plus pricing was more likely to be used for revising the prices of existing products than for pricing new products, or as a general pricing method. The survey gave no evidence for this hypothesis, as 57 per cent of the companies who used cost-plus pricing used it for pricing all products, and of the remainder, slightly more used it for pricing new products than for revising existing prices. Another hypothesis that was tested, and for which no evidence was found, was that firms which compute prices only on receipt of inquiries from potential customers (what can perhaps be called 'jobbing' firms) would be far more likely to use cost-plus pricing than firms which have a scale of fairly standardized prices or charges determined in advance of receiving orders. Seventy-five per cent of 'jobbing' firms (53 out of 71) claimed to use cost-plus pricing, compared with 67 per cent (68 out of 101) of firms which compute prices in advance; the difference between these

---

[11] W. S. Eitman, *Price Determination—Business Practice* v. *Economic Theory* (Ann Arbor, Mich.: Michigan University Press, 1949).

proportions is not statistically significant.[12] In addition, the alternative uses of cost-plus pricing (all prices, new prices, revising existing prices) was very little different (statistically not significant) between the two types of company.

The cost-plus pricers were asked how often they reviewed their profit mark-up; 55 per cent said yearly, and a further 38 per cent said they reviewed it more frequently than yearly, or irregularly, as and when necessary. They were further asked whether, between reviews, they applied the same percentage mark-up to all products and orders, and 68 per cent (80) replied 'No'. Of those 80 companies, 81 per cent varied their mark-up according to the force of competition, 53 per cent according to the strength of demand and 26 per cent to take account of other factors, mainly on the supply side (for example, the level of stocks or the existence of surplus capacity). A result that is surprising to accountants, but which is in accordance with the findings of Andrews,[13] is the large proportion of cost-plus pricers (80 per cent) whose mark-up is designed to cover both profit and some overhead, rather than profit only; the telephone inquiry revealed, however, that a few respondents had interpreted the question (rather surprisingly) as asking whether they attempted to recover overhead in their prices. This finding on the use of composite mark-ups, together with that on flexibility in the application of mark-ups, provides some (rather weak) evidence for Fog's contention (pp. 97–100) that firms may well, in effect, adjust not only profit margins, but also unit costs, to take account of competition and demand. A somewhat disturbing (although not surprising) feature of cost-plus pricing is the small proportion of firms (11 per cent in this survey) which base their profit mark-up on a desired rate of return on employed capital; the great majority base it on a desired percentage profit on cost or sales value, or on a desired total profit for the year. (The results described in this paragraph are discussed further in the last section of this paper, dealing with accounting methods.)

---

[12] The chi-squared test was used for differences between proportions, including the proportions giving each answer in questions where alternative answers were indicated. The t test was used on differences between means, including the mean marks allotted in questions where marks were called for. 'Not significant' means not significant at the 5 per cent level. The levels of significance used were (in percentages): 5, 2·5, 2, 1, 0·5 and 0·1.

[13] P. W. S. Andrews, *Manufacturing Business* (London: Macmillan, 1949).

The flexibility of prices which is likely to result from the comparatively frequent review of mark-ups by cost-plus pricers was not confined to 'jobbing' firms. Thirty per cent of those who issue list prices revise them yearly, and 54 per cent more frequently than yearly, or irregularly, as required. The main cause of a change in list prices was a change in costs (9 marks out of 10); the need for more or less profit was allotted 5 marks, as was a change in competitors' prices; a change in customers' ability or willingness to pay was given only 3 marks.[14] A point that is stressed by Oxenfeldt[15] in his study of steel prices is the comparative rigidity of list prices, but the frequent adjustment of dealers' margins. This practice seems not to apply generally: of the firms in this survey who gave trade or quantity discounts on list prices, only 34 per cent varied them from time to time depending on trade conditions.

Further evidence as to the weight given to competition and demand in pricing was obtained by asking how important these factors were in computing prices generally (Q. 20) and in computing the price of a new or improved product or service (Q. 24). The former question was stated to apply only to 'jobbing' firms; the latter question was put to all the firms, but would obviously apply less well to 'jobbing' firms than to others. A firm's own costs and profit were allotted 9 marks (out of 10) in both questions, competition was given 7 marks in the former question and 8 in the latter, and demand was given 6 marks in both questions. The relative importance of these factors is consistent with what is widely believed about British industry—that it is rather less 'market-oriented' than is, say, American industry, and that within the marketing field it is somewhat less 'customer-orientated'.

The significance of these results for the interpretation of cost-plus pricing is that cost and profit is likely to be the most important factor in arriving at a price, but that it is by no means the only factor to which importance will be attached. To explain the use of the description 'cost-plus' in such circumstances, an analogy may be drawn with other aspects of management practice, such as work study, production planning, or incentive payments: a company may, for example,

[14] In reporting the results of questions where marks (out of 4) were asked for, the average marks allotted have been converted to a scale from 0 to 10 (see Appendix B).

[15] A. R. Oxenfeldt, *Industrial Pricing and Market Practices* (Englewood Cliffs, N.J.: Prentice-Hall, 1951).

describe its remuneration system as a payment-by-results scheme, even if only a comparatively small part of its total wage payments (even to those under the scheme) is computed on an incentive basis. The investigation provided virtually no evidence for any extreme or pure form of cost-plus pricing. A 'pure' cost-plus pricer can perhaps be defined as one who uses the method for all his prices (not just for revising existing ones); between reviews of his mark-up applies the same rate to all orders (irrespective of competition and demand); revises prices *upwards* if sales volume is lower than expected (since unit costs will be higher at the lower volume);[16] changes only his prices if he has a permanent change in his costs (rather than, for example, his profit or the design of the product); and bases his product cost calculations on sales volume in the previous accounting period or periods (rather than on a forecast for the next period). Of the companies in this survey, only 1 out of the 121 who claim to use cost-plus pricing does all these things. The picture that emerges fairly clearly is of considerable sensitivity to the effects of competition and demand, as well as to cost and profit, in setting prices.

PROFIT POLICY

Price-determination is a very difficult subject to study in isolation, because it is often not possible to separate it from other elements in the marketing 'mix'. (One respondent felt unable to answer some of the questions for that reason.) For example, it cannot be isolated from other objective factors such as quality and delivery dates, from more subjective factors such as design and appearance, and from irrational factors such as the effects of persuasive advertising. If, however, the scope of an inquiry is widened beyond price alone, the investigator is then likely to become involved with everything that goes on in a company: if, say, a stable employment policy is followed, a firm may have to adjust prices to dispose of any excessive stocks it builds up. The questionnaire did in fact attempt to investigate the relationship between price and other elements in the marketing 'mix'.[17] Only one aspect of company-wide policies was inquired about, however, namely, profit policy.

Profit policy is even more difficult to study than price-determination. Businessmen seem almost as ready to quote profit maximization

[16] See Haynes, p. 31 of the book.
[17] These results are not reported here.

as their objective (or, less extremely, to state that they are 'in business to make a profit') as they are to describe their pricing method as being cost-plus. The difficulties are similar: it is notoriously difficult to attach any meaning to the phrase 'profit maximization'. No clarification of meaning emerged as regards this phrase, as it was desired to keep the survey to a manageable size by concentrating on pricing. The profit to be maximized is often interpreted as being the total amount of profit for a period of time. On this interpretation little evidence was found for it: only 12 per cent of cost-plus pricing firms aimed for this, the majority (75 per cent) aiming for a given percentage profit on cost or sales value.

The firms who determined prices in advance were asked (in Q. 8) whether they could (if they wanted) increase their profit by changing their prices: 48 per cent of the respondents said 'Yes'. During the telephone inquiry, those who had replied in the affirmative were asked whether they had interpreted the question as applying to their firms' *long-run* profit, and they all said they had. Where an explanation was offered, it was that some or all of their products had a distinct competitive edge, of which further advantage could be taken in terms of price; a few respondents said that, within fairly wide limits, price was not important in securing sales. Those who could increase their profit by means of price changes are presumably not profit-maximizers, but it does not follow that the remainder are: owing to competitive pressures they might not be able to change their prices, even if they wanted to. Those who answered in the affirmative were further asked whether their competitors would probably follow their price change, and 60 per cent said 'No'. Not surprisingly, in most cases (87 per cent) the price change involved would need to be upwards rather than downwards.

The topic of price changes was pursued further (in Q. 9), where it was asked whether the firm could estimate what effect a price change would have on its sales volume: 32 per cent said they could. The weighted average change in price (up or down) necessary to produce a noticeable effect (suggested as being 1 per cent or more) on sales volume was 6·7 per cent (the simple average of the price changes was 7·0 per cent).[18] The average price reduction necessary to increase sales volume was slightly greater than the average price increase that would reduce volume. There is an apparent anomaly

[18] These are averages of the four price-change figures quoted in the second part of Q. 9 in Appendix B.

between the number who gave the affirmative answer to this question (40) and to Q. 8 (62); in other words, some of the firms which thought that they could increase their profit by changing prices could not estimate the effect of a price change on sales volume. Some respondents who had originally answered 'Yes' to Q. 9, inquired about the effect of a price change on sales volume, had altered their answer, presumably when they discovered that the second part of Q. 9 asked them to quantify their reply. This suggests a possible explanation of the anomaly: that demand is insensitive to price changes, but only within certain, not at all well-defined, limits. A company may, for example, be fairly sure that a price change of, say, 2–3 per cent would not affect sales volume (and would therefore affect profit), while not being at all sure whether or not a 5–6 per cent price change would affect volume. This explanation is to some extent borne out by a recent survey of *industrial* purchasing by Buckner,[19] where it was found that, whilst price was the most important factor in determining a purchase, about 40 per cent of the firms surveyed would require a price difference of 5–9 per cent to induce them to change from their best supplier for an *identical* product, and about 20 per cent would require a difference of 10 per cent or more.

A further question relevant to profit policy was Q. 26, the first part of which inquired whether the firm had ever pioneered a new product or service: 71 per cent of the respondents said they had. This proportion certainly seems high: it is probably a result of the vast amount of product differentiation that exists nowadays, some of it highly artificial, of course, but some of it due to the sophistication of modern technology. One of the 'new' products mentioned during the course of the telephone inquiry was a plant food designed specifically for rose bushes, which the company had developed as an improvement on the more general-purpose products previously used on those plants—not an earth-shattering invention perhaps, but one that can reasonably be called a new product. The second part of Q. 26 inquired about the alternative pricing policies for new products distinguished by Joel Dean.[20] Forty-six per cent of the respondents had initially charged a cost-plus price, 33 per cent a 'skimming' price, and 17 per cent a 'penetration' price. The cost-

[19] H. Buckner, *How British Industry Buys* (London: Hutchinson, 1967).
[20] See note 5 above.

plus pricers were presumably not profit-maximizers, whereas the 'skimmers' probably were: the 'penetrators' may have been either.

A question which was relevant to profit policy, although not directly so, was Q. 27, which inquired about the phenomenon reported, in particular, by Fog[21]—the 'backward-sloping' demand curve. Thirty-nine per cent of the respondents claimed to have had experience at least occasionally of a given price generating a greater sales volume than a lower price would have done. This provides further evidence for the attention usually paid to demand factors, as presumably pure cost-plus pricers would not be aware of the phenomenon. It was assumed that such an experience would be far less common among firms selling only to other industrial and commercial organizations or to public authorities, than among firms selling only direct to the general public or to wholesale or retail distributors. This proved not to be so, however: 3 per cent of respondents in the first category (2 out of 71) had had frequent experience of a backward-sloping demand curve, and 31 per cent (22 firms) had occasionally experienced it. These proportions do not differ significantly from those for companies selling, directly or indirectly, to the general public.

Those parts of the questionnaire relevant to profit policy, whilst not providing support for profit maximization as a realistic generalization about the majority of firms, did provide more support for it than was originally thought would be the case. A possible explanation may lie in the comparatively low average size of the firms surveyed.[22] If competition is likely to be stronger for small firms than for large, a small firm may have to give major emphasis to profit earning, whether it likes it or not, in order to be sure of earning even a reasonable profit. A large firm, moreover, may, for a number of reasons, have a greater degree of social consciousness, and be less subject to pressures from shareholders. In view of the vagueness surrounding the whole idea of profit maximization, however, no attempt was made to test this hypothesis.

ACCOUNTING METHODS

Even if cost-plus pricing means only that cost plus profit is the most important factor out of a number in computing prices, 'progressive' accounting methods in computing cost and profit are likely to be

[21] 44–6 (see note 4 above). [22] See Appendix A.

important in order to ensure that firms achieve a reasonable sales volume, rate of growth and profit. Four aspects of accounting methods were examined, and the practices of large firms were compared with those of the smaller.[23] All but the last of these four practices (variable costing) have already been briefly mentioned. Two definitions of large were used: respondents employing 100 or more (70 firms), and of these, those firms employing 1,000 or more (15 firms). Firms with fewer than 100 employees will be described as 'small', those with 100 or more as 'large', and those with 1,000 or more as 'very large'. There were too few very large firms to permit significance tests to be carried out on their results.

The cost-plus pricers were asked how their profit percentage mark-up was calculated initially and, as mentioned earlier, only 11 per cent (12 out of 106) of the respondents calculated it as a percentage on employed capital. The proportion for large firms, at 17 per cent (7 out of 41), was not significantly different from that for the small firms (8 per cent); the proportion for the very large firms was 29 per cent.[24] A number of respondents mentioned in their questionnaires, or during the telephone inquiry, that they were thinking of changing over to this basis. It is perhaps worth noting that, for a firm which is not growing in terms of either sales or net assets, the calculation of profit as an amount for the year, or as a percentage of cost or sales value, will give the same end result as the return on capital method.

The cost-plus pricers were asked whether, between reviews of their mark-up, they applied the same percentage to all products and orders. It is reassuring that 68 per cent (80 out of 117) said they did not, but usually varied it according to the force of competition and the strength of demand. In view of this quite high proportion, it is not too surprising that the proportion for large firms, at 76 per cent (34 out of 45), was not significantly different from that for the small (65 per cent); the proportion for the very large firms was 89 per cent.

[23] In making this comparison, the replies of 3 firms, which gave no information about their numbers employed, were ignored.

[24] Large firms in America may be more progressive in this respect than those in Britain: see A. D. H. Kaplan, J. B. Dirlam and R. F. Lanzillotti, *Pricing in Big Business* (Washington, D.C.: The Brookings Institution, 1958) (summarized in R. F. Lanzillotti, 'Pricing Objectives in Large Companies', *American Historical Review*, vol. 48 (Dec. 1958)).

All the firms were asked how they usually arrived at the capacity utilization figure on which their product cost calculations were based. Only 46 per cent (53 out of 116) forecast their usage for the next period.[25] It is perhaps worth mentioning, however, that for a firm whose capacity utilization does not vary from year to year, the usage figure for the previous period (or periods) will give the same result as a forecast. The proportion for large firms, at 67 per cent (36 out of 54), was significantly higher (at the 0·1 per cent level) than that for the small (26 per cent); 91 per cent of the very large firms forecast their capacity utilization.

The most surprising aspect of accounting methods revealed was the widespread use of variable costing.[26] The firms were asked (in Q. 18) whether they had analysed their costs into fixed and variable elements, and if so, whether they normally made any use of the distinction in setting selling prices. Seventy-three per cent (122 out of 166) of the respondents said they had made the distinction, and of these, 60 per cent used it in price-determination. The proportion of large firms who had made the distinction was even higher at 85 per cent (57 out of 68), which is significantly different (0·5 per cent level) from the proportion for the small firms (66 per cent); almost all the very large firms (93 per cent) had made the distinction. A separate question asked all the firms (whether or not they distinguished between fixed and variable costs) whether they were able to estimate the effects on their costs of an increase or decrease in sales volume; the number (and proportion) of affirmative answers to this question were, not surprisingly, almost the same as in Q. 18.[27]

The findings on variable costing are out of line with the results of

[25] The remainder employed the utilization figure of the previous accounting period (24 per cent), or an average of several previous periods (30 per cent). The mean rate of capacity utilization reported was 84 per cent.

[26] As understood by accountants, variable (or direct or marginal) costing means the analysis of costs into fixed and variable elements, and the use of the distinction, primarily, to predict the effects on costs of changes in sales (or production) volume.

[27] In fact there were 3 more affirmative answers to Q. 18, which seemed somewhat anomalous, as it implied that some of those who had made the distinction did not use it. Two such firms were contacted during the telephone inquiry. One said that its difficulty arose over predicting the behaviour of costs which were neither strictly fixed nor strictly variable. The other reported that its accountants had made the distinction, but had not had occasion to use it to predict the effects on costs of a change in sales volume.

other British investigations, which are described by Sizer.[28] The most recent of these was carried out in 1963, and they all showed very little use of variable costing. The findings are, however, remarkably similar to those of an American survey carried out by Early[29] about 1955: about 90 per cent of his sample of 'excellently managed companies had made the distinction between fixed and variable costs, and of those about 70 per cent made use of it in setting prices. A possible explanation of the discrepancy between the earlier British surveys and this one is that perhaps changes do occur in British industry after all, and perhaps more rapidly than is sometimes thought! Or it may be that firms on Merseyside are more progressive than those in other parts of the country. Neither of these explanations is particularly plausible. The reason is more likely to lie in the nature of the question asked. A non-accounting manager may well not understand the meaning of such a question as 'Do you use marginal costing?' Having never heard this description of the technique, he will probably reply 'No' to the question.

The results of the survey relating to accounting methods tend to confirm what is widely believed about British industry: that in this area (as no doubt in many others) it is 'patchy'. Firms generally are progressive in some accounting practices but not in others. Large firms are more progressive than small in some aspects of accounting, but not in others.

APPENDIX A

THE SURVEY

Of the 1,903 despatched, 179 completed questionnaires were returned. In addition, letters and telephone calls were received from 81 organizations giving various reasons for not participating. These were mostly non-trading organizations and professional firms. If one excludes Chamber of Commerce members in these categories (about 180), the response rate works out at 10·4 per cent. Some idea of how representative the respondents were can be obtained because they were asked to state how many people they employed, and 98

[28] See J. Sizer, 'The Accountant's Contribution to the Pricing Decision', *Journal of Management Studies*, vol. 3 (May 1966). They are also out of line with the findings reported in Heiznes's book (see note 4 above), pp. 43–5.

[29] J. S. Early, 'Marginal Policies of "Excellently Managed" Companies', *American Economic Review*, vol. 46 (Mar. 1956).

per cent of them did so. The average number employed by respondents in manufacturing industries only was 448, with a standard deviation of 1,188.[30] The *Report on the Census of Production for 1958* shows that the average size of manufacturing enterprise on Merseyside was then 146.[31] These two means are significantly different from each other (at the 2 per cent level). To put the difference in perspective, however, it should be remembered that, over manufacturing industry as a whole (in Britain in 1958), enterprises with 100 or more employees, while comprising less than 20 per cent of manufacturing enterprises, accounted for over 80 per cent of both manufacturing employment and net output, and the average number employed by such enterprises was 689.[32]

Replies were received from all Order numbers in the Standard Industrial Classification except Gas, Electricity and Water (Order 18) and Public Administration and Defence (Order 24). Some Orders, however, had very few representatives, but it was possible to combine these with others without increasing the diversification already existing within each Order. On the other hand, replies were numerous in Transport and Communication (Order 19) and Distribution (Order 20); the former was therefore split into two industry groups, and the latter into three. In all, the replies were analysed into 17 industries, comprising 8 manufacturing industries (96 companies), 7 service industries (67), Construction (8), and a group of 8 companies which did not give their names or any information about their industries. The replies were examined for statistically significant differences between industries. In the case of many questions, however, there were too few replies in each industry to permit tests of significance. Where tests were possible, most of the differences were not significant. The significant differences that were revealed were of little interest, merely reflecting such facts as that Food, Drink and Tobacco is more of a consumer-goods industry than others. Manufacturing companies together and service companies together were tested to see if their results differed from those for all the

[30] The average number employed by all the respondents was 337, with a standard deviation of 1,017.

[31] Board of Trade (London: H.M.S.O., 1963), Part 134, Table 7. Similar data from the 1963 census are not yet available. No comparable information is available for service industries, apart from retail distribution.

[32] This average figure, and that quoted earlier for Merseyside firms, is based on the assumption that, for enterprises with fewer than 25 employees, each enterprise comprises only 1 establishment.

respondents. Replies to all the questions were tested, which revealed 3 significant differences, the only one of interest being that firms in service industries were significantly less well able (2 per cent level)[33] to estimate the effects on their costs of changes in sales volume. This was no doubt partly due to the fact that fewer service firms (although not significantly fewer) had analysed their costs into fixed and variable elements; the questionnaire did not reveal, however, whether this was because they were not able to do so, or had not chosen to.

The respondents were asked to give the name of their organization, and 83 per cent (149) did so. All the respondents asked for a copy of the results summary.[34] Fifty-one per cent (92) agreed to discuss their replies at an interview. From these three pieces of information (as managers' names and posts were usually quoted), it was possible, in respect of most of the replies, to ascertain who had completed the questionnaire, and in all cases these were proprietors, directors or senior managers. Telephone inquiries were made of 26 of the firms who had agreed to answer further questions; the basis of selection were firms who had given apparently ambiguous answers to some of the questions. In the case of 2 respondents, this inquiry revealed what could be classed as a mistake in answering a question, but in all the other cases it revealed complex situations that could not be simply described; if the ambiguity could not be finally resolved, their replies to those questions were ignored. The main object of the telephone inquiry, however, was to ascertain how some of the questions had been interpreted; these results are reported in the text. The inquiry was not carried further as regards the interpretation of questions, partly through lack of time, but mainly because it was felt that no further useful information would emerge: of the 5 questions inquired about, the interpretations of 2 (including Q. 8) were unanimous and emphatic, and there were very few departures from unanimity on the other 3 questions.

[33] Comparing the results for manufacturing and service industries with each other, the difference is significant at the 0·5 per cent level.

[34] It is assumed that this was so, as the number of requests was the same as the number of completed questionnaires: as the respondents did not have to quote their names in their questionnaires, it was possible for a firm to send in a request for the summary without submitting a questionnaire.

APPENDIX B

THE QUESTIONNAIRE

This appendix reproduces only those questions referred to by their numbers in the text. For each question the percentage and number of replies are stated; the percentages are of the replies to each question, unless otherwise indicated. The number of replies to each question seldom equals the total number of questionnaires, as some questions did not apply to all organizations, and some respondents refrained from answering all the questions that did apply to them. For questions where marks on a scale from 0 to 4 were asked for, the average marks allotted have been converted to a scale from 0 to 10 by multiplying each average by 2·5; this was done in order to make the marks more intelligible.

8. (i) Taking account of all relevant factors, including the reactions of your competitors, could you at present (if you wanted) increase your profit by changing your prices?
     Yes *62* (*48%*)   No *68* (*52%*)   (Tick one)

    (ii) If so,

       (a) Would your competitors probably follow your price change?
            Yes *24* (*40%*)   No *36* (*60%*)   (Tick one)
       (b) Would the price change need to be upwards or downwards?
            Up *52* (*87%*)   Down *8* (*13%*)   (Tick one)

9. (i) Are you able to estimate what effect a change in price would have on your sales *volume*?
     Yes *40* (*32%*)   No *85* (*68%*)   (Tick one)

    (ii) If so, what is the minimum percentage change in price that would have a noticeable effect (say, 1% or more) on your sales volume:—

	No. of replies
(a) Minimum *reduction* in price necessary to increase sales volume:	
(i) Assuming your competitors did not react *6·1%* (*mean*)	29
(ii) Assuming your competitors did react *9·8%* (*mean*)	19

No. of
replies

  (b) Minimum *increase* in price that would re-
     duce sales volume:
    (i) Assuming your competitors did not
       follow your increase   5·3% (*mean*)   31
    (ii) Assuming your competitors did follow
       your increase   6·8% (*mean*)   23

(The above two questions were stated not to apply to firms which
'normally quote a price only on receipt of inquiries from potential
customers'.)

12. (i) Do you ever use cost-plus pricing?
      Yes *121* (*70%*)   No *51* (*30%*)   (Tick one)
        (If No, go on to Question 16)
  (ii) If Yes, in what circumstances do you use it?   (Tick one)

                                                   %
  (a) Pricing all products   *62*   57
  (b) Pricing new products   *22*   20
  (c) Revising the prices of existing products   *19*   18
  (Other uses   *5*)   (5)

18. (i) Have you analysed your costs into fixed and variable ele-
      ments?
      Yes *122* (*73%*)   No *44* (*27%*)   (Tick one)
  (ii) If so, do you normally make any use of the distinction
      between fixed and variable costs in setting selling prices?
      Yes *82* (*69%*)   No *37* (*31%*)   (Tick one)

20. How important is each of the following factors in computing
    your prices?   (Mark each out of 4)

                                        Mean mark
                                        (*out of 10*)
  (a) Your costs and profit   *76* (*84%*)   9
  (b) Competitors' prices   *73* (*80%*)   7
  (c) Customers' ability and willingness to pay
      71 (*78%*)   6

(d) Other factors (Please specify and allot mark)
  7 (*8%*)   7
  No reply: 88

(The percentages above are of the number of questionnaires, less no replies.)

(The above question was stated to apply 'to organizations which compute prices only on receipt of inquiries'.)

24. For a new product or service, how important is each of the following factors in deciding on its price? (Mark each out of 4)

<table>
<tr><td></td><td>Mean mark
(out of 10)</td></tr>
<tr><td>(a) The prices of your competitors 134 (90%)</td><td>8</td></tr>
<tr><td>(b) The estimated costs of your competitors 109
(73%)</td><td>4</td></tr>
<tr><td>(c) Your estimated costs and profit 144 (97%)</td><td>9</td></tr>
<tr><td>(d) The probable effect of price on demand 120
(81%)</td><td>6</td></tr>
<tr><td>(e) Other factors (Please specify and allot mark)
 9 (6%)
 No reply: 30</td><td>9</td></tr>
</table>

(The percentages above are of the number of questionnaires, less no replies.)

26. (i) Have you ever pioneered a new product or service?
   Yes *113* (*71%*) No *47* (*29%*) (Tick one)
 (ii) If so, how did you price it *initially*? (Tick one)

<table>
<tr><td></td><td>%</td></tr>
<tr><td>(a) At the price which would probably prevail eventually when competitors had entered the market 18</td><td>17</td></tr>
<tr><td>(b) At the highest price you thought you could get for your initial output 36</td><td>33</td></tr>
<tr><td>(c) At cost plus a normal margin of profit 50</td><td>46</td></tr>
<tr><td>(d) Other bases (Please specify) 4</td><td>4</td></tr>
</table>

(The above two questions were stated to apply 'to new goods or new services; this includes improved ones, and the use of new methods or new techniques for existing ones'.)

27. Sometimes a higher price generates a *greater* sales volume than a *lower* price would. Has this happened to you?   (Tick one)

		%
(a) Frequently	*5*	3
(b) Occasionally	*60*	36
(c) Never	*100*	61

9

Price Theory and Petrol Prices

by Harry Townsend

Twenty years ago Lord Robbins resumed the main Economic Principles course at L.S.E. We sat at his feet, impressed by his erudition and devotion to economics, wondering whether what he had to say was of any use whatever. This is a belated apology for such undergraduate scepticism.

There was no difficulty in recognizing the purpose of monetary theory, national income theory or the theory of international trade. Great issues of state hung upon the forces we analysed. The trouble lay with the core of economic theory, with price theory, that elegant logical structure carefully constructed by generations of scholars.

The assertion that Marshall's notions of elasticity were a great contribution to knowledge, that they pervaded the analysis of almost any economic problem sounded splendid enough. Yet did the responsiveness of quantity demanded to price matter very much?

One could see that if Commodity A were produced alone for a cost of £7 and Commodity B produced alone for £6, but that they could be produced together for £10, A and B would be produced together. One could further see that the difference made by not producing B of the combination would be £3, and the cost-saving of not producing A would be £4, so that £3 of the total cost could be attributed to B and £4 to A. There would remain a joint cost of £3 that could not be allocated to either commodity separately. This knowledge gave one a feeling of superiority over the more con-

From *Essays in Honour of Lord Robbins*, ed. Peston and Corry (Weidenfeld and Nicolson, 1972), pp. 369–79. Reprinted by permission of the publishers.

ventional type of accountant who persisted in allocating the un-allocable, but did it have further use?

We seemed to be getting nearer to the world in which we thought we lived when we were introduced to oligopoly, perhaps because here it seemed anything might happen. It was easy to see that competition could easily get out of hand if only a small number of rivals was involved. Decisions would be interdependent with the wisest thing one competitor could do depending upon what he thought his rival would do, who in turn would decide on the basis of what he thought the first competitor would do in the light of the first competitor's expectations of what he would do, and so on in an infinite regress. There would be search for strategies to which rivals could not react with identical countermoves: competition might be in quality of product, methods of production or ingenuity of advertising. Price competition might be avoided because one price-cut could be matched by another in a downward spiral. Alternatively rigid prices might be explained by each competitor thinking in terms of a kinked demand curve. If each expected price-cuts to be matched and thus to be associated with only *pro rata* increases of shares in total market sales, whilst price increases were not copied so that rivals could gain increased market shares, there would be a kink in individual demand curves at the going price, a discontinuity in marginal receipts curves at the same price, and the possibility of changes in costs which resulted in no changes in prices or outputs.

In this paper we use the concepts of price and income elasticity of demand, joint costs and oligopolistic competition in an explanation of two features of petrol distribution, the retail price of petrol and the prices of filling stations in the property market. These prices are of special interest because of the system of exclusive dealing in petrol retailing, the 'solus system'.

THE SOLUS SYSTEM AND PRICING PROBLEMS

Petrol is usually distributed through outlets which sell only one brand of petrol. Eighty per cent of retail outlets belong to inde-pendent property-owners, owner-dealers or multiple garages. The dealers operating these outlets almost all restrict their sales to one brand in return for an exclusive dealing rebate and often for addi-tional financial assistance from oil companies such as loans on favourable terms. The remaining 20 per cent of outlets are owned by oil companies and operated by tenants: the leases restrict the tenants to the landlord's brand of petrol. There are about 37,000 petrol stations in the U.K., 30,500 independently owned and operated as solus stations, 5,500 owned by oil companies, and 1,500 multi-brand outlets.

Solus trading began in Britain in 1951 when petrol brands were re-introduced in place of the wartime pool petrol. Esso began tying stations and the other oil companies quickly followed suit. At first there were simply gentlemen's agreements of a year's duration arranging exclusive supplies in return for an additional rebate of $\frac{1}{2}d.$ per gallon and small loans to repaint filling stations. As the oil companies vied with one another for outlets, formal contracts were drawn up offering larger and larger rebates and loans in order to attach dealers to particular suppliers for periods of increasing length. It is doubtful whether the courts would now enforce exclusive contracts of more than three years' duration; but as the solus system was built up oil companies made contracts of up to twenty years. They also bought filling stations outright. Before 1951 they had not owned any retail outlets.

In 1960, the supply of petrol to retailers was referred to the Monopolies Commission for investigation. It would not be surprising if the Monopolies Commission asked oil companies a question something like 'does solus trading result in the public paying a higher price for petrol than they would otherwise have to pay?' They may also have asked 'does competition to acquire company-owned sites result in inflation of site values?'

How does one answer such questions? A layman would possibly reply that of course solus trading must lead to motorists paying higher prices for petrol: oil companies would not make such arrangements if there were not something in it for themselves rather than their customers. He would also probably reply that oil companies would bid up the price of filling-station sites. If Shell-Mex and B.P. compete against Joe Bloggs, what else could happen? A tyro-economist might answer that exclusive dealing restricts entry to a market and restricted entry leads to higher prices. He might argue that oil companies are oligopolists and if they bid against one another for sites this may easily generate an inflation of property values. These answers may seem fair. They have one thing in common: they have been made without any appeal to the facts. Theory has not guided factual analysis, it has replaced it. Let us see what happens when we attempt to use price theory to sort out the facts.

DOES SOLUS TRADING RESULT IN A HIGHER PRICE FOR PETROL?

We may begin by examining the demand for petrol, market structures and costs of supply. This leads to an examination of competition at the wholesale and retail levels.

Market Demand

Petrol is sold branded, in three main qualities described by different superlatives by different companies, and according to a British Standards classification which allows petrols with different performance characteristics to be sold as falling within the same class. There are some real and fancied differences between brands of petrol of about 90 octane (two-star, standard petrol), 97–99 octane (four-star, premium petrol) and 100-plus octane (five-star, super petrol); but competition in quality ensures that petrols in each class will be close substitutes for one another.[1] The Consumers' Association reached the conclusion after testing different brands that they had 'found little difference between different brands of petrol, all brands performed their function well'.[2] Petrols of a given grade are therefore sufficiently alike to permit inquiry about the nature of the total market demand for petrol as well as the demands facing individual wholesalers or retailers.

The main feature of the demand for petrol as a whole is that it is price inelastic. Estimates of the price elasticity range from 0·1 to 0·5: a guesstimate for Britain would be 0·2. The main reason for the low elasticity is the absence of direct substitutes for petrol. There is no other fuel available to the motorist and so, if petrol prices rise, his

---

[1] The octane number most commonly quoted, and used above, is the research octane number. Research octane numbers are obtained by comparing petrols, in a single cylinder laboratory engine, with a reference fuel whose properties are known. The comparison may be made in a four-cylinder motor car engine running on the road. This gives a road octane number which is always lower than the research octane number but which differs in relationship to the research octane number with different petrols. There is also a distribution octane number.

[2] *Which?* (Jan. 1964), p. 11.

only adjustment can be to substitute something else for motoring or pay up for the petrol. A second reason is that petrol is not bought on its own but together with the other outlays on motoring. Petrol accounts for about 60 per cent of the running cost of a car. A 10 per cent increase in the price of petrol would therefore represent a 6 per cent increase in running costs. In the long run it is possible to buy smaller cars which give more miles per gallon; but then we have to consider the total cost of a car and not just its running cost. Petrol accounts for about 25 per cent of the total annual cost of a car, and thus a 10 per cent increase in the price of petrol would represent a 2·5 per cent increase in the total cost of motoring.

Demand appears even more price inelastic from the point of view of petrol suppliers. An oil company sells premium petrol to retailers for about 1s. 3½d. per gallon net. The retailer sells it for 6s. 3d., but 4s. 4d. of this is tax. If an oil company should reduce its price by 25 per cent (i.e. by 4d. per gallon) this would make possible a reduction in the post-tax retail price of 5 per cent. Taking the market elasticity of demand as 0·2, the quantity demanded would increase by 1 per cent. A 25 per cent change in price for the oil company is associated with a 1 per cent change in the quantity demanded. The elasticity of demand for the oil company is not 0·2 but 0·04.

The unresponsiveness of demand to price changes means that wholesale suppliers will be reluctant to engage in price competition as this would be at each other's expense. There is little possibility of expanding the total market by lowering prices. Securing retail outlets by long-term exclusive contracts or outright purchase of petrol stations will appear especially attractive as this allows an oil company to achieve its sales target without increasing the amount of competition in the retail market. There is the further point that the inelasticity of demand would make possible monopoly profits if it could be exploited.

A second feature of the demand for petrol is that it is income elastic. Demand has grown over the post-war years by about 7 per cent per year whilst real incomes have increased by just over 2 per cent per year, which suggests an income elasticity of more than 3·0. The growth in demand for petrol has meant that the British market has been an attractive one to enter. Mobil, Total and Gulf are among the more notable companies who have responded to the attraction.

The growing ownership of new and second-hand cars mediates

between increasing incomes and increasing demand for petrol. Low price elasticity means that annual consumption may be predicted with considerable accuracy by multiplying the number of cars by the average number of miles run each year. This second quantity, 7,000 miles per year, is one which motorists, perhaps understandably, exaggerate when asked to report their mileage. Just as they underestimate their consumption of alcohol and tobacco, they overestimate their mileage. The average reported is 9,000 miles per year.

Retail Demand and Market Structure

Demand has a special appearance to the individual retailer. We cannot divide the total demanded by 37,000 in order to get a representative local picture. The total market is made up of thousands of small market areas where quantities sold are almost entirely independent of sales in contiguous areas. Local market areas consist of clusters of dealers in direct competition with one another. An increase in the market share of one dealer would be at the expense of a small number of neighbours. The boundaries of market areas might be defined as lying between pairs of dealers experiencing low cross-elasticity of demand, or low conjectural price flexibility. They are drawn in more matter-of-fact ways by oil companies. Oil companies in planning marketing strategies divide the country into such areas and seek a national position by successful penetration in each local area.

Local markets are sometimes obvious, e.g. a group of filling stations on a main road at the edge of a town, but often their geography is more complicated, depending upon the habitual routes of motorists living in a neighbourhood or the convenient routes for through motorists. A railway line, river or main road may place petrol stations separated by only small distances in different markets. A dual carriageway or thick traffic flow may place stations on opposite sides of a road in different markets. Filling stations on each corner of a crossroad may even be in only limited competition with one another. Traffic approaching a simple crossroad may turn left, go straight ahead or turn right. A motorist turning left has the choice of only one station; a motorist going ahead might choose the station before or beyond the junction but will find it more convenient to rejoin the traffic if he makes the second choice; a motorist turning right will be in the outside lane, away from the first station he passes, and so can only conveniently call at the station at the right-hand egress from the junction.

Within local market areas the operator of a filling station may well consider that he faces a kinked demand curve. If he should reduce his prices his neighbours would be forced to follow, and they would each gain few additional sales because of the low price elasticity of demand in the total market. If he should raise his prices the other dealers would be unlikely to follow since they could gain sales at his expense. The demand for petrol at a particular station is likely to depend upon the traffic flow, the density of the local motoring population, the convenience of its location, the popularity of its brand of petrol, the amount and quality of service offered, the appearance of the station and the credit facilities offered.

Supply

When we turn to the costs of supplying filling stations with petrol we run into immediate difficulties. Oil companies supply petrol along with a wide range of other products, from chemical feedstocks to fuel oil. Refinery flexibility makes possible estimates of costs of adding to the output of particular products, but in the end there remain joint costs which cannot be attributed to any one product in isolation. The problem of determining the cost of petrol to an oil company is made even more difficult because such companies do not simply refine and market products. They also explore for, produce and transport crude oil. The accounting cost of refining is therefore affected by the transfer price at which the crude oil is brought into the refinery. This transfer price is influenced by the incidence of taxation in different countries and on different stages of production, and by the exigencies of concession negotiations in oil-bearing countries. There is no means of knowing what petrol costs to supply, and so no means of knowing what the profit is on supplying petrol alone.

In connection with the question we face of the effects of solus trading on petrol prices we may make a little more progress. If we do not know the total cost of supplying petrol we may still inquire whether solus trading is likely to increase or decrease the unknown quantity. Oil companies were asked by the Monopolies Commission to estimate cost savings which they thought attributable to solus trading. The methods of making the estimates differed from company to company, but they all arrived at cost savings of the order of 1*d*. per gallon.[3] These estimates suffer from the limitation which is common to all attempts to quantify the effects of features of industrial structure. The effects can only be discovered by comparing a known situation with a conjectural one. In this instance, if petrol retailers should continue to buy only one brand of petrol in the absence of solus contracts there would be no cost saving attributable to exclusive dealing. The estimates were made on the basis that the alternatives to solus trading would be situations with varying amounts of multibrand trading, and so they show cost-savings resulting from having a single wholesaler instead of a number supplying a retail outlet.

The major saving lies in delivery costs. Suppose that four filling stations take fortnightly deliveries of 4,000 gallons, first in 4,000 gallon drops from single oil companies, and secondly in four 1,000 gallon drops from four different oil companies. In the first case four road tankers would journey straight between the depot and a filling station, setting out full and returning empty. In the second case the tankers would have to journey round, calling at all four stations, before disposing of their loads. The tankers would make longer journeys because of the cross-hauling, and they would take much more time because they would have to manoeuvre on to four stations, make and break four linkages with storage tanks and carry out four invoicing procedures. In addition to savings on physical distribution there are further economies in stock-holding when fewer brands are retailed, in wholesaling when orders have to be filled rather than solicited, and in clerical work. It may therefore be that solus trading reduces the costs of distribution. Oil companies have sought economies in distribution throughout the period of solus trading. What has happened to prices?

Wholesale Prices

The prices which motorists pay for petrol have risen continuously since 1945. However, one needs no economics to explain this. The excise duty on petrol has been increasing again and again. The prices which call for explanation are the prices before tax. Here experience has been unusual.

[3] The Monopolies Commission, *Petrol: A Report on the Supply of Petrol to Retailers in the United Kingdom* (London: H.M.S.O. 1965), p. 91.

Wholesale prices have fallen not simply relative to other commodities but also in absolute terms. The net price received by oil companies for standard petrol fell by 10 per cent between 1953 and 1969, and the net price of premium petrol fell by 13 per cent. Super petrol, introduced in 1957, fell by 19 per cent in the following twelve years. Prices in general rose by 60 per cent from 1953 to 1969. Moreover the size of the price reductions is concealed by the monetary terms as petrol improved in quality. Between 1953 and 1969 standard petrol was raised in octane number from 75 to 91, and premium petrol was raised from 90 to 97–99 octane.

In addition to selling their petrol more cheaply, oil companies have offered financial assistance to dealers on favourable terms which represent in effect a concealed price reduction. The Monopolies Commission mention that a twenty-five-year loan of £1·2 million at 2 per cent was extended, in 1964, by an oil company to a multiple retailer in return for representation at twenty-three outlets. Taking 6½ per cent, a low figure, for the commercial rate of interest, the annual loss of interest to the oil company would be £54,000. If the twenty-three stations were exceptionally good ones offering average annual throughputs of 300,000 gallons each, this would be equivalent to a price reduction of 2d. per gallon; on more likely throughputs the equivalent price reduction would be correspondingly higher. This loan is an extreme example, but it emphasizes that price rebates of the order of 1¾d. per gallon for exclusive representation are only part of the story of price competition at the wholesale stage.

The solus system has certainly not prevented price competition between oil companies. It has provided the institutional framework for such competition. We cannot, of course, prove that competition would not have been fiercer in the absence of solus distribution. There were a large number of forces making for price reductions over the 1950s and 1960s. Crude-oil production expanded rapidly in the Middle East and North Africa, Russian oil re-entered world markets, oil has been diverted from the U.S. market by quota restrictions, tanker freight-rates have fallen, and refinery balance has been constantly threatened by the rapid inroads made by fuel oil into coal's traditional markets. Oil companies have been seeking markets for a swelling volume of petrol.

Retail Prices

Despite the falling wholesale prices, retail prices, excluding tax, of standard and premium petrol have remained steady. They have fallen relative to prices in general, but the lower wholesale prices have resulted in larger retail margins and not lower absolute retail prices. If solus trading has kept prices up to the motorist the explanation would have to be found mainly in the retail trade. Here there are a large number of small local oligopolistic markets displaying price rigidity. There have been instances of price competition but they have usually been associated with the sale of little-known brands or with sales through new or isolated outlets. Gift stamps have been used more widely as a means of offering price reductions as within each market area the franchise of the stamp companies prevents rivals being able to retaliate with identical stamps should one of their number offer stamps.

Muted price competition is what one would expect in oligopolistic markets, especially if the demand envisaged by dealers may be represented, as we have argued, by kinked demanded curves. There is no reason to suppose that the competitive behaviour of retailers would change if they were supplied on other than solus terms. Their behaviour is explained by the market structure in which they sell rather than by the contractual terms on which they purchase.

The influence of market structure is most clearly seen in the exceptional and extreme cases of the motorway service areas. The Ministry of Transport requires that these be multibrand stations but they are operated by single retailers who enjoy geographical monopolies. They have no rivals for fifteen or twenty miles. The operators of service areas enjoy the lowest wholesale prices of any petrol retailers in the country, and they sell at the highest prices. They are multibrand but they are monopolists, and any other behaviour would be unexpected.

Large retail margins enjoyed on the motorways do not make service areas especially profitable to operate. The rents of motorway filling stations are also among the highest in the country. This brings us to our second question.

DOES COMPETITION FOR COMPANY-OWNED SITES INFLATE SITE VALUES?

If we are correct in attributing price behaviour in retailing to the structure of retail markets it follows as a corollary that purchase of filling stations by oil companies, which does not change that structure, will not affect property values. An oil company may seek custom by offering price rebates and loans on favourable terms, or by purchasing outlets to be operated by its tenants. If it is attempting to maximize profits it should pursue the various methods to the point where net receipts per gallon are equal. In this case, the price which an independent dealer could offer for a filling station should equal the offer price of an oil company. The retail price of petrol is determined by the market structure so the offer price of an independent dealer for a site depends on the net wholesale price he would have to pay for petrol.

The fact that oil companies do attempt to maximize profits is suggested by the fact that they employ discounted cash-flow techniques to evaluate investments in petrol stations. It is further substantiated by calculations that show that the cost per gallon of petrol in terms of rebates to independent dealers equals the cost of smaller rebates plus rent concessions offered to company tenants. There is no advantage in supplying one type of customer rather than the other.

The situation is reflected in the course of property values. Property values in petrol retailing have risen over the years. This is to be expected as sales have increased and retail margins have widened. However, the prices of filling stations have not risen more rapidly than those of other properties. For example, in S.E. England house prices and prices of filling stations have increased in step with one another and to much the same extent.

It may therefore be seen that with property prices and petrol prices things have not been as the layman would expect. Economic theory helps one to understand more of the working of the economy even though this often seems unlikely in undergraduate days.

PART III

Demand and Consumers

Introduction to Part III
Demand and Consumers

This section concentrates on demand. The first reading is composed of extracts from the chapter 'On Empirical Determination of Demand Relationships' in W. J. Baumol's textbook. The purpose of this reading is to present the problems faced by the economist undertaking empirical work in demand determination. Although the course deals with such problems it was felt that these extracts would provide a useful introduction to the four other readings in this part.

The first paper of these by A. P. Koutsoyiannis presents the results of an interesting international analysis of the demand for tobacco. Despite some questionable statistical manipulation, in particular the decision not to deflate the price and income data, but to work in 'money' rather than in 'real' terms, this analysis does give a very full discussion of the preliminary work necessary before any empirical demand study is undertaken. It sets out the *a priori* reasoning clearly and the expected outcome of the hypothesized relationships, and assesses the strengths and weaknesses of the data gathered and methodological procedures adopted. It also provides a detailed discussion of the results obtained from the analysis and some of the statistical difficulties associated with regression analysis are raised. Their presence in the study is partly the result of the decision referred to above.

One of the major difficulties experienced in empirical demand estimation is that of the 'identification problem'. This is dealt with at length in W. J. Baumol's extract where the problem is discussed with the use of diagrams. The article by C. M. Allan on the demand for herring shows that in a case where the good is highly perishable so that good market clearing is likely, and where the supply is fixed exogenously, identification becomes possible and the demand curve can be adequately specified with the use of a simple equation model. Such is the case with herring landings. The article shows that the price-elasticity is high for this particular fish and that it fluctuates considerably through the year. The price-elasticities in Table 2 are calculated from the estimating equation by differentiating with respect to Q_t as follows:

$$\frac{d}{dQ_t}(\log P_t) = \frac{d}{dQ_t}(\log a + b \log Q_t + c \log Q_{t-a} + U_t)$$

$$\frac{1}{P_t}\frac{dP_t}{dQ_t} = \frac{b}{Q_t}$$

The price elasticity is then $\frac{dQ_t}{dP_t}\frac{P_t}{Q_t} = \frac{1}{b}$ where b is the coefficient of the second term in the estimating equation. Note that Table 2 contains a minor error. The price-elasticity derived from the second model for the second half of 1965 should be 5·2 and the elasticity in the same model for the first half of 1966 should be 2·6.

An example of the determination of demand for a consumer durable is given in the third reading by H. J. Buxton and D. J. Rhys. As the authors comment, most of the estimates of car demand to date have relied on an aggregated model employing car price and income levels as the independent variables. These are found to explain most of the variation in ownership demand. In this study the model is disaggregated in attempting to assess the impact of the density and age structure of the population on the demand for car ownership as well as that of income, the analysis tends to confirm the hypothesis that car ownership is positively related to income and inversely related to the density of the population, though it seems to imply that the age structure of the population is negatively related to car ownership as well. A weakness of the approach might be that the dependent variable, demand for cars, is specified in terms of the 'average numbers of cars' rather than the now more usual 'stock' of cars used in aggregative studies, which takes into account the age structure and size of cars—see the *National Institute Economic Review*, number 17 (September 1961), 'Prospects for the British Car Industry'—though such data on a disaggregated level may be made harder to find.

One interesting question raised, among others, in the last article by K. T. W. Alexander, is the effect on the demand for new commodities of the existence of markets in which these can be resold. Most durable and even non-durable goods are characterized by the existence of second-hand markets, though little economic analysis has been directed towards such markets. The article sets forward some preliminary thoughts on the nature and working of this important area of the economy. It further provides a useful four-fold classification of such markets concentrating predominantly on the second-hand markets for durable and investment goods.

10

On Empirical Determination of Demand Relationships
by W. J. Baumol

WHY DEMAND FUNCTIONS?

Demand functions, as they are defined in economic analysis, are rather queer creatures, somewhat abstract, containing generous elements of the hypothetical and, in general, marked by an aura of unreality. The peculiarity of the concept is well illustrated by the fact that only one point on a demand curve can ever be observed directly with any degree of confidence, because by the time we can obtain the data with which to plot a second point, the entire curve may well have shifted without our knowing it. A more fundamental but related source of our discomfort with the idea is the fact that the demand relationship is defined as the answer to the set of hypothetical questions which begin, 'What would consumers do if price (or advertising outlay, or some other type of marketing effort) were different than it is in fact?' We are, then, dealing with information about potential consumer behaviour in situations which consumers may never have experienced. And, since we have very little confidence in the constancy of consumer tastes and desires, all of these data are taken to refer to possible events at just one moment of time—e.g., consumer reactions to alternative possible prices if any of them were to occur tomorrow at 2.47 p.m.

In view of all this, there should be little wonder that people with an orientation towards applied economics occasionally become

From *Economic Theory and Operations Analysis* (Prentice-Hall, Inc., 1972), pp. 234–54. 3rd ed. Copyright 1972. Reprinted by permission of the publishers.

somewhat impatient with the economic theorist's demand function. Yet no matter how ingenious the circumlocutions which may have been employed, they have been unable to find an acceptable substitute for the concept. For the demand function must ultimately play a critical role in any probing marketing decision process, and there is really no way to get away from it.

For example, to decide on the number of salesmen which will best serve the interests of the firm, it is first necessary to know what difference in consumer purchases would result from alternative sales force sizes. But this is precisely the sort of odd and hypothetical information which goes to make up the demand relationship. It is for exactly the same reason that many large and reputable firms in diverse fields of industry are conducting ambitious research programmes whose aim is the determination of their advertising-demand curves, that is, the relationship between their advertising outlays and their sales. So far, these efforts have met with varying degrees of success, and it must be admitted that many of them have not come up with very meaningful results. For the empirical determination of demand relationships is no simple matter and there are many booby traps for the amateur investigator and the unwary. It is no trick at all, on looking over a small sample of the published demand studies, to come up with horrible examples of just about every available type of mis-step.

This chapter is designed primarily to point out some of the pitfalls which threaten the investigator of demand relationships. Its aim is to warn the reader to proceed with extreme caution in any such enterprise. No cut-and-dried solutions are offered to the problems which are discussed. This is true for two reasons. First, because many of the methods for dealing with these difficulties are highly technical matters of specialized econometric analysis. Second, and more important, solutions are not listed mechanically because there simply are no panaceas; the problems must be dealt with case by case as they arise, and the effectiveness with which they can be handled is still highly dependent on the skill, experience, and judgement of the specialist investigator.

INTERVIEW APPROACHES TO DEMAND DETERMINATION

Before turning to statistical methods for the finding of demand functions, it is appropriate to say a few words about a more direct method for dealing with the problem—the consumer interview approach. In its most blatant and naïve form, consumers are simply collared by the interviewer and asked how much they would be willing to purchase of a given product at a number of alternative product price levels.

It should be obvious enough that this is a dangerous and unreliable procedure. People just have not thought out in advance what they would do in these hypothetical situations, and their snap judgements thrown up at the request of the interviewer cannot inspire a great deal of confidence. Even if they attempt to offer honest answers, even if they had thought about their decisions in advance, consumers might well find that when confronted with the harsh realities of the concrete situation, they behave in a manner which belies their own expectations. When we get to the effects of advertising on demand, the problems of such a direct interview approach become even more apparent. What is the consumer to be asked—how much more of the company's product he would buy if it were to institute a 10 per cent increase in its spot announcements to its television budget?

Much more subtle and effective approaches to consumer interviewing are indeed possible. Indirect, but far more revealing, questions can be asked. Consumers may, for example, be asked about the difference in price between two competing products, and if it turns out that they simply do not know the facts of the matter, one may be led to infer that a lower product price may have a relatively limited influence on consumer behaviour, just because few consumers are likely to be aware of its existence. A clever interview designer may in this way build up a strategy of indirect questions which gradually isolates the required facts.

Alternatively, consumers may be placed in simulated market situations, so-called consumer clinics, in which changes in their behaviour can be observed as the circumstances of the experiment are varied. An obvious approach to this matter is to get groups of housewives together, give them small amounts of money with which they are offered the opportunity to purchase one of, say, several brands of dishwasher soap which are put on display at the clinic, and observe what happens as the posted prices on the displays are varied from group to group. Here again, much more subtle variants in experimental design are clearly possible.

But even the best of these procedures has its limitations for our purpose, which is the determination of the precise form of a demand relationship. Artificial consumer clinic experiments inevitably introduce some degree of distortion because subjects cannot be kept from realizing that they are in an experimental situation. In any event, such clinics are rather expensive and so the samples involved are usually extremely small—too small for confidence in any inferences which are drawn about the magnitudes of the parameters the demand relationships for the body of consumers as a whole. And large sample interviews which approach the determination of consumer demand patterns by subtle and indirect questions are often highly revealing, but they rarely can supply the quantitative information required for the estimation of a demand equation.

DIRECT MARKET EXPERIMENTS

A second alternative approach which is sometimes considered as a means for finding demand relationship information is the direct market experiment. A company engages in a deliberate programme of price or advertising level variation. Suppose it increases its newspaper advertising outlay in one city by 5 per cent, in another city it increases this outlay by 10 per cent, and in still a third metropolis a 10 per cent reduction is undertaken. In some ways such a direct experimental approach must always be the most revealing. It gives real answers to our formerly hypothetical questions and does so without subjecting the consumer to the artificial atmosphere of the interview situation or the consumer clinic.

However, direct experimentation has its serious limitations as well.

1. It can be very expensive or extremely risky for the firm. Customers lost by an experimental price increase may never be regained from competitive products which they might otherwise never have tried, and a 10 per cent increase in advertising outlay for any protracted period may be no trivial matter.
2. Market experiments are almost never *controlled* experiments, so that the observations which they yield are likely to be coloured by all sorts of fortuitous occurrences—coincidental changes in consumer incomes or in competitive advertising programmes, peculiarities of the weather during the period of the experiment, etc.

3. Because of the high cost of the experiments and because it is often simply physically impossible to try out a large number of variations, the number of observations is likely to be unsatisfactorily small. If, for example, it is desired to determine the effects of varied advertising outlay in a national periodical, the company cannot increase the size of its ads which are seen by Nashville readers and simultaneously reduce those which are seen in Lexington, Kentucky. This difficulty has been eased to some extent by the fact that a number of national magazines now put out several regional editions, but by and large the problem remains: market experiments usually supply information only about a very limited number of alternatives.

4. For similar reasons, market experiments are often of only relatively brief duration. Companies cannot afford to permit them to run long enough to display much more than impact effects. And yet the distinction between impact effects and long-run effects of a change are often extremely significant, as was so clearly demonstrated by the sharp but very temporary drop in cigarette sales when the first announcement was made about the association between smoking and the incidence of cancer. How often has a rise in the price of a product caused a major reduction in purchases for a few weeks, with customers then gradually but steadily drifting back?

Market experiments do have a role to play in demand relationship determination. They can be important as a check on the results of a statistical study. Or they can provide some critical information about a few points on the demand curve in which past experience is entirely lacking. In some special circumstances experimentation is particularly convenient and has been used in the past, apparently with a considerable degree of success. For example, some mail-order houses have employed systematic programmes in which a few special experimental pages were bound inconspicuously into the catalogues distributed to customers within restricted geographic regions, thus permitting observation of the effects of price, product, or even catalogue display variations. However, it should also be clear that market experiments cannot by themselves be relied upon universally to provide the demand information needed by management. Economics is just not a subject which lends itself readily to experimentation, largely because there are always too many elements beyond the control of the investigator and because economic experimentation is often inherently too expensive, risky, and difficult.

STANDARD STATISTICAL APPROACHES

The third, and generally most attractive, approach to demand function determination attempts to squeeze its information out of sources such as the accumulated records of the past (a time-series analysis), or a comparative evaluation of the performance of different sectors of the market (a cross-sectional analysis). The available statistics on sales, prices, advertising outlays of the most relevant varieties, and other marketing data are gathered together and then analysed with the aid of the standard statistical techniques.

The basic procedure is simple enough; in fact, as we shall see presently, it is often far too simple. Suppose, for example, that the data in Table 1 on company sales and advertising outlays have been accumulated.

TABLE 1

Year	1950	1951	1952	1953	1954	1955	1956	1957
Sales (millions of dollars)	67	73	54	62	70	75	79	83
Advertising (millions of dollars)	12	15	13	14	18	17	19	15

Once the figures have been plotted, the pattern formed by the dots can be used in an obvious manner to fit a straight line (see Figure 1) or a curve to them. This line is then taken as the desired advertising-demand curve. Its slope can be used as a measure of advertising effectiveness, that is, it measures the marginal sales productivity of an advertising dollar, Δ sales/Δ advertising outlay. This line can be determined impressionistically simply by drawing in a line that appears to fit the dots fairly well, or any one of a variety of more systematic methods can be used.

The most widely employed and best known of these techniques is the method of least squares, in which the object is to find that line which makes the sum of the (squared) vertical deviations between our dots and the fitted line as small as possible, where the deviations are defined as the vertical distances such as *AB* or *CD* in Figure 1. The idea is inherently attractive. We wish to minimize deviations because a line which involves very substantial deviations from the dots representing our data surely does not represent the information in a very satisfactory way. But if, in our addition process, a large negative deviation such as *AB* (that is, a case where the line under-

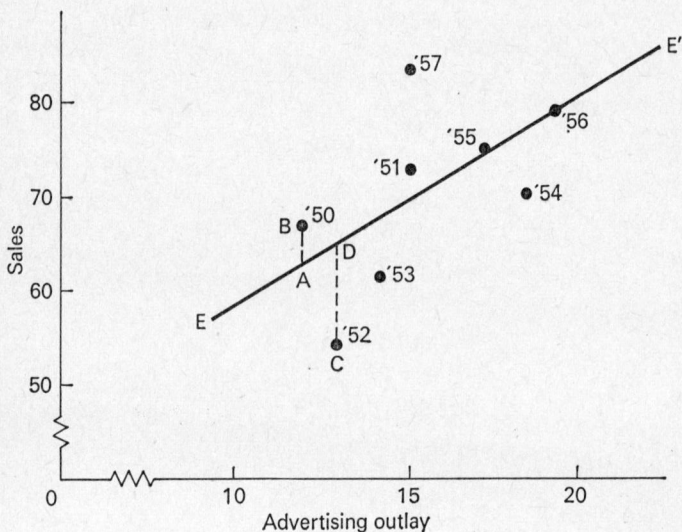

Fig. 1

estimates the vertical co-ordinate of our dot) happens to be largely cancelled out by a positive deviation, *CD*, the sum of the deviations can turn out to be small. This is surely not what we want in looking for a line which does not deviate much from the dots. One can avoid ending up with a line which fits the facts rather badly but in which the positive and negative deviations add up to a rather small number, by squaring all the deviation figures before adding them together. Since the square of a negative real number as well as that of a positive real number is always positive, large, squared negative deviations cannot offset large squared positive deviations, and the sum of squared deviations will never add up to a small number unless our line happens to fit the dots closely.

OMISSION OF IMPORTANT VARIABLES

Clearly, sales are affected by other variables in addition to the company's advertising expenditure. Prices, competitive advertising, consumer income variations, and other variables also play an important role in any demand relationship. If, therefore, we try to extract from our statistics a simple equation relating sales to advertising outlay alone, and in the process we ignore all other variables, our results are likely to be very badly distorted. We may ascribe to the company's advertising outlays sales trends which are really the result of the behaviour of other economic changes. The behaviour of other variables can thus conceal and even offset the effects of advertising. To show how serious the results can be, consider the illustrative demand equation

$$S = 50 + 4A + 0.02Y \qquad (1)$$

where S represents sales, A advertising expenditure, and Y consumer income. The values given in Table 2 can easily be seen to satisfy the equation precisely, and any standard estimation procedure based on such information can be expected to yield the correct equation.

TABLE 2

Date	1956	1957	1958
Y	3,000	4,000	3,500
A	2	3	2·5
S	118	142	130

But a *two*-variable, straight, least-squares line which gives us a (perfect!) correlation between S and A alone (ignoring Y) and which is based on these same values will yield the equation

$$S = 24A + 70. \qquad (2)$$

This equation asserts that each added dollar of advertising expenditure brings in \$24 in sales, instead of the true \$4 return shown by equation (1). In addition, because of the perfect correlation there is, in this case, no residual unexplained variation in S which is left to be accounted for by a subsequent correlation between S and Y, i.e., *this incorrect procedure appears to show that consumer income has absolutely no influence on demand*! The advertising coefficient has been inflated by usurping to itself the influence of Y on sales.

Incidentally, if, instead of proceeding as we just did, we had started off by finding a least-squares equation relating sales to consumer income alone, we would have obtained from the same statistics the equation

$$S = 0 \cdot 024 \Upsilon + 46$$

which this times overvalues the influence of income on sales and ascribes absolutely no effectiveness to advertising.[1]

It is clear, then, that more than two variables must usually be taken into account in the statistical estimation of a demand relationship. And, in fact, this is ordinarily done, the estimation usually employing what is called a least-squares *multiple regression* technique. However, it should be remembered that, even if we include five variables in our analysis but omit a sixth rather important variable, precisely the same difficulties will be encountered. That is, the omission of any important variable, however defined, from the statistical procedure can lead to serious distortions in its results.

This might appear to constitute an argument for the inclusion in the analysis of every variable which comes to the statistician's mind as a factor of possible importance, just as a matter of insurance. Unfortunately, however, we are not at liberty to go on adding variables willy-nilly. The more variables whose influence we want to take into account, the more data we require as a basis for the estimation. If we only have statistical information pertaining to three points in time, it is ridiculous to try to disentangle the influence of fifteen variables. In fact, the statistician requires many pieces of information for every variable he includes in his analysis, if he is to estimate his relationship with a clear conscience.

However, large masses of marketing data are not easily come by. Records are often woefully incomplete; additional data can sometimes be acquired only at considerable expense, and in any event, statistics which go too far back in time are apt to be obsolete and irrelevant for the company's current circumstances. We must, therefore, very frequently be contented with skimpy figures which force us to be extremely niggardly in the number of variables which we take into account, despite the very great dangers involved.

[1] The correlation between Υ and A creates another difficulty in this example. The resulting problems are discussed in the next section.

INCLUSION OF MUTUALLY CORRELATED VARIABLES

Another difficulty which, to some extent, can help to make life easier as far as the problem of the preceding section is concerned arises when a number of the relevant variables are themselves closely interrelated. For example, one encounters advertising effectiveness studies in which income and years of education per inhabitant are both included as variables. Now education is itself very closely related to income level both because higher-income families can afford to provide more education and larger inheritances to their children and because a more educated person is often in a position to earn a higher income.

It may nevertheless be true that education and income do have different consequences for advertising effectiveness. For example, an increase in income without any change in educational level could increase the person's willingness to purchase more in response to an ad, whereas more education not backed up by larger purchasing power might have the reverse effect. But, in general, there is no statistical method whereby these two consequences can be separated, because, for the bulk of the population, whenever one of these variables increases in value, so does the other. Hence, the statistics which can merely exhibit directions of variation might show that, other things remaining equal, whenever sales increased, income also increased, and so (as a consequence?) did education.

In such circumstances if we include both the income and the educational level variables in the statistical demand-fitting procedure, the chances are that the mechanics of the procedure will provide a perfectly arbitrary ascription of the sales changes to our two causal variables. And sometimes the results may turn out completely nonsensical because the standard computational procedure has no way to apply common sense in imputing the total sales change to the separate influences of education and income changes.

Therefore, if in a demand relationship there occur several variables which are themselves highly correlated, it is usually wise to omit all but one of any such set of variables in a statistical study. If this is not done, another powerful source of nonsense results is introduced.

SIMULTANEOUS RELATIONSHIP PROBLEMS

The difficulties which have so far been discussed, while they can be extremely important and are often overlooked in practice (with rather sad consequences) may, by and large, be considered rather routine and in retrospect, fairly obvious matters.

We come now to a far more subtle and perhaps a far more serious problem which was only brought to our attention in 1927 by E. J. Working and which has only received serious and systematic attention quite recently, largely as a result of the work of the Cowles Foundation. The problem in question, in a sense, follows from the difficulty which was discussed in the previous section. If there is a close correlation between two variables, it is likely to mean that they are not independent of one another and that there is at least one other relevant equation in the system which expresses the relationship between them. For example, in our illustrative case there might be an equation indicating how income level is ordinarily increased by a person's education. We then end up having to deal with not just a single demand equation, but with a system of several equations in which a number of the variables interact mutually and are determined simultaneously.

Economics is characterized by such simultaneous relationships. The standard example is the price determination process in which a supply equation is involved as well as our demand relationship. Similarly, simultaneous relationships constitute the core of national income analysis. National income depends on the demand for consumer's goods which helps determine the level of profitable production. But the consumption demand equation, in turn, involves national income (as a measure of the public's purchasing power) as a variable. To mention another simultaneous relationship example, the coal mining industry is a customer for steel whose volume of demand depends on coal sales, but the demand for coal itself depends heavily on the amount of coal to be used in producing steel. It is possible to expand the list of simultaneous relationships in economics indefinitely.

The empirical data which are generated by such a set of equations are the information source on which the statistician must base his estimates of the relationships. But since these data are the result of a number of such relationships, the difficult problem arises of separating out the relationships from the observed statistics.

Unless steps are taken to make sure that the influences of the several simultaneous relationships on the data can be and have been separated, there is not the slightest justification for the use of any estimation procedure, such as that depicted in Figure 1, to compute a statistical relationship. Yet it will readily be recognized how frequently this completely fallacious procedure is employed in practice in the form of simple or multiple correlations computed without any attempt to cope with the simultaneous relationship problem. Let us see now how serious are the distortions which can be expected to result.

THE IDENTIFICATION PROBLEM

In rather general terms our basic problem can conveniently be divided into two parts.

1. In some circumstances the simultaneous relationships (equations) will be so similar in character that it will be impossible to unscramble them (or at least some of them) from the statistics. Such relationships are said to be *unidentifiable*. Presently it will be shown how such an unhappy situation can arise, and it will be indicated that it is unfortunately not unheard of in marketing problems. Clearly, in such a case, we are wasting our time in a statistical investigation of the equation in question. There do exist some mathematical tests which show whether or not an equation is *identified* (i.e., whether or not it is in principle possible to separate it from the other relationships in the system). These tests should always be applied before embarking on the type of statistical investigation under discussion. It must be emphasized that if an equation happens not to be identified, it is impossible even to approximate the true equation from statistical data alone. Market experiments or other substitute approaches must be employed to obtain this information.

2. Even if an equation turns out to be identified, precautions must be taken to ensure that a statistically estimated equation is not distorted by the presence of the simultaneous relationships. We will see in the next section that an ordinary least-squares procedure is likely to lead to precisely this sort of distortion.

In this section we deal with the first of these, the identification problem—the circumstances under which it is, at least in principle, possible to unscramble our simultaneous relationships statistically.

To illustrate, let us consider what is involved in finding statistically an advertising-demand curve such as the one which Figure 1 attempted to construct in a rather primitive fashion. Now while sales are doubtless affected by advertising, as the advertising-demand function assumes, this function is often accompanied by a second relationship in which what we might call the direction of causation is reversed. It is well known that a firm's advertising budget is frequently affected by its sales volume. In fact, many businesses operate on a rule of thumb which allocates to advertising expenditure a fixed proportion of their total revenues. For such a business, then, we will have two advertising expenditure demand relationships: (1) the demand function which shows how quantity demanded, Q, is affected by a firm's advertising budget, $A: Q = f(A)$ and (2) the budgeting equation which shows how the firm's advertising decisions are affected by the demand for its product: $A = g(Q)$.

Both of these relationships may actually be of interest to the businessman. The first, as already stated, is directly relevant to his own optimal expenditure decision. The second, if obtained from industry records, will give him vital information about the behaviour patterns of his competitors.

The firm's actual sales and its actual advertising expenditure will, of course, depend on both its advertising budgeting practices (the budgeting equation) and on the demand-advertising relationships. In Figure 2 the graphs of two such hypothetical relationships are depicted.

In Figure 2a we show the two curves which the statistician is seeking. We make ourselves, as it were, momentarily omniscient and thus have no difficulty envisioning the true relationships. However, the information available to the statistician is much more restricted as we shall now see. In our situation the actual advertising expenditure, A, and the volume of sales, Q, are determined, as for any simultaneous equation, by the point of intersection, P of the two curves.

We now can describe two cases of non-identification.

Case 1: *Neither curve identified*. If the two curves were to retain their shape from year to year, that is, *if neither of them ever shifted*, all the

inter-section points P would coincide or at least lie very close together (Figure 2b). There would only be a single observed point,
as in the figure, or the tightly clustered points would form no dis-
cernible pattern, and so the shape of neither curve could even
approximately be found from the data. We see then, though it may
be a bit surprising, that curves which never shift are from this point
of view the worst of all possibilities.

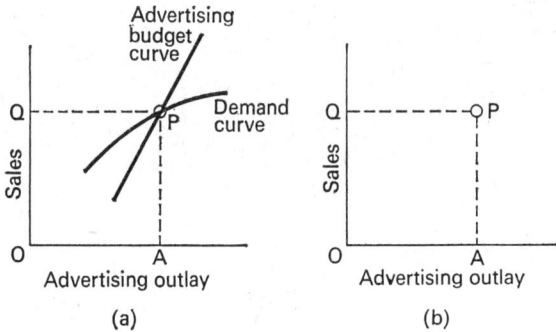

FIG. 2

Case 2: *One of the curves not identified* (but the other curves identifiable). This is a case frequently encountered in practice when the
demand curve of one firm is investigated. The data form a neat and
simple pattern, but what they describe is the firm's inflexible advertising budgeting practices rather than the nature of the demand
for its product. In such circumstances what happens is that the
budget curve never shifts but the demand curve does. There will
then be a number of different intersection points, such as P, P', and
P'', but they will always describe only the shape of the advertising
budget line (Figure 3). The reader can well imagine how often
statistical attempts to find the advertising-demand curve have produced neat linear relationships (and spectacularly high correlation
coefficients), though what the triumphant investigator has located
(without his knowing it) is a totally different curve from the one he
was seeking. The situation which we have just examined is really
ideal from the point of view of the statistician, *provided the relationship
which is not shifting happens to be the one he is seeking.* But the question remains; How is he to know when one relationship is standing still,

and even if he somehow knows this, how does he determine which one it is? We will see that in the answers to these questions lies the key to the solution of the identification problem.

It will be shown presently that only where both curves shift over time or from firm to firm or from geographical territory to territory can they ordinarily both be identified. However, in this case the difficult task of unscrambling the two relationships becomes par-

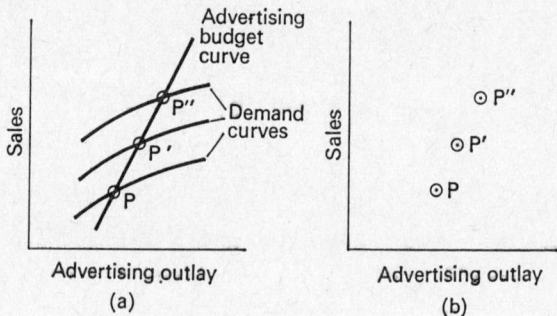

FIG. 3

ticularly acute. Figure 4 illustrates how three points, A, B and C, in a diagram similar to Figure 1 might have been generated by three different (shifted) pairs of our curves. It is noteworthy that the negatively sloping (!) 'advertising curve' FF' estimated statistically from these points bears not the slightest resemblance to any of the true curves. Nor, since it is merely a recording of points of inter- section, is there any reason why it should. *The shape of* FF' *is not even any sort of 'compromise' between those of the budget and advertising demand curves*! We conclude that where simultaneous relationships are present the standard curve-fitting techniques described in Section 4 and Figure 1 may well break down completely. *Their results are likely to bear absolutely no resemblance to the equations which are being sought*! Such a naïve approach may therefore well be worse than no investigation because misleading information is usually worse than no information at all.

Let us now see how one can, in principle, test whether the rela- tionship we are seeking is identified (potentially discoverable by statistical means).

First we note that, as the model has so far been described, there is no way of accounting for any shifts in either relationships which, as we have observed, are crucial for our problem. The reason is that only two variables, A and Q, have been considered in the relationships $Q = f(A)$ (the demand relationship) and $A = g(Q)$ (the advertising budget equation).

There must, in fact, be some other influences (other variables) which disturb the relationships between Q and A and produce the

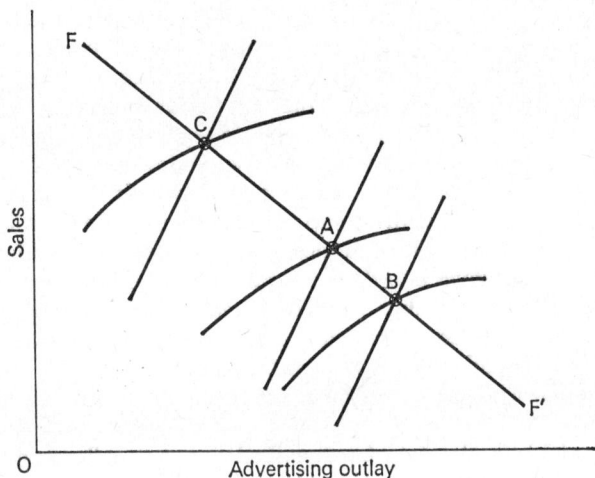

FIG. 4

shifts in their graphs. These additional variables must be taken explicitly into account. As we know, the demand relationship is likely to involve many variables in addition to A. For example, consumer's disposable income is a variable which affects the volume of sales resulting from a given level of advertising expenditure though, very likely, it does not enter the firm's budget calculation explicitly but only indirectly via the effects of income on the sales of the company's product. Similarly, the firm's budget policy may be affected by its past dividend payments, which determine how much it can currently spare for advertising expenditure, but this dividend policy will have little or no effect on the demand curve for its products. Suppose, for the sake of simplicity, that the four variables

Q, A, Y (the disposable income), and D (the total dividend payments in the preceding year) are the only ones that are relevant to the problem. Our two relationships then become:

the advertising-demand function $Q = f(A, Y)$ (3)

and

the advertising budget equation $A = g(Q, D)$. (4)

Here changes in the value of Y are what produce the shifts in the graph of the demand equation which have been discussed. Similarly, changes in D produce shifts in the advertising budget curve.

Now that we have examined how shifts in the two curves are produced we can return to the question of identification. Let us see, intuitively, how the presence of the shift variables in equations (3) and (4) makes it possible, in principle, to separate the relationships from the statistics (i.e., how the shift variables identify the equations). It will be shown now that Y and D permit the statistician, at least conceptually, to divide up the statistical information in such a way that he is left with situations like that depicted in Figure 3. Such a situation gives him the information that permits him to infer which of the relationships is shifting and which is standing still. That is, he can determine when one graph is not moving while the other shifts around, so that the resulting dots trace out the graph of the equation which is not shifting, the equation he is trying to estimate. The reader should first be warned, however, that the procedure which is about to be described is not usually a practical estimation (curve-finding) procedure and that other, more sophisticated measures are normally employed for the purpose.

In Figure 5 we replot the data of Figure 1. Let us, in addition, determine for each point the level of income Y for that particular year. Suppose this information is as shown in Table 3 (the corresponding sales and advertising figures are in Table 1).

TABLE 3

Advertising Demand point	1950	1951	1952	1953	1954	1955	1956	1957
Disposable Income Y (\$ billions)	360	297	295	307	428	381	420	300

We note that the income values for the points representing 1951, 1952, 1953 and 1957 are fairly close together. Hence, if we are convinced that Y is the only variable which makes for sizeable shifts in the advertising-demand curve, it is reasonable to assume that all four points lie on (or close to) the same curve; that is, among these points there has occurred little or no shift in the curve. We may, therefore, use these four points (ignoring the others) to locate a demand curve UU' (for income level approximately 300 billion) as shown. Similarly, we can use points for years 1954 and 1956 alone to find the shape of the advertising-demand curve VV' which per-

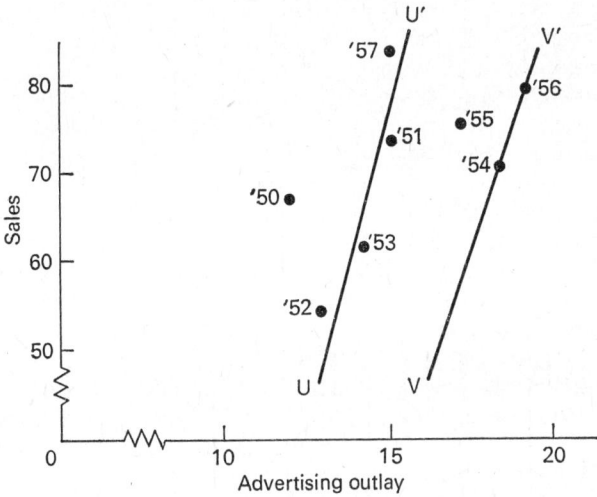

Fig. 5

tains to income level approximately 420 billion, etc. In other words, the additional information on the value of Y for each point has permitted us, in principle, to ignore all points which contain information irrelevant to a given advertising-demand curve.

We see, then, that if variable Y is present in one equation but not in the other it permits us, in principle, to discover statistical points over which the budget line has shifted but through which the demand curve remains unchanged, thus enabling us to trade out the corresponding *demand curve*.

In an analogous way we were able to trace out a *budget line* in Figure 3, for there the position of the demand curve changed while the budget line remained stationary. But while this enabled us to find the budget line in Figure 3, there the demand curve was un-identifiable because the budget relationship postulated at that point which moves the budget line about and yet permits the demand curves to stay still. This gives us the following result: *one of a pair of simultaneous relationships will be identified if it lacks a variable which is present in the other relationship.* A change in the value of that variable will not affect the position of the curve corresponding to the relationship we are seeking, but it will shift the other curve.

The relevance of the shift variables Y and D for identification can also be seen in another way. Assume that on the basis of *a priori* judgement we have already constructed our model consisting of equations (3) and (4) in which we postulate in advance that the variable Y is present only in the first of these equations and the variable D appears only in the second. Suppose now that we use any simultaneous-equation estimation procedure to find some statistical relationships among the variables Q, A, Y and D. The system is identified if it is possible, in principle, to obtain one such statistical relationship which is known to be an approximation to equation (3) (the demand function) and another statistical function which approximates (4) (the budget function), and if it is possible to find out whether any given statistical curve derived in the process represents (3), (4) or neither. Suppose, then, we have obtained some such statistical function from our data on Q, A, Y or D. How might we be able to tell whether it represents a demand function, a budget function or a hodge-podge combination of the two? There are three possibilities:

1. Suppose, after our calculations are completed, we discover that the statistical relationship turns out to take the form $Q = (A, Y, D)$ in which all four variables are present (*all* of their coefficients are significantly different from zero). In that case we know that the statistics have given us a mongrel function resembling neither of the relationships we are seeking, for the equations of our model tell us that neither of the *true* relationships contains *both* variables Y and D.

2. Suppose now that the statistical relationship turns out to have an equation of the form $F(A, Y) = Q$; i.e., D plays no role in the equation. Then we can be fairly sure that no budget function component has sneaked into our statistical equation;

for, if the budget equation had somehow gotten mixed into our calculation, the variable D would have shown up in our calculated equation, since it is present in the budget curve (4). The presence of the variable D would have shown at once that the budgeting relationship had intruded into our computation. But since, in the case we are discussing, we obtain an equation $Q = F (A, Y)$ *from which D is absent*, we conclude that our statistical equation must be an estimate of the demand relationship (3) alone.

3. Similarly, if the form of the statistical equation is $F (A, D) = Q$, it must represent the budget relationship (4) alone.

Thus the two variables Y and D, each of which appears in one and only one of the two *a priori* relationships in our model, have permitted us to identify both equations. For example, the presence of the variable D, which occurs only in the budget equation, acts as a warning signal which notifies us at once when the budget equation has somehow got itself mixed in with our demand information.

LEAST-SQUARES BIAS IN SIMULTANEOUS SYSTEMS

Even if it transpires that a set of simultaneous relationships is identified so that it is appropriate to investigate them statistically, the analyst's troubles are not yet over. For the statistical methods which yield satisfactory results in determining the nature of a single relationship are apt to yield seriously biased results in the presence of simultaneous equations.

To show one way in which they may come about notice first that any economic relationships are constantly subject at least to small shifts as the result of minor random occurrences. A sudden change in the weather or a newspaper strike affects department store sales, rumours of a price rise may lead housewives to stock up on a product, and so on. Consequently, a demand curve can never be expected to stand still for very long. Rather, it is likely to shift back and forth so that its position will (at least) vary within a (more or less) narrow band.

Figure 6a illustrates the band within which our illustrative advertising-demand curve usually varies as the result of random disturbances. Suppose first that this is a single relationship situation so that the advertising-demand curve is the only relevant curve. Observed statistics are then likely to fall throughout this band as shown by the points in Figure 6a. The dots form a pattern very similar in shape to the demand curve itself. A least-square line fitted to these data will then tend to follow the same pattern and it will be a rather good representation of the true demand curve which the statistician is seeking.

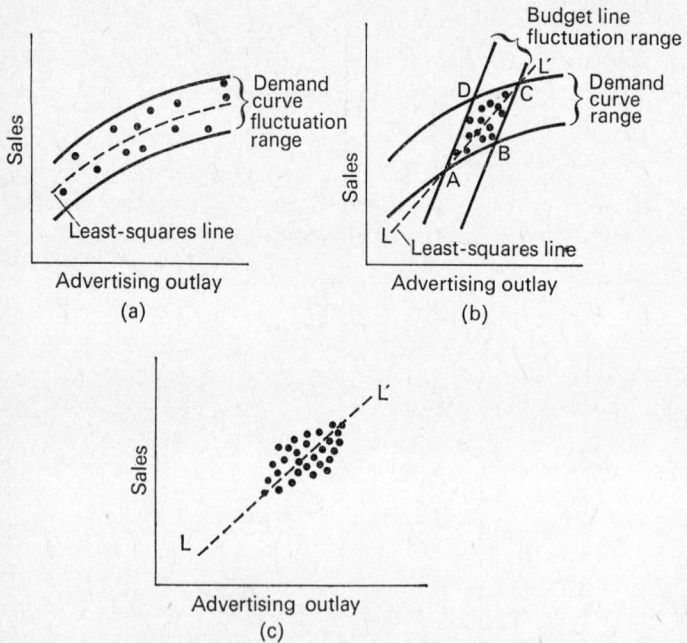

Fig. 6

Now let us contrast this with what happens when there is a second relationship present—our advertising budget line. The range of variation of these two curves is shown in Figure 6b, where both curves may be expected to shift about simultaneously. This means that the intersection points of the two curves are likely to move about within the diamond-shaped region *ABCD*. The dots within that region, then, represent the information which the statistician observes.

This time it will be noted that the pattern of dots does not resemble either curve closely. Moreover, a least-squares line, LL', fitted to these dots will generally pass approximately through a diagonal of the diamond moving upward and to the right from corner A to corner C. It should be clear to the reader that a diagonal line of this sort should appear to yield a good fit to such a diamond-shaped collection of dots (see Figure 6c). But from our state of omniscience in Figure 6b we can easily see that this least-squares line is really a very poor approximation to the advertising-demand curve.

All sorts of alternative methods have been devised for simultaneous-equation estimation to avoid these difficulties of the standard least-squares approach. Aside from the full maximum-likelihood method, which is generally too expensive and cumbersome to be employed in practice, several alternatives have been designed and employed extensively. Noteworthy are the limited-information method, the instrumental variables method, and the multiple-stage least-squares method (which employs several repeated applications of the least-squares technique, designed to correct for its deficiencies). All of these are intended to serve as approximations to the maximum-likelihood method.

There is no point in trying to describe these methods here. It is enough for our purpose that the reader has been made aware of the statistical problems caused by the presence of simultaneous relationships and of the fact that methods exist for dealing with these difficulties.

CONCLUDING COMMENTS

We have seen, then, how difficult it is to find actual demand relationships in practice. These problems are, to a large extent, a consequence of the very peculiarity of the demand function concept itself —the fact that it represents the answers to a set of purely hypothetical questions and that the information is taken to pertain simultaneously to the same moment of time. Unfortunately, this odd demand relationship turns out to be indispensable to sophisticated decision-making within the firm. We simply have to learn to live with it, and to face up to the difficulties involved in its empirical determination. An essential part of this process is knowledge of the pitfalls which await the unwary investigators who set out to beard the demand function in its lair.

11

Demand Functions for Tobacco

by A. P. Koutsoyiannis

In this article[1] an attempt is made to establish the demand function
for tobacco manufactures for fourteen countries; the United States,
the United Kingdom, France, Italy, the Netherlands, Belgium,
Sweden, Norway, Austria, Finland, Greece, Canada, Australia and
Ireland, a group which includes some of the world's most important
tobacco consumers. These countries were the ones for which data
were available.

The demand function for tobacco manufactures has considerable
theoretical interest. Tobacco manufactures have no direct substitutes, except other kinds of tobacco manufactures, mainly because of
the extraordinary nature of the need which tobacco fulfils. Thus
there are strong *theoretical* implications as to the price- and income-
elasticities of demand for tobacco products. Furthermore, tobacco
is such an important source of tax revenue to almost all countries,
even those where there is no tobacco monopoly, that these elasticities
assume a great *practical* importance.

Although tobacco might be considered a 'luxury' compared with
the more basic needs of food, drink, etc., the consumption of tobacco
products seems to be far more widespread than that of most other
'luxuries'. The smoking habit can be found in all income groups,

From *The Manchester School*, 1963, pp. 1–20. Reprinted by permission of the
author and the editor of the journal.
[1] This article arose out of research undertaken as part of the thesis requirement
for the degree of Ph.D. in the Faculty of Economics and Social Studies at the University of Manchester. I am indebted to my supervisor, Prof. C. F. Carter, to Prof.
J. Johnston and Mr. D. D. Bugg.

and it is generally recognized that for many people the habit is extremely difficult to break. This is one of the reasons why demand for tobacco products may show a much smaller price- and income-elasticity than the demand for other 'luxuries'.

A further reason for low elasticities of demand for tobacco manufactures is the fact that there is no similar commodity that could be used as a 'direct substitute' to meet the demand to smoke. Moreover, tobacco has only one possible function as a part of final consumption, namely to be smoked. Of course there are indirect substitutes for tobacco, in the sense that all commodities purchased by the consumer compete for part of his income. Tobacco manufactures, however, are extraordinary to such a degree that the extent to which other goods compete for the consumer's income is likely to be small over a much wider range of incomes and prices than in the case of almost any other 'luxury' commodity.

One suspects that there is some substitution between the various types of tobacco products (cigarettes, pipe, etc.) and an even greater substitution between the many varieties of the same product (cigarettes of various brands, tobacco of various qualities, etc.). But this type of substitution raises questions different from those of substitution between tobacco goods and other goods in the consumer's final 'basket of goods', and these are not relevant to the present study.

BASIC PROCEDURES

For each of the fourteen countries we estimated a demand function of the form

$$Q = aM^\beta P^\gamma \ \pi^\delta n^\epsilon e^{rt} \tag{1}$$

where: Q = quantity of tobacco demanded, M = money income, P = price of tobacco goods, π = index of prices of other commodities, n = adult population, e = base of natural logarithms, and t = time in calendar years.

Such a relation assumes that:

1. The relationship between the dependent and the explanatory variables is non-linear. By taking logarithms we come to the following function (linear in logarithms):

$$\log_{10} Q = \log_{10} a + \beta \log_{10} M + \varepsilon \log_{10} M + \ldots$$
$$\gamma \log_{10} P + \delta \log_{10} \pi + rt \log_{10} e \quad (2)$$

the parameters of which we estimated by least squares.

2. $\beta, \gamma, \delta, \varepsilon$, are constant elasticities. In other words the elasticities of demand for tobacco with respect to income, price of tobacco, prices of other commodities, and population are taken as constant over time.

3. The trend takes the form of a constant rate of change per unit of time.

Our analysis covers the ten-year period 1950–1959. The time series of the variables used in the study of the consumption function are taken mainly from United Nations' statistics.[2]

Regarding the variables included in the demand function the following points should be noticed:

First, in empirical demand analysis it is customary to work with real prices and real income.[3] The theory of consumer demand rests on the assumption that money is a scale factor. Thus inflationary or deflationary pressures are regarded simply as changes in the monetary unit and are therefore assumed to have no influence on consumer behaviour. However, we decided to use money income series in our analysis. We made the assumption that consumers react to changes in money incomes and are much less conscious of changes in the real purchasing power of those money incomes. Experience suggests that this is a reasonable assumption, at least in periods where there are no violent movements in price levels, and therefore in real incomes. It is observed that in periods of depression consumers, and especially wage and salary earners, are influenced in their consumption patterns by money income, and the same seems to be true in periods of slow increases in prices. It is only when price increases take the form of rapid inflation that money income ceases to be the predominant guide in consumption patterns.[4] Therefore it is money income which is important for the demand function, especially for the countries studied and the period under considera-

---

[2] See Koutsoyiannis and Kokkora, *An Econometric Study of the Leaf Tobacco Market of Greece* (Athens, 1962).

[3] See H. Wold and L. Juréen, *Demand Analysis*, Wiley publications in statistics, 1953, pp. 15–16.

[4] See also R. P. Congard, *Étude économetrique de la demande de tabac*, (Paris, 1955).

tion, during which increases in prices were moderate and never took the form of uncontrolled inflation.

Furthermore we believe that during this period there has been money illusion at work. Using nominal prices and income, the condition for the absence of money illusion would be indicated by $\beta + \gamma + \delta = 0$. If one uses nominal prices and real income[5] then the absence of money illusion would be indicated by the sum of the two price-elasticities being equal to zero. However, for reasons which will be explained below, we will make use of formulations using relative prices P/π as an explanatory variable. In such cases the use of real income in the relation would explicitly rule out the possibility of money illusion. Consequently when P/π appears in the relation, the use of money income M is essential, when in fact it is believed that money illusion has not been absent.

A third reason for using money income in our analysis is the fact that it is easier for economic interpretation and more convenient for practical computations to have the whole price effect (substitution plus income effect) measured by a single coefficient for each of P (price of tobacco) and π (prices of other commodities). We normally are interested in measuring the percentage change in the quantity demanded of a commodity as a result of a percentage change in its own price (P) or in prices of other commodities (π), not bothering to split this change into an 'income effect' and a 'substitution effect'.

In other words we are usually interested in the type of question: 'What will the change in Q be when we change P and/or π by a given percentage?' The answer to this question necessitates measurement of the elasticities of P and π by a single coefficient. This is not feasible if we introduce in the formulation real income and absolute prices, as for example in Stone's relation:

$$Q = aR^b P^c \pi^d e^{rt} \qquad (3)$$

where: Q = quantity demanded, R = real income, P = price of the commodity, π = prices of other commodities, e^{rt} = trend factor, b,c,d = constant elasticities.

In Professor Stone's formulation P and π appear explicitly and they also enter into the function for a second time in computing real

[5] See, e.g. R. Stone, 'The Analysis of Market Demand', *Journal of the Royal Statistical Society*, vol. cviii (1945).

income. Thus the coefficients c and d reflect only part of the effect of price changes, namely the substitution effect. The income effect of a price change is lumped together with the 'pure' income-elasticity,[6] and thus the coefficient b measures partly the 'pure' income-elasticity and partly the income effect of a price change.

If we call money income M, and Π the cost of living index, which for simplicity we can assume is of the simple form $\Pi = P^{w_1}\pi^{w_2}$ (and $w_1 + w_2 = 1$), we have $R = \dfrac{M}{\Pi} = \dfrac{M}{P^{w_1}\pi^{w_2}}$, and substituting in equation (3) we get:

$$Q = aM^b P^{c-bw_1}\pi^{d-bw_2}e^{rt} \qquad (4)$$

In equation (4) the coefficients of P and π, namely $c - bw_1$ and $d - bw_2$ respectively, clearly comprise the whole price effect of the change in prices, i.e. a substitution effect (measured by c or d) plus the income effect of the price change (measured by $-bw_1$ or bw_2). These income effects, however, are absorbed into the coefficient of real income R in Stone's formulation (3). (Our formulation $Q = aM^\beta P^\gamma \pi^\delta e^{rt}$ is in fact identical with (4) with $\beta = b$, $\gamma = c - bw_1$ and $\delta = d - bw_2$.)

Second, our equation $Q = aM^\beta P^\gamma \pi^\delta e^{rt}$ involves absolute prices P and π. In other words the coefficients γ and δ (which we have seen represent total price-elasticities) are left to 'float free'. without restriction. *A priori* we expect, in fact, that $-\gamma > \delta$; i.e. that demand for tobacco is more sensitive to changes in the price of tobacco than to changes in other prices. By leaving γ and δ unrestricted, such a hypothesis can be tested directly, in terms of the estimated values of $\hat{\gamma}$ and $\hat{\delta}$.

An additional indirect examination of the hypothesis may be made by examining the results of calculations on a relation involving relative prices P/π, i.e. $Q = aM^h(P/\pi)^f e^{rt}$. Here the restriction is imposed upon the coefficients of P and π that $-\gamma = \delta = f$. We shall compare results of this 'restricted' formulation with those of our 'unrestricted' form.

Third, in our analysis the variable 'price of tobacco products' is an average price for all tobacco products, computed by dividing total expenditure on tobacco during each year by the quantity consumed. The average price computed in this way will be a

[6] i.e. the percentage change in Q as a result of a percentage change in money income.

weighted average of the retail prices of all varieties during the year in question.

Thus the regression coefficient of P will be an average price-elasticity for one time period of a year. It is impossible to measure point elasticity, because of lack of data for short periods. One should know the retail prices over the whole year, the consumption figures and the changes in stocks. But even if it were feasible to measure the short-run elasticity, it would be of limited practical value. It is the long-run elasticity which is important for empirical analysis.[7] The reaction of consumers to any change in price in the short run is usually capricious. In particular for tobacco, experience shows that the immediate effect of a change in retail prices tends to be a turning to lower quality types of tobacco goods, so that the total quantity will be practically unaffected. After a short period (perhaps one to three months) consumers resume the old pattern of their demand.[8] Thus it is the long-run elasticity which is most significant from an economic point of view.

Similar considerations hold for the regression coefficient of income, which is the long-run income-elasticity (average elasticity of demand with respect to income over one time period).

Fourth, since tobacco has no obvious direct substitutes, we need not concern ourselves with the influence on tobacco consumption of the change in price of any other *particular* product. Instead, we examine the influence of changes in the prices of all other commodities as reflected by a general price index which should, of course, exclude the price of tobacco. Unfortunately we had to use the cost of living index of each country, which includes the price of tobacco, because we could not obtain an index excluding the weight of the tobacco price. However, the error introduced from this source can be expected to be small. Even if the price of tobacco could be extracted from the cost of living index, it would make no perceptible difference to the price index of the remainder.[9]

Fifth, the distribution of income has been suggested by economic theory as an important factor for demand analysis. In the post-war period in most Western countries there may well have been a tendency towards greater equality in the distribution of income. We think, however, that the influence of this factor on consumption

[7] See also H. Wold and L. Juréen.
[8] See also *Tobacco*, published by Barclays Bank D.C.O. (London, 1961), p. 62.
[9] See also R. Stone.

cannot be important in the short run. If there has occurred any variation in Q because of changes in the distribution of income, we assume that it will be absorbed by the coefficient of income and the trend factor.

Sixth, there is the problem of population. One should take into account in a demand function changes of population and its distribution by age and sex. This might be done either by working with *per capita* data, or by introducing adult population as a separate variable in the equation. The two methods differ in that the inclusion of population as a separate variable implies an attempt to measure directly the influence of population change upon quantity demanded Q; while the use of *per capita* data (of consumption and income) is equivalent to the assumption that the coefficients of income and population—in the formulation involving population 'n' explicitly—sum to unity.[10]

Alternatively, over the period considered one might reasonably expect any influence of the 'population' factor to be absorbed by the trend factor introduced in the equation, since in most cases 'n' and 't' are highly correlated. In fact, our series of population 'n' and 't' show a high correlation, as do the 'n' and M series (money income). The dangers here are, therefore, that singularity of the moment matrix of explanatory variables may make regression calculations impossible, or worse, that a slightly less than perfect correlation between, say, 'n' and 't' may cause rounding errors in the computations to yield spurious (though apparently valid) results.

Thus, we decided to attempt the measurement of the influence of population 'n' on Q using *per capita* data (which assumes that the coefficients of n and M sum to unity, a hypothesis which might not be true), though in some cases we also experimented with functions including 'n' as an explicit variable.

In general, where the function is expressed in aggregate, as distinct from *per capita*, terms, we assume that the influence of population is absorbed by the residual trend factor. We prefer to drop n out of our relation rather than t, since we anticipate that t

---

[10] For consider a formulation involving *per capita* consumption and income

$$Q/n = a(M/n)^\beta P^\gamma \pi^\delta e^{rt}$$
$$= aM^\beta P^\gamma \pi^\delta n^{-\beta} e^{rt}$$
$$Q = aM^\beta P^\gamma \pi^\delta n^{1-\beta} e^{rt}$$

i.e. this *per capita* form is identical with a formulation involving population 'n' explicitly, with the sum of the coefficients of M and n equal to unity.

should reflect other 'autonomous' factors which may be important for the consumption of tobacco, e.g. changes in the proportion of smokers to non-smokers which may not correspond exactly to changes in 'n'.

Seventh, we introduced time as an explanatory variable in our equation, in order to take care of continuous variation of variables which have not been introduced explicitly into the relationship. In particular in our analysis we expect this factor to account for changes in consuming habits, changes in the distribution of income, changes in the age and sex distribution of population etc. Furthermore, t is expected to absorb the influence of factors like income, population etc., which have a strong trend in them, in formulations where such factors are not explicitly included.

EXPECTED ELASTICITIES

We come now to our *a priori* expectations about the signs, magnitudes or relative magnitudes of the regression coefficients.

(a) The income-elasticity of demand for all tobacco goods is expected to be positive. Tobacco is not an inferior good. This may be so for some of the lower-grade types of tobacco manufactures, but is not true for tobacco as a whole.

(b) The elasticity of demand with respect to the price of tobacco is expected to be negative. In our relation, which is formulated in terms of nominal income and absolute prices, the coefficient of the price variable measures both the substitution effect and the income effect of the price change. The substitution effect is always negative as a necessary consequence of the 'preference hypothesis'.[11] The income effect is positive for normal goods, but negative for inferior goods. If the good is inferior and the substitution effect is smaller in absolute value than the income effect, i.e. if $|c| < |bw_1|$, the whole price effect will be positive. For this 'Giffen' case to arise, firstly the good must be inferior, secondly a considerable proportion of income must be spent on it, so that the income effect of a price change is important, and finally the substitution effect must be small. The first two conditions clearly do not apply to

[11] See J. R. Hicks, *A Revision of Demand Theory* (Oxford: Clarendon Press, 1956), pp. 59–68.

tobacco and consequently we must expect the price-elasticity to be negative.

(c) The elasticity of demand with respect to the average level of all other prices (π) is expected to be positive, since a rise in all other prices will render the commodity in question relatively less expensive and vice versa. However, as we shall see below, the influence of π on the quantity of tobacco demanded is expected to be unimportant.

As regards the magnitudes of the coefficients, we expect none of the elasticities to be large. In other words the demand for tobacco goods is expected to be inelastic with respect to their own price, income and prices of other commodities. On the other hand we expect the influence of population—especially the increase in the proportion of smokers to non-smokers—on the quantity demanded to be important.

First, the elasticity of demand with respect to tobacco price is expected to be low: (1) because smoking has become a very powerful social habit, so that tobacco is considered among the 'necessity' products; (2) because of lack of direct substitutes; (3) a third reason derives from the fact that the average price computed above is a 'statistical' price and the elasticity of demand with respect to changes in this 'computed price' cannot be high, and is not a 'true' elasticity. A *fall* in the 'statistical' average price may be due to a shift of the demand to lower quality products, due either to a fall in income or even to *increases* in the retail prices of the various tobacco goods, which attracts consumers to lower (cheaper) brands of tobacco manufactures. Similarly an *increase* of the 'statistical' average price may disguise either an increase in income, with no price change, or a *fall* of the retail prices of the various types of tobacco manufactures, both factors leading to a shift of the demand to higher quality—more expensive products.

Second, as regards income-elasticity, we notice that tobacco, being a 'necessity', is bought in quantities adequate to satisfy more or less the need of smoking. Thus when income increases tobacco consumption may be expected to increase less than proportionally, especially in the countries under consideration where income is already high. A low income-elasticity might be expected for an additional reason. Unlike most other 'necessity' products, tobacco is offered at a very wide variety of prices, according to the quality of the type of tobacco goods. When income decreases, the consumer has the alternative of turning to cheaper brands without being obliged to curtail the total quantity consumed. Thus when income falls, the quantity of tobacco consumed may not be much affected, though there may be a shift of consumption to lower quality tobacco products. Similarly when income increases the effect on the quantity of tobacco consumed may well be expected to be small, while it may be expected to cause a shift of the demand to higher quality (more expensive) varieties. This substitution cannot be measured because of lack of data. One would need analytical data of 'real' consumption by types, retail prices of each type, changes in stocks etc. One would, of course, expect that such influences would reflect themselves in a positive correlation between the time series of money income and average tobacco price. However, the inverse observation, that the observed correlation does reflect such influences, need not be valid, since it ignores other 'trend' influences on both series. Thus we content ourselves with the *a priori* expectation of a low income-elasticity.

Third, as for the prices of other commodities, tobacco does not have direct substitutes, and cannot substitute for other commodities, so that changes in the prices of other commodities are expected to have practically no influence on the demand for tobacco, at least in the fourteen countries examined.

Fourth, the influence of changes in adult population which we are assuming to be reflected in 't', is expected to be important for the consumption of tobacco. Furthermore, one of the most important factors in the increase of tobacco consumption has been the increase in the proportion of smokers to non-smokers, mainly because of the extension of smoking among women and members of lower age groups.

STATISTICAL PROCEDURE

In our calculations we adopted a procedure which combined the theoretical considerations discussed above with empirical observations, designed to extract the maximum of information from our observed statistical series. That is, we performed least squares regression calculations on a demand function (linear in logarithms) of the form of (2) above. However, we began by calculating the regression of Q on just one explanatory variable, namely money income M (which on *a priori* grounds we believed to be the most significant variable in explaining variations in tobacco consumption). As calculations were then carried out by adding other explanatory variables in various combinations, we were able to observe the statistical effects of such additions in an attempt to use our data to the full in throwing light on our function. Each time a new variable is introduced because it is thought to explain a significant part of the variation in the dependent variable of the relation, three statistical effects on the relation will normally result.

1. The new variable will have some effect, minor or major, on the 'systematic part' of the relation. In other words, the new variable will or will not be shown to explain a significant part of the variation of the dependent variable.
2. It will affect the 'non-systematic' (residual) part of the relationship, for example because of errors of observation in this new variable.
3. It will have some minor or major effect upon the *coefficients* of the variables already included in the equation. We should notice that if an important variable is omitted, not only may the over-all fit of the relation be worse, but the coefficients of the included variables may well be distorted from the values which would be obtained from a complete analysis. In this case the introduction of the new variable will 'correct' the value of the coefficients of the other explanatory variables.[12]

Clearly we need some criteria to decide whether the introduction of a new variable or variables into our relation has proved 'significant' and meaningful, or not.

The criteria, which we used for deciding whether to accept or reject the newly introduced variable, were the following.

1. A new variable was judged useful if it improved the multiple correlation coefficient (R^2), thus indicating a better fit of the regression plane. This is an important indicator for acceptance of the new variable, but not a sufficient one.
2. The introduction of the new variable should furthermore affect the coefficients of the other explanatory variables in a meaningful way. By this we mean that the new variable would not

[12] See R. Stone.

be acceptable if it gave the 'wrong' signs to the other coefficients, or ascribed to them unreasonably high or low values. There is always the question of the *a priori* expectations about the parameters. In most cases these are rather restrictive, so that if we find 'wrong' signs of the coefficients, for example, we must look elsewhere for a better formulation of our model, irrespective of the apparent goodness of fit of the expression in which these results are found.

3. The new variable must not be linearly correlated with the other independent variables. If the explanatory variables are perfectly intercorrelated it is not possible to partition the variation in the *dependent* variable between the explanatory variables: in other words the structural coefficients of the regression will be arbitrary, although the over-all relation may still be useful for prediction. If the explanatory variables are highly but not perfectly intercorrelated, estimates of the structural coefficients can be obtained, but they will be subject to large sampling errors. Here the decision to retain the new variables will depend on *a priori* economic criteria as well as statistical considerations.

4. The '*F*' tests on the estimated coefficients must show that the new variable is significant, though in attempting to apply tests of significance, especially when the number of observations is small, we should bear in mind that by introducing additional variables we lose degrees of freedom, a fact that is expected to render the statistical tests of significance less reliable. Thus in this case also the *a priori* expectations about the signs and values of the coefficients will be important in deciding about the acceptance or rejection of the new variable.

Autocorrelated residuals in any of our formulations are a possible source of error, casting some doubt upon the validity of the '*F*' tests used as a criterion for choosing between the various formulations. However, in all our computations the number of observations is small. Consequently we do not consider the Durbin-Watson '*d*' statistic to be sufficiently reliable, either as an additional criterion for choice between relations, or to suggest further statistical investigation of the structure of the residuals.

THE RESULTS

We carried out regression calculations on the following combinations of factors for each of the fourteen countries.

A. Absolute prices—Money income. Aggregate data of Q and M.

$$1.\ Q = f(M)$$
$$2.\ Q = f(M,P)$$
$$3.\ Q = f(M,t)$$
$$4.\ Q = f(M,P,\pi)$$
$$5.\ Q = f(M,P,t)$$
$$6.\ Q = f(M,P,\pi,t)$$

B. Absolute prices—Money income. *Per capita* data of Q and M.

$$7.\ Q/n = f(M/n)$$
$$8.\ Q/n = f(M/n,P)$$
$$9.\ Q/n = f(M/n,P,\pi)$$
$$10.\ Q/n = f(M/n,P,t)$$
$$11.\ Q/n = f(M/n,P,\pi,t)$$

C. Relative prices—Money income. Aggregate data of Q and M.

$$12.\ Q = f(M,P/\pi)$$
$$13.\ Q = f(M,P/\pi,t)$$

D. Relative prices—Money income. *Per capita* data of Q and M.

$$14.\ Q = f(M/n,P/\pi)$$
$$15.\ Q/n = f(M/n,P/\pi,t)$$

We started by computing models including only income as an explanatory variable. Countries with high income rates are the heaviest consumers of tobacco. Consumption per adult tends to be lower in the less industrialized countries with generally lower *per capita* incomes. On the other hand, high proportions of smokers are found even in the low income groups of the United States and the United Kingdom, both heavy consuming countries, and this is probably true also for most other countries with high total consumption.

Experience, furthermore, suggests that changes in price have little permanent effect on consumer demand for tobacco. Despite the very high levels to which taxes on tobacco have risen in many countries, demand has survived and consumption has, in general, increased. The immediate reaction against an increase in price is often a falling off in the quantity consumed, but it is common experience that within a short period demand recovers. It also seems true that when price rises, or when incomes decline, the consumer tends to turn to a cheaper 'smoke' rather than cut down his smoking, so that even in the short run the quantity consumed is not seriously affected.

Thus it seems justifiable on empirical grounds to consider income as the main factor determining the demand for tobacco.

Starting with aggregate money income as a single explanatory variable, $Q = f(M)$, we obtain a fairly good fit in most countries. Only in the case of Belgium and Austria is R^2 very low, and in Ireland and Austria the coefficient of M takes the 'wrong' (negative) sign. The value of the income-elasticity is in all cases less than unity (with the exception of Australia) but is significantly different from zero according to the 'F' test.

If we introduce price of tobacco as a second explanatory variable, $Q = f(M,P)$, we obtain an improved fit in the case of the United States, France, Italy, Belgium, Sweden, Finland, Ireland and Australia. The coefficients of price and income acquire expected signs and values, with the exception of Italy, where the price-elasticity is rather high, and Australia, where the coefficient of M is higher than expected. Furthermore, the income-elasticity is significant in all these countries except Ireland, while the coefficient of P satisfies the 'F' test only in four cases, France, Italy, Finland and Ireland (significant at least at 5 per cent level).

In the remaining six countries the coefficient of price takes the 'wrong' (positive) sign and is insignificant. In most cases the overall correlation coefficient is slightly higher, though less significant than in the formulations including only aggregate income as independent variable. In the case of Austria both coefficients acquire unexpected signs. In general the results of aggregate models in the case of Austria do not give plausible results.

The formulations including aggregate income and a trend factor as explanatory variables, $Q = f(M,t)$, give in general worse results than the previous formulation involving P and M, with the exception of the Netherlands.

If we introduce π (prices of other commodities) as a third explanatory variable, $Q = f(M,P,\pi)$, we obtain in all cases a slightly higher but less significant R^2. The coefficient of π acquires in some cases the 'wrong' sign, while in all countries it is statistically in-significant. The only case in which the coefficient of π seems to be somehow significant, despite its negative sign, is Greece, where special conditions permit the formulation of different expectations about the sign and significance of the coefficient of π. Greece has the lowest income per head of all the fourteen countries under con-sideration. Thus it would seem realistic to expect the demand for tobacco to be sensitive to changes in the cost of living, and, more-over, for Q to change in the opposite direction to changes in π. As prices of other commodities increase, low income consumers cannot afford to spend as much of their income as before on tobacco, and consequently reduce the quantity smoked.

If instead of π we introduce time as a third explanatory variable, $Q = f(M,P,t)$, in an attempt to reflect mainly the influence of population changes on the demand for tobacco, we obtain in general 'better' results for Italy, the Netherlands, Sweden, Finland, Ireland and Australia. In the cases of the United States $(Q = f(M,P,n))$ and the United Kingdom $(Q = f(M,P,n,t))$, introduction of adult population (n) as a direct explanatory variable appears to yield quite satisfactory results.

In the remaining countries neither 't' nor 'n' seems to improve the results obtained from the formulation containing P and M as ex-planatory variables. Despite a higher (though less significant) R^2, the sign of at least one of the coefficients of the explanatory variables cannot be accepted on theoretical considerations.

If we introduce all four explanatory variables M, P, π, t, simul-taneously in the equation, once more we reach the conclusion that π (prices of other commodities) is not a significant factor in the explanation of the variation of the quantity of tobacco demanded, with the exception perhaps of Greece.

The formulations involving *per capita* data give in most cases worse results than the equivalent combinations of aggregate data from the statistical point of view. The only exceptions are Austria and Canada, where the results obtained from the models including *per capita* data are considerably more satisfactory. In all other cases, however, the conclusions about the significance of the explanatory variables, their signs, values and their interpretation in general are broadly the same as those derived from the equations expressed in terms of aggregate consumption and income.

On the basis of the above considerations, we arrive at the functions shown in Table 1 as the most satisfactory explanation of the variation in the quantity of tobacco demanded for each of the 14 countries examined.

COMMENTS ON THE TESTS OF THE HYPOTHESES $-\gamma \neq \delta$ AND $-\gamma > \delta$

The formulations including absolute prices P and π permit a direct comparison of the coefficients of P and π. This comparison shows that $-\gamma \neq \delta$ in all models. Furthermore:

1. in 7 countries (the U.S.A., France, Italy, Finland, Austria, Greece and Australia) our hypothesis that consumers are more sensitive to changes in price of tobacco than in prices of other commodities is true; in other words for these countries we found that $-\gamma > \delta$;
2. in two countries (Norway and Ireland) the opposite seems to be true, in other words consumers appear to be more sensitive to changes in π than in P; thus $-\gamma < \delta$;
3. in the remaining countries (the U.K., the Netherlands, Belgium, Sweden and Canada) in some models we observed $-\gamma > \delta$, while in others we found that $-\gamma < \delta$.

Another indirect test of the hypothesis that $-\gamma \neq \delta$ is to compute models including relative prices P/π. Such formulations assume that $-\gamma = \delta$. Thus if these models yield 'worse' results than the relations including absolute prices P and π, this suggests that the two price-elasticities are different.

The results of the models including P/π show that: In eight countries (France, Italy, the Netherlands, Sweden, Finland, Austria, Canada, Australia) the formulations with relative prices give 'worse' fits, in general. In three countries (the U.S.A., Norway, Ireland) the models including relative prices seem to give a better fit. Finally in three countries (the U.K., Belgium and Greece) the results of models with relative prices are equally as 'good' as those of formulations including absolute prices. Thus, in most cases, our results suggest that consumers of tobacco do not act according to the usual suggestions of economic theory. Though the evidence is by no means unambiguous it seems plausible to accept that $-\gamma \neq \delta$.

In analysing our results, we should notice several possible sources of error.

1. The number of observations is small. Sampling errors in a ten-year period may be expected to be considerable.
2. Errors in the variables have been inevitable in our study and may well give misleading estimates of the true parameters. Thus: (a) the data for consumption of tobacco are in fact figures of the manufacturing production of tobacco goods. Unfortunately data of tobacco consumption, like most consumption statistics, are scarce. Of course, demand is not the same as supply, since consumption and production in general are not in perfect equilibrium, especially if we consider data for a limited period. Thus, production data should be corrected to account for changes in stocks, as well as for imports and exports.[13]

However, the error introduced from this source is probably unimportant. For one reason, changes in stocks of tobacco manufactures are negligible. Tobacco products cannot be stored for a long time without losing their special characteristics (flavour, humidity, etc.); thus manufacturers stockpile leaf tobacco instead, with which they can fairly easily meet abrupt changes in demand, since the manufacturing process is rather short. Imports and exports of tobacco manufactures on the other hand offset each other to a certain degree. Furthermore, they are relatively unimportant when compared with total consumption in each country. Despite that, some error cannot be avoided from the use of production data, since in particular any error may be amplified and carried through into the 'average statistical price', which, as we saw, is computed by dividing total expenditure on tobacco by the total manufacturing production of tobacco goods.

(b) Ideally, one should use personal disposable income in a demand function. Unfortunately the required series of disposable personal income were not available, and we used 'total national income at factor cost' instead.

(c) The cost of living index used as an index of changes in prices of other commodities, includes the price of tobacco. However, the weight of a single commodity is usually small

[13] See also H. Wold and L. Juréen.

in the cost of living index. Thus, even if we extracted the price of tobacco, it would make no perceptible difference to the price index of the remainder.

3. Some distortions of the parameter estimates may well be expected, because most time series used in the formulation of the demand function are highly correlated. We tried to detect and take into account such distortions by introducing each explanatory variable separately into the equation and studying its effects on the other coefficients and the over-all fit, both statistically and in relation to our *a priori* economic criteria. However, because of multicollinearity we must view the actual numerical values of our estimates with a certain amount of suspicion.

4. The observed 'd' statistic often suggests autocorrelation in the 'disturbance term', a fact which invalidates statistical tests on the coefficients. Another reason for suspecting that the statistical tests are not reliable is the limited number of observations, which leaves vey few degrees of freedom.

However, bearing in mind these deficiencies, we can draw the following tentative general conclusions regarding our hypotheses postulated above.

First, the assumption of constant elasticities has yielded plausible results. In all fourteen countries the formulation finally selected is capable of explaining the greatest proportion of the variation in consumption of tobacco (i.e. R^2 is fairly high in all cases).

Second, price- and income-elasticities are low. Demand for tobacco manufactures in the countries and the period under review has been rather inelastic to changes in price of tobacco or in incomes. In all countries both price- and income-elasticities are well below unity.

Third, in all countries (except Greece) the prices of other commodities do not appear to have influenced the consumption of tobacco manufactures. In all countries it seems true that $-\gamma \neq \delta$, in other words consumers do not react to relative prices. Furthermore, in most cases tobacco consumers tend to be more conscious of changes in the price of tobacco than in the prices of other commodities, i.e. $-\gamma > \delta$. This result is supported both directly by the results of the formulations including unrestricted prices (P, π), and indirectly by the 'poorer' results of most relative price models.

TABLE I

Final Results for the Demand Function of the Fourteen Countries

	Countries		$\log_{10} a$	$\dfrac{\gamma}{P}$	$\dfrac{\beta}{M}$	$\dfrac{\delta}{n}$	$\dfrac{\epsilon}{n}$	$\dfrac{r}{t}$	R^2	d
1	U.S.A.	$Q = f(P,M,n)$	-11·84419 (2·13)	-0·93726 (5·63)	0·33698 (1·18)	—	2·18760 (3·20)	—	0·722 (5·21)	1·134
2	U.K.	$Q = f(P,M,n,t)$	-30·43041 (45·93)	-0·03647 (0·17)	0·06628 (1·07)	—	4·26654 (28·24)	0·00637 (1·28)	0·997 (493·1)	1·633
3	France	$Q = f(P,M,t)$	19·40504 (2·06)	-0·54394 (14·90)	0·82818 (12·87)			-0·02351 (1·60)	0·937 (30·23)	1·887
4	Italy	$Q = f(P,M,t)$	-14·20161 (1·18)	-0·82040 (4·61)	0·48480 (2·11)			0·02213 (1·32)	0·989 (186·3)	1·540
5	Netherl.	$Q = f(P,M,t)$	-9·73522 (1·08)	-0·07837 (0·16)	0·10303 (0·82)			0·01913 (2·37)	0·986 (147·4)	2·526
6	Belgium	$Q = f(P,t)$	-19·26284 (4·80)	-0·67797 (7·04)				0·03332 (9·07)	0·574 (4·72)	1·048
7	Sweden	$Q = f(P,M,t)$	-14·87188 (0·34)	-0·41373 (1·83)	0·26324 (0·17)			0·02339 (0·40)	0·789 (7·49)	1·292
8	Norway	$Q = f(M)$	4·82726 (209·9)	—	0·18124 (31·21)			—	0·796 (31·21)	2·627
9	Finland	$Q = f(P,M,t)$	-22·99165 (10·57)	-0·41495 (30·03)	0·13224 (2·65)			0·03493 (14·05)	0·918 (22·58)	2·715
10	Austria	$Q/n = f(P,M/n,t)$	-29·24782 (31·02)	-0·95120 (98·72)	0·11482 (3·42)			0·03684 (31·53)	0·987 (16·3)	1·698
11	Greece	$Q = f(M,\pi,t)$	-22·13187 (12·73)		0·06545 (0·36)	-0·36525 (4·96)		0·03430 (17·78)	0·965 (55·77)	1·698
12	Ireland	$Q = f(P,M,t)$	24·17338 (1·76)	-0·14709 (1·04)	0·55557 (1·07)			-0·02595 (1·00)	0·722 (5·19)	2·996
13	Canada	$Q/n = f(P,M/n,t)$	-16·53282 (6·08)	-0·20938 (0·30)	0·08983 (0·17)			0·02008 (5·38)	0·902 (18·35)	2·015
14	Australia	$Q = f(P,M,t)$	-32·46265 (2·54)	-0·36186 (3·43)	0·42580 (0·81)			0·04232 (2·08)	0·977 (86·84)	1·445

Note: The numbers in brackets are the values of the 'F' tests on the estimated parameters.

Fourth, the results of our analysis gave inconclusive evidence concerning the existence of money illusion. In our formulation the absence of money illusion would be indicated by $\beta + \gamma + \delta = 0$. However, the variable π was dismissed as insignificant to the relation for all countries excepting Greece, reducing the condition for the absence of money illusion in the final formulation for each of those thirteen countries to $\beta + \gamma = 0$. ($\beta + \delta = 0$ in the case of Greece.)

Significance tests based on the estimated variance–covariance matrix of parameters in each case showed $\beta + \gamma$ to be significantly different from zero (at the 5 per cent level) in only six out of the final fourteen formulations selected. Further investigation based on wider information as it became available would therefore seem to be necessary before we can (a) produce more satisfactory significance tests after a more serious investigation of serial correlation in the residuals, and (b) arrive at firmer conclusions concerning our money illusion hypothesis.

Fifth, tobacco consumption in most countries seems to be influenced mainly by changes in the number of smokers either as a result of increase in total population or of increase in the proportion of smokers to non-smokers. Such influences in the functions for many countries have adequately been absorbed by the residual trend factor.

The above conclusions about the magnitudes and the significance of the regression coefficients are confirmed by computations with *per capita* data of consumption and income.

Thus for most of the countries examined the results obtained appear fairly satisfactory, though more confident conclusions, based upon more satisfactory functions, must await further investigation with more observations when they become available.

12

The Demand for Herring: A Single-Equation Model[1]

by Charles M. Allan

This article reports on the successful estimation of demand equations for herring. This work claims the attention of economists on two grounds. First the prices observed, unlike the vast majority of prices, are *equilibrium* prices being achieved by auction. And secondly because the *identification problem* is avoided, which enables demand to be estimated using a simple one equation model.

Since H.L. Moore[2] investigating the demand for pig-iron found a positive sign on the regression line of Price on Quantity the problem of separating and identifying supply and demand has been recognized. As E. J. Working in his famous article[3] showed, what Moore observed was a series of market equilibria. Each point represented the intersection of *a* supply curve with *a* demand curve but there was no reason for thinking that the same demand or supply curve was common to any two observed equilibria. Moore either observed a supply curve (Fig. 1) or a regression line produced

From *Scottish Journal of Political Economy* (Feb. 1972), pp. 91–8. Reprinted by permission of the author, the editor and the Longman Group Ltd.

[1] I am indebted to the Herring Industry Board for statistical information and the opportunity to do this work. I should also like to acknowledge the technical help I received from Mustafa A. Ali and the helpful comments of A. B. Jack, A. J. Phipps and E. Ramm.

[2] *Economic Cycles: Their Law and Cause* (1914).

[3] 'What Do Statistical "Demand Curves" Show?', *Quarterly Journal of Economics*, vol. 41 (1927), pp. 212–35; reprinted in H. Townsend (ed.), *Price Theory* (Harmondsworth: Penguin, 1971).

by the movement of the demand and to a *lesser* extent also the movement of supply (Fig. 2). This regression line has no meaningful equivalent in the static theory of price.

One can never be quite sure in the statistical measurement of the demand that what one is measuring is 'demand'. Indeed one only has to consider that both demand and supply are functions of price

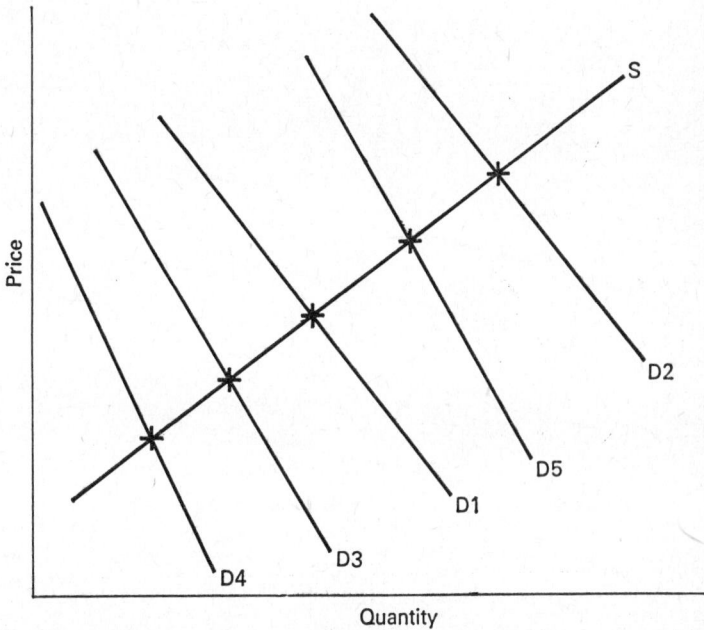

Fig. 1

to see that the problem of identifying which blade is doing the cutting is considerable.

The most usual approach to the problem is to estimate demand and supply using simultaneous equations. This procedure is subject to stochastic variation and does not often yield convincing estimates of demand. This paper gives an interesting example of the successful statistical estimation of demand using two simple single-equation three-variable models not unlike those used by Moore.

A second barrier to the successful estimation of demand curves is the fact that by far the majority of prices are not equilibrium prices at all. Market analysis of the classical type, which forms such a large part of undergraduate training and which lies at the back of so much of economists' thinking about market, assumes that prices are made by the intersection of demand and supply schedules and that prices will be determined on the basis of market-clearing; that there will be equilibrium prices. Whilst we all believe that some-

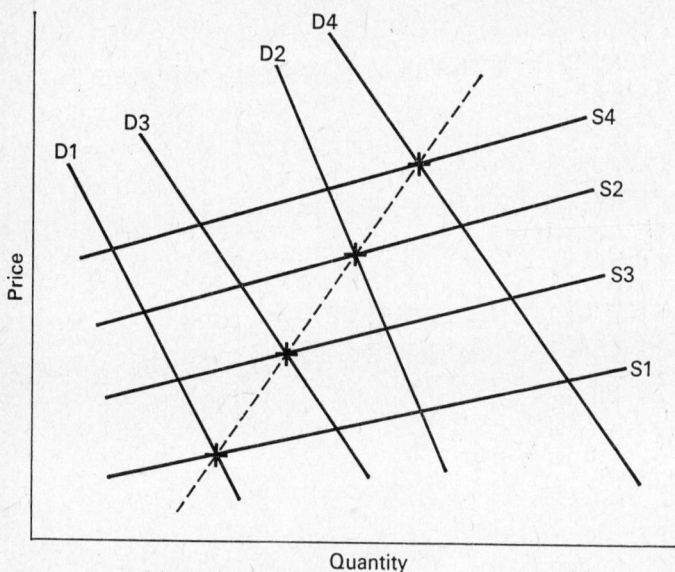

FIG. 2

thing, not altogether unlike the classical market mechanism, does exist statistical investigation is not easy. The only statistical information available is actual prices paid and received and quantities bought and sold. Most prices are not in fact equilibrium prices. They may reveal points which are neither on the supply curve nor on the demand curve: stocks are normally being increased or decreased and queues are common. As Eckstein and Fromm[4] have

[4] O. Eckstein and G. Fromm, 'The Price Equation', *American Economic Review*, vol. 58, No. 5, Part 2 (1968), pp. 1159–83.

observed, 'the continuous clearing case where production equals supply and supply equals demand is probably an exception. Disequilibrium is the more common situation.' Market clearing is achieved in this case of the British quayside market for herring as there are no stocks and all of each day's catch is sold immediately by auction.

One set of conditions sufficient for the successful statistical estimation of demand using single-equation estimating techniques is:

1. A highly perishable product
2. A unified market
3. A homogeneous and divisible product
4. Adequate accurate statistical information
5. Supply which varies in response to exogenous influences
6. Demand which remains constant for long enough to enable a sufficient number of observations to be made.

If these conditions are met it will be possible to identify demand by plotting successive market equilibrium quantities and prices as in Fig. 3.

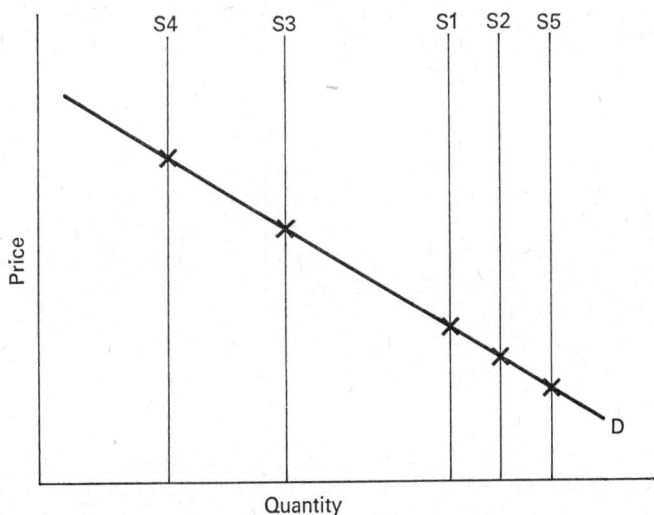

Fig. 3

These conditions were all met to a satisfactory degree in the case of the British Quayside Market for herring.

1. The herring is very highly perishable. Herring must be sold on the day of landing. Sale is by auction which ensures market clearing. If a glut forces the price down the meal manufacturers will buy (at a low minimum price of 75p per cran) any surplus for making into fish meal.

2. The British market for herring consists of several major and several minor centres. They are linked by an efficient transport system and the buyers of all but a few fish consumed locally have efficient telecommunications with all major ports. Thus price differentials are principally determined by differences in transport costs. A change in landings may be expected to have the same effect on prices irrespective of where it occurs.

3. The quality of herring varies considerably due to variation in size, time since catching and oil content. Although each catch is described by the Herring Industry Board representative at the port, it proved impossible to use this information on quality. The principal difference in quality appeared to be between summer (oily) and winter (dry) fish. It was therefore decided to estimate two demand equations per year—one for summer quality fish and one for winter quality. Herring is a divisible product.

4. A great deal of statistical information was available from the Herring Industry Board. But the only usable material giving both quantity and price for the same fish is the annual figures and the weekly figures for *all ports* together. This then was the information from which demand was estimated.

5. Supply is determined by the number of boats going out to hunt herring. This is vitally affected by the day of the week. There is nothing on the Sabbath as most of the boats are Scots. There is nothing on Monday because catching fish for Monday means setting out on Sunday. Tuesday is a good day and so is Thursday because this gets the fish into the shops for Friday. Saturday is less good, demand being less as Saturday's fish can't be sold until Monday and discriminating housewives will know that the fish is not fresh. The problem then is that, on this account supply *is* determined by demand to some extent—we do have some identification problem.

It was attempted to overcome this problem by estimating demand separately for each day of the week. The information necessary to do this was not available. The problem was then overcome by taking weekly average sales and average prices. In this case supply in any one week is very largely determined by the biology of the herring and the weather. These are exogenous factors which affect supply and indeed alter it daily.

6. It is 'common knowledge' that the quality of herring increases dramatically in early June each year and stays high until around Christmas when quality declines drastically. This is reflected in the demand for herring at the ports. It was therefore assumed that demand was stable between June and December and between January and May. There may be some circularity here but the veracity of this assumption is supported by the high R^2 achieved in the equations 1–16 estimated in this paper.

To a greater or lesser extent the conditions 1–6 have not been completely fulfilled. It was felt that they were sufficiently nearly met to make the attempt to estimate statistical demand equations worth-while. The proof of this matter rests largely on what extent the models tested proved to be statistically significant.

THE MODELS TESTED

Two, three-variable equations were estimated.
The first:

$$P_t = f(Q_t, Q_{t-a})$$
where P_t = Price in period t
Q_t = Quantity in period t
$Q_{t-a} = [Q_{t-1} -$ antilog 4·2] Zero if negative.

Q_{t-a} was included because it was widely held that landings of over 26,000 crans (=antilog 4·2) in $t - 1$ reduced P_t. The asymmetry of the effect of Q_{t-1} on price—having a negative effect on price above 26,000 crans but no effect if smaller—is related to the size of the cold storage capacity. Thus landings in Q_{t-1} will have no effect on price as long as there is plenty of storage space. However, a Q_{t-1} of over 26,000 crans has the effect of causing a shortage of available storage and so of reducing the quantity demand for freezing.

U_t is an error term.

The estimating equation was:

$$\log P_t = \log a + b \log Q_t + c \log Q_{t-a} + U_t$$

1964 1st half	1·492	− 0·232	− 0·662
SE	(0·296)	(0·079)	(1·130)
t	5·04	2·94	0·59
R^2	0·396		
1964 2nd half	2·798	− 0·490	− 0·360
SE	(0·404)	(0·098)	(0·215)
t	6·91	4·99	1·67
R^2	0·608		
1965 1st half	1·500	− 0·217	− 0·686
SE	(0·121)	(0·034)	(0·301)
t	12·41	6·36	2·28
R^2	0·814		
1965 2nd half	1·502	− 0·173	− 0·673
SE	(0·204)	(0·051)	(0·472)
t	7·37	3·42	1·43
R^2	0·398		
1966 1st half	2·311	− 0·429	+ 0·116
SE	(0·266)	(0·075)	(0·352)
t	8·69	5·69	0·33
R^2	0·792		
1966 2nd half	2·673	− 0·473	− 0·482
SE	(0·209)	(0·051)	(0·147)
t	12·81	9·27	3·28
R^2	0·814		
1967 1st half	0·925	− 0·047	− 0·940
SE	(0·109)	(0·029)	(0·198)
t	8·48	1·69	4·78
R^2	0·687		
1967 2nd half	2·741	− 0·492	− 0·503
SE	(2·731)	(0·068)	(0·202)
t	10·04	7·24	1·81
R^2	0·787		

The second:

$$P_t = f(Q_t, Q_{t-n})$$

where $Q_{t-n} = (0.6 \ Q_{t-1} + 0.3 \ Q_{t-2} + 0.1 \ Q_{t-3} - \text{antilog } 4.2)$
Zero if negative. Q_{t-n} was a weighted average of the previous three quantities as it seemed plausible to suppose that past quantities would affect price and that such effects would diminish through time. Like Q_{t-a} in the previous equation this variable was specified in such a way that only the effects of large landings on price were estimated.

Here the estimating equation was:

$$\log P_t = \log a + b \log Q_t + c \log Q_{t-n} + U_t$$

1964 1st half	1·490 —	0·232 —	0·351
SE	(0·327)	(0·088)	(1·187)
t	4·56	2·63	0·30
R^2	0·329		
1964 2nd half	2·945 —	0·530 —	0·128
SE	(0·506)	(0·124)	(0·421)
t	5·82	4·28	0·30
R^2	0·569		
1965 1st half	1·381 —	0·175 —	0·790
SE	(0·117)	(0·035)	(0·216)
t	11·84	5·04	3·65
R^2	0·896		
1965 2nd half	1·508 —	0·175 —	0·812
SE	(0·206)	(0·051)	(0·658)
t	7·33	3·44	1·24
R^2	0·387		
1966 1st half	2·179 —	0·386 —	0·195
SE	(0·340)	(0·101)	(0·376)
t	6·42	3·84	0·52
R^2	0·801		
1966 2nd half	2·629 —	0·462 —	0·371
SE	(0·211)	(0·052)	(0·112)
t	12·43	8·92	3·30
R^2	0·814		
1967 1st half	1·721 —	0·275 —	0·058
SE	(0·255)	(0·729)	(0·218)
t	6·74	3·78	0·27
R^2	0·785		

1967 2nd half	2·739	—	0·491	—	0·503
SE	(0·254)		(0·063)		(0·224)
t	10·9		7·79		2·25
R^2	0·800				

Both models give results which are acceptable. All show high R^2s and have at least one explanatory variable which is highly significant and in all but one case the sign is as expected. Although the R^2s are roughly the same with the two models the second is preferred for the following reasons.

1. With the first model 1966 1st half there is an unexpected sign for Q_{t-a}.
2. With the first model an odd result for 1967 1st half emerges. The result that Q_t is not significant is unlikely.
3. The variance of the constant term (a) and the price-elasticity of demand is much smaller in the case of the second model. This is shown in Tables 1 and 2.

TABLE 1

Values of Constant Term (a) *by Model*

	First model		Second model	
	Jan.–June	July–Dec.	Jan.–June	July–Dec.
1964	1·5	2·8	1·5	2·9
1965	1·5	1·5	1·4	2·2
1966	2·3	2·6	1·5	2·6
1967	0·9	2·7	1·7	2·7

TABLE 2

Price-Elasticities of Demand by Model

	First model		Second model	
	Jan.–June	July–Dec.	Jan.–June	July–Dec.
1964	4·3	2·0	4·3	1·9
1965	4·6	5·2	5·2	2·6
1966	2·3	2·1	5·2	2·1
1967	21·3	2·0	3·6	2·0

It seems intuitively more plausible that the more stable relationships are produced by the most appropriate model although there is no *a priori* proof that it is so.

Because of the paucity of equilibrium prices in modern economies the possibility of deducing demand curves by observation of price changes is confined to such cases where market clearing is achieved. Indeed the applicability of this type of simple one-equation model to problems of demand estimation is likely to be limited. Its chief interest is that of the limiting case where supply is determined exogenously. However there will be other cases where, because the product is perishable and subject to supply variations in response to natural phenomena like the weather, where such an approach may be worth attempting. Fresh fruit, such as strawberries, and of course all other fish come near to fulfilling the conditions mentioned above—conditions sufficient for overcoming the identification problem and the need for models using simultaneous equations.

13

The Demand for Car Ownership: A Note

by M. J. Buxton and D. G. Rhys

Existing statistical estimates of the aggregate demand for cars suggest that the main explanatory variables are price and some measure of *per capita* income. Whilst other factors, such as socio-economic indices of various kinds and variables relating to credit conditions have been tried, none of these have tended to add much to the explanatory power of the models involved. In fact price and income variables alone, in some cases, have been found to explain up to 95 per cent of the variation in demand.[1]

These main econometric studies have yielded values for the long-run elasticity of demand in the range 1·1 to 4·2. For instance Evans[2] suggests that a 1 per cent change in income would lead to a 1·1 per cent change in the expenditure on cars (although he measures the short-run elasticity as 2·2). At the other end of the scale, Suits[3] estimates the income elasticity of the demand for new cars as 4·2. Similarly the empirical studies place the long-run price-elasticity

From *Scottish Journal of Political Economy* (June 1972), pp. 175–81. Reprinted by permission of the authors, the editor and the Longman Group Ltd.

[1] For example, G. C. Chow, 'Statistical Demand Functions for Automobiles and Their Use for Forecasting', in A. C. Harberger, *The Demand for Durable Goods* (Chicago, 1960), expressing the stock of automobiles in new-car equivalent units finds that price and disposable income variables together explain 85–90 per cent of the variance in the stock of cars. Using expected income instead of disposable income the function can explain 90–95 per cent of the variance.

[2] M. K. Evans, *Macroeconomic Activity, Theory, Forecasting, and Control* (New York: Harper and Row, 1969).

[3] D. Suits, 'The Demand for Automobiles in the U.S.A., 1929–1956', *Review of Economics and Statistics* (1958), pp. 273–80.

of the demand for cars between -0.6 and -1.5, although Evans calculates a short-run coefficient of -3.1. These studies however, were concerned with aggregate demand functions, and were not intended to examine variations in demand response according to area, or on a regional basis. A study by Bennett[4] introduced the rural or urban location of the family unit as an explanatory variable. He found that the higher the ratio of rural to urban families the higher the level of the demand for cars.

Our basic model followed upon the work of Sleeman[5] and Tanner,[6] and consists of a cross-section analysis, on a geographical basis, of the level of car ownership. Basically it uses car ownership per 1,000 population as the dependent variable and population density, average income *per capita*, and an index of the age structure of the local population as independent variables. A stepwise multiple regression programme[7] was used to computer analyse the data which was for 1968 and 1969.

Car ownership: This is the average number of 'private cars and private vans' licensed in the particular licensing authority in the relevant year per 1,000 population (Ministry of Transport, *Highway and Statistics, 1968* and *1969* (London: H.M.S.O., 1969 and 1970)).

Population density: Estimated population per square mile in June of the relevant year (General Register Office, 1969 and 1970).

Average income: This is perhaps more accurately described as an *index* of average income. It uses the official figure for the counties' total net personal incomes (excluding persons with an income of less than £275), divided by the counties' population figures (Board of Inland Revenue, *Inland Revenue Statistics, 1968* and *1969* (London: H.M.S.O., 1970 and 1971)).

Age structure: This figure was perforce the same for each of the two years analysed, being based on the 1966 Sample Census of

[4] W. B. Bennett, 'Cross-Section Studies of the Consumption of Automobiles in the United States', *American Economic Review* (Sept. 1967), pp. 841–50.

[5] J. F. Sleeman, 'The Geographical Distribution of Motor Cars in Great Britain', *Scottish Journal of Political Economy* (Feb. 1961), pp. 71–81; and 'A New Look at the Distribution of Private Cars in Britain', ibid. (Nov. 1969), pp. 306–18.

[6] J. C. Tanner, 'Car and Motorcycle Ownership in the Counties of Great Britain in 1960', *Journal of Royal Statistical Society*, Series A, Part 2 (1963), pp. 276–84.

[7] Stepwise Regression Programme (BMD02R), from *Biomedical Computer Programs*, University of California Press, 1970.

Population. It represents the percentage of the local population between the ages of 15 and 60 at the census date (General Register Office, *Sample Census, 1966, County Reports* (London: H.M.S.O., 1967)).

In addition a fourth independent variable was used for part of the analysis: as no Inland Revenue figures for incomes were available that distinguish between administrative counties and the county boroughs, the main part of the analysis had to use population statistics for counties including their county boroughs. However, it was appreciated that the population density of some county boroughs might be considerably higher than that of the administrative county with which they had to be included.

Skew variable. This was therefore introduced and defined as the percentage of the total population of the county living in the county borough(s) divided by the percentage of the total area of the county lying within the county borough(s). Where there was no county borough the variable was given the value 1·0. The value of this variable thus ranges upwards from 1·0 as the population density of the county boroughs increasingly deviates from that of the administrative county with which they have been included. Thus it can be said to give a measure of the variance of the population density from the mean figure used basically.[8]

This analysis was carried out on the data for England and Wales: both together and separately. Table 1 summarizes these results. What seems immediately noteworthy (though in no way unexpected) is the consistency of the direction of the relationship between the dependent variable (car ownership) and the independent variables of average income and population density. This clearly supports the hypothesis that car ownership is positively related to income and inversely related to population density. (It is not claimed that the latter is necessarily a causal relationship. It may well be that the density of population is in effect a 'proxy' variable for the adequacy of public transport service, or the distances involved in home-to-work, business, shopping or social journeys.) The R^2 (or apparent explanatory power of the models) varies from a weak 28 per cent

---

[8] There seems intuitively a strong possibility that there may be a relationship between 'skewness' as measured here and the distribution of total income: the greater the 'skewness' the greater the influence of the county borough(s) in the county as a whole, and possibly the greater the concentration of incomes.

to a fairly strong 78 per cent. The log-linear models (which used logs of all variables) are neither consistently better nor worse than the arithmetic-linear models. It is interesting, however, to note that in all the Welsh models population density is a better explanatory variable than average income. In all other cases the 'T' statistic (viz. the coefficient divided by its standard error) for average

TABLE I

Ref.	Area	Year	Transf.	R^2	Constant	Av./Inc.	Pop./Dn.	Age/St.	Skew.
1.	E.+W.	1968	—	0·3543	18·5402	0·2028 (0·0532)	−0·0090 (0·0025)	n.s.	−1·4765 (0·4207)
2.	E.	,,	—	0·4032	−71·7770	0·2761 (0·0712)	−0·0083 (0·0025)	n.s.	−1·0556 (0·4580)
3.	W.	,,	—	0·7815	28·9457	0·2159 (0·0717)	−0·0709 (0·0123)	n.s.	n.s.
4.	E.+W.	,,	LOG.	0·5171	−1·3499	1·2973 (0·2506)	−0·0874 (0·0169)	n.s.	−0·0402 (0·0123)
5.	E.	,,	LOG.	0·4851	−2·0701	1·5374 (0·3654)	−0·0925 (0·0229)	n.s.	−0·0370 (0·0149)
6.	W.	,,	LOG.	0·7139	2·6171	n.s.	−0·1125 (0·0215)	n.s.	n.s.
7.	E.+W.	1969	—	0·2795	558·5928	0·1531 (0·0588)	−0·0052 (0·0032)	−8·4403 (2·9394)	−1·2525 (0·5449)
8.	E.	,,	—	0·5623	407·0872	0·4733 (0·0716)	−0·0048 (0·0025)	−12·7709 (2·5411)	n.s.
9.	W.	,,	—	0·4944	265·7790	n.s.	−0·0681 (0·0208)	n.s.	n.s.
10.	E.+W.	,,	LOG.	0·4380	1·7504	1·3262 (0·3004)	−0·0921 (0·0232)	−1·8112 (0·6341)	−0·0324 (0·0151)
11.	E.	,,	LOG.	0·5759	−0·1814	2·5595 (0·3790)	−0·0620 (0·0229)	−2·9334 (0·6346)	n.s.
12.	W.	,,	LOG.	0·6868	2·6613	n.s.	−0·1250 (0·0255)	n.s.	n.s.

Notes: (i) The data for E. (England) is based upon 46 observations and that for W. (Wales) upon 13 observations.
(ii) n.s. Not statistically significant at the 5 per cent level.
(iii) Figures in parentheses are the appropriate standard errors.

income is superior to that for population density. One reason for this is the higher significance of the skew variable in the English models, reflecting the importance of the county boroughs. The R^2 is also higher in the Welsh cases. One possible reason for this is that the dichotomy between urban and rural administrative counties is much more clear-cut in Wales than in England, where in the latter a seemingly rural county may have a number of significant urban areas, which this analysis cannot distinguish. In Wales, however, the rural counties include only small towns which are less significant than the English ones in terms of the proportion of the population of the administrative county they account for.

A further analysis was also carried out disaggregating administrative counties and county boroughs, so eliminating the need for the skew variable. These results are summarized in Table 2. Unfortunately, no figures for average income are available on this basis, so the results are not totally comparable; however, it is interesting to see that the 'T' statistic for population density is much higher.

Sleeman (1969) also comments upon the relationship between car density and population density; however, the sensitivity of his analysis is reduced by his consideration of regions rather than counties (a result again of the availability of data at the time of his writing). By looking at the level of car ownership in regions, important variations within these regions are averaged out and so the exact nature of the relationship is further obscured. In a footnote[9] he gives some details of his statistical analysis which looks at the

TABLE 2

Ref.	Area	Year	Trans.	R^2	Constant	Av./Inc.	Pop./Dn.	Age/St.
13.	E. + W.	1968	—	0·4327	234·4135	N.A.	−0·0063 (0·0006)	n.s.
14.	,,	,,	LOG.	0·4185	2·5964	N.A.	−0·0909 (0·0090)	n.s.
15.	E. + W.	1969	—	0·4101	243·2905	N.A.	−0·0064 (0·0006)	n.s.
16.	,,	,,	LOG.	0·3856	2·6207	N.A.	−0·0877 (0·0094)	n.s.

Notes: (i) The data for E. + W. (England and Wales) are based upon 142 observations.
(ii) N.A. Relevant data not available.
(iii) n.s. Not statistically significant at the 5 per cent level.
(iv) Figures in parentheses are the appropriate standard errors.

relationship between car density, and population density and/or average income in two groups of regions, which he describes as 'more urbanised' and 'less urbanised'. For comparative purposes the present authors ran similar regressions on the basis of 'more urbanised' *counties* and 'less urbanised' *counties*, using the same operational dividing point as used apparently by Sleeman (viz. 450 persons per square mile). Unfortunately, Sleeman does not give his figures for the values of R^2, but as far as is possible Table 3 includes details of his published results and summarizes our own.

[9] Sleeman, 1969, p. 315.

TABLE 3

Ref.	Area	Year	Transf.	R^2	Constant	Av./Inc.	Pop./Dn.
17.	L.U.R.	1966	LOG.	V.N.S.	V.N.S.	1·76 (0·45)	0·02 (0·03)
18.	M.U.R.	,,	LOG.	V.N.S.	V.N.S.	2·89 (0·96)	−0·10 (0·10)
19.	L.U.C.	1968	LOG.	0·2398	0·8094	0·5793 (0·3276)	−0·0849 (0·0342)
20.	L.U.C.	1969	LOG.	0·2413	1·1175	0·5200 (0·3447)	−0·1380 (0·0483)
21.	M.U.C.	1968	LOG.	0·7749	−6·6475	3·0621 (0·3366)	−0·1334 (0·0271)
22.	M.U.C.	1969	LOG.	0·5617	−6·2341	2·9198 (0·5453)	−0·1407 (0·0447)

Notes: (i) Sleeman's data for L.U.R. (less-urbanised regions) is based on 6 observations, that for M.U.R. (more-urbanised regions) on 9 observations. The data for L.U.C. (less-urbanised counties) is based on 30 observations, that for M.U.C. (more urbanised counties) on 29 observations.

    (ii) V.N.S. Values not stated.

    (iii) Figures in parentheses are the appropriate standard errors.

The most surprising aspect of Sleeman's findings is that although he obtains the now familiar relationship of car density being positively related to average income and negatively related to population density in his 'more urbanised regions', in the 'less urbanised regions' he finds car ownership positively related to both these variables. Furthermore, the 'T' statistic for the population coefficients suggests that neither are in fact significant. Using the county basis, however, this unexpected sign reversal does not appear, and indeed although income is still the more significant, the population density variable is in each case significant at the 5 per cent level. However, it is clear that for the less urbanised counties the model has a low explanatory power (viz. $R^2 = 0.24$) and other factors must be important. For instance, socio-economic groupings and social ethos may vary considerably within the group of counties, and perhaps in these essentially rural (or at least non-urban) areas the skewness of the distribution of incomes may be greater. By this last point we mean that the income distribution deviates from the normal national pattern with perhaps a greater discontinuity between low and high income groups. Thus as incomes increase, the low-income groups may still consider the car outside their effective demand, whilst the high-income groups have already achieved their optimal level of per capita car ownership (at least in terms of numbers of vehicles, even if not in terms of quality or type of unit).

Our findings are much more in line with the results of the study carried out by Tanner (1963), using much earlier data (1960). He obtains, however, a very strong correlation for car-ownership against his variable 'distance north'. The biggest problem in using this in our particular context is to understand its causal significance. Clearly it is a proxy variable: but a proxy for what? If indeed it is, as he suggests, an expression of difference in climate, it seems surprising that so simple a proxy for such an intricate variable as climate has such a high explanatory power. Certainly as far as transport policy is concerned, it gives little help in anticipating or being able to influence future trends in car ownership in any particular area. However, one point of his that we investigated further was the effect of the age structure of the population. He suggests that 'Sussex has a low number of cars probably because the proportion of the population over the age of 65 is particularly high' (Tanner, p. 281). The implication of this is presumably that persons over that age are unlikely to own or drive cars. (The question of financial ability of old-age pensions to run vehicles should be covered by the average income variable.) Clearly, however, there is also the question of young persons unlikely to own, or indeed prohibited from owning, motor vehicles. Thus our age structure variable measured the percentage of the population within the likely car-owning age brackets. For the most part, however, the resulting coefficient was not statistically significant at the 5 per cent level. However, where it was significant, the relationship was negative, i.e. car ownership was lower in areas with a higher proportion of persons in the potentially car-owning age bracket! This perhaps deserves further analysis: one tentative explanation may be that families with a large number of children consider the car as more of a necessity than other sectors of the community. From an economic point of view it is true that the larger number of persons travelling in a vehicle the lower the average costs per person per mile. This cost saving is not fully reflected in public transport fare structures as far as the family is concerned, and so makes the car relatively cheaper the larger the family.

Clearly this type of analysis is severely restricted by the limitations of the available statistics. Unfortunately, county boundaries do not enclose areas with a homogeneous population density; average income is a poor indicator of the diversity of actual income distributions. Aggregate studies suggest that a meaningful price variable (including perhaps a measure of the relative costs of private and public transport) would increase the explanatory power of the functions. However, our results show that even the use of county statistics improves the explanatory power of such disaggregated models, as compared with earlier studies, and leads to theoretically more acceptable results.

14

Markets in Second-Hand Goods

by K. J. W. Alexander

Many goods change hands more than once. There has, however, been little interest in the economics of second-hand markets (the phrase is used to include third-, fourth-, fifth-, etc., hand markets as well), despite their importance. The market for older houses is something of an exception, though here too there is scope for greater study. Yet, not only the quantitative importance of second-hand markets commends them as topics for investigation. An examination of second-hand market behaviour can bring out especially clearly the way in which markets function.

In particular, that costs of production are not immediately important can demonstrate that their influence affects only part of the supply side. The scope for substitution—between products performing the same function but of different ages—can also contribute to a fuller understanding of market processes. The demand for new commodities is also much affected by the existence of efficient markets in which these commodities can be resold. Demand is encouraged, since goods bought can be sold for cash, or used to provide backing for credit, but it may be depressed by the availability of close substitutes at lower prices. The interesting relationship between the pace at which new designs and models of products may be introduced and the re-saleability of earlier designs indicates one way in which the working of second-hand markets may increase or decrease the rate of innovation in an economy.[1]

From *Lloyds Bank Review*, No. 97 (July 1970), pp. 37–49. Reprinted by permission of Lloyds Bank Ltd.

[1] Some of these topics are discussed in Arthur H. Fox, 'A Theory of Second-Hand Markets', *Economica*, New Series, vol. 24 (1957).

TYPES OF MARKET

Second-hand markets may be classified into four main types, the basis of classification being determined by the use to which the commodity being sold is to be put. This classification is not water-tight and there are certain difficulties associated with it, as we shall see. However, it provides a useful starting-point. These four classifications are: superior re-use; inferior re-use; reclamation; disposal.

Superior and Inferior Re-Use

The distinction between superior and inferior re-use is not an easy one to define clearly. One approach is to compare the market price of a second-hand article with that of its new close substitute, defined in terms of use, making allowances for expected length of life from the time of resale. Account has to be taken of comparative maintenance costs where these are relevant. But the difficulties of establishing what are close substitutes defined solely in terms of use make this approach a difficult one to apply in practice. An alternative method is to establish normal depreciation rates for particular articles and to classify those articles which resell *at* or *below* the value derived by applying this depreciation rate to their original price as inferior use and those which sell at prices *above* their 'normal value' as superior use.

Both of these methods are vitiated by the possibility of short-run fluctuations around the longer-run trend of 'normal values', which are assumed to be determined by depreciation. Any such longer-run trend would be derived from historical experience,[2] which would not be mirrored in all subsequent periods because, for example, of changes in technology and in taste. In addition, the practical application of these concepts is complicated by changes in the value of money. Like many other concepts in economics which aid clear thinking, those of inferior and superior re-use are not capable of being clearly specified. In the case of particular objects being resold, however, it is usually fairly easy to distinguish in practice whether resale is for inferior or superior re-use. The classification of goods in auction rooms provides a practical illustration.

[2] R. Stone and D. A. Rowe, 'The Market Demand for Durable Goods', *Econometrica*, vol. 25 (1957), provides an illustration of this approach.

Antiques are the best example of goods being resold for superior re-use. The simple cottage-style chair of one hundred years ago today fetches a much higher price than do contemporary chairs manufactured to serve the same purpose. In some cases, the superior re-use is a different use: the brass balance-scales now being resold for use in interior decoration. In the market for older houses, there are the artisans' terraced houses in certain districts which become highly prized, and the farm labourers' cottages whose value multiplies many times in response to the demand for week-end retreats. In both of these housing cases, the somewhat indeterminate notion of 'amenity' plays a major part: the combination of quietness and accessibility being the important feature in town houses, and seclusion and view the features most affecting the value of country properties. The factor spanning both the antique and older-house sectors of the superior-use market is design, style or, more generally, aesthetic appeal. The influence of length of life remaining, qualified by maintenance costs, is more dominant in inferior than in superior re-use markets. The market for second-hand cars is probably the best example, certainly from the point of view of the extent to which experience of its workings is diffused throughout the population. With second-hand cars, furniture and clothes, style is of considerable importance, however, demonstrating the impossibility of keeping the inferior and superior categories completely distinct.

Goods which could sell in the superior re-use market may, in fact, sell at much lower prices in the inferior re-use market, because of imperfections in the degree of market knowledge in second-hand markets generally. Sellers, in particular, may be unaware that possessions have a value far in excess of the cost of replacing them with new substitutes. For this reason, the antique market, for example, is made up of several tiers up which goods may pass, each successive tier having a greater awareness of the potential market for particular commodities. Shifts in taste may also reclassify second-hand commodities from inferior to superior or superior to inferior markets. Indeed, such reclassification may arise for reasons other than of taste, and commodities may be pushed right out of the re-use classifications by social and legislative influences. For instance, the proportion of the total number of cars of a given age being scrapped for reclamation has increased as a result of statutory tests of road-worthiness; the market in used dentures virtually disappeared with Mr. Bevan's National Health Service Act; and the market in used spectacles has become export-oriented.

Reclamation

The reclamation market, through which raw materials are cycled for re-use, takes over when the price which a commodity can fetch for inferior re-use falls below that which it can get as 'scrap'. This price comparison is complicated by the costs of reclamation, on the one hand, and by the costs of finding a buyer for a low-grade inferior-use commodity, on the other. These factors must qualify the use of relative prices as the explanation of why commodities move from one level of second-hand market to a lower one. Because the market prices of new raw materials fluctuate quite widely (copper fell from over £600 per ton in 1966 to £350 in 1967, rising again to over £700 recently) there can be related fluctuations in the prices paid for scrap, even influencing the length of life in use of those commodities which embody raw materials in a reclaimable form. The possibility of fairly wide fluctuations in the free-market price of scrap has led in one case—the ferrous scrap market in U.K.—to the use of controls to stabilize prices.

Disposal

One of the sources of scrap for re-use after reclamation is disposal, when a commodity is discarded as valueless by its owner and re-channelled into the reclamation market by those concerned with disposal—either formally, as in the case of the sale under contract of waste paper by municipalities to paper and board manufacturers, or informally, as when refuse collectors sell goods thrown out for disposal to scrap-metal merchants. The distinguishing characteristics of the disposal market is that to the person disposing of or 'selling' the commodity the price is zero or negative —negative in the sense that rates are paid to have waste removed or (and this can be quite important in the case of industrial disposers) a price is actually paid for removing specific quantities of waste product.

Among factors which complicate the study of second-hand markets is, of course, inflation. The attempt to draw a distinction between inferior and superior re-use would be easier if the value of money remained constant. The demand for works of art and for antique furniture has become affected by the capacity of some such commodities to appreciate at a rate faster than the decline in the purchasing power of money, so that they offer a hedge against inflation. Changes in the cost of production of cars, houses and raw materials also will affect the money value of substitutes in the re-use and reclamation markets. Further, technological changes can depress second-hand prices either because the old product becomes increasingly unacceptable or because the cost of production of its new close substitutes is reduced by improved methods of production.

Before examining the characteristics of these overlapping second-hand markets in some detail it is of interest to see the scale and structure of such markets for which there is information. Unfortunately, some of the data available are not very up to date, but the picture given is probably still fairly representative.

SCRAP METAL TRADES

Since 1958 these trades have been dropped from the census of production, so that the latest information is for 1954. In that year, there were 723 'scrap establishments' in the U.K., employing nearly 13,000 workers. But this excludes factors and merchants. At an even earlier date, 1950/51, there were 1,463 scrap-metal merchants and processors listed in the censuses of production and distribution, with gross output and receipts of £107 millions and employment of 31,800. The British Scrap Federation has lost around a fifth of its members over the last decade—as a result of mergers and of dropouts from the trade—and it is probable that this total of 1,463 firms should be written-down to something nearer to 1,100 for the late sixties.

The nature of the industry suggests that considerable unrecorded collection and merchanting of scrap metal goes on. More important, these figures do not include refiners, re-smelters and re-rollers and, therefore, they cover only one end of the metal reclamation industry. The most important specialist activity of scrap processors is that of dismantling old motor vehicles. Rather more than half of all processors dismantle. It has been estimated that over 1·5 million vehicles were dismantled annually in the late 1960s. The rapid increase in the junking of cars in the U.S.A. provides a pointer to future growth in Britain. Over the sixties the proportion of cars junked to those in use in America rose from 6 per cent to nearly 10 per cent and the number of cars junked was coming close to the number of new cars sold each year, that is, a constant stock situation was being approached.

The other major specialist type is that of ship-breaker, of which there are only a few and most of these are among the largest scrap processors in the business. These large firms are not limited to ship-breaking, however, and indeed not only span the whole range of scrap-metal processing and merchanting but have diversified into other activities. Plant-hire is an obvious extension of purchasing used capital equipment for scrapping. The manufacturer of garden furniture is less obviously associated—he uses the teak decks of ships being broken up. Sometimes, integration can take place in the reverse direction: for example, a firm which used shot for stone-polishing took over a scrap merchant producing shot, scrap ultimately completely overshadowing the stonemason's business.

ANTIQUES

Figures for some of the other important identifiable second-hand markets are given in Table 1, derived from the 1961 census of distribution.

TABLE 1
Antique and Other Dealers, 1961

	Number of establishments	Average turnover £'000
Antique dealers	1,652	9·6
Second-hand furniture dealers ...	1,315	3·2
Pawnbrokers	573	13·9
Second-hand book sellers	431	4·1
General second-hand dealers ...	1,107	1·7

The continuing boom in 'antiques' (interpreted rather loosely) means that the 1961 census figure of 1,652 dealers is certainly too low today. *The British Antiques Yearbook* lists around 3,000 dealers, and even this figure underestimates the numbers who deal in 'antiques'. Many of these 'firms' are very small. Thus, three-quarters of the antique dealers in 1961 had no more than two employees, and over half the second-hand furniture dealers and book sellers had only one employee.

There is one sense in which it is near-tautology to point out that prices in the superior re-use market rise faster than the general level of prices. It is the reasons for this which are of interest.

The examples of antiques and of houses with 'amenity' may be taken together. First, the supply of any given type is fixed. The quantity coming on to the market at any one time is unlikely to be very responsive to price changes. Supply is thus relatively inelastic. Indeed, in both cases there are forces at work which are reducing the total stock. Antiques wear out and an increasing proportion of

TABLE 2

Increases in Prices of Selected Antiques, Pictures and Books 1951–1969

	%
French furniture	+ 400
Oriental porcelain	+ 2,350
English porcelain	+ 300
English silver	+ 750
English glass	+ 750
English pictures	+ 950
Italian pictures	+ 650
Old Master drawings	+ 2,050
Old Master prints	+ 3,050
Old Master pictures	+ 600
Impressionist pictures	+ 1,600
Modern books	+ 800
Old books	+ 1,050

Source: The Times–Sotheby Index.

the total stock is withdrawn permanently from the market into museums and art galleries. In addition, there is an expanding export market for British antiques in North America, Italy and elsewhere. The sharp increase in the prices of British antiques after the 1967 devaluation in part reflected the importance of these export markets. Houses, too, wear out, but more important are the encroachments on amenity by roads, new building and other factors. On the supply side, therefore, we have diminishing stock and inelastic supply. On the demand side, we have demand rising with affluence. Rising prices, quite distinct from the effect of inflation, are the consequence, and there is every reason to expect this tendency to continue and even to accelerate. A few price movements of recent years bring the point home very forcibly.

It should be remembered, of course, that whilst investments in art and antiques may yield capital appreciation they do not yield an annual money income. On the other hand, such investment can yield a considerable psychic income which, taken together with average annual price rises in a range from 7 to 18 per cent, must more than compensate for the forgone money income.

Even so, there are risks. Snuff-boxes—for long a favourite of the small collector—suffered a sharp price decline some years ago. Last year saw sharp declines in the prices fetched by some types of English silver. The one safe rule seems to be that the higher the quality of the article the smaller relative price decline it suffers in a general fall, demonstrating the effectiveness of extreme scarcity as a price prop even in conditions of slackening demand. Investors had turned to English silver because both hallmarking and the fairly frequent sale of the large supply of 'standard' items established a more perfect market than exists for most antiques and works of art. There was some 'bunching' of this shift into English silver for investment purposes in the mid-sixties and this appears to have accelerated the annual rate of price increase and taken prices beyond a level which could be sustained. The similarity between such sectors of the second-hand market for superior re-use and for investment in the stock market is quite clear. It should also be noted that the exclusion of antiques from tariff duties, the tax relief concession given by the U.S. government to collectors who covenant to will their purchases to museums, and the U.K. estate duty exemptions all stimulate demand in the antique market.

HOUSES AND MOTOR VEHICLES

The two most important parts of the 'inferior re-use market' are housing and motor vehicles. Both are subject to the powerful influence of government policies for economic management, in the form of interest rate and hire-purchase restrictions. To a lesser extent, the vehicle market is affected by changes in the levels of purchase tax (on new cars), motor-fuel tax and of vehicle licensing. There is scope for study of how changes in such variables have affected the volume and prices of new and second-hand vehicle sales.[3] Apart from anything else, there have been twenty changes in hire-purchase restrictions on cars and motor vehicles since 1952.

These two markets are very large. In 1969 over 1·1 million hire-purchase contracts were recorded in connection with sales of second-hand cars and other vehicles, to which must be added sales made without hire purchase. Old houses made up about 70 per cent of all housing loans by building societies in 1968. The statistics of one of the largest societies show that its mortgage lending on old houses amounted to over three-fifths of its total lending in 1969.

In both the second-hand vehicle and house markets there are sectors which should be classified as for 'superior use' rather than 'inferior use', and particular items may change their classification, particularly in the house market. A similar situation exists in the second-hand furniture market, in which, although the majority of items are sold for inferior use, some move up into the superior use category. Taste is obviously important in this respect.

The prices of newly built houses are a more important determin-ant of the prices of relatively modern second-hand houses than of the older stock but, with demand high and the annual addition to stock a fairly low proportion of total stock, there is an obviously strong influence exerted by new house prices on those of older houses. Were it not for this combination of demand and slow-changing stock, it would seem reasonable to expect rising incomes, together with people's preferences for modern housing design, to produce a widening gap between new and old house prices, and there are slight indications that such a widening is taking place.

Apart from the influence of taste, it would seem that trends in new building and land costs will together continue to exercise a strong influence on second-hand house prices. On the supply side, a decline in the current market price of second-hand houses can have a very marked impact on numbers offered for sale. The relation-ship between mortgage commitments, the recoupment price of an old house and the cost of a new house together produce a reluctance to sell when prices level off or decline. The extent to which inflation

---

[3] J. S. Cramer, 'The Depreciation and Mortality of Motor Cars', *Journal of the Royal Statistical Society, Series A,* vol. 121, Part 1 (1958), is a pioneering study using British data. There have been a number of studies since which have concentrated on the effect of hire purchase controls, e.g. A. Silberston 'Hire Purchase Controls and the Demand for Cars', *Economic Journal* (Mar. 1963). The factors included in this study are new car prices, age of model and scrap value.

qualifies the influence of the mortgage commitment is counteracted by the tendency of new house prices to rise faster than the general level of prices. All analysis of house markets is complicated by the unusual relationship between supply and demand arising from the fact that a substantial proportion of sellers are simultaneously buyers. We shall see that there is a similar phenomenon in the reclamation and re-use markets. The market in second-hand houses, however, suffers from great imperfections of knowledge which can produce results for individual buyers and sellers very different from those reflecting general conditions in the market.

CAPITAL GOODS

A sector of the inferior re-use market which is of especial interest is that of second-hand capital goods sold for re-use by other producers. Such business has usually developed out of scrap-metal marketing, when a merchant has decided that the price for resale to users would be higher than to processors for reclamation. An early example was the resale to Italy of the entire stock of broad gauge rail when the Great Western Railway converted to standard gauge in 1892. The supply of capital equipment for scrap or for re-use can be affected by government policy for inducing new investment, with generous depreciation provisions increasing both the total supply and the proportion within it of equipment suitable for re-use. On the other side, there is a growing demand for second-hand capital equipment from developing countries, in line with the concept of 'intermediate technology' which is becoming increasingly fashionable.

Thus, we have a market in which the supply side is directly affected by government policies in developed countries to secure faster growth and reduce regional imbalance, whilst the demand side is affected by the aid policies of these same governments to developing economies. The transfer of capital equipment from developed to developing country can, of course, take place without passing through a second-hand market. An international company can re-equip in a developed country with the assistance of capital grants and transfer the older capital equipment to a developing country where, again, locational inducements are available. Assuming such transfer can promote economic growth in developing countries, we should consider how government policies for inducing capital replacement in developed countries could be integrated with programmes of aid to developed countries.

It would be a mistake to assume that resale abroad must always be to poorer countries. The resale of ships (an important part of the re-use capital market) can operate in the other direction, as evidenced by the sale by a merchant on behalf of Cunard of the cruise liner *Caronia* to the American-owned Star Line. This company is registered in Panama, however, which somewhat blurs the point. The export of ships for re-use is related to higher foreign prices for ferrous scrap, which will be discussed next. Ships for scrapping are the one exception to the present ban on the export of good quality ferrous scrap, which has resulted in a decline of tonnage being broken in British yards and in considerable overcapacity in the British ship-breaking industry.

SCRAP AND RECLAMATION

Scrap and reclamation are a major indigenous source of raw materials for British industry. Some measure of their importance is indicated by the figures in Table 3.

TABLE 3
Consumption of Reclaimed Materials, U.K., 1968

	Total use '000 tons	Approximate proportion of 'new' production derived from reclaimed materials %
Rags, waste ropes, etc.	79·1	n.a.
Waste paper	1,765·0	42
Copper	138·3	20
Lead	105·8	28
Zinc	84·8	25*
Ferrous scrap	15,331·0	50

*Scrap zinc has several uses. 28 per cent of the output of slab zinc was based on home scrap.

It has been estimated that the scrap and reclamation trades save approximately £1,000 millions on our annual import bill. These 'waste trades' might have had more attention given them had they the more appropriate name of *anti-waste trades*. The recent proposal

(May 1970) to establish a Confederation of Reclamation and Processing Industries is an indication of the increasing importance of this field of economic activity.

Scrap is classified as: (1) *Home Scrap*, generated in primary metal production. In iron and steel production, for example, the sheared-off ends of ingots, blooms, etc. can amount to as much as 25 per cent of total production. (2) *Process Scrap*, the waste metal generated in manufacturing processes. It is estimated that about 13 per cent of the total steel bought by manufacturing firms in Britain and as much as 35 per cent of the steel purchased by the motor-manufacturing industry comes into this category. (3) *Capital Scrap*, the metal embodied in equipment which is sold or otherwise disposed of and not kept in use thereafter.

Of these three broad classifications of scrap, only capital scrap really affects the supply of scrap as a substitute raw material. The ratio of the input of a metal at a particular time in the past which is recovered will be determined partly by the current market value of the metal and partly by the difficulties of cost of recovery.

FERROUS SCRAP

The market for ferrous capital scrap is the largest and most important capital scrap market in the U.K., but there are no statistics of the prices paid by merchants or of the volume of their purchases. The view among merchants—which there seems no reason to doubt—is that supply is highly inelastic. Estimates of the additional flow of scrap which a substantial price increase might induce have ranged from 100,000 to 200,000 tons a year, small in comparison to the total supply of ferrous scrap and small even in relation to the increase of 500,000 tons of scrap which is implied by the planned expansion of steel production in 1970.

The market in which merchants buy ferrous capital scrap has three important features. First, there is a high degree of imperfection caused by the wide variation in the market knowledge of sellers. Second, supply can be subject to sudden changes unrelated to the price offered but caused by factors of technology and taste, and by the bunching of investment decisions in both the past and the present. Third, the price elasticity of supply is low. The demand for ferrous scrap is a function of current steel production, and thus of demand for steel.

Because there can be quite sizeable fluctuations in steel production, the combination of sizeable shifts in demand and inelastic supply could produce considerable fluctuations in the price paid by steel-makers for scrap. In a steel boom, rising prices for scrap would reflect competition between steel manufacturers for scarce scrap. The total supply of scrap would not increase much in response to such a price increase. Hence, the result is regulation of the market by agreement between steel manufacturers and scrap-metal merchants. This regulation has kept scrap prices low.

The steel industry has had to deal with two problems faced by any monopoly buyer: the rationing of supplies between participating firms and the distribution of the gains made at the expense of the owners of capital scrap and, to a lesser extent, the merchants. These problems have been handled within the steel industry by adjusting the effective cost of using scrap and pig-iron through the operation of a self-balancing fund raised by a levy on the use of all scrap and distributed as a remission on pig-iron used in steel-making. In the early sixties the levy was 89/- and the remission 33/- per ton. These internal problems need not trouble a steel industry under unified control, unless the British Steel Corporation wishes to allocate its gains between plants or divisions for 'management accounting' purposes.

British prices can be regulated at levels very substantially below world prices only if the export of scrap from Britain is also regulated, the wider this price gap the more rigorous the restriction of exports. These arrangements have survived the scrutiny of the Restrictive Practices Court. The saving on imports of scrap is not an important consideration; even if free market prices prevailed, the transport cost advantage would still operate in favour of British steel-makers using British scrap. Keeping costs low in the interests of the export of new steel makes a stronger case. Whereas farmers, for example, are subsidized to encourage import substitution, scrap prices are so regulated that the owners of ferrous scrap subsidize exports. The difference between the two policies stems from the inelasticity of supply of scrap, compared to the responsiveness of farm produce to price and profit stimuli.

If Britain joins the Common Market any agreement to regulate scrap prices would have to be abandoned, as the Community prohibits agreements affecting scrap which fix prices, allocate markets, customers or sources of supply, and it is taking steps to ensure that there are no distortions to 'the normal play of competition'. The regulatory mechanism practically stabilized prices for more than ten years up to the end of 1969, a very remarkable phenomenon given the rising costs of labour, transport and overheads. There is a possibility that the very diverse activities of scrap merchants have allowed for some cross-substitution of the supply of ferrous scrap at the expense of other commodities being reclaimed. A small price increase, equivalent to around $1\frac{1}{2}$ per cent, was agreed by the British Steel Corporation in December 1969. This will give the scrap industry some easement, which would be increased should there be S.E.T. relief and the extension of investment grants to the scrap-metal trades, both actively advocated by merchants in recent months. Considerable new investment has already taken place and the dismantling, sorting and stocking of scrap has become much less labour intensive than it was only a decade ago.

WASTE PAPER

The waste-paper trade is currently providing another example of a combination of rising demand and unresponsive supply resulting in substantial price rises and costly imports. The difference between ferrous scrap and waste paper is that the supply of waste paper is capable of considerable expansion, as only a small proportion of the total flow of paper is recovered, whereas a high proportion of the metal which can be reclaimed is recovered. The costs of collection are high relative to the price of reclaimed paper, partly because the quantities held by individual owners at any one time are too small to make it worth while to send waste direct to merchants. In addition, there are technical difficulties that make the cost of some reclamation processes high. There is a risk that, because of the high and rising costs of collection, supplies will actually decline, despite substantial rises in pulp prices. To increase import saving, the government has recently proposed investment grants to encourage the adoption of more economic reclamation processes. Earlier, the Industrial Reorganization Corporation had put up around £$1\frac{1}{2}$ millions for new processes for de-inking newsprint. The economic importance of the so-called 'waste trades' is receiving increasing recognition.

CONCLUSION

The diversity of second-hand markets makes it difficult to generalize about them on the basis of this brief review. One aspect stands out, however: the imperfection of these markets, closely associated with the tendency of the sellers of many second-hand goods to value them in relation to their lack of a continuing use to themselves rather than in relation to market considerations. Allied to this is the tendency for the quantities of commodities supplied in many second-hand markets to be determined by 'wear and tear' and considerations of fashion rather than in response to the level of demand and of prices. In those second-hand markets where buyers are relatively few, prices have reflected the situation. When buyers are many, competition breaks through and the inelasticity of supply produces substantial fluctuations in prices in response to demand changes. When circumstances produce substantial upward shifts in demand —as when rising affluence stimulates the demand for 'amenity'— prices will rise permanently, as there can be no consequential expansion of supply. For this reason, an increasing number of certain commodities will be bought for investment rather than for 'use', and this will add further to demand and rising prices. It is hardly surprising that some newspapers have begun to publicize price movements for pictures, prints, silver, porcelain and other classified antiques.

PART IV
Contemporary Problems

Introduction to Part IV

Since economics is by no means immune to the influence of current fashion and public concern it follows that the problems at the forefront of academic discussion vary from time to time. In the field of microeconomics, an increasing public interest in matters relating to the quality of life has been paralleled by a growing involvement of economists with problems in this area. The main aim of these readings is to show a sample of their work. Economists are of course interested in other microeconomic problems and some economists would no doubt select questions relating to the distribution of incomes as being *the* contemporary economic problem. The neglect of distributional and other questions follows simply from a desire to achieve some degree of coherence in these readings by focusing upon a particular class of problems.

To a considerable extent, the economist's interest in 'the quality of life' boils down to the way in which resources are, or should be, allocated. In mainstream economics the market mechanism is assumed to be the main allocator of resources. It is widely recognized however that the market cannot be relied upon to generate socially desirable results in certain situations, perhaps most notably in the presence of externalities.

The general posture adopted in these papers is a 'reformist' one. In other words, the values and institutions characterizing a modern capitalist society are taken as given. The concern is to improve the workings of that system by guiding private and public decision-makers to take a fuller account of their actions rather than to ask questions about the desirability of that system in relation to other alternatives.

Somewhere in the region of 40 per cent (about £4,000 million) of total fixed investment in the U.K. is now accounted for by the public sector. Since much of this public expenditure clearly has implications for the quality of life, the basis on which decisions about this expenditure are taken is of considerable importance. The technique of cost–benefit analysis is often proposed as a seemingly rational method for allocating public resources efficiently from the point of view of the community rather than merely the actual decision-maker.

The intellectual roots of the cost–benefit approach can be traced back to Dupuit, a nineteenth-century French engineer, and Pigou, a later English economist. However, it was not until the 1930s that the technique was put to practical use in discriminating between alternative water development schemes in the U.S.A. With a few notable exceptions, little use of cost–benefit analysis was made in the U.K. prior to 1960, although since then a great interest has been shown in the technique.

A comprehensive survey of the current state of the art is provided by Mishan in his 'ABC' article. He shows that cost–benefit is simply an application of the orthodox principles of resource allocation modified to take account of non-marketed costs and benefits. Some consideration is given to theoretical and practical difficulties inherent in the use of the technique and his conclusion is well worth close attention.

The articles by Newton on slums and Mishan on Roskill provide some idea of just how difficult it is to conduct an actual cost–benefit study. Thus Newton concludes by describing his study as a 'crude first experimental step' as judged by the standards set by Prest and Turvey in their now classic 1965 survey of cost–benefit analysis. The critique of the Roskill study by Mishan highlights the difficulties of putting a meaningful value on intangibles such as noise and architectural treasures, with resulting danger of biased recommendations. The paper by Smith has been included as an example of a narrower, less ambitious study which attempts to discriminate between two urban mass-transit alternatives and which also complements the Lennan article on urban traffic congestion.

In his survey of some alternative ways of tackling the problem of traffic congestion in towns, Lennan lends his support to the orthodox view that motorists should be charged for the full costs of the scarce road space, including parking space, that they use. Apart from certain theoretical objections to the use of the implied marginal cost pricing rule, it is also necessary that the full social costs can be measured since otherwise the appropriate congestion tax cannot be established. This problem is dealt with by Baumol and Oates in their paper, which is highly sceptical of so-called optimal solutions. It is also noteworthy that whereas Smith assumes the existence of some form of metering, i.e. pricing of urban road space, Lennan pays scant attention to alternative ways of tackling traffic problems in towns, such as the creation of traffic-free precincts or promotion of public transport.

Although their paper is not based upon empirical study, Baumol and Oates set out to be thoroughly practical. Their argument is that it is simply not possible to devise the optimal taxes proposed by theoretical economists to deal with externality problems because, as they put it, 'the optimal world has never been experienced or even described in quantitative terms'. In other words, it is meaningless to talk about the 'optimal amount of pollution' or 'optimal amount of traffic congestion'. They propose instead the establishment of acceptability standards and the imposition of taxes to bring those who cause net social damage into line with these standards, after which the standards could be progressively raised. This is, of course, merely one way of tackling externality problems through the price mechanism. Some economists would prefer more direct methods such as the use of legislation. A final comment is that, from the point of view of the environment as a whole, it is by no means clear that the Baumol and Oates proposal would succeed in preventing, say, producers from substituting one form of pollution for another e.g. air instead of river pollution.

The paper by Douty may at first sight seem to be the odd one out. Whereas the other papers look at problems of resource allocation within a fairly predictable environment, the Douty paper considers resource-allocation questions in situations where the environment has been subjected to sudden and unexpected changes. How do societies cope under these circumstances? On the basis of a number of case studies Douty argues that a temporary shift in economic behaviour appears to result, so that predictions derived from hypotheses about assumed 'normal' behaviour do not hold. In particular, firms do not appear to take advantage of the situation by increasing prices to market-clearing levels. With the aid of some sophisticated reasoning Douty attempts to show that orthodox utility-maximizing economic theory is still capable of shedding light on behaviour even in disaster situations. Since disasters are not all that uncommon there is perhaps a need for further empirical work in this area.

15

The A B C of Cost–Benefit
by E. J. Mishan

Cost–benefit analyses are in high fashion. Scarcely a week goes by without an authoritative voice asserting that, in connection with some project or other, a thorough cost–benefit study is needed. No matter how heated a controversy, a government spokesman can still the protests of the critics and be assured of a respectful silence simply by announcing that a cost–benefit analysis is in progress. The popular belief is that this novel technique provides a 'scientific' assessment of the social value of a project or at least an 'objective' assessment. True, if every benefit and every cost associated with a proposed project or investment is properly evaluated and brought into the calculus in a systematic way, the resulting sum—whether an excess of benefits over cost or the other way round—can hardly be challenged. Yet such a statement is not much more than a tautology. The fact is that evaluating 'properly' all relevant economic data is a guiding ideal, not a current practice. For, although the procedure used in cost–benefit analysis follows certain conventions, the outcome may vary according to the economist in charge of the study, because of differences in judgement with respect both to *what* is to be included and *how* it is to be evaluated. With the passage of time, one can hope that such differences of judgement will narrow but, in the meantime, and in the absence of a consensus, the individual judgement of whoever is in charge is an important factor in the outcome.

One question that a cost–benefit study sets out to answer is

From *Lloyds Bank Review*, July 1971, pp. 12–25. Reprinted by permission of Lloyds Bank Ltd.

whether or not a particular investment project, say project A, should be started. More generally, the question is whether a number of projects, A, B, C, D, etc. should be introduced and, if the investible funds are limited, which one, or which two or more, should be selected. Another question to which cost–benefit analysis addresses itself is that of determining the level at which a plant should operate, or the combination of outputs it should produce. I follow custom, however, in confining my attention largely to the former questions concerning the choice of investment projects.

COSTS AND BENEFITS

In order to appreciate some of the issues raised in the technique of cost–benefit analysis, we can ask the question: Why cost–benefit analysis? Why not plain honest-to-goodness profit and loss accounting? The simple answer is that what counts as a benefit or a loss to one part of the economy—to one or more persons or groups—does not necessarily count as a benefit or loss to the economy as a whole. And in cost–benefit analysis we are concerned with the economy as a whole; with the welfare of a defined society, and not any smaller part of it. A private enterprise, or even a public enterprise, comprises only a part of the economy, often a very small part. More important, whatever the means it employs in pursuing its objectives, the private enterprise, at least, is guided by ordinary commercial criteria that require revenues to exceed costs. The fact that its activities are guided by the profit motive, however, is not to deny that a large number of people other than its shareholders benefit from it. It confers benefits on its employees, on consumers and—through the taxes it pays—on the general public. Yet, the benefits enjoyed by these others continue to exist only so long as they coincide with profits to the enterprise. Without a public subsidy the enterprise will not survive if it continues to make losses. If it is to survive as a private concern and to expand, it must, then, over a period of time, produce profits large enough either to attract investors or to finance its own expansion.

There is, of course, the metaphor of the invisible hand; the *deus ex machina* discovered by Adam Smith which directs the forces of private greed so as ultimately to confer benefits on society. And one can, indeed, lay down simple and sufficient conditions under which the uncompromising pursuit of profit acts always to serve the public interest. These conditions can be boiled down to two: that all effects relevant to the welfare of individuals be priced through the market, and that perfect competition prevail in all economic activities. Once we depart from this ideal economic setting, however, the set of outputs and prices to which the economy tends may not serve the public so well as some other set of outputs and prices. In addition to this possible misallocation of resources among the goods being produced, it is possible also that certain goods which can be economically justified do not get produced at all, whilst others which cannot be economically justified continue to be produced. Again, certain goods having beneficial, though unpriced, 'spill-over effects' qualify for production on economic grounds, notwithstanding which they cannot be produced at a profit. The reverse is also true, and more significant: profitable commercial activities sometimes produce noxious spill-over effects to such an extent that on a more comprehensive pricing scheme they would be unable to continue.

The economist engaged in the cost–benefit appraisal of a project is not, in essence, then, asking a different sort of question from the accountant of a private firm. Rather, the same sort of question is asked about a wider group, society as a whole, and is asked more searchingly. Instead of asking whether the owners of an enterprise will be made better off by the firm's engaging in one activity rather than another, the economist asks whether *society* as a whole will be made better off by undertaking this project rather than not undertaking it, or by undertaking, instead, any of a number of other projects.

Broadly speaking, for the more precise concept of revenue to the private firm, the economist substitutes the less precise, yet meaningful, concept of *social benefit*. For the costs of the private firm, the economist will substitute the concept of *opportunity cost*—or the social value forgone when resources are moved away from other economic activities and into the construction and running of the project in question. For the profit of the firm, the economist will substitute the concept of *excess social benefit over cost*, or some related concept used in an investment criterion.

However, it cannot be stressed too strongly that the result even of an ideally conducted cost–benefit analysis does not of itself constitute a prescription for society. Since it simulates the effects of an ideal price system, an ideal cost–benefit analysis is subject also to its limitations. This means that any adopted criterion of a cost–

benefit analysis requiring, as all such criteria do, that benefits exceed cost, can be vindicated only by a social judgement that an economic arrangement which *can* make everyone better off is an improvement. Such a judgement does *not* require that everyone actually be made better off, or even that nobody be made worse off. The likelihood—which, in practice, is a virtual certainty—that some people, occasionally most people, will be made worse off by introducing the investment project in question is tacitly acknowledged. A project that is adjudged feasible by reference to a cost–benefit analysis is, therefore, quite consistent with an economic arrangement which makes the rich richer and the poor poorer. It is consistent also with manifest inequity. For an enterprise that is an attractive proposition by the lights of a cost–benefit calculation may be one that offers increased profits and pleasures to one group, in the pursuit of which substantial injury may be suffered by other groups.

In order, then, for a mooted enterprise to be socially approved, it is not enough simply to show that the outcome of an ideal cost–benefit analysis is positive. It must also be shown that the resulting distributional changes are not regressive, and that no gross inequities are perpetrated.

Sophisticated cost–benefit analysis clearly requires a high order of skill in the application of quantitative techniques. More important still, it requires thorough familiarity with the economics of resource allocation. For it is more important to be measuring the right thing in a crude sort of way than to be measuring the wrong thing with impressive refinement. This dictum will be more readily appreciated after we have touched upon some of the problems that arise in the application of cost–benefit methods, problems which fall conveniently into three categories. In the largest group are the problems of designating the relevant magnitudes and evaluating them. Having evaluated the benefits and costs over time there is, secondly, the problem of choosing an investment criterion to enable us to select and rank alternative investment projects. There is, however, always some uncertainty about the expected values of future benefits and costs. This leads to the third problem: that of making allowance for uncertainty.

WHAT AND HOW TO MEASURE?

We can divide this group into four sub-groups, beginning, first, with the question of relevance.

Relevance

The treatment of direct taxation offers a simple instance. Whether a domestic enterprise is private or public, the net benefit in any year is taken to be equal *not* to net profit or net benefit, less tax, but to net social profit or benefit *before* tax. For the tax payments are simply that portion of the net benefit that is transferred, through the government machine, to the rest of the community. If, however, the enterprise is established in a foreign country the taxes paid to the foreign government *do* represent a transfer of net benefits to foreigners. Consequently, such taxes have to be deducted from the net profits or net benefits available to the home country. Moreover, if new investments in a particular foreign country have the incidental effect of lowering the rate of return there on previous investments from the home country, the losses suffered on all these older investments have to be deducted from the net profit or net benefit on the prospective new investments.

Other instances will illuminate the nature of this kind of problem. Consider investment in a railway. The rise in the rents of sites near the railway station might, on first thoughts, be regarded as one of the benefits. But the rise in such rents is nothing more than the capitalized value of the annual worth of the extra convenience provided by sites that are close to the new railway station. If the cost–benefit analysis has calculated future benefits year by year, as it ought, this increase in annual worth has already been included. Adding the rise in capital values would, therefore, amount to counting the same benefit twice, once as an annual flow and then, again, as the capital value of that flow.

Again, suppose an increase in the retail sales of a small town, the result of the movement of staff associated with the establishment of a new airport in the vicinity. The increase in profits cannot be counted as benefits of the new airport. Most, or all of it, is simply a transfer of purchasing power from one part of the country to another; in so far as sales and profits rise in the new town they fall off in other parts of the country.

Shadow or Accounting Prices

In the absence of spill-over effects (which I discuss presently) and excise taxes, a highly competitive full-employment economy would, it is believed, provide an ideal background to a cost–benefit analysis, inasmuch as the 'true', or *opportunity*, cost of all productive services would be equal to their market prices. This is valid, however, only if the owner of such services, a skilled workman, say, is indifferent as between one occupation and another. But such an assumption is too restrictive. In general, therefore, the economist will conceive of the true cost of a man's labour as equal to the value it produces in the occupation from which it is to be transferred *plus* any additional sum above his existing wage that is required to induce a worker to transfer his labour into the new project.[1] This direct method of calculation provides a guiding rule for estimating the 'shadow prices' of all productive services needed in any investment project.

It follows, therefore, that it is wrong to value productive services at their *market* prices, if they are transferred from the production of goods subject to excise taxes. If, say, tax added 50 per cent to the price of a competitively produced good, the value associated with the labour of a worker to be withdrawn from the production of this good would be 50 per cent more than his wage-rate there—at least, if we assume the labourer to be indifferent as between his present occupation and that of the investment project in question. If he is not indifferent, but prefers his existing occupation, then the premium necessary to induce him to move into the new enterprise has (as indicated above) to be added.

Again, if a man is unemployed, his labour is not to be valued at his unemployment pay, say £10 a week, since this is not the value of his current work, but simply a transfer payment to him from the rest of the community.[2] It may be that his apparent contribution to national income is zero. However, he himself may place some value on his 'non-market activities' or, if entirely idle, he may enjoy his

---

[1] If, instead, he prefers to work in the *new* project, we have to subtract from his value in the old occupation a sum equal to the difference between his old wage and the minimum wage he would accept to work in the new project.

[2] In a popular sense, he may have 'earned' his unemployment insurance money by paying regularly his unemployment insurance premiums. But such insurance transactions are wholly 'transfer payments' within the economy.

idleness to the extent that some minimum sum, say £12 a week, has to be paid to induce him to accept work in a new enterprise. The true cost to the economy of his work in the enterprise is this minimum sum of £12 less the £10 transfer payment, or £2. For, in agreeing to work for £12, he no longer receives his unemployment pay of £10, which now reverts to the rest of the community. Since the cost to the community of engaging his labour is only £2 a week, there is a gain if his weekly labour adds a value in excess of £2.

In general, however, new investment in one sector of the economy has repercussions in all sectors. The total numbers brought into employment as a result of this initial investment, and their costs to the economy, can be estimated, provided that the average unemployment rate for each sector and/or region is available. For there is a known relationship between the unemployment rate in a sector, and/or area, and the probability that any newly employed labour there will come from the unemployment pool. (In the United States, for example, this probability approaches 100 per cent when the percentage unemployment in a sector or area is about 25 per cent.) Investment projects which would not be economically feasible in conditions of virtually full employment may, of course, become so in conditions of low employment.

For a final example of shadow prices, consider the imports of goods by countries that are chronically short of foreign exchange. If the additional imports of some material, say copper, can be afforded *only* by relinquishing other imports to an equal value in terms of the scarce currency, the shadow price of these additional copper imports has to be taken as equal to the domestic value of the particular goods that are no longer imported. For this is the value that has to be forgone in order to obtain the additional copper. If, on the other hand, the additional copper imports are paid for by additional exports, their shadow price is the domestic value of the particular goods exported to raise the needed foreign currency.

Spill-over Effects

The pricing of 'intangibles' or 'spill-over effects' can be thought of as the limiting case of a shadow price. For the market prices of spill-over effects are generally zero. In the manufacture and use of certain goods, incidental by-products are generated such as smoke, pollution, noise and so on[3] which are not recorded by the market. However, those people who have to put up with these noxious effects are not compensated in any way. It is the task of the economist, therefore, to bring them, as Pigou would have said, 'into relation with the measuring rod of money'.

The principle used is the straightforward one of accepting the scale of values of the people directly concerned. The loss of any good —including such 'free' goods as quiet, clean air, pleasant scenery, etc.—is to be valued, therefore, at the minimum sum people would be willing to accept as just compensation for their loss. These spill-over costs, together with resource costs, have to be less than the value of the total benefits if an investment is to be accepted as economically feasible.

Although the principle is straightforward enough, difficulties are encountered in obtaining reliable approximations to the value of spill-over effects. In attempting to evaluate aircraft noise, for example, the Roskill Commission made use (among other information) of replies to a questionnaire by a sample of those householders who would have to move if their neighbourhood were to be taken over for the third airport site. The key question was framed as follows:

Suppose that your house was wanted to form part of a large development scheme and the developer offered to buy it from you, what price would be just high enough to compensate you for leaving this house (flat) and moving to another area?

A number of weaknesses are apparent in the Commission's procedure.[4] First, although 8 per cent of the householders interviewed asserted that they would not move at any price, the compensatory sum attributed to them was an arbitrary £5,000. One suspects that a good interviewer might well have elicited a finite sum from them, though one probably well in excess of £5,000. If, however, it were true only of a single case that nothing money could buy would suffice to compensate for the losses suffered in moving from the neighbourhood, then, strictly speaking, no cost–benefit analysis would admit a third London airport.

[3] Though spill-over effects can also be beneficial, their treatment is symmetric with that of adverse spill-over effects.

[4] For a highly critical appraisal of the Roskill Commission's Report, the reader is referred to my paper, 'What is Wrong with Roskill?', first published in the *Journal of Transport Economics and Policy* (Sept. 1970), and reprinted as reading 17 below.

Secondly, no allowance was made for the disturbance suffered by people subjected to aerial disturbance below 35 NNI (NNI is an abbreviation for noise and number index and was developed as an index of aircraft annoyance by the Committee on the Problem of Noise). Symmetry of treatment would require that no benefits be entered for people whose enjoyment of an air journey fell below a particular point on some arbitrary index. No physical measure of pleasure is available, however, so that no matter how impulsive the decision, and no matter how marginal the benefit, each trip was valued at its full fare. Finally, the framing of the question gave the impression to householders that only a limited move was contemplated—a question of making land available for some new development. The disruption involved in parting from old friends, in changing jobs, in moving the children to new schools, may not have occurred to them. What is more, even if the purpose of the questionnaire had been made perfectly explicit, the compensatory sum required by the family would vary with circumstances about which it could not hope to have accurate information. The sum would be smallest if as quiet a neighbourhood could be found only a short distance away. It would be larger if the number of such neighbourhoods within commuting distance of work and schooling were limited. And it would be largest if no comparable neighbourhoods could be found anywhere. Again, the compensatory sum would vary according to the spread and intensity of traffic noise expected elsewhere over the future, being lower for expectations of a gradual abatement than for the reverse, and more likely, expectations. If, however, the spread of noise were expected to engulf the original neighbourhood in any case, then, with respect to the noise factor, it would not matter where the family moved, and the sum would be nil—notwithstanding which the family's welfare would decline over time, though not as a result alone of the establishment of a third London airport.

The Problem of Constraints

In any cost—benefit analysis there will be a number of political or institutional conditions, more or less restrictive, which the economist has to accept. The issues they raise can be illustrated by the unlikely example of a man lawfully installing a steam hammer in his back yard. In response to the outcry, the enterprising town council hires an economist to undertake a cost–benefit study to determine whether all the houses in the neighbourhood should be sound-proofed. The total costs of the sound-proofing of all the houses affected is reckoned at £85,000. But, since the benefits over the future of the sound-proofing are reckoned to exceed £100,000, the scheme is approved.

If the economist were able to move away from his terms of reference, however, he would propose a court order preventing the operation of the steam hammer. The loss by the would-be entrepreneur might be of the order of, say, £1,000 a year or a capital value of £15,000, but the savings to the rest of the community would be £85,000. Indeed, in the absence of the court order, the council should be willing to pay the £15,000 to bribe the man not to operate his steam hammer—provided the law is able to uphold such contracts. The trouble about bribing a potential offender where the law is permissive of noise and smoke pollution is that it lends itself inadvertently to blackmail.

Consider now a more topical example: a proposal to widen a road so as to allow for three lanes of traffic each way, instead of the existing two. As before, the economist, keeping strictly to his terms of reference, may come up with a positive figure for the benefit 'enjoyed'. Allowed more latitude, however, he might point out that the traffic is already so heavy on the two-lane highway that a sizeable net gain can be achieved by a system of tolls, or taxes, calculated to reduce the traffic to an 'optimal flow'. Once the traffic approaches this level, it may transpire that an efficient public transport service is profitable and, in these new circumstances, a cost–benefit calculation can no longer justify the road-widening scheme. Moreover, the economist might wish to point out that the improvement of an existing rail service would cost much less, and yield at least as much benefit, as the road-widening scheme.

Such alternatives, however, will not emerge if the economist has to work strictly within his terms of reference or if, for political reasons, the alternatives are to be regarded as 'impractical'. Indeed, it is not too often that the economist is asked to consider all alternatives relevant to a broad problem before choosing that which offers the greatest net benefit to the community. It is more common to enlist his expertise in order to reach a decision about a particular kind of investment. Yet no matter how uneconomic they are, if political or administrative constraints are expected to remain operative during the period of time covered by the cost–benefit calculation, the economist has no choice but to accept them as part of the data.

CRITERIA FOR INVESTMENT PROJECTS

The benefits from an investment project by the government come to fruition over the future, and some of the costs may also be incurred over the future. In general, then, there is a distinct 'time-profile' of benefits and costs corresponding to each of the investment projects under consideration. Thus, the time-profile for one project may have large net benefits during, say, the first three years and small net benefits thereafter. For another project, the time-profile may be the reverse of this. Yet a third project may have more modest net benefits spread evenly over a longer period than the other two. For an unambiguous comparison of the value of such projects it is clearly necessary to reduce all these time profiles to a single figure.

Of the two usual methods used, the more popular is the discounted present value (DPV) method, which consists of discounting all future benefits and outlays to a present value by means of some appropriate rate of interest. If that rate of interest were, say, 10 per cent per annum, a certain benefit valued at £1,100 next year, or one valued at £1,210 in two years' time, would have a discounted value of £1,000. The alternative method is that of calculating the internal rate of return (IRR) of the stream of future benefits and costs. The resulting figure purports to be an average rate of growth of (the present value of) the sum invested. An IRR of 15 per cent calculated for a twelve-year investment stream indicates an average annual growth rate of 15 per cent per annum of the present value of the total outlay.

An investment criterion can base itself on either of these two methods. If the DPV method is adopted, it might be thought that any public project is economically advantageous if the DPV of its benefits exceeds that of its outlays. Alternatively if the IRR method is adopted it might be thought that any project having an IRR greater than the market rate of return should be undertaken. But it is not so simple as that. In fact, the investment criterion to be adopted depends on three related factors: on political and administrative constraint (on which I have touched earlier); on the uncertainty surrounding the size of expected future benefits and out-lays (which I discuss in the following section); and on the alternative opportunities open to the investible funds which the government raises either by borrowing, by taxation or by a combination of the two.

If, say, it is doubled to raise £10 millions through taxes that fall wholly on current consumption, and to spend this sum among several public projects from a list of approved investment projects, provided it is 'economically justifiable', the task of the economist is straightforward. Suppose he elects to use a DPV criterion. If there is agreement that society as a whole regards the consumption of £105 worth of goods next year as equivalent to the consumption of £100 today, he can use 5 per cent as the appropriate discount rate. Any of the approved projects is then eligible for the short list if, using this 5 per cent rate, the DPV of its benefits exceeds that of its costs. Should it happen that the total cost of the number of public pro-jects that are eligible on this criterion exceeds the £10 millions available, the economist simply ranks the projects in descending order and goes down the list until the total outlay required does not exceed £10 millions.

If, to take another example, it were decided instead to raise the whole of the £10 millions by borrowing (the effect being supposed to reduce private investment by £10 millions) the economist may not regard any public investment as justifiable unless it can earn at least as much as is being earned by private investment. An expec-ted yield of, say, 12 per cent in private investment then justifies his choice of 12 per cent as the appropriate discount rate. Clearly, if only a part of the £10 millions is to be raised by reducing current consumption and the remainder by reducing current private invest-ment, the criterion has to be adapted accordingly. Finally, if there is no constraint whatever placed on the use of the £10 millions then, *no matter how the sum is raised*, the economist is justified in using a dis-count rate of 12 per cent. For now all, or any part of, the £10 mil-lions made available for public projects may be invested instead in the private sector at a 12 per cent yield.

In practice, DPV is the more popular of these two methods, for two reasons: first, the use of IRR criteria occasionally produces a ranking of investment projects contrary to that produced by DPV criteria, and the logic of the DPV method appears unassailable. Secondly, a DPV criterion invariably produces a single benefit–

cost ratio whereas, for some investment streams, there can apparently be more than one internal rate of return.

UNCERTAINTY

In the evaluation of any project there is sure to be some guesswork about the size of future costs and future benefits, arising in the main from technological innovations, shifts in demand and political changes. The problem of how to reach decisions in situations where knowledge of the past affords little guidance for the future is one that continues to attract attention.

The more familiar methods of allowing for future uncertainty may be grouped into two categories: those operating through a choice of the rate of interest in a DPV criterion; and those operating through revisions of expected future prices.

The Rate of Interest

Since the risk of loss is not compensated by an equal chance of gain, one method is to add a percentage point or two on to a pure, or riskless, rate of interest. This was the method, for instance, that was used in evaluating the Channel tunnel project. The benefits were projected up to a 50-year period, and a 7 per cent rate of discount was adopted as being the conventional rate for long-term planning in France and Britain. There is, of course, the practical problem of discovering this riskless rate of interest, to allow for future uncertainty. Although the concept of a riskless rate of interest —one reflecting society's preference of present over future consumption—is clear, the difficulties of measuring it in an existing dynamic economy are formidable. In the event, the riskless rate of interest on long-term government bonds has been proposed as a tolerable proxy (riskless, that is, in respect of default only: obviously, government bonds may fall in value over time, either in money or real terms without any fear of default on the nominal interest payments). This bond rate, it is acknowledged, is likely to be much lower than the current rates of return on commercial investments. But, then, a private firm is more likely to default than a central government.

Whilst this is undoubtedly true, it may not always be relevant, which brings me to the second method of choosing the rate of interest in a DPV calculation: to adopt the rate of return in private industry as the appropriate rate of discount. As those favouring this method point out, any funds raised by the government for public projects can, in principle, at least, always be invested in private industry. Now, the riskier the type of private investment the higher, in general, is the actuarial rate of return—a result arising both from risk-aversion and tax disadvantages under the existing fiscal system. But, whatever the reasons for this higher actuarial return on risky private investment, they do not of themselves weaken the argument. If the placing of government funds in the riskier types of private investment can, in fact, realize over time these higher returns, then no public investment should be undertaken that yields rates of return below them. To the extent, however, that political constraints are imposed on the use of investible public funds, the appropriate rate of discount is below the private investment yield.[5]

Future Prices

We can also allow for risk by estimating or guessing (in addition to the most likely future price, and quantity, of each input and output over the future) upper limits and lower limits. In this way three cost–benefit estimates are produced: a most likely, a most optimistic and a most pessimistic net benefit for each project. Although this is better than a single most likely estimate, it has the distinct disadvantage that the chance of the most likely cost–benefit occurring can turn out to be very small. One can go some way to remedy this by consulting with experts on the likelihood of each uncertain future price or quantity having different values. From such information a 'probability' table can be constructed.

This resulting 'probability' table cannot, of course, be any more accurate than the subjective estimates of the experts on which it is based. But it does bring out the full implications of these estimates, and enables us to say much more than before. In some hypothetical project, we should be able to say, for example, that there is a 90 per cent chance of the net benefit falling between £150,000 and

---

[5] If, as is common, estimated future benefits and costs are calculated in terms of current prices, the market rate of return on private investment has to be deflated for the annual expected price rise. Expectations of a rise in prices of, say, 6 per cent per annum entail a reduction of a nominal yield of, say, 25 per cent per annum to a real yield of approximately 19 per cent per annum.

£210,000; that there is only a 2½ per cent chance of the net benefit being zero or negative, and so on.

If public investment in the economy is large enough to be spread over a great many projects to be undertaken within a year, then it is not unreasonable to decide each project on the basis of a single most likely cost–benefit outcome, using as discount rate the highest average rate of return accruing to risky commercial investment. Such a procedure will tend to produce for public sector investments an average rate of return above that which the same total amount of investment would have obtained if, instead, it had been invested in the private investment sector of the economy.

If, on the other hand, only a few large public investments are undertaken from time to time, it would be advisable to be guided in any decision by the sort of subjective probability table briefly described above.

CONCLUSION

I conclude by summarizing the phases in a cost–benefit study in which judgements may differ. Following the order in which we have treated the subject they are to be found in the choice of which items are to be valued at market prices and which are to be valued at shadow prices; in the methods used to evaluate the shadow prices; in the range of 'intangibles' to be included in the study; in the methods used to evaluate these 'intangibles'; in the choice of an investment criterion; and in the devices used to make allowance for future uncertainty.

It must not, however, be supposed that all such sources of potential discrepancy are of equal importance, or that judgement in the above respects is evenly diffused among all economists. It is probably true to say that it is easier, at present, to secure agreement among economists on the first five of the above phases than on the last. Moreover, for many projects, the differences remaining may have little effect on the final recommendation. Nevertheless, there can be occasions where, as between one economist (or one group of economists) and another, differences in the evaluation of large public projects are critical and arise largely from differences in skill and care.

It is well to bear in mind that, in the present stage of its development, cost–benefit analysis—and, for that matter, all systems analysis—is an imperfect calculus, as much an art as a science or, more precisely, as much a matter of judgement as a technique. In many a large project it is quite possible for an economist to be swayed by prevailing fashions or the public mood or by political biases, conscious or otherwise, in favour of or against the scheme— especially in the choice of prices to be attributed to spill-over effects and in the method used to allow for uncertainty. For this reason, the interests of society are better served by making public not merely the findings of a cost–benefit study, but also the methods employed and the sources of data. Thus, although there may be good reasons for dissatisfaction with the findings of the Roskill Commission, it had the great merit of making its methods explicit.

It remains only to remind the reader that, even if repeated scrutiny by fastidious and disinterested economists confirms the positive findings of cost–benefit study, the question of equity remains to be debated by the public. But there is nothing in the literature of economics to support the current prejudice that considerations of equity should defer to those of allocation.

16

Urban Redevelopment and the Social Cost of Slums: A Survey and Case Study

by T. Newton

INTRODUCTION

This paper, which is written in four distinct parts, expresses the view that a narrow economic criterion based on financial profita-bility is often irrelevant as a basis for decision-making in the public sector. First, it describes an established theoretical framework for the evaluation of urban redevelopment schemes, using the narrow profitability criterion. Secondly, it introduces a specific cost–benefit approach to the analysis of town centre redevelopment projects in Britain. Thirdly, it discusses the view that certain urban conditions (popularly described as 'slum' housing) involve the community in tangible social costs. And fourthly, it describes a recent attempt to devise a methodology aimed at measuring these social costs.

THE ECONOMICS OF URBAN RENEWAL: A NARROW VIEW

The objectives of urban renewal are many and varied. Each type of urban redevelopment process will therefore involve distinct sets of costs and benefits. This paper is concerned with two types of urban renewal which are significant so far as local and central govern-ment in the United Kingdom are concerned, namely, town centre redevelopment, and programmes of slum clearance and rehousing.

From *Cost Benefit Analysis in Administration* (George Allen & Unwin, 1972), pp. 155–75. Reprinted by permission of the publishers.

Generally, their economic problems have the same basic cause, the phenomenon of 'blight'.

The centres of many English towns and cities suffered heavily from bombing during World War II. The devastation of shopping and commercial centres provided a stimulus to large-scale re-development in the late fifties and early sixties. Added to this is the fact that most town centres were just not built to accommodate the huge influx of motor vehicles experienced in the sixties. This and other changes in social behaviour led many planners to believe that the outworn fabric of our town centres had to be replaced to cater for new demands. One interesting fact has, however, emerged from personal observation of the process of town centre redevelopment; this is that really large-scale and comprehensive redevelopment has not been an activity which the private market has been eager to promote (with certain notable exceptions, e.g. in London and one or two other large cities). It has been left to the local authorities to secure 'integrated' redevelopment of town centres, often at a finan-cial cost to themselves as a result of subsidizing private enterprise.

Part of the explanation of this phenomenon may lie in an analysis of the causes of blight—especially housing blight. The problems of areas of old housing are, on the surface, similar in many respects to the problems of obsolescent town centres. The impact of industry and motor vehicles added to the factors of age and condition of the housing stock have had the result of turning many areas of housing (usually those areas in or near city centres) into 'slums'. The terms 'blight' and 'slum' are often used synonymously. However, this is based on a confusion of the *ethical* and the *economic*. The word 'slum' has ethical and emotional connotations which in many respects defy objective analysis. The word 'blight' refers to a market situation which can be explained in economic terms. It is not to be confused with so-called 'planning blight' which can arise in an area because of local authority planning procedures. Whinston and Davis in their study 'The Economics of Urban Renewal',[1] attempted to de-fine the nature of and explain the existence and persistence of blighted areas. Their objective in doing so was to provide a cost–benefit criterion to be used in evaluating urban renewal programmes.

Blight stems essentially from a situation where individual property owners, *acting rationally*, fail to keep their property in a state of

[1] O. A. Davis and A. B. Whinston, 'The Economics of Urban Renewal', *Law and Contemporary Problems* (Winter 1961).

adequate repair. Continuance of this kind of behaviour results in blighted property, and if neighbouring owners pursue such a course of action a whole neighbourhood may become blighted. Whinston and Davis stated three conditions by which blighted property could be identified. These are where:

(1) strictly individual action does not result in redevelopment;
(2) the co-ordination of decision-making via some means could result in redevelopment;
(3) the sum of benefits from renewal could exceed the sum of costs.

Why these conditions are important is now examined.

The slum clearance and rehousing programme of a local authority is a response to a number of pressures. In economic terms, it is a response to a peculiarity of the urban property market. The value of a piece of property, like a house, depends not only on its structural condition but also on attributes of the neighbourhood in which it is located. That part of the value which is due to its *location* is called the 'neighbourhood effect value'. To maintain or increase the neighbourhood effect value requires the co-ordination of decisions of property owners as to repairs and improvement of their properties. Where such co-ordination is not possible, an individual property owner may reason that the benefits of repairs and improvements to his property may not exceed the costs of such repairs and improvements and so refrain from keeping his property in an acceptable state of repair.

The decisive factor in the mind of the property owner in reaching his decision is the state of repair and the improvements needed in surrounding properties. These may be such that the individual considers that they depress the neighbourhood effect value of his property so much that he has nothing to gain by committing his own resources to repairs and improvement. The paradox of this decision is that other property owners in the neighbourhood reason along the same lines and come to a similar conclusion about their own properties. The net effect of *all* their decisions is to lead to underestimation of the benefits to be gained from repairs and improvements. If, by chance, all had simultaneously engaged in repairs and improvements, the effect would be an increase in the neighbourhood effect value of each property. A like result could be produced if some means of co-ordination of individual decision-making had been visible. An important consequence of an individualistic calculation about the allocation of resources to repairs and improvements to properties in a neighbourhood is that it can result in a vicious circle of deteriorating structures changing the image of the neighbourhood, thereby reducing further the neighbourhood effect value of properties. This, in turn, may lead to further underestimation of the benefits of repairs and improvements needed, and so the vicious circle continues. The key feature of a blighted area is that co-ordination of decisions may result in the benefits of repairs and improvements exceeding the cost of such repairs and improvements. In the absence of co-ordination, the benefits are likely to be less than costs. Finding a means of co-operation is the key problem. Voluntary co-operation may or may not be too difficult where there are a few properties concerned. However, where there are a large number of properties, such co-operation is most improbable as some property owners may reason correctly that by opting out of a repair and development scheme they can realize some of the benefits of the decisions of other property owners without incurring any of the costs.

With voluntary co-operation unlikely to succeed, the next seemingly obvious solution is for a private developer to buy out all the properties and profitably undertake repairs and improvements. Such private development is likely to be frustrated by price gouging and stubborn tenants. Price gouging is particularly important where assembling tracts of land is an essential condition for re-development.

Voluntary co-ordination has, therefore, practical difficulties which would not exist if there were only one property owner, but a single property owner's attempts to develop may be frustrated. Unless these difficulties can be eliminated, a blighted area will persist. In these circumstances there is a role for the public sector. In some cases, the extreme position can be avoided by the application by local authorities of codes as to minimum standards of repair and upkeep of property, although such codes are extremely difficult to apply in practice. However, areas which are already severely blighted cannot be treated by preventive policies and the more usual action is for a local authority to use its powers of compulsory purchase in order to gain ownership of the whole area and engage in comprehensive demolition and redevelopment.

The whole point of cost–benefit analysis is to provide local authorities with a criterion with which they can make choices about priorities for redevelopment. Clearly, some areas are more blighted than others and the benefits of redevelopment may therefore be correspondingly higher. The criterion suggested by Whinston and Davis is one which considers solely the revenues and expenditures of a redevelopment project as the relevant benefits and costs. Their cost–benefit framework is a simple 'profit and loss account' (see Table 1), counting only the financial costs and benefits accruing to the local authority.

TABLE I

Benefits	Costs
1. Receipts from sale of land to private developers.	1. Acquisition of land, demolition and site improvement.
2. Net additions to local authority tax revenues.	2. Cost of relocating (and compensating) displaced tenants.
3. Income from public amenities.	

There are two major criticisms to be made of this cost–benefit framework. The first derives from the distinction made earlier between the terms 'blight' and 'slum'. 'Blight' is defined by Whinston and Davis in terms of a misallocation of resources in a neighbourhood, whilst the term 'slum' is used to convey an ethical judgement about the physical conditions of a neighbourhood in which people live. The solution to the problem of blight is by means of a redevelopment programme, whilst the solution to slums may well be achieved by means of an income redistribution policy. However, it can usually be shown empirically that a blighted area contains a preponderance of defective, unsafe, insanitary and overcrowded dwellings—conditions usually associated with the popular conception of a slum. The cost–benefit framework in Table 1 does not identify the wider social effects arising from these conditions. It may well be the case that the spill-over effects of physically poor housing may impose costs on a community. Clearly, these factors should be considered in any cost–benefit analysis of housing redevelopment proposals in order to make the 'best' set of choices. This argument is developed further later in this paper.

The other criticism made of the 'profit and loss criterion' is that it only takes account of the financial benefits and costs accruing to the *local authority*. It makes little attempt to identify the impacts of redevelopment schemes on the many sectors of the community affected, and this sort of information is vital to decision-makers concerned with the complex issues of large-scale redevelopment. One approach to this particular problem is described below.

TOWN CENTRE REDEVELOPMENT: A SPECIAL CASE OF COST—BENEFIT ANALYSIS

The methodology developed by Professor Nathaniel Lichfield is not primarily concerned with *measurement* of benefits and costs, although some progress has been made in this respect. The main emphasis has rather been on the issue of the *incidence* of benefits and costs, i.e. who receives the benefits and who bears the costs of public investment decisions concerned with large-scale redevelopment. This is merely a recognition of the fact that no matter what economists might like to think, decisions on the allocation of public resources are not usually taken on economic grounds alone. In a democratic society, these complex decisions must, in the final analysis, be taken by politicians who are swayed more by *people* than by economic analysis. It is not enough to be told that the discounted net present value of scheme A exceeds that of scheme B. 'Value to the community' is not a meaningful criterion to the politician—he is often more concerned with the effects of public decisions on groups of people *within* it.

Town centre redevelopment is a perfect example of a complex decision situation which responds to this sort of analysis. A town centre scheme affects many different (and overlapping) sectors of the community: shoppers, shopkeepers, pedestrians, car drivers, house owners, office workers and many others. Apart from considering how any redevelopment scheme is likely to affect these groups of people, the decision-maker will have to weigh other factors, some of which are tangible (e.g. the effect on the finances of the local authority), and some of which are rather more imponderable (e.g. the 'prestige' value of any scheme). The rest of this section describes briefly how Lichfield treats some of these complex issues and how the decision-making process can be assisted by the drawing up of a 'planning balance sheet' which attempts to present the choice to be made in terms of the effects of a decision on different groups and organizations within the local community.

As stated earlier, the essence of Lichfield's methodology is to identify the impacts of a redevelopment scheme on various homogeneous groups within the community, and wherever possible to make a comparative assessment of these impacts in quantitative terms. The corollary to this, of course, is that the decision-maker, faced with this information, is able to make a choice in the light of the weight or significance he attaches to each of the various sectors of the community identified in the analysis.

The first stage in the analysis is to enumerate the various groups affected by the project. These are classified as either 'producers' (groups who produce or operate the project) or 'consumers' (groups who consume the services produced by the project). So far as is possible, each producer is linked directly to a consumer; for instance, in the case of a town centre redevelopment project, current property owners who are to be displaced are classed as producers and the new occupiers are classed as the corresponding consumers. Each pair of producers and consumers may be considered as engaging in a 'transaction', as a result of which each side incurs costs and receives benefits. These costs and benefits can be valued in many cases at market prices, especially so far as producers (e.g. local authorities) are concerned. However, some categories of costs and benefits to consumers have no market price. In these cases, Lichfield advocates that they should be included in the planning balance sheet as dimensions of utility or welfare (usually a crude ranking or preference system). It is recognized that failure to measure these costs and benefits in monetary terms places a limitation on the planning balance sheet as a basis for decision-making. However, there is no doubt that this approach highlights the number and the kind of value judgements which the decision-maker has to make in coming to a final decision. The balance sheet presents for his information all the groups involved in a public decision, and the differences in all their respective costs and benefits (where possible in absolute monetary terms, or otherwise in relative terms). With this information, he is in a position to make a decision in accordance with some concept of 'equity', and he is able to discern the cost (if any) of the decision in terms of 'efficiency'.

THE SOCIAL COST OF SLUMS: A SURVEY

In addition to identifying the impact of redevelopment proposals on various groups in the community, it is obviously important to make some attempt to measure the spill-over costs and benefits involved in the decision, many of which are usually considered as 'intangible'. The narrow profit-and-loss criterion does not take account of these wider social effects and little research has been undertaken to *measure* the spill-over effects of slum housing redevelopment.

The association of certain social effects and slum housing conditions has fascinated researchers for many years. Many empirical studies have shown (especially in the U.S.A.) that slum areas exhibit rates of illegitimacy, juvenile delinquency, violent crime, mental illness, residential fires, tuberculosis and other communicable diseases far in excess of the average for major cities. The data shown in Table 2 relating to Los Angeles in 1944 are typical. Ignoring for the moment the issue of *causality* (i.e. do slum housing conditions create these social pathologies?), the association of housing conditions and social pathology clearly has implications for local authorities, concerned as they are with the provision of public services to alleviate ill-health and to combat crime and fire.

TABLE 2

Incidence per 10,000 Persons

	Blighted area	'Good' area
Tuberculosis	705	91
Communicable diseases	69	14
Venereal diseases	13	1
Health service visits	356	54
Fire alarms	256	142
Police arrests	350	100
Juvenile delinquency cases	69	10

Source: J. Rumney, 'The Social Cost of Slums', *Journal of Social Issues*, vol. 7 (1951), Nos. 1–2.

Rothenberg was one of the earliest writers to consider this question in cost–benefit terms.[2] He saw two types of social costs arising from slums: costs to the slum dwellers themselves and costs to the community at large. His view is summarized as follows:

Given overcrowding, filth and inadequate sanitary facilities, slums are a health menace, increasing the frequency and severity of illness for both inhabitants and outsiders through contagion. Through subsidized medical

[2] J. Rothenberg, *Economic Evaluation of Urban Renewal* (Washington, D.C.: Brookings Institution, 1967).

care for some slum dwellers, the costs are borne in part by the tax payer. Other costs are borne at large through the effect of illness on the welfare of individual citizens and on the overall productivity of the economy.

Slums breed crime: overcrowding and lack of privacy tends to undermine respect for the individual and for property, create frustration over the constant obtrusion of others, and promote opportunities for crime and recruitment into criminal sub-cultures.

Personality difficulties result from poverty, despair and bitterness, and hinder many in their attempts later in life to join the dominant culture of society.

Such a generalized statement is, however, of only limited assistance in practical terms. The real crux of the problem, is, of course, as always in cost–benefit analysis, the *measurement* of social cost. If we enumerate the social costs of slums as (*a*) increased fire hazards, (*b*) increased menace to health and social welfare of inhabitants of the slums and the city or town in which they are treated, (*c*) increased crime rate, and (*d*) personality difficulties, then we must attempt to include meaningful assessments of these factors in any analysis of alternative slum clearance/redevelopment programmes. The next section describes some of the difficulties of quantification which were encountered in our own research exercise. The remainder of this section reviews some earlier empirical studies which provided valuable insights into some of the problems.

Although Rothenberg was one of the first to see the relevance of social costs to the selection of housing redevelopment projects, he was not notably successful in providing quantitative estimates of such costs for use in analysis. Table 3 shows the cost–benefit framework used in his appraisal of five housing redevelopment projects. Clearly, the part of the analysis which was capable of evaluation is very similar to the narrow profitability criterion of Whinston and Davis. Item 2(*b*), the spill-over effect on neighbouring land, is included in the analysis on the argument that the value of the housing services provided by a dwelling unit is a function not only of the unit itself, but also of the character of the surrounding neighbourhood (this is what Whinston and Davis call the neighbourhood effect value). A redevelopment project will therefore lead to an improvement in quality of *surrounding* dwelling units, and this improvement should be included as a social benefit in the analysis. The twin problems of determining the extent of the 'impact neighbourhood' (the cut-off point) and measuring the improvement benefit were found by

TABLE 3

Benefit Cost Summary of Five Redevelopment Projects in Chicago
($000)

Benefit and cost categories	Blue Island	Hyde Park 'B'	Hyde Park 'A'	Michael Rees	Lake Meadows
1. Resource cost of project					
(a) Gross project costs	396	638	10,534	6,235	16,761
(b) Less initial value of land	46	49	6,449	1,596	8,777
(c) Total resource costs	350	589	4,085	4,639	7,984
2. Benefits produced by the project					
(a) Increased productivity of site land	29	30	5,016	1,719	12,711
(b) Increased productivity of neighbouring real estate (spill-over)	+	+	+	+	+
(c) Decreased social costs associated with slums	+	+	+	+	+
3. Total costs not offset by site land benefit (1c−2a)	321	559	−931 (gain)	2,920	−4,727 (gain)

Rothenberg to be extremely complex and, although methods of solving the problems were suggested, no numerical results were obtained for inclusion in the Table. So far as item 2(c) is concerned, Rothenberg was content simply to acknowledge that the quantification problem requires a treatment that goes far beyond the scope of his study. However, although no measurements appear in Table 3, he did sketch out the nature of some of the social costs identified earlier (fire risk, health hazard, crime and personality difficulties).

An estimate of the benefit of reduced fire risks may be obtained by comparing the total value of fire damage and the value of fire protection services in slum areas with that in non-slum areas. Property damage data may be available in many cases and the value of human life lost and damaged can be estimated, although some controversy surrounds the issue. Differential fire protection costs can be roughly approximated to actual fire department expenditures, although actual service levels might in any case be inadequate in slum areas as opposed to non-slum areas. The slum health hazard can be measured in two ways: (a) the value of medical goods and services, and (b) the value of human life and costs imposed by illness. Both methods have disadvantages. The level of police protection will probably bear a closer relationship to the amount the public is willing to pay to avoid losses due to crime than the level of services in the two previous categories. However, in practice it would seem reasonable to assume some correlation between the police budget and the cost of crime. The costs of personality and social adjustment difficulties pose very special measurement problems. The influence of housing conditions on family and social relationships cannot be described in terms of black and white, and it is probably wise to be realistic and accept that quantified assessments of these effects are not likely to be forthcoming in the near future.

Another illustration of cost–benefit analysis in redevelopment projects is provided by a study undertaken by Mao[3] in relation to a housing project in East Stockton, California. Table 4 sets out measured benefits and costs of the project.

It will be noted that the Mao Table refers to *tangible* benefits and costs of the project. This is a reminder that only items capable of measurement have been included in the cost–benefit framework. It would seem that Mao has gone somewhat further than Rothenberg in providing monetary estimates of benefits and costs. But many of his measures are not wholly satisfactory from a conceptual point of view. Some figures in Table 4 may therefore be but a crude monetary measure of the appropriate concept.

The Rothenberg and Mao studies relate to renewal or replacement housing projects. Under the provisions of a recent Housing Act greater emphasis is now being placed on rehabilitation instead of renewal. The background to this shift is discussed in *Old Houses into New Homes*.[4] With the passing of this Act there should be

[3] J. C. T. Mao, 'Efficiency in Public Urban Renewal Expenditures through Benefit–Cost Analysis', *Journal of the American Institute of Planners* (Mar. 1966).

[4] Cmnd. 3602 (London: H.M.S.O., 1968).

greater scope for the use of code-enforcement procedures to improve housing conditions. Some of the difficulties of code-enforcement have been mentioned earlier. On the positive side, code-enforcement is usually assumed to be the least costly and most convenient method

TABLE 4

Summary of Tangible Social Benefits and Costs of the East Stockton Urban Renewal Project

($000)

Benefit	Amount ($)	Cost	Amount ($)
1. Increase in the value of project area land	228	1. Survey and planning	113
2. Increase in the value of neighbourhood properties	416	2. Project execution expenditures	
		(a) Administrative, travel and office furniture	202
3. Value of public improvements: schools and parks*	823	(b) Legal services	114
		(c) Acquisition expenses, salaries of relocation staff and other related items	387
4. Reductions in costs of municipal services		(d) Site clearance	93
(a) Savings in fire protection cost	700	(e) Disposal, lease, retention costs	59
(b) Savings in health protection costs	425	(f) Project inspection	33
(c) Savings in police protection cost	1,167	(g) Value of improvements demolished	2,342
		3. Site improvements	701
		4. Public and supporting facilities	552
		5. Relocation payments	85
	3,759		4,681

* It is assumed that these public investments have social values equal to their costs. On the right side of the Table, these costs are included under 3 and 4 (dates of reckoning have been omitted).

for both the city and its property owners to achieve better quality housing, whilst lessening the threats to public health and safety posed by decayed housing. The merits and demerits of code-enforcement have long been argued, but in the end the advantages one way or the other can only be resolved by examining a code-enforcement project against a renewal project for the neighbourhood in question.

The main problem then is to decide a cost–benefit framework for a code-enforcement renewal programme. Case[5] suggests a possible framework and provides estimates of tangible costs and benefits for a project relating to the Beacon Light District in California. The results are summarized in Table 5.

TABLE 5

Estimated Tangible Costs and Benefits of a 10-Year Code Enforcement, Neighbourhood Rehabilitation, and Property Conservation Programme, Beacon Light District, 1965

Estimated costs	$000
1. Costs of administering the programme	2,100
2. Public expenditures to provide improved public services and facilities	11,500
3. Private expenditures	
(a) Repairs and rehabilitation of properties	8,100
(b) Demolitions	900
Total estimated costs	22,600
Estimated benefits	
1. Reduction in city service costs	6,900
2. Increases in private property values	31,900
3. Increases in property tax revenues	6,400
Total estimated benefits	45,200

Before leaving Case's results, it is of interest to reproduce some other results from his paper. The Beacon Light District, he notes, conforms to the pattern of a blighted area. Public expenditures are much greater and tax revenues much lower than in other areas of the City of Los Angeles, as can be seen from the data in Table 6. The collection of this type of information is a prerequisite to the use of cost–benefit analysis in housing project selection, but as anyone with a cursory knowledge of local government finance will

[5] F. E. Case, 'Code Enforcement in Urban Renewal', *Urban Studies*, vol. 5 (Nov. 1968), No. 3.

know, requests for information of this type are likely to be met with a blank stare by treasurers and accountants in many local authorities in Britain.

The role of cost–benefit analysis as reviewed here places emphasis on the spill-over or external effects associated with unsatisfactory housing conditions. These effects are reflected in *real* costs, not only

TABLE 6

Direct per capita Expenditures in the Beacon Light Study Area, 1965

per capita cost

Beacon Light

Type of expenditure	Dollar totals	As percentage of Los Angeles expense	City of Los Angeles
	($)	(%)	($)
Police	36·87	180	20·49
Refuge and sewage disposal	4·34	100	4·34
Public assistance	34·58	864	4·00
Fire service	14·04	105	13·33
Parks and recreation	3·90	84	4·52
Street maintenance	7·16	100	7·16
Education	5,020·86	153	3,280·97
Health	4·48	188	2·38
Other items	24·60	100	24·60

to the individuals living in them and the local community, but also to the wider community of which they are a part. Which categories of externalities are important in British housing conditions is difficult to say. The subjective evidence of social workers in the field varies, whilst quantitative evidence is scanty and results can usually be queried on methodological grounds. This raises the whole question of causality which has been neglected until now. The causal relationship between slum living and external social costs is complicated and interrelated with other causal factors. For example, standards of health are influenced by such factors as income, occupation, ethnic background, age and environment, factors which *themselves* are interrelated. Fire risk is not only a function of housing conditions, it depends also on human behaviour. A redevelopment project may demolish buildings, but it only *redistributes* the human population. Furthermore, information about these factors, whether qualitive or quantitative, is often imprecise and the probabilistic element in the relationships makes it difficult to distinguish between pure chance and significant variations. Most of the empirical studies which have been carried out have found that shifting social factors tend to obscure the statistical relationships found between classes of housing conditions and health. What *is* certain is that an enormous research effort will be needed to make any impact on these problems.

THE HARINGEY CASE STUDY

The Haringey study was an attempt to examine the problems of measuring the social cost of slums. It is necessary, however, to make one initial qualification to what follows—no serious investigation of the causality issue was attempted. Such an investigation would have required a far more ambitious investment in interdisciplinary research effort than was available to the Royal Institute of Public Administration research team.

The study started from an investigation of a so-called 'twilight area' in the London Borough of Haringey. The houses in the area were 70–90 years old and generally too large for single family use. The area was experiencing a great deal of multiple occupation, in the sense that, although houses became occupied by several households, they were not physically adapted to maintain acceptable standards. The *structural* condition of most of the houses was reasonably good and many of them had a remaining life of 25–30 years. From a policy point of view, three alternative solutions were possible:

(1) undertake early comprehensive rehabilitation of the area;
(2) undertake early demolition and renewal;
(3) postpone demolition and undertake renewal at a future date when constraints on (2) are not operative.

Using a purely financial investment criterion, the choice between (1) and (2) could be determined along lines suggested by formulae developed by Needleman.[6] Such formulae were subsequently in-

---

[6] L. Needleman. 'Comparative Economics of Improvement and New Building', *Urban Studies*, vol. 6 (June 1969), No. 2.

corporated into Ministry of Housing and Local Government Circular 65/69 under the 1969 Housing Act which followed up *Old Houses into New Homes*. However, because of constraints, only (1) and (3) could be considered as feasible policy alternatives. Under a postponed renewal policy, the council would merely have been required to maintain minimum code-enforcement standards (with regard to health, sanitation, fire regulations, multiple occupation, etc.). The question therefore arose as to whether this kind of policy would result in significant *social* costs to the community which might be avoided if *immediate* comprehensive rehabilitation were undertaken. It is this question to which our study was addressed.

There were two distinct parts to the problem. First, it was necessary to assess the externalities of bad housing conditions in *physical* terms. Secondly, it was thought desirable to evaluate these externalities in terms of money in order to assess the scale of social cost incurred. We saw earlier that previous American research into these questions had not gone very far, so any attempt to identify even the existence of these externalities in British conditions clearly had to start in unexplored territory. Our first objective, therefore, was to determine by empirical investigation whether the general statements about bad housing conditions and their alleged externalities could be supported. The original intention was to undertake an exercise similar to that illustrated in Table 2, i.e. some kind of cross-sectional analysis to determine whether areas of 'bad' housing exhibited different social characteristics from areas of 'good' housing. The first major difficulty presented itself immediately. The problems involved in delineating 'bad' and 'good' housing areas proved to be a major obstacle and so the scope of our inquiry had to be widened to attempt to provide a measure of housing quality against which to compare measures of the physical incidence of externalities.

The objective of the case study was therefore an extremely limited one in terms of cost–benefit analysis. In a nutshell, it was to explore the feasibility of estimating statistically significant relationships between quantitative measures of housing quality and various aspects of social behaviour which could be described as spill-over effects of housing conditions. Our feeling was that if a link could be established between housing quality and such factors as crime rates, fire incidence and other social pathologies, then knowledge of the impact of public investments designed to improve housing standards would have taken a step forward, paving the way for more ambitious attempts at cost–benefit analysis in this field.

In the light of the novelty of the study, to us at least, a pragmatic approach seemed to offer a fruitful source of investigation. This took the form of contacting departments of the local authority and other community services as seemed appropriate (police, probation and fire services). It became apparent from discussions with many of the officers of the services concerned that there was no clear answer to the causality aspect of the study. Experiences of different officers varied; however, it became clear that any investigation in depth would require the examination of a wide range of data. This was not always possible because of confidentiality requirements, the type of data kept by the service departments and the length of time records were kept, as well as the form in which they were kept. The striking feature that emerged was the absence of comprehensive information systems likely to be of use in cost–benefit studies. The data collected are summarized in Appendices 1 and 2. It is important to emphasize that the data collected represent what it was possible to collect over a period of nine months with the co-operation of several local authority departments and the police, probation and fire services.

From the outset it was clear that it was not operationally useful to talk about 'slums' and 'twilight areas'. Instead, it was decided to think in terms of an index of housing quality, and therefore the first task was to find criteria for measuring housing quality. An examination of previous attempts to do this revealed a broad measure of agreement on the principal factors to be considered, namely, the level of amenities offered by a housing structure, its physical condition, and the intensity at which it is used, i.e. the level of occupation. However, the *relative* contribution of each of these factors to the *over-all* assessment of housing quality is a matter which has to be agreed. In the construction of an index of housing quality, a system based upon penalty scores for deficiencies is often favoured, and this was the approach we adopted. In the absence of a universally agreed weighting system, we decided to allot a penalty weight to each deficiency in accordance with our own value judgements, (these weights are shown in Appendix 1). It was felt that factors associated with the *level of occupation* were of greater significance in the assessment of housing quality than the physical condition of the dwelling structure (i.e. state of internal and external repair), which in turn was considered to be more important than the lack of any single amenity such as a bath or shower. (It is a matter of simple arithmetic to recalculate the index with different penalty weights.)

The index shown at Appendix 1 is based on *weighted* housing penalty scores for the *electoral wards* of the London Borough of Haringey. The use of such large areas was an unfortunate necessity, governed more by considerations of data availability and compatibility than by the research objectives. Data from two secondary sources (the 1966 Census and the Housing Age and Condition Survey of the G.L.C.) were used to obtain measures of the percentage of the housing stock in each ward which was 'deficient' in any of the indicators of housing quality covered by the index. This percentage was then multiplied by the penalty weight assigned to that deficiency to produce a penalty score. Consider as an example hot water facilities: 8·2 per cent of the dwellings in ward A were shown to have no hot water facility; the penalty weight assigned to this deficiency was 6, and the penalty score for the deficiency was calculated as 49·2 (8·2 × 6). Individual penalty scores were aggregated first to give penalty scores for amenities, condition and occupancy, which together made up the total penalty score on which wards were ranked. The lowest penalty score (ward A) indicates the highest level of housing quality (ranked 1) and vice versa.

The index revealed a number of interesting features. The ward rankings produced bore a close resemblance, at least at the two extremes of the scale, to subjective assessments of comparative housing conditions made by the council's officers. This fact encourages the opinion that the factors included in the index and the penalty weights assigned to each are reasonable as a basis for quantitative assessment. It is also clear that there is no consistent relationship between existence of amenities, the condition of dwellings, and the level of overcrowding. The area designated as a twilight area has a high penalty score, and the ward of which it forms a part is ranked eighteenth in terms of over-all housing quality. However, its major deficiency is shown to be the high percentage of above-average occupancy levels and shared accommodation; in this respect, it is by far the worst area in the Borough. In terms of amenities and physical conditions, however, it is by no means abnormal.

Having established a basis for a quantitative inter-ward comparison of housing quality, the next stage in the exercise was to obtain measures of various social activities which may give rise to external effects. If it could be shown that wards with 'poor' housing quality produced a high incidence of certain social pathologies, a *prima facie* case could ultimately be put forward for the measurement of housing externalities in so far as they involve resource costs to the community.

We were able to obtain data for only five types of social pathology. Appendix 2 ranks wards in terms of these five characteristics, which are discussed individually below. It is important to emphasize that there was nothing definitive about selecting these particular types of social stress; it merely happened that we were able to collect and process data relating to them.

Several studies undertaken in the United States have indicated the existence of a significant statistical relationship between slum housing conditions and high crime rates. For this reason, considerable effort was put into analysing crime in Haringey by ward areas in the hope that the pattern which emerged would bear some resemblance to comparative housing quality. The results clearly disappointed our hopes for they do not support a consistent relationship between our measures of housing conditions and crime rates experienced in the electoral wards of Haringey. For instance, the area with the best housing conditions, ward A, is almost the worst area in terms of crimes committed per thousand population, and the worst housing area ranks only midway in the crime table. However, these rather confused results may in large part be explained by the type of data available. The available data related to the physical incidence of indictable crime in Haringey in 1966. This information was then analysed by ward and the result gives a picture of the location and incidence of crime in the borough. It is not, therefore, surprising that the figures show that the area offering the richest pickings attracts a lot of crime. Ideally, the measure of crime which should have been used is not one based upon the geographical location of the offence, but one based on the neighbourhood of origin of the *criminal*. It was unfortunately not possible to obtain such information for two reasons: (*a*) it would require a 100 per cent detection rate for all types of crime—for obvious reasons such a detection rate is not practicable, and (*b*) it is police policy not to disclose the addresses of criminals in research exercises of this nature. In fact, therefore, our statistics relate only to the neighbourhood origin of reported crime and the use of this measure in U.K.

conditions may well have blurred the statistical evidence. A more detailed analysis of the data did reveal some evidence of a link between bad housing conditions and certain types of crime, notably some categories of petty larceny (stealing milk bottles and robbing gas meters!). However, factors such as police 'purges' on certain offences (e.g. shoplifting) tended to further distort the figures. One final point to be made is that parallels with American experience in this field are rather dangerous. Compared with crime rates in the U.S.A., the situation in Britain, especially in the area of *violent* larceny and physical assault which might reasonably be considered as 'slum-oriented', is nothing like so bad. In these circumstances it is not altogether surprising that our results did not tend to confirm the results of similar investigations in the United States.

Data on juvenile delinquency in the Borough were also collected. The data made available related to the *stock* of cases on the books of the Probation Service at the end of 1968. Once again, the data were not ideal—it is clear that the Probation Service does not deal with *all* delinquents but only with those who are apprehended and assigned to probation officers by the courts. However, this time we were at least able to obtain information on the location of the delinquent rather than the location of the offence. However, once again the results are not consistent with our initial hypothesis. It was clear from talking to probation officers at the outset that the major problem areas for juvenile delinquency were not the areas with the worst physical housing conditions. They considered that post-war housing estates with their relative lack of social and community facilities for young people had the worst record of juvenile delinquency. Our investigation confirmed this. Wards C, I and L all include substantial areas of local authority housing and exhibit relatively low levels of housing stress. Yet the delinquency problems in these areas are more serious than in many areas with poorer housing conditions.

The data and results relating to the incidence of fires were more encouraging. It is possible to detect a positive relationship between housing quality and fire incidence by examining the respective ward rankings in Appendix 2, e.g. ward A is the best housing ward and ranks second so far as fire incidence is concerned. (A rank correlation exercise produced a coefficient of rank correlation of 0·62.) However, it was not possible to analyse the fire data by cause of fire, i.e. chimney fires and fires caused by cooking were included along with types of fire which could be caused by bad housing conditions, e.g. fires caused by oil heating appliances and faulty electrical wiring. If it had been possible to isolate these occurrences, it seems probable that a more detailed analysis would have improved the results.

The other broad area for which we were able to collect data was the local authority social services, i.e. the welfare of the aged and the care of deprived children. The results in Appendix 2 do not show a consistent positive relationship between the incidence of children or old people taken into local authority care and the quality of housing. Yet again, there are obviously many causal factors involved and housing condition is likely to be only one of them, especially in regard to the incidence of children taken into care through the influence of bad housing on parental relationships and personality difficulties.

In considering other possible areas of social behaviour in which housing might be considered a factor, discussions were held with officers of several departments of the local authority. Data problems became a serious constraint at this stage. The impact of housing conditions on health, both physical and mental, was clearly a strong contender for investigation. However, it proved impossible to collect the necessary data during the course of the study. Certain diseases, notably tuberculosis, are nurtured in conditions of dark and damp housing, and improvements in domestic sanitation have of course played an important part in reducing the incidence of other diseases in this country. In the absence of empirical investigation, it is only possible to speculate that a significant link between housing and physical health would not be substantiated, except possibly in very small and localized areas of appallingly low housing quality. Fortunately, areas of this type are relatively few and far between in our cities today.

The case of *mental* health is rather different. It seems likely that housing conditions play an important part in many kinds of mental illness. However, it is not necessarily the *quality*, as measured by our index, which is the key factor—modern blocks of high-rise apartments would clearly score a low mark for housing deficiency as defined here. There is increasing evidence that the breakdown of traditional community relationships (often seen at their best in so-called 'slum' areas) is the basic causal factor in many cases of mental illness. This should serve as a salutary reminder to the planners that merely to improve the quality of the *physical* environment does not by itself guarantee an improvement in the 'quality of life'.

One final area which we hoped would produce numerical results is concerned with the educational development of children. However, in the event, it was not possible to obtain data. In any case we found considerable difficulty in establishing which sort of data available to us could be used as a surrogate for educational achievement. Many educational experts now believe that poor housing

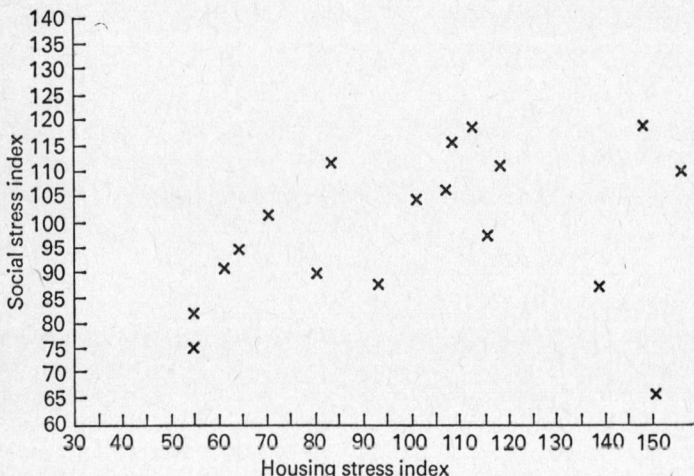

FIG. 1. Relationship between social stress and housing stress.

conditions, especially over-crowding, have a major influence on a child's educational standards. The causal element involved here is intuitively more obvious than in most of the other social characteristics considered in this study and, with hindsight, it is clear that the research should have concentrated more heavily on this aspect.

Appendix 3 is an attempt to summarize all the results in order to compare an index of social stress with the index of housing stress. The indices are different from those in Appendices 1 and 2 in that each ward is expressed as a percentage of the whole borough average. In spite of the fact that no positive relationship between the two indices can be claimed in terms of *statistical* significance, it is clear from Figure 1 that social stress generally does increase with housing stress.

This is not a particularly world-shattering conclusion, yet it does give some basis for encouragement of further work in this field. Such research will need to overcome two major difficulties (*a*) the problems of establishing purely *quantitative* measures of social pathologies, and (*b*) the shortcomings of much of the available data. Both types of problem were experienced during this exercise. However, the statistical validity of the results would probably have been much improved if data relating to smaller geographical areas than electoral wards could have been used. Most of the wards contained a mixture of different types of housing, exhibiting fairly wide-ranging conditions. It is possible that analysis of data by enumeration distinct might have produced more positive correlations of housing quality with some of the social pathologies identified. It is certainly probable that analysis on these lines would provide local authorities with a useful guide to establishing priorities in policies for housing renewal and rehabilitation.

Nevertheless, the final conclusion must be that we are a long way from applying cost–benefit analysis as defined by Prest and Turvey[7] to problems in the housing and social fields. This study can only be regarded as a crude first experimental step. Nevertheless, it has provided an insight into some of the conceptual issues to be resolved. More important, it has highlighted some of the operational hurdles likely to be encountered in developing cost–benefit analysis as a working tool in this area of public policy.

FURTHER READING

LICHFIELD, N., *Cost–Benefit Analysis in Urban Redevelopment*, Research Report of the Real Estate Research Programme (Berkeley, Calif., Institute of Business and Economic Research, University of California, 1962).

——'Cost–Benefit Analysis in City Planning', *Journal of the American Institute of Planners*, vol. 26 (Nov. 1960).

——'Cost–Benefit Analysis in Plan Evaluation', *Town Planning Review*, vol. 35 (1964–5).

——*Cost–Benefit Analysis in Town Planning: a Case Study of Cambridge* (Cambridge and Isle of Ely Council, 1966).

——'Cost–Benefit Analysis in Town Planning. A Case Study: Swanely', *Urban Studies* (Nov. 1967).

[7] See *Economic Journal* (Dec. 1965).

—— and McKEAN, R., 'Costs and Benefits from Different View-points' in H. G. Schaller (ed.), *Public Expenditure Decisions in the Urban Community* (Washington, D.C., Resources for the Future, 1963).

—— and MARGOLIS, J., 'Benefit–Cost Analysis as a Tool in Urban Government Decision-Making', in Schaller, op. cit.

APPENDIX I

Housing Quality Index: Haringey Wards

Penalty Scores Based on Weighted Percentage Deficiencies in Housing Amenities, Condition and Occupancy Levels

Penalty weight

Ward	No stove/sink (4)		Share inside w.c. (4)		No inside w.c. (10)		Housing deficiencies Share bath/shower (3)		No bath/shower (10)		Share hot water (3)		No hot water (6)		Total penalty score (Amenities)
	%	Score	%	Score	%	Score	%	Score	%	Score	%	Score	%	Score	
A	1.3	5.2	13.1	52.4	4.1	41.0	14.4	43.2	5.9	59.0	8.2	24.6	8.2	49.2	274.6
B	3.7	14.8	27.1	108.4	2.6	26.0	31.1	93.3	2.0	20.0	11.2	33.6	8.1	48.6	344.7
C	4.6	18.4	35.4	141.6	3.4	34.0	42.0	126.0	1.1	11.0	14.1	42.3	11.8	70.8	444.1
D	6.6	26.4	28.9	115.6	13.4	134.0	30.0	90.0	15.9	159.0	16.5	49.5	18.7	112.2	686.7
E	4.3	17.2	28.1	112.4	13.6	136.0	46.0	138.0	8.6	86.0	20.9	62.7	19.9	119.4	671.7
F	3.8	15.2	21.5	86.0	2.5	25.0	26.0	78.0	1.6	16.0	10.1	30.3	4.0	24.0	274.5
G	4.7	18.8	43.7	174.8	6.5	65.0	55.5	166.5	2.6	26.0	16.3	48.9	16.1	96.6	596.6
H	9.5	38.0	53.5	214.0	5.6	56.0	65.6	196.8	9.7	97.0	29.6	88.8	23.7	142.2	832.8
I	3.6	14.4	3.8	15.2	21.8	218.0	5.9	17.7	19.1	191.0	5.2	15.6	18.5	111.0	582.9
J	1.3	5.2	11.6	46.4	30.4	304.0	11.0	33.0	30.0	300.0	7.1	21.3	28.9	173.4	883.3
K	2.0	8.0	13.4	53.6	11.2	112.0	32.6	97.8	8.2	82.0	13.9	41.7	12.4	74.4	469.5
L	2.3	9.2	13.6	54.4	24.2	242.0	25.8	77.4	23.3	233.0	11.3	33.9	23.5	141.0	790.9
M	1.2	4.8	8.0	32.0	39.2	392.0	6.8	20.4	43.0	430.0	4.2	12.6	40.7	244.2	1,136.0
N	4.6	18.4	32.2	128.8	18.3	183.0	35.6	106.8	23.6	236.0	14.5	43.5	29.1	174.6	891.1
O	4.6	18.4	12.9	51.6	46.6	466.0	12.9	38.7	48.4	484.0	6.1	18.3	37.7	226.2	1,303.2
P	3.9	15.6	16.0	64.0	30.4	304.0	14.1	42.3	37.8	378.0	4.1	12.3	35.6	213.6	1,029.8
Q	5.0	20.0	15.7	62.8	27.4	274.0	23.6	70.8	25.2	252.0	11.6	34.8	22.0	132.0	846.4
R	1.6	6.4	20.2	80.8	5.0	50.0	27.3	81.9	3.4	34.0	8.1	24.3	9.4	56.4	333.8
S	1.0	4.0	19.5	78.0	10.3	103.0	22.6	67.8	10.8	108.0	6.4	19.2	18.5	111.0	491.0
T	1.9	7.6	9.5	38.0	31.1	311.0	14.5	43.5	24.7	247.0	6.5	19.5	26.9	161.4	828.0
Twilight Area (part of Ward H)	12.6	50.4	59.1	236.4	3.6	36.0	66.4	199.2	11.7	117.0	35.6	106.8	21.1	126.6	872.4

APPENDIX I—*Continued*

Penalty weight

Ward	'Fair' Condition (5) %	Score	'Poor' Condition (20) %	Score	Total penalty score (Condition)	Housing deficiencies — Persons per room 1·0–1·5 (5) %	Score	Persons per room > 1·5 (20) %	Score	Net dwelling shortage (10) %	Score	Total penalty score (Occupancy)	Total penalty score	Rank
A	14·4	72·0	1·2	24·0	96·0	5·2	26·0	2·0	40·0	4·4	44·0	110·0	481	1
B	23·2	116·0	0·7	14·0	130·0	6·8	34·0	2·3	46·0	30·6	306·0	386·0	861	5
C	29·3	146·5	2·9	58·0	204·5	4·9	24·5	5·7	114·0	30·6	306·0	444·5	1093	7
D	27·6	138·0	7·5	150·0	288·0	12·8	64·0	7·0	140·0	27·8	278·0	488·0	1463	12
E	29·2	146·0	2·5	50·0	196·0	18·9	94·5	5·6	112·0	34·8	348·0	554·5	1422	11
F	29·0	145·0	0	0	145·0	7·2	36·0	2·2	44·0	22·9	229·0	309·0	729	3
G	31·2	156·0	1·8	36·0	192·0	12·5	62·5	8·3	166·0	47·6	476·0	704·5	1493	13
H	41·5	207·5	4·9	98·0	305·5	15·2	76·0	11·3	226·0	50·2	502·0	804·0	1942	18
I	29·3	146·5	10·4	208·0	354·5	12·4	62·0	4·0	80·0	2·5	25·0	167·0	1104	8
J	37·7	188·5	11·9	238·0	426·5	9·2	46·0	4·1	82·0	10·7	107·0	235·0	1545	14
K	4·6	23·0	0	0	23·0	11·0	55·0	4·0	80·0	19·4	194·0	329·0	822	4
L	11·1	55·5	0·7	14·0	69·0	10·5	52·5	5·7	114·0	22·6	226·0	392·5	1252	9
M	31·4	157·0	13·3	266·0	423·0	8·8	44·0	5·4	108·0	12·9	129·0	281·0	1840	17
N	24·4	122·0	3·9	78·0	200·0	11·7	58·5	5·8	116·0	28·6	286·0	460·5	1552	15
O	41·1	205·5	13·6	272·0	477·5	11·4	57·0	3·7	74·0	15·7	157·0	288·0	2069	20
P	27·9	139·5	21·7	434·0	573·5	12·6	63·0	9·8	196·0	15·5	155·0	414·0	2017	19
Q	24·1	120·5	21·8	436·0	556·5	6·7	33·5	6·5	130·0	19·5	195·0	358·5	1761	16
R	23·8	119·0	1·5	30·0	149·0	8·2	41·0	2·1	42·0	14·6	146·0	229·0	712	2
S	21·8	109·0	4·1	82·0	191·0	6·1	30·5	4·7	94·0	13·1	131·0	255·0	938	6
T	46·7	233·5	5·0	100·0	333·5	8·3	41·5	2·2	44·0	10·5	105·0	190·5	1352	10
Twilight area (part of ward H)	41·5	207·5	4·9	98·0	305·5*	14·9	74·5	13·1	262·0	50·2	502·0	838·5	2016	18

* No breakdown of ward H figures was available from the GLC survey.

Notes:

1. Penalty scores are calculated by multiplying the ward percentage of each deficiency by the penalty weight. Highest penalty score indicates lowest housing quality.
2. Data on amenities and occupancy are from the 1966 Census.
3. Data of physical condition are from the GLC Housing Age and Conditions Survey, 1967.

APPENDIX 2

Incidence in Haringey of Various Social Phenomena by Ward

Ward	Housing deficiency (i.e. penalty score) total		Indictable offences per 1,000 population		Fires per 1,000 dwellings		Juvenile probation cases per 1,000 children		Children taken into care per 1,000 children < 16 yrs		Admissions, etc., to welfare homes per 1,000 population > 65 yrs	
	Score	Rank	No.	Rank	No.	Rank	No.	Rank	No.	Rank	No.	Rank
A	481	1	48·0	19	4·85	2	2·34	2	1·13	14	5·08	3
B	861	5	50·4	20	9·52	16	6·78	7	2·67	2	5·37	4
C	1,093	7	45·8	18	5·75	7	10·77	16	4·12	4	3·40	2
D	1,463	12	29·7	9	12·80	18	4·76	4	12·84	17	7·66	14
E	1,422	11	27·9	7	5·5	5	7·56	10	10·24	15	11·19	19
F	729	3	23·5	3	7·2	12	8·74	11	2·90	3	6·97	9
G	1,493	13	36·6	13	6·98	11	7·41	9	11·97	16	11·52	20
H	1,942	18	32·2	12	9·92	17	11·33	17	9·30	12	9·46	17
I	1,104	8	21·2	2	6·70	8	15·23	20	10·10	14	7·04	11
J	1,545	14	36·7	15	12·96	19	8·80	12	8·36	10	5·42	6
K	822	4	17·9	1	7·41	13	6·95	8	9·52	13	8·12	16
L	1,252	9	25·1	4	4·39	1	12·16	19	4·53	5	7·36	13
M	1,840	17	37·8	16	7·99	14	4·88	5	5·11	6	6·98	10
N	1,522	15	30·3	10	6·78	9	9·68	15	7·76	9	6·72	8
O	2,069	20	31·8	11	9·01	15	8·87	13	13·27	18	7·05	12
P	2,017	19	29·5	8	6·86	10	0	9	8·91	11	2·38	1
Q	1,761	16	36·6	13	13·28	20	11·54	18	14·12	19	7·83	15
R	712	2	25·6	5	5·71	6	4·74	3	7·33	8	5·38	5
S	938	6	26·3	6	5·33	3	5·97	6	17·84	20	5·96	7
T	1,352	10	42·6	17	5·51	4	8·94	14	5·52	7	9·95	18
Twilight Area (part of Ward H)	2,016	18	30·7	10/11	9·76	16·17	13·04	19	N.A.	—	8·40	16/17

Notes:

1. Crime figures are for 1966 and relate to indictable offences occurring in each ward.
2. Fire figures are for 1966 and relate only to fires in inhabited dwellings.
3. Juvenile delinquency figures relate to the *stock* of cases at the end of 1968, i.e. to the location of *offenders* rather than offences.
4. Children in care figures relate to 1967.
5. Welfare figures relate to admissions to local authority welfare homes during 1967/8; also to the current waiting list for admission.

APPENDIX 3

Indices of Social and Housing Stress in Haringey

Ward		Social stress						Housing stress	
	Indictable offences (100·0)	Fires (100·0)	Juvenile probation cases (100·0)	Children taken into care (100·0)	Admissions to welfare homes 60 yrs and over (100·0)	Total (100·0)	Rank	Housing deficiency score (100·0)	Rank
A	147·2	63·8	29·2	12·9	72·6	65·2	2	36·4	1
B	154·6	125·3	84·5	30·6	76·7	94·4	9	65·2	5
C	140·5	75·7	134·3	47·2	48·6	89·2	7	82·7	7
D	91·1	168·4	59·4	147·1	109·4	115·0	17	110·7	12
E	85·6	73·4	94·3	117·3	159·9	106·0	13	107·6	11
F	72·1	95·7	109·1	33·2	99·6	82·0	4	55·2	3
G	112·3	91·9	92·4	137·1	164·6	119·6	13	113·0	13
H	98·9	130·5	141·3	106·5	135·1	122·4	19	147·0	18
I	65·0	88·2	189·9	115·7	100·6	111·8	14	83·6	8
J	112·6	170·6	109·7	95·8	77·4	113·2	15	117·0	14
K	54·9	97·5	86·7	109·1	116·0	90·8	8	62·2	4
L	77·0	57·8	151·6	51·9	105·1	88·6	6	94·8	9
M	116·0	105·1	60·8	58·5	99·7	88·0	5	139·3	17
N	92·9	89·2	120·7	88·9	96·0	97·6	10	115·2	15
O	97·5	118·6	100·5	152·0	100·7	113·8	16	156·6	20
P	99·5	90·3	8·2	102·1	34·0	65·0	1	152·7	19
Q	112·3	174·8	143·9	161·7	111·9	141·0	20	133·3	16
R	78·5	75·1	59·1	84·0	76·9	74·8	3	53·9	2
S	80·7	70·1	74·4	204·4	85·1	103·0	11	71·0	6
T	130·7	72·5	111·5	63·2	142·1	104·0	12	102·3	10
Twilight area (part of ward H)	94·2	128·4	162·6	106·5	120·0	122·4	(19)	152·6	(18)

Note: Borough = 100.

17

What is Wrong with Roskill?[1]

by E. J. Mishan

The *Papers and Proceedings* of the Commission on the Third London
Airport run to nine volumes, covering between them the first three
stages of the Commission's planned procedure. Under review here
is the seventh volume, pertaining to Stage III.[2] It runs to over 500
pages, and embodies both the method of approach and the quantitative assessment of the Commission's research team led by Mr. F. P.
Thompson, an economist formerly employed in the Ministry of
Transport. I doubt whether an economist who, like myself, has had
no hand in the writing of this volume could become familiar with
all the aspects discussed in less than a couple of months of uninter-
rupted study. Nor would he be able to check all the calculations in
less than about six months, and then with a goodly amount of research assistance. Since I can claim only to have perused a number
of chapters—though I believe they are the more important chapters
—the over-all impressions left on me have to be regarded as provisional only. Some of the more critical judgements, especially those
put forward under the heads 'Is a Third Airport Justified' and
'Social Costs and Equity', are put forward with less reservation,
since they were reached only after a close scrutiny of the text. The
more general reflections at the end of this review depend neither on

From *Journal of Transport Economics and Policy* (Sept. 1970), pp. 221–34.
Reprinted by permission of the author and the editor of the Journal.

[1] I am very much indebted to Mr. A. Flowerdew for prior discussion and to Mr.
D. L. Munby for later comments on a first draft of this paper.

[2] Commission on the Third London Airport *Papers and Proceedings*, vol. vii (Parts
1 and 2), Stage III Research and Investigation Assessment of Short-Listed Sites
(London: H.M.S.O., 1970).

my over-all impressions of the Report nor on the more critical findings. They arise from a consideration of the relevance of such cost–benefit evaluations for the world we are living in.

COST OR COST–BENEFIT

It may be useful first to remind the reader of the limitations of cost–benefit techniques. A cost–benefit analysis purports to measure in money terms all the benefits and all the costs to be expected over the future of some mooted project, and to admit the project if the sum of the benefits exceeds the sum of the costs by a sufficient margin. Under ideal conditions, the adopted criterion of a cost–benefit analysis—requiring that benefits exceed costs—can be vindicated only by a social judgement, that an economic rearrangement which *could* make everyone better off is 'a good thing'.

There are two points to notice about such a judgement. First, nothing is said about existing institutions, economic, political or legal. But in order to be a valid judgement, the criterion adopted must be *independent* of existing institutions. This is far from being an esoteric refinement, as we shall see later on. Second, and more obvious perhaps, such a judgement does *not* require that everyone shall be made better off, or even that some people shall be made better off while no others are made worse off. The likelihood—a virtual certainty—that some people, possibly most, will be made worse off is tacitly acknowledged. The criterion is met simply if it can be established that, on the adoption of the project, hypothetically costless transfers of money *could* make everyone better off than he was before. A project admitted on a cost–benefit analysis is, therefore, quite consistent with an economic arrangement which makes the rich richer and the poor poorer. It is consistent also with transparent inequity: irrespective of the income groups involved, the opportunities for increased profit or pleasure provided by the new project may inflict direct and substantial injury on others.

In order, then, for a project to be socially acceptable, it is not enough to show that the outcome of a cost–benefit calculation is positive—allowing, always, that the evaluation of each of the component items has been thorough and consistent. It must also be established that the resulting distributional effects are not unduly regressive, and that no gross inequities are perpetrated.

In the light of an ideal cost–benefit procedure, what can be said of this Report?

The first thing that ought to be said is that, for Britain at least,[3] the Report has aimed at a level of sophistication that will not be easy to exceed. For the most part it is clearly written and well organized. The theoretical underpinning—much of it summarized in Part I, *Proposed Research Methodology*, and in chapter I of Part II— is respectable, and the tone is suggestive of a determination not to forsake principle for facility of calculation. The so-called intangibles are believed to be in principle quantifiable, and the research team has not yielded to the temptation to hand back part of its brief to the political process, which had offered it to the economists in the first place.[4] There are occasional manifestations of resourcefulness and ingenuity, as well as determination, in bringing disparate considerations 'into relationship with the measuring rod of money'. Nevertheless, paragraph 1.22 (on page 43) makes it plain that the conditions mentioned above, relating to distribution, and equity— though their relevance is acknowledged—are *not* to be taken into

---

[3] Cost–benefit studies on the grand scale are more common in the United States, a large proportion being concerned with water resources and construction of dams.

[4] Nevertheless, there are one or two blemishes in the proposed methodology which could be damaging in a cost–benefit analysis, though, if they were corrected in this cost-comparison report, they would not be likely to make much difference to the ranking of sites in Table 29.1. (i) On p. 38 (para. 1.7), for instance, it is asserted that goods and services are to be valued at their resource costs on grounds that they 'most clearly represent the real cost to the community . . . in terms of resources embodied in their production. Indirect taxes and subsidies . . . are excluded'. This is a valid convention for estimating changes in national income aggregates, but it is an *incorrect* principle for cost–benefit evaluations. The cost to the economy of a resource to be used in the project is determined by the value it creates in the use from which it is to be moved. Consequently, if the resource is moved from the production of some good subject, say, to a 100 per cent tax, its cost to the project must be valued as equal to the price, which is not equal to, but twice, the resource cost. (ii) Again on pp. 32–3 (para. 1.19), in the discussion on the costs of journeys to the airport, mention is made of the preference of some people for using their own cars, and the paragraph ends with the sentence: 'The measure of this benefit is found deductively by observing what the travelling public is prepared to pay, in time and money, for the convenience, at least in their own eyes . . . of using their own car.' Fair enough, but no allowance is made for the additional congestion costs that are imposed on all *other* vehicles, or for the additional spill-over effects on the rest of the population of private transport as compared with public transport.

consideration in the assessment. For this reason, if for no other, the quantitative findings of the Report cannot be used alone to decide the issue.

The second thing that ought to be said is that the urgency is apparently not so great as we had been led to believe. If their projections of future air traffic are accepted (and they are large enough in all conscience), the airlines could go on until about 1982 using the existing facilities at Heathrow and Gatwick. Although congestion costs at the existing airports are expected to increase year by year, it will not be until 1982 that they will exceed £22 million, which is the estimated annual worth of postponing construction of the third airport.

The third thing that ought to be said is that the assessment in this volume is *not*, properly speaking, a cost–benefit analysis. It consists only of a comparison of the costs of the four alternative airport sites on the short list: Cublington, Foulness, Nuthamstead and Thurleigh. And in this connection it is important to notice that the full costs of each item are *not* always compared; sometimes only the differences in costs are entered, or a portion of the costs in which the differences are captured. We shall find it revealing to dwell a whilst on this peculiarity of the Report.

This choice of a relative cost evaluation rather than a cost–benefit evaluation carries with it an implicit presumption that a third airport at any one of the four alternative sites can be justified on economic grounds. There are reasons to doubt this presumption, and we shall turn to them later in this paper.

In the next section we concern ourselves only with the weight to be attached to the comparative figures produced by the Commission in order to rank the four alternative sites on the scale of economic desirability.

COSTS TO PASSENGERS AND AIRLINES

A comparison of the costs of the four sites discounted to 1975[5] is given by row 22 of Table 29.1 (pp. 490–1). They are ranked below in order of increasing cost:

[5] If the costs are discounted to a later date, 1982, the figures above are all roughly doubled, since a discount rate of 10 per cent per annum has been adopted.

Cublington	£2,265 million	(0)
Thurleigh	£2,267 million	(£2 million)
Nuthampstead	£2,274 million	(£9 million)
Foulness	£2,385 million	(£120 million)

(The figures in the brackets indicate by how much the cost of that particular site exceeds the cost of the lowest site at Cublington.)

It is clear that the differences between the first three sites are too slight in proportion to likely errors to be taken seriously. Foulness—except for bird-lovers, the conservationists' favoured site—stands out clearly as the most costly of the four. One reason is that a loss of potential benefit amounting to about £44 million is chalked up against Foulness in consequence of the smaller air traffic it is expected to generate as compared with the three inland airports, all of which happen to be on the right side of London to attract traffic from the North and the Midlands. In the year 2000, for example, the total number of air passengers in the country is expected to be something between 6 and 10 million less if Foulness is chosen rather than one of the others.

How significant is this difference in cost for the Foulness site? The two largest items in Table 29.1 are those for 'Airspace movement' and 'Passenger user cost'. They account for over 80 per cent of the total costs in the table, and they both depend heavily on the value placed on passengers' time. In particular, it is the additional time and cost of reaching the Foulness Airport site that forces the figure for 'Passenger user cost' there to £1,041 million, or £152 million more than the figure for the next most costly site in this respect, Thurleigh.

Value of Travel Time

It is at such points that one is tempted to challenge the figure of 46s. per hour placed on business travel in 1968, rising to 72s. per hour (all at 1968 prices) by the year 2000. The figure is derived from an estimate of business firms' average annual expenditure on their airborne representatives of £4,626 (in 1968), which sum includes an average business travellers' income of £3,200. For 'leisure passengers', in contrast, a mere 4s. 7d. an hour is deemed appropriate. Both figures are assumed to rise over time at 3 per cent per annum.

Since these estimates, made in consultation with the Ministry of Transport, are likely to be controversial, the Report makes some additional calculations on the side, based on alternative evaluations of the worth of people's time. If, for instance, the value of business time is reduced by 25 per cent of the above figure, and leisure time is not valued at all, the total costs are so revised that the bracketed figures giving the *differences* in cost for the four airports become those shown below:

Thurleigh	(o)
Cublington	(£10 million)
Nuthampstead	(£28 million)
Foulness	(£42 million)

Clearly there is some margin to be attained by playing around with such figures, and this makes any choice on economic grounds alone appear somewhat less satisfactory. The figures would appear less reliable still, and the differentials would narrow further,[6] if one could reasonably object to the notion of basing the value of time on a person's earnings. First of all, it is meaningful to say of a person that he values his leisure very little but that he dislikes his work a lot. Travel time for, say, a holiday-maker is simply one way of using his leisure. And it is not to be regarded as equivalent to work unless, at the margin, the person is indifferent as between, say, an hour spent on the train and an hour at work.

Secondly, the assumption of putting a positive value on the extra hour or so of businessmen's time if Foulness is chosen is also open to challenge. Dividing a firm's annual expenditure per travelling representative by the number of hours he is supposed to work produces an average hourly figure which, it can be argued, has no economic significance in this connection. The correct economic concept is the 'opportunity cost' to the firm, or rather to the country, of an hour or so's delay to its representative. Notwithstanding, assertions to the contrary, indivisibilities of time are important here. If the delay were of a full day, it could matter to the individual firm—

---

[6] In the limiting case, if no value at all were placed on the time required to reach the airports, the cost ranking of the four airports (with the cost differences given in brackets) would be: Thurleigh (o), Foulness (6), Cublington (7), Nuthampstead (21).

though, again, it might not matter that much for the country. If the difference in delay were of an hour's duration, one might think up circumstances in which it would matter. But such circumstances would not be relevant to the choice under consideration in the Report. If Foulness is chosen, it is not to be supposed that many firms could make profitable use of the extra hour or so of representatives' time saved in travelling to the airport. To most firms, I should imagine, it would make no difference at all. The representative would simply have to get up a little earlier on the appointed day and travel a little longer. And if this is a disutility for him, it has to be taken out of the category of business time and put into the category of passengers' leisure time.

Airline Operation Costs

Let us suppose, however, that we accept the figures in Table 29.1 as not seriously misleading. We may still wonder what importance we are to attach to them. Large though the absolute figure of £120 million is, it appears as only about 5 per cent of the total discounted costs of any of the sites. Actually, it is a very much smaller proportion of the total future resource costs of any of the airports; for, as mentioned, the table does not reveal all of the costs. The full airport construction costs are given. So also are all the 'passenger user costs'—the resource costs of travelling to each of the four sites, *plus* any difference in the 'disbenefits' of travelling to one airport site rather than another. But the cost of the largest item in the table, 'airspace movement', is only a fraction—presumably unknown—of the total airline operation costs over the future. For, on the assumption that, whichever site is chosen, all the aircraft will fly the same distances to their destinations from some common boundary containing the four sites, the authors of the Report simplified their work by calculating only the costs of reaching this boundary from each of the four sites (allowance being made for the somewhat smaller air traffic expected if Foulness were chosen). If, instead, total airline operation costs were included, the discounted value of *total* resources could be more than double the figures given in row 22 of Table 29.1. Accepting the Report's valuation of time, the excess cost of Foulness would be more like $2\frac{1}{2}$ per cent of the value of the total resources involved. On the Report's optional calculation of business and leisure time, the excess of £42 million for Foulness comes to less than 1 per cent of the value of total resources. On margins thus small, an economic case against the choice of Foulness cannot be seriously maintained.

Supersonic Flight

Finally, nothing is said about the particular sorts of damage currently associated with supersonic flight. I have been told that the omission was deliberate, and predicated on the recent White Paper of the previous governments, in which it was stated that the Concorde would not fly at supersonic speeds over land. Such a statement of intent may reasonably be regarded with suspicion. If we suppose that there is a chance that, for any of a half-dozen reasons the aircraft industry or the airline companies can think up, supersonic speeds over land may some day become 'essential' the choice of any site other than Foulness would leave us in a sorry and angry state.[7]

[7] There are deficiencies also in the measurement of other disbenefits. Their potential impact is probably less significant than that of aircraft noise, but they are worth touching on. For churches located off the airport site, the social losses entered are no more than the costs of strengthening the structures to withstand vibration. On the other hand, the social loss resulting from the demolition of churches and other buildings on the airport site is taken to be equal to the sum of their current market costs, as indicated by their insurance values. For architecturally undistinguished churches there need be no objection on secular grounds. But for irreplaceable churches of unique architectural value, this is obviously unacceptable. If Westminster Abbey is insured for £200,000 against destruction by fire, it does not follow that the nation at large is indifferent as between having Westminster Abbey or the £200,000. But this is the implied logic of accepting the fire insurance figure as the loss equivalence. The loss arising from damage to recreational activities is conventionally treated and arbitrarily quantified. Thus, on p. 418 (para. 24.24) we read: 'Most of the recreational activities affected by aircraft noise, of which visiting historic houses, hunting, golf, fresh water fishing, predominate, are located within moderate noise levels. It was therefore assumed that visits would, on average, be reduced by 10 per cent, and that this would be directly reflected in lower admission revenues. It can be deduced from conventional demand analysis that this reduction in participation could correspond to a reduction of about 20 per cent in the consumer surplus enjoyed by those continuing to visit.' The tone is tentative here: 40 per cent, perhaps 60 per cent, would be no less acceptable. But, frankly, the statement makes no sense as it stands. Admissions could change very little, and yet the loss be far in excess of '20 per cent in the consumer surplus enjoyed by those continuing to visit'. Indeed the method is in conflict with the guiding principle laid down on p. 39 and elsewhere: that the loss of an existing facility is to be measured by the sum necessary to restore the person's original welfare.

IS A THIRD AIRPORT JUSTIFIED?

Let us now turn to what I regard as the major defect of the Report: that the economic case for the construction of a third London airport was not a part of its terms of reference. In a brief chapter on 'The Value to the Nation of a Third London Airport' a number of considerations were put forward to convince the public that the benefits were almost self-evident: the popularity of the post-war package tour, it was pointed out, is sure to grow immensely. So also is business travel, conceived as a 'lubricant' of international trade through which the blessings of technology are spread throughout the world. Besides, airports are generators of high income in the surrounding areas, and the growth in traffic should benefit the aircraft construction industry and industry in general; and much more of the same sort of froth. I suspect that this industry sales talk got included in the Report only on the insistence of interested parties. It contrasts with the more professional judgement shown elsewhere and is perhaps not expected to be taken seriously. There is, however, another argument in the earlier part of the chapter which, if it were accepted, would go some way towards establishing a presumption in favour of sufficient benefits to justify the undertaking. This takes the form of a belief that the expected revenues from passengers will be able to cover all the future resource costs involved in airline flights, and that, in addition, the estimated cost of all 'disbenefits'—noise, disamenity, demolition of historic buildings, etc.—could be more than covered by an increase in revenue from raising landing fees.

The Intangibles

Before this presumption is accepted, it is necessary to examine the estimates made of the value of the 'intangibles', more particularly of the value of the loss of amenity and recreation to the community, or rather to examine the methods used by the authors to estimate these values. For in a comparative cost analysis, whatever the magnitudes of the 'intangibles', one of the alternative projects has to be chosen. Under this constraint, the only relevant question is whether or not introduction of the 'intangibles' will alter the cost ranking of the alternative projects. In a cost–benefit analysis, in contrast, one question to be answered is whether or not any one of the alternative projects is economically feasible. The magnitude of the 'intangibles' can, therefore, be decisive.

By and large, the conceptual underpinning of the report is, as indicated earlier, sound enough. It is in making the transition from the concepts to the measurement of the relevant effects that one begins to feel critical of the particular devices, ingenious though they sometimes are, which the authors make use of in order to place money values on the damages suffered by others. Thus, in evaluating the potential disbenefits, the authors lay it down on page 39 that 'The analysis has been guided by the principle of accepting the scale of values apparently held by the people concerned, as revealed by their choice and behaviour. For *potential* possessions or activities, they are valued at what people would be prepared to pay to acquire them. For *existing* possessions or activities, things are valued at the minimum which people would be prepared to accept as just compensation for their loss.' As a statement of intent, this reflects the doctrines of modern welfare economics, and is unexceptionable. But, in the event, what do they do?

Households Displaced

For those households moving out because of the airport, the loss suffered is reckoned as (*a*) estimated depreciation of their property, plus (*b*) removal expenses, plus (*c*) 'consumer surplus'. Thus, if the market value of a house before the airport is sited in the area is £10,000, but the family enjoys a consumer surplus of £2,000 on it (that is, the family would not sell it below £12,000) and would require £500 for removal expenses, a fall in the market price to £7,000 would involve the family in a total loss of £5,500—equal to (*a*) £3,000, plus (*b*) £500 plus (*c*) £2,000. The estimate of (*a*), depreciation, was derived from consultations with estate agents and by reference to depreciation of properties in those areas around Gatwick and Heathrow that are subject to various degrees of aircraft disturbance. The estimates for (*b*) and (*c*) together, removal expenses plus consumer surplus, resulted from a sample survey in which householders were asked the following question: 'Suppose your house was wanted to form part of a large development scheme and the developer offered to buy it from you, what price would be just high enough to compensate you for leaving this house (flat) and moving to another area?' (p. 381). Subtraction from this subjective price of the existing market price provided an estimate for (b) and (c). A truthful answer to this question would be a satisfactory measure of the subjective value of the house only if the move contemplated by the householder were one that would take him completely out of the noise area (or, more precisely, if there already was some noise in the area, to another area suffering from no greater noise). Yet the question posed does not state how far the householder will have to move. Mention of a developer must surely give the householder the impression that a few acres, within which his house happens to be situated, are required. It would not occur to him that he would have to leave the neighbourhood. And it is, indeed, entirely a different affair if the household is to be displaced either because the site is needed for an airport or because the noise will be all but unbearable. This can be a real wrench for the family. A change of job location, to say nothing of a loss of friends and neighbours, have then to be anticipated. The figures used by the Report in this connection are, therefore, certain to have understated the value of expected losses.

A more obvious reason why the figures derived from the sample answers to the above question understate the amount of compensation is that 8 per cent of those asked said they would not move at any price. The compensatory sum for such a householder was placed, arbitrarily, at £5,000. If these people mean what they said, the compensatory sum would be 'infinite' and this would obviously wreck any cost–benefit criterion. Yet, if the answers are believed, consistency of principle requires that an 'infinite sum' be entered. It may be that a good interviewer would have elicited a finite sum, though well in excess of £5,000—perhaps £50,000? or £5 million? And, though unlikely, it is not altogether inconceivable that for some older, or unworldly, people all that money could buy for them would not suffice as compensation for having to live elsewhere. What is certain, however, is that by setting this arbitrary upper limit of £5,000 the authors' figure for 'consumer surplus' can be made much smaller than the 'consumer surplus' figure that would have emerged by an uncompromising application of their own adopted principles.

The disbenefits of an increase of the number of flights associated with the establishment of a third London Airport is an underestimate for another reason, one which the Report itself touches upon—though possibly without recognizing its full significance (inasmuch as it applies to the evaluation of traffic noise in general). On page

368 (para. 20.12) it is observed that 'People buying a house affected by aircraft noise would be very naïve if they did not expect an increase in noise, at least for the next ten years or so.' Precisely! If noise is to increase over the next ten years—and, on present trends, who doubts it?—a family will have to search very much farther afield if they are to discover an equally congenial neighbourhood with the same degree of quiet. It is scarcely possible for them to discover an area which has reasonable amenities and facilities within commuting distance of work and at the same time is expected over the future to be as quiet as is their present habitation today. Anticipating the spread of noise everywhere, the family, in effect, have only a limited choice: that of staying in the existing area or of moving to a new one, where *both* areas are expected to become much noisier. Indeed, as the level of noise in general increases, the perceived differences are likely to decrease, and so also, therefore, will the sum of money necessary to induce the family to move. But the disbenefit suffered from each contribution to a rising noise level is properly valued only by a sum of money large enough to compensate the family for the loss of the original low-noise situation, this being the sum that will enable them to maintain their original level of welfare.

Households Remaining in Neighbourhood

The expectation of an increase over the future in the volume and spread of noise is yet more significant in evaluating the loss to the larger population who will continue to live within the noisier zones about the airport—those remaining within the 35 NNI contour line.[8] The statement quoted on page 39 of the Report implies that the measure of the loss experienced by such people would emerge from a truthful answer to the question: 'What is the minimum sum you would accept to reconcile yourself to the increase in aircraft noise to which you are, and in the future will be, subjected?' Yet the loss for this larger group was measured, ultimately, by the expected depreciation of their property alone—that is, no more than the (a) component of the loss to the household that is moved from the airport site. A good deal of finesse was, of course, employed in working

[8] NNI is an abbreviation of Noise and Number Index. It was developed as an index of aircraft noise annoyance by the Committee on the Problem of Noise (Cmnd. 2056).

out the exact depreciation to be used for each sort of house in each sort of zone, allowance for sensitivity being made by using the figure for depreciation as the median point of a distribution of noise sensitivity. Again, however, if noise is expected to increase over time, such measures are sure to understate the loss. For as noise grows over time the absolute difference in noise between any two points on a map may be unchanged, and the difference in property values will also remain unchanged—yet people living in areas about these two points will be worse off. Indeed, as noise increases over time, it is far more likely that *differences* in noise will diminish within a given area, and the effect therefore on property values will be smaller—a prospect with which the estate agents consulted can be assumed to be familiar. In such circumstances, the use of differentials in property values does not only understate the loss; as an index of loss it is wholly perverse. In the limiting case in which there is no escape whatever from aircraft noise in all inhabited areas of the country, noise being everywhere uniformly unbearable, noise-induced differences in property values will vanish; the measure of loss for all of us, on this indicator, being zero.

In connection with noise, there is yet another weakness, which at first glance may seem a quibble but in fact is a critical weakness of the cost–benefit technique when extended to non-market disbenefits: its almost unavoidable asymmetry in the weighting of 'imponderables'. To illustrate in the present instance, the authors confine themselves to noise within the 35 NNI contour line, apparently on the grounds that the effects of aircraft disturbance below 35 NNI are difficult to determine. Now the population within the zones between, say 20 NNI and 35 NNI is several times as large as that within the area enclosed by the 35 NNI contour. Despite the admirable statement of intent on page 39, no loss of welfare is imputed to this larger population. That decision can be justified only if it is known that all families are perfectly indifferent to the increase in noise up to 35 NNI. Yet there will surely be a proportion of such families who, at least will come to resent the extra noise.

Illusory Benefits of Air Travel

Clearly the reaction of numbers of people in the larger population to noise levels below 35 NNI involves a judgement about significance. It is a purely subjective judgement, however, and it is in just such circumstances that the economist can be misled by a 'misplaced concreteness'. I am not suggesting that the economist is visibly stirred, as we imagine the technocrat to be, by a vision of a vast airport having all the familiar manifestations of highly organized bustle and breathlessness. I am suggesting, however, that market-formed prices and quantities are regarded as somehow more solid than the values attributed to the 'intangibles'. If a person is willing to pay £50 for a flight from London to Palma, there is, indisputably, a figure of £50 of benefit to play with. If the resource cost of the flight were shown to be £40, the economist would have no hesitation in claiming an excess benefit of (at least) £10. Such a flight may well be, for the greater number of future passengers, a whimsical form of indulgence, a fashion good of which the deprivation would be resented in varying degrees—though probably much less as time passed and alternative opportunities were discovered.[9]

For business travellers, the case is simpler yet. For most of them the company pays air fares from business expenditures, so that, taking income and corporation taxes into account, the true cost to the firm is less than half the fare. Thus, the marginal value of the air trip to the business firm is, presumably, well below the marginal resource cost.

With the advent of air travel, the number of conferences, business, professional and academic, has been growing at an exponential rate. The same people who now rush about the world reading the same paper at a dozen conferences in as many months are those who, in quieter days, would have found time to read, write and reflect. At any rate, the value of such trips cannot be measured by the air fare, simply because air travel is not, in such cases, one of the alternative goods a man can buy subject to a budget constraint. The conferees do not pay their own fares. And it is doubtful if the benefit they personally expect to derive from these occasions is such that many would attend the conference without additional inducements. Only the conveners of the conference can be said to benefit. Calling a conference is one among the alternative ways of disposing of

---

[9] I do not underestimate the extent of the potential protest, initiated by business interests with the support of mass media and inflated by the sheer joy of expressing protest. I speak only of the individual discomfort after the ban against this sort of travel has been generally accepted. Anger at being deprived, or the pleasure of expressing it, is no measure of the loss of utility of a thing.

funds provided by governments and businesses guided by the principle of self-promotion. Conference-creating activity is one of many growth industries produced by aircraft travel, and one of the many prestige uses of the massive funds accumulated by business foundations. The social benefit of all this hectic to-ing and fro-ing, however, is difficult to evaluate—which is no reason for not assuming that it is probably negative.

There is room for speculation here, but not for doubt, that much of the assumed benefit of air travel is illusory.

Asymmetry in Cost–Benefit Analysis

The purpose of carping at the nature of these assumed benefits is to draw attention to the asymmetry referred to, which arises, in the last resort, from institutional limitations. Whether he is motivated by strong desire, by the spirit of over-indulgence, or by spurious business need, if a man pays £50 twice a year for an air trip a benefit of at least £100 will be entered against the cost of the resources used in the two flights. In contrast, the disbenefit suffered by a person living within the 35 NNI–20 NNI zone, whether it verges on fury for a hypersensitive minority[10] or whether it is the bearable annoyance of the majority, does not enter the grand computation at all. Yet it is, at least, a moot point whether the loss of welfare to any person subjected daily (and perhaps nightly also) to this *initially* lower level of noise-annoyance should properly be thought of as meriting no consideration as compared with the gain in welfare of any person who, at some time in the year, does the flight to Palma, or to Hong Kong for that matter.[11] If institutions happened

---

[10] On p. 365 the authors refer to the survey conducted by the Committee on the Problem of Noise. In the *quietest* areas covered by the survey, 10 per cent of the population were classified as 'seriously annoyed'. In the noisiest areas, on the other hand, only 10 per cent denied that aircraft noise was a nuisance, and 10 per cent claimed a 'minimal degree of annoyance', leaving 80 per cent claiming more than a minimal degree of annoyance.

[11] It might be objected that the person on the ground may, at some other time, be an air passenger on his way to Palma or Hong Kong. But this, as it happens, makes not the slightest difference to the calculation. His losses are no less real for his having benefits also, and vice versa. Nor does the fact that a person who resents aircraft noise also travels by air constitute evidence that, *on balance*, he prefers air travel along with the accompanying disbenefits to no air travel at all. Evidence of the latter proposition must await developments in which he is given the choice

to be the reverse of what they are for this particular case; if, say, the universe were so designed that people could freely sell their quiet in a competitive market at the ruling price whilst, on the other hand, owing to some institutional factor (say, the cost of fare-collecting was fantastically high), a market in airline services were not possible, we should appreciate the asymmetrical treatment better. For then, *all* the disbenefits from noise would be priced on the market, and they would grow with the increasing noise of aircraft. They would be counted as part of the 'solid' price-quantity data, and would be added to the resource costs on the same economic principle—that payment has to be made to induce people to part with things they value, whether it be their property rights, their leisure or their peace and quiet. And both in virtue of the change to a correct method of evaluating these disbenefits, and in virtue of the extension of the market to the population as a whole, the resulting loss figure would probably be many times that estimated in the Report. On the other hand, in keeping with the current methods used in estimating the values of non-market items, the benefits of the trips would be calculated only for a fraction of the potential number of beneficiaries. This would be the fraction having greater claims according to some benefit-scale beyond which the economist would declare it difficult to believe that benefits were at all substantial. Moreover, if the methods used in estimating benefits were deficient in the same respects as those used by the Report in estimating disbenefits, the total value of the benefits calculated even for this fraction of the beneficiaries would be an underestimate.

In sum, under such hypothetical institutions, the outcome of a cost–benefit calculation conducted on the lines of this Report would be vastly different from that reached under the existing institutions, and could fail entirely to justify the building of a third London airport—from which we may conclude, at the very least, that the methods employed in the Report do not meet the conditions of an ideal cost–benefit analysis as laid down at the beginning of this article.

----

of being 'grounded' without any aircraft noise or of putting up with the noise along with the opportunity of flying. This sort of choice is not provided by the market, nor does the government at present look like presenting it to us.

SOCIAL COSTS AND EQUITY

The conclusion of the section dealing with costs to passengers and airlines was that, on alternative—and, in my opinion, more plausible—estimates of the value of passengers' time over the future, the cost differences between the four sites as a proportion of total resource costs become so small as to be unreliable for the purpose of economic ranking.

In the next section I gave some reasons for doubting whether, indeed, the construction of a third London airport could be justified by a respectable cost–benefit analysis. The chief reason I gave was that the methods used for the estimate of the benefits and the disbenefits are not independent of existing institutions: because the benefits are registered largely as market phenomena, and disbenefits largely as 'intangibles' the asymmetry of treatment tells heavily in favour of the benefits.

This reason is reinforced when it is discovered that a number of 'intangible' disbenefits have been omitted altogether from the Commission's calculation. There may be some justification for these omissions in a study of cost comparisons; the evidence may suggest that they differ little as between one site and another. But in a cost–benefit study undertaken to establish economic feasibility such disbenefits must be counted. I mention two of these below, neither of which is negligible.

(a) *Loss of life.* Per million passenger miles fatalities may be falling. But what matters in a cost–benefit calculation is the expected rise in absolute numbers attributable to the rise in numbers of passengers brought about by a third London airport. If choice of Foulness implies fewer passenger flights over the future, loss of life will be correspondingly smaller also—something the Commission did not take into account.

(b) Most important of all, however, is the *destruction of natural beauty* at home and abroad. This disbenefit is sometimes rudely referred to as 'tourist blight'—a phenomenon of post-war affluence that has already caused irreparable destruction, all over the Mediterranean area and far beyond, to places of once rare scenic beauty, woodland, coastline, lakes and islands.[12]

[12] I refer not only to the disfiguration of innumerable coastal resorts, once famed for their beauty, as a result of frantic 'development' in the attempt to accommo-

The social costs inflicted as a result of air travel facilities may be ignored by governments, but a comprehensive cost–benefit analysis simply cannot ignore them. If they appear intractable to existing methods of computation, the economist must say so, in which case an otherwise favourable cost–benefit calculation must be deemed inconclusive.[13]

Finally, the economist is interested not only in the question whether a given project yields an excess of benefit over cost, but also in the *optimal* operation of an existing or future project.

From Table 4.6, on page 86, one gathers that the number of air passengers taking off in the London area is expected to increase from 18 million per annum in 1969 to 294 million in 37 years' time. Reference to such figures would seem to leave no room for doubt of the 'need' of a third London airport, and probably of a fourth and fifth also. After all, for every single air passenger today there will be, according to these predictions, as many as seventeen in 37 years' time. And if fares continue to remain much the same relative to the prices of other services, and if there is no restriction on airports or air travel, some of us may live to witness the grand spectacle. But, inasmuch as air travel does impose disbenefits on the public, proper concern with allocation requires that fares be raised to take account of them. If this were done, the numbers would not rise nearly so rapidly. They might hardly rise at all, and the need for a third London airport might not then be in the least apparent. For the disbenefits do not consist only of the noise annoyance, fearful as this is going to be,[14] and increased air pollution—which disbenefits,

---

date increasing numbers: these are losses to be borne by future generations as well as ourselves. I refer also to the increasing discomforts endured in popular resorts in consequence of the greater numbers of people and the greater traffic. Indeed, in the expectation that in this respect matters can only get worse, there is every incentive to add to the crowds by visiting such places sooner rather than later. The reader will readily appreciate that the economic issue is not *who* should travel, but (thinking in terms of the spill-overs borne by the intra-marginal tourists today and other generations to come) *how many*.

[13] The *otherwise* excess benefit over cost may be provided by the economist so allowing the public to judge whether such a figure compensates for the damage to be expected over the future.

[14] Unless some effective aircraft-noise preventive device is invented. This does not seem too likely just now, particularly as private and public airlines have no strong incentive to undertake such research—an incentive they would have if they were required to compensate the victims of noise pollution.

be it noted, contribute to a spreading background of pollution and perpetual noise, by reference to which further aircraft and automobile projects are the more easily justified by cost–benefit techniques, since the perceptible contribution of each project to noise and air pollution that are already so bad is obviously limited.[15] As already indicated, the chief disbenefit, tourist blight, is the most difficult of all to measure. The popularity of package tourism need not be questioned. Let us accept airline receipts as a measure of benefit. We need attend only to the 'spill-over effects' each additional person imposes on all others, present and future, but of which he himself takes no account. Indeed, not being 'very naïve' either, the would-be traveller will expect tourist blight to rise over the future and will hasten to travel the sooner before the destruction is complete.

Measuring these adverse spill-over effects would, as suggested, present some difficulties. In view of the commercial interests at stake, and in view of the commitment of governments to compete for a share in this growing market (for fear of losing on balance-of-payments account), research into methods for their quantification would also be a thankless task. As things stand, however, the process of destruction through mass tourism, instead of being slowed down by taxes high enough to cover the marginal spill-over effects, is, on the contrary, accelerated by subsidies. In view of the magnitude of these spill-overs, it is high time that governments began to think in terms of stiff taxes on air travel. Where the fare may cover only a small part of the social cost, a very roughly calculated tax is almost certainly better than no tax at all—even if it should eventually be found to reduce air travel below the optimum level.

Growth of Public Protest

Let me conclude with a more general reflection. There are the beginnings in this country and abroad, particularly in the United States, of a strong anti-disamenity movement among the public. At present, political parties are trying to absorb some of its force.

---

[15] As has been pointed out frequently during the controversy on noise, the ground traffic is already so heavy in built-up areas that the addition of aircraft noise makes no great difference. So, too, once a third airport is built and the aircraft noise level rises over time and extends over the country, it will be that much easier to justify further noise-creating projects, including a fourth and fifth London airport.

My belief is that they underrate the passion behind the protest, and its growing appeal, not least among the young. The movement shows every indication of growing rapidly in the next few years, and also every inclination to achieve its aims by large-scale political changes rather than by 'tinkering with the system'.

Cost–benefit techniques are, indeed, becoming more sophisticated. But they may be too late to exert much influence in the choice of projects which can be related to the 'quality of life' issue. A Report such as the present one, excellent as it is, paying lip service to right principles and secure within its terms of reference, may have the unexpected effect of contributing only to the public's growing impatience with economic expertise, and perhaps with economics in general.

One reason for this impatience is that in such economic calculations *equity* is wholly ignored. If indeed, the business tycoons and the Mallorca holiday-makers are shown to benefit, after paying their fares, to such an extent that they *could* more than compensate the victims of aircraft spill-over, the cost–benefit criterion is met. But compensation is *not* paid. The former continue to enjoy the profit and the pleasure; the latter continue to suffer the disamenities. Another reason for growing impatience is even more compelling. In an age of supposedly increasing prosperity, the choice of a more wholesome life than that we seem to be moving into should, it seems, be technically feasible. Yet, despite a succession of governments overtly obsessed with economic growth, we are being offered year by year continuously less choice in the one factor most crucial to our welfare—the physical environment in which we live, and in which we are fast being submerged.

18

An Economic Examination of Traffic Congestion in Towns

L. K. Lennan

Despite the present plethora of new ideas on measures to combat congestion, little public discussion has taken place in Ireland on the subject of road pricing. This article has been written in the conviction that road pricing has much to contribute to combating traffic problems.

THE PROBLEM

The reasons for the increasing proportion of the population living in urban areas have been discussed by a number of writers. Clark says that the process of urbanization is a case of to him who has, more shall be given—districts which already have abundant industries tend to attract still more.[1] Before the advent of the motor car, industry was concentrated in compact and densely populated industrial towns. With the coming of fast rail and road transport, the so-called 'sprawl' of cities occurred, where workers could live some distance from their place of employment. Industry, however, continued to be attracted to the centre of the complex and consequently access problems arose.

For every country for which information is available the number

From *Administration*, summer 1972, pp. 50–61. Reprinted by permission of the author and the editor of the journal.
[1] C. Clark, 'Transport—the Maker and Breaker of Cities', *Town Planning Review* (Jan. 1958).

of motor vehicles per head of population is increasing. The minimum rate of increase over the period 1966–8 was 4·5 per cent per annum in the U.S.A., a country which in 1968 had slightly over 40 cars for every 100 inhabitants. In Ireland there has been a growth of nearly 20 per cent over the two years 1966–8, the latest available figure being 12 cars per 100 inhabitants; this means 0·52 car per family.[2] In the U.S.A. at this time 50 per cent of all white-collar workers are in two-car families.[3] Obviously the same patterns are developing here: in some areas up to 20 per cent of households at present own two cars. Together with the rapid increase in urbanization, the popularity of motoring must lead to serious traffic congestion in our cities—indeed the problem is already with us.

Measurements over the years in city centres indicate that traffic speeds are falling. In Central London the mean journey speed has been decreasing fairly steadily at 1·9 per cent a year, and is now under 10 m.p.h. during working hours. In Dublin the average speed during working hours is 18 m.p.h. Although the number of car licences in the City and County of Dublin has trebled, the volume of traffic in the central city has doubled.[4] Why not trebled? The reasons are probably numerous but an important one is the deterrent effect of traffic jams in central Dublin.

Every vehicle using the road system in the city causes delays to other vehicles. Although these time losses are often small they mount up, especially where the average speed is already low. It has been calculated that an extra car travelling for one mile on a road where the average speed is 5 m.p.h. causes a cumulative loss of 0·56 vehicle hours on that stretch of road.[5] An extra bus causes time losses of about three times as much. An extra car where the journey speed is 25 m.p.h. does not cause any appreciable congestion to other vehicles. When the traffic flow on roads in a city increases beyond a certain point, vehicle operating costs per mile (fuel consumption, etc.) will increase. Average speeds will be reduced so that the costs of lost time must also be considered. We show the situation dia-

[2] 'The OECD Member Countries', *OECD Observer*, various issues.

[3] D. McIlwraith, 'Are We Highwaymen? Traffic Management and Road Planning in Irish Cities', *Management* (Feb. 1971).

[4] D. J. Reynolds, *Road Transport—The Problem and Prospects in Ireland*, E.S.R.I. Paper No. 17.

[5] R. J. Smeed, *The Traffic Problem in Towns* (Manchester Statistical Society, 1961).

grammatically in Figure 1. (For a more elaborate exposition see Walters's article[6] and the Smeed Report.)[7]

The average cost curve (AC) shows that as the flow of cars increases the cost per vehicle rises. The marginal cost curve (MC) depicts the increase in average costs caused by the addition of each extra car. The demand curve indicates that as the cost per vehicle

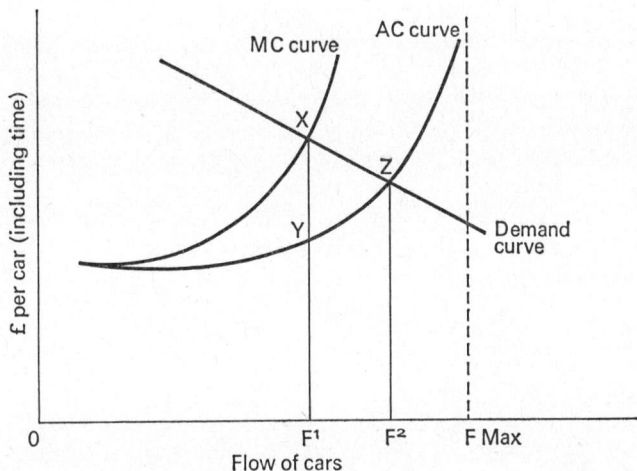

FIG. 1

decreases the flow will increase. The point of equilibrium will be at Z where the flow is F_2. Between traffic flow F_1 and F_2 the cost to each individual (as shown by AC) will be less than the value he places on the journey (as shown by the demand curve). However beyond traffic flow F_1, each extra road user will add more to average costs (see MC curve) than he himself would be willing to pay (MC curve above the demand curve). If a charge XY reduces the flow of traffic from F_2 to F_1 where the demand curve intersects the MC curve, journeys will not be made unless they are valued at the same or more than the costs they cause.

[6] A. A. Walters, 'The Theory and Measurement of Private and Social Cost of Highway Congestion', *Econometrica*, vol. 29 (1961).
[7] Ministry of Transport, *Road Pricing—The Economic and Technical Possibilities* (London: H.M.S.O., 1964) (Smeed Report).

In this example it has been assumed that all cars have the same costs, etc. There is the difficulty that some cars may pay more or less than the costs they cause others. Some small cars might get only 15 m.p.g. while some buses might have no higher cost per mile using diesel oil. But buses cause more congestion and charges should be varied in proportion to the costs the individual vehicle imposes on others. This variation could also apply to less or more congested times of the day, month or year.

The essence of the traffic problem is that an equilibrium brought about by free individual decisions fails to minimize total cost. Every individual is presumed to seek to minimize his own cost, therefore the failure lies with the allocation of total costs to the individual road users. There is a good case for cutting down the volume of road traffic generally from that which would obtain under a free system with neutral taxation. On heavily congested roads traffic should be reduced, whilst on lightly travelled alternative routes the flow should be increased.

SOME SOLUTIONS: A SUMMARY

1. Incentives

The cost of providing for additional rush-hour traffic in or near the centre of the city can be very high. To take a practical example, we might suppose a cost due to congestion on Butt Bridge of £300 per day or for 250 days £75,000. The planner's way of dealing with this situation is to build a wider bridge or a new bridge to eliminate the bottleneck. If this can be done for an outlay of, say, £600,000 everybody is happy. If you offered incentives, say a free special bus service (which might or might not have to traverse Butt Bridge) to motorists who daily use that bridge, the cost of the incentive package might be so contrived as to be lower than the cost of widening Butt Bridge or of building a new bridge, while achieving the same effect on traffic flow. It can also be seen that a charge on people using the Butt Bridge route could be used to discourage drivers who were not willing to pay the full cost of their use of this route.

2. Expansion of the Road System

The idea of this is simply that, as more cars come on the road, road capacity should be increased. Capacity is increased in order to diminish congestion; then more people are attracted to cars when they see how easy it is to get through town and with the taxes they pay the road system is further improved, and so on. It seems very logical but unfortunately it is not all that simple. There is the major problem with a universal tax that the people paying for the new roads, bridges, flyovers, etc. may not necessarily be the people using them. And, more emphatically, people may not wish to tolerate the environmental changes needed to adapt a graceful and historic city from coach transport to multi-lane traffic.

There is repeated emphasis on the need to increase the capacity of roads in the Buchanan Report[8] and also in Buchanan's book *Mixed Blessing*,[9] yet in Los Angeles some of the most congested routes are expressways built recently to relieve congestion.

In some circumstances it is necessary to construct new roads with a large capacity. For example, ring roads are needed or at least desirable if a congestion tax is to work for a city centre.[10]

3. Physical Controls

Could congestion be cured by physical controls on cars entering certain central city areas? This method is also suggested in the Buchanan Report. Physical controls could have the undesirable effect of barring from the road the person who is willing to pay the full social cost of his journey, but who falls into a low-priority class of road user. Physical controls are manifestly a crude solution unless they are specially justified, perhaps for environmental reasons.

4. Differential Fuel Taxes

Walters mentions this as an addition to a road pricing policy.[11] It is possible that this solution would create more problems than it

---

[8] Ministry of Transport, *Traffic in Towns*, Report of the Steering Group and Working Group appointed by the Minister of Transport (London: H.M.S.O., 1963) (Buchanan Report).

[9] C. D. Buchanan, *Mixed Blessing—the Motor in Britain* (London, 1958).

[10] C. D. Foster, *The Transport Problem* (London, 1963).

[11] 'Theory and Measurement'.

would solve. If fuel taxes were differentiated by area the urban motorist, let us say, could either ignore the difference (if small enough), or buy outside the area (if the difference was large enough).

It would be possible also to increase fuel taxes sharply leaving it to 'essential' motorists to claim a rebate. But motoring is now so much woven into the fabric of our lives that above a very low and a very crude level we cannot readily distinguish between essential and non-essential motoring.[12]

5. Differential Licences

Another idea suggested is a more costly licence for congested areas. This system would have the advantage of simplicity but would not discriminate effectively between different times of the day, etc. without losing this simplicity. However, one major difficulty of this system is that once a motorist buys a licence he can spend as much time as he likes in a problem area. To be in any way effective it has been calculated that the congested areas licence would need to cost between £50 and £100 per annum.[13]

6. Poll Tax

A poll tax on employees in congested areas has also been advocated. However, whatever the merits of this in other respects, it would have little effect on road congestion. Low-income workers (the majority probably not owning motor cars) would move out of the centre city area and high-income workers would move in, having a higher ratio of cars per head. A high poll tax would also encourage the mechanization of labour in the city but it is unlikely this would have a significant effect on car travel as the jobs mechanized would be those held by the less affluent who have fewer cars.

7. Parking Policy

This is studied in the section of this paper dealing with parking.

[12] J. McGilvray, 'The Economics of Roads', *Administration* (Summer 1962).
[13] Ministry of Transport, *Better Use of Town Roads*. The Report of a Study of the Means of Restraint of Traffic on Urban Roads (London: H.M.S.O., 1967).

DIRECT CHARGING

To introduce the idea of direct charging I would like first of all to present a simple analogy, first given in the Smeed Report.[14]

Suppose a man runs a small ferry-boat continuously across a river and that it costs 4p a minute to run the boat including his own wages. When he has no passengers it takes him 8 minutes to cross the river. The boat can seat 10 passengers comfortably but can hold as many as 20 passengers, with crowding and discomfort. It is reckoned that within that range (0 to 20) each passenger adds half a minute to the time of the crossing. If there were, say, 16 passengers in the boat and a seventeenth joined them he would increase the ferryman's cost by 2p and he would also cost the 16 passengers $\frac{1}{2}$ minute delay. Assuming time to be worth 1p per minute the additional passenger would be costing every other passenger $\frac{1}{2}$p: he would be in effect adding 2p to the ferryman's costs and, by delaying 16 other people, he would be adding 8p in all to their personal costs, in addition to appreciable discomfort on their journey.

The ferryman might cover his costs if he let each passenger on for only 4p but at this price there might be considerable crowding and delay. One possibility of solving this situation is to introduce regulations; it might be decided that regardless of demand not more than 15 passengers would be allowed on the boat on the grounds that more than this number created too much delay and discomfort. The problem of which passengers should be allowed on could be dealt with on the principle of first come first served, or a system of priority could be developed on some merit principle.

If we drop the assumption, which we made earlier for convenience, that time is worth 1p per minute to *all* passengers we arrive at a more realistic situation where some people value their time more than others do. Two further possibilities now emerge.

1. The passengers could bargain among themselves. Thus for instance a man who valued his time at 50p a minute could pay 20p to another who valued his time at $\frac{1}{2}$p per minute to wait for the next boat. In this way both men would be happy.
2. An alternative would be for the ferryman to raise his price. A higher price would deter those passengers not prepared to pay the cost in time, money and discomfort that their journeys

[14] See above, n. 7.

would cause to the ferryman and the other passengers. As the numbers were thus reduced the associated costs would also be reduced and if the price to the remaining passengers was set so that it just covered these costs this would ensure that journeys were not made if they were valued at less than the costs they caused. In this way there would be an aggregate gain but how this gain was distributed between the passengers and the ferryman and the rest of the community would depend on many other factors.

The use of the road involves similar problems to those of the ferry. A wide variety of regulations is possible or people could bargain with each other to change their modes of transport, though, of course, there are so many road users that no system of direct bargaining is conceivable. But there is also the third possibility— direct charging.

Some rationing of road space results from the variable part of our system of road-user taxation, i.e. the duty on road vehicle fuels which is about 20p per gallon. Taxation paid per vehicle mile varies directly with fuel consumption which is in turn related to the size and technical characteristics of vehicles. There is thus an incentive to economy in the use of fuel and as a result to the development of smaller cars. (Vehicle licences are also 'progressive' in this way but not to the same extent.) In practice tax paid per vehicle mile varies from about $\frac{1}{2}$p–$1\frac{1}{2}$p under uncongested conditions. Rates are about 50 per cent higher under severely congested conditions such as occur in Central London.[15] The full cost of vehicle operation on existing roads includes rent, the costs of road maintenance, the value of resources used in the operation of the vehicle itself and the costs imposed on other vehicles by additional congestion. In order that the individual vehicle should cover its full costs on existing roads, taxation per vehicle mile should equal road maintenance costs, costs imposed on other vehicles and users plus a rent element.

Road maintenance costs are relatively low (less than $\frac{1}{2}$p per vehicle mile in most instances).[16] Marginal social costs only become significant under congested conditions when they are likely to be comparatively large. The Report on Road Pricing estimated that

[15] Smeed Report.

[16] D. J. Reynolds, *Economics, Town Planning and Traffic*, Institute of Economic Affairs (London, 1966).

costs imposed on other vehicles by the passage of one vehicle may approach 30p per mile at 8 m.p.h., 17p at 10 m.p.h., 5p at 15 m.p.h. and 2p at 20 m.p.h.[17] Thus there is a very large gap between the price paid and the full cost of vehicle operation under congested conditions. To rectify this discrepancy a 'fair' general level of taxation of vehicles should be supplemented by charging for road use under congested conditions.

What is a 'fair' level of motor taxation? There are two basic ways of looking at motor taxation. The first is that motor taxes do not differ in kind from other indirect taxes, that the proceeds of motor taxation over and above that which can be attributed to rent should be used for the general purposes of the community, and that there should not necessarily be a relationship between the costs of providing roads and the amounts raised by motor taxation.

The other view is that road taxation should be used simply for the maintenance and expansion of the road system. Those who hold this view are likely to complain that the amount paid in by way of road-licence taxation exceeds that spent on improving and maintaining the road system. Although this may be true, it is not the whole story. If motor taxation is to be regarded as a payment for the roads, each individual should be expected to pay in *road tax an amount equivalent to the costs arising from his use of the road system.* It is obvious that this is not happening. Much of the real cost of travel when traffic is snarled and congested is not borne in full by those causing the congestion; as a result the basic economic nature of the problem is concealed.

The idea of direct charging would be to balance supply of, and demand for, road space, especially road space which is invariable, such as in central city areas and in areas of special amenity. Elsewhere the same principle would apply but supply and demand might both be variables. A perfect balance would be impossible but, by means of direct charging, prices for different roads or areas at different periods of the day or on different days of the week could be fixed. For the sake of argument let us assume three degrees of congestion (A,B,C) and these could be applied to particular roads making sure that the road user would know in advance what particular roads 'cost'. These classifications could be varied at intervals. It is perfectly feasible to measure mileage done in con-

[17] Road Research Laboratory, *Research on Road Traffic* (London: H.M.S.O., 1965).

gested areas by means of a taxi-type meter which displays outside coloured lights to facilitate enforcement. (Congested area A = purple light, B = yellow light, etc.) The British Ministry of Transport report contains details of this and other systems.[18]

Direct charging would cut down congestion and encourage motorists to avoid rush hours and congested streets. If, however, they insisted on travelling in such conditions it would make them bear the full social cost attributable to their journey. This charging system could also take other social costs into account—noise, fumes, etc. although the effects of these might have to be subject to arbitrary measure. It is estimated that the economic benefits to be expected in Britain from an efficient system of road pricing would be of the order of £50m to £100m a year under present traffic conditions.[19]

PROBLEMS IN IMPLEMENTATION

Measures such as those suggested to improve the efficiency of transportation would be opposed by many, and by most motorists, who would regard them as oppressive—an infringement of the ancient right of the freedom of the highway. The object would of course be the opposite, to prevent motorists from oppressing one another. It is surprising that many economists and planners still believe solely in expansionist rather than interventionist doctrine in this area.

Sharp raises some problems about road pricing.[20] He says that the imposition of a congestion tax is in no way an attempt to use a 'normal' price system in selling road space and that a price for road space arrived at by the normal processes of the market would not include the major constituents of a congestion tax. He gives the example of a profit-maximizing road corporation which sold not only road space but also transport, hiring out cars and lorries to users and charging for the use of vehicles and for road space. He says:

Its cost would not be influenced (except in relatively minor matters of fuel consumption and vehicle and road maintenance) by increasing congestion. Any increase in these costs with increased traffic flow would probably be more than offset by spreading the fixed interest charges arising from the

[18] *Better Use of Town Roads.*
[19] Road Research Laboratory, *Research on Road Traffic.*
[20] C. Sharp, 'Congestion and Welfare—An Examination of the case for a Congestion Tax', *Economic Journal* (Dec. 1966).

buildings of the road over a large number of vehicles. The increased journey time would merely represent a decline in the quality of the service which the corporation was selling. There would be no means it could arrange for those road users willing to pay for a higher quality service to pay others to leave the road clear for them, nor would the corporation have any motive for doing so . . .

Sharp's analogy is faulty in that where the road company in question is a monopoly one can hardly speak of the normal processes of the market. If some competition exists, congestion would influence the attractiveness of the roads to traffic and therefore the price necessary to maximize profits. If there was a perfectly competitive road market, congestion costs would be included in the pricing.

Another criticism made by Sharp of the proposals is that the case for a congestion tax rests on the value judgement that some motorists' time is worth more than others. This is not true. The congestion tax case recognizes that some people's time is more costly than others. Sharp in support of his case gives the analogy of the National Health Service and a proposal to reduce waiting time in doctors' surgeries by deterring all those who are not prepared to pay the social cost of waiting time. The point is that Sharp here regards the provision of road space as a social service whereas it is suggested in this work that it is also to some appreciable degree a commodity in trade.

A picture thus conjured up of a city centre cleared of all but Rolls Royces and Bentleys is quite wrong. The idea of road pricing would be that say about 10–20 per cent of present motor traffic would be cut off and volume held constant at that level. The aim might be to cut the *general* tax on the motorist and increase the revenue from *specific* taxation under congested conditions by the same amount. Neither the poor nor the rich motorist need in general be worse off. The ratio of general to specific taxes could be varied and the revenue could be put to whatever use you please. The present free-for-all on congested urban roads means that the private motorist, who in general is better off than the average man, raises the cost of all movement on those roads; the resulting chaos imposes extra costs on everyone, motorist, bus users, even pedestrians. Thus the average man is paying the piper though he has not called the tune—and what a tune it is!

The other problem is that of commercial vehicles and, as Sharp puts it, the 'fairly widespread inflationary consequences' which would result if a congestion tax were imposed on them. There does

not seem to be any major reason why firms should get any concessions; they are contributing to congestion, they are reaping the
advantage of the concentration of business life in the city, and they
should therefore pay for this privilege.

On the question of buses it is suggested that they should pay the
price also. The charge on buses would be small *per passenger*, as
according to Smeed, a bus causes only three times the amount of
congestion caused by cars.

PARKING

Until all cars are charged for the use of the road there is no rational
way of allocating road space between parked cars and moving ones.
There is of course a very widely held attitude that moving traffic
should be given priority over standing traffic because 'streets were
made for movement and not for parking'. As against that the object
of city streets is to provide facilities for access, which requires
parking as well as movement. Street parking should be forbidden
where it causes exceptional danger and interference with movement. Consider for example the case where a car parks for 10
minutes 25 ft. from an intersection on a road 16 ft. wide with 1,000
cars passing per hour; this can be reckoned to cause time losses of
290 minutes to cars travelling along this road.[21] There are many
streets, however, in which the benefits to car parkers outweigh
any conceivable losses to moving traffic even under the present
system of charging.

The consequences of the scarcity of parking space are no different
in kind from those of the scarcity of shops for renting, etc. Since
space in towns is scarce the demand for it must compete with the
demand for other land uses. Space should be allocated to car parking only if car parkers put a higher value on it than people who
wish to use it for other purposes. Parking space in towns should be
made available to people with most need of it. The price system is
the main mechanism for allocating scarce goods and services. What
is different about parking space? If car owners are unwilling to
pay parking costs in full they are simply seeking a subsidy from
others.

There are three methods used to decide who should use the
available car parking space:

[21] Read Research Laboratory, *Research on Road Traffic.*

1. Time limits—priority here is given to the short-term parker.
2. First come, first served—discriminates against the late arrivals. It also leads to 'mobile parking'—cruising around looking for space which adds to congestion.
3. Paying an economic price for the use of parking facilities.

Paying for the use of car parks on an open market is the most direct means of providing parking space. We rely on private enterprise to supply us with most of the commodities for which there is a demand at prices that cover costs: motor cars, petrol, housing, etc. In a rational world we would expect private or public enterprise to step in and provide parking space when it becomes profitable to do so. Unfortunately, in many cities adequate parking space is not provided even when charges could cover costs. This is due partly to a reluctance on the part of the public to pay for what they regard as a free good (this was seen to be true when parking meters were first introduced in Dublin but this reluctance was soon overcome) and also to the existence of free street, or off-street, parking. Local authorities supply the rest of the parking space, usually free, or at small rents. But one does not expect Dublin Corporation to run a hotel at nominal charges and have long queues of would-be guests forming every night!

This attitude towards the justice of free parking is prevalent everywhere. Even the regulation governing parking meters in Ireland authorizes the use of the surplus revenue from parking meters for the provision and maintenance of off-street car parks.[22] This attitude is again to be seen in the approach of Brierley: 'Without some over-all control of car parking in the business areas of our cities conditions will become ripe for the exploitation of the motorist by unscrupulous businessmen. It will be possible for huge profits to be made out of traffic congestion for a limited period at the expense of the motorist and the business life of the city.[23] Parking space should be made available by local authorities at an economic rent within the framework of a road pricing policy, and if private companies (unscrupulous businessmen, by Brierley's definition) are able to compete with the local authorities on this level, let them do so.

[22] Department of Local Government, *Road Traffic (Parking Fees) Regulations 1969*, S.I. No. 169 of 1969 (Dublin: Stationery Office, 1969).
[23] J. Brierley, *Parking of Motor Vehicles* (London, 1962).

The fundamental difficulty with proposals to relieve traffic congestion by parking restrictions is that there is no definite relationship between parking space and traffic flow. Any attempt to discourage the use of road space by restricting the use of a commodity associated with it—such as parking space—is likely to succeed only if there is a close and binding connection between the use of the road space and the use of the commodity chosen for restriction. Thus if all whisky drinkers—and only whisky drinkers—were to drink from glasses it would be feasible to discourage the consumption of whisky by a tax on glasses. But of course the hypothesis does not hold.

The relationship between the use of road space and of parking space is also loose. Many people do not park in the city but still congest the streets. The introduction of a policy of penalizing parking would cause a shift towards more space for movement. It is not only that parking controls would not deter 'non-parking' traffic; the very success of parking controls in reducing congestion (by forcing some of the parking traffic off the roads) would make the area more attractive to the 'non-parking' traffic. In London for example parking controls would result in an increase in the amount of goods traffic being sent to the docks by heavy lorries rather than by rail.[24]

The Buchanan Report advocates, paragraphs 451–2, the use of parking policy to relieve congestion.[25] It goes on to say 'it would not, we think, be sufficient to say that "economic charges" should be levied for parking, we think it is necessary to levy whatever the circumstances demand'. This idea that parking should be subject to restraints above the costs of providing parking space, if the degree of congestion warrants it, runs the risk of confusing the real issue and may unduly penalize the central city parker if a system of road pricing is already in operation. Through traffic can often avoid central areas without loss; not so traffic with destinations in central areas.

It is interesting to note that Thompson who did a comparative study on the results of restraints in Central London—the restraints being daily town entrance licences and a system of parking taxes—concluded that little advantage was seen in the proposal for a

[24] G. J. Roth, *Paying for Parking* (London: Institute of Economic Affairs, 1965).
[25] See above, n. 8.

parking tax.[26] He said that the maximum benefit of such a tax on all parking space is only half that of the daily licence. This finding does not seem to be reflected in the ideas of the Buchanan Report.

The most recent U.K. Report on congestion problems, *Better Use of Town Roads*, comes down in favour of road pricing, saying that the basic objective of traffic restraint is defined as 'to get the best use of scarce land space by inhibiting those uses of the road which cost more to others than they benefit the users.[27] The influence of the Smeed Report is seen throughout the new report which concludes that the advantages of road pricing are so great that it has advised the Ministry of Transport to carry out a full research and development programme on the subject.

SUMMARY AND CONCLUSIONS

It would appear, therefore, that to relieve congestion in towns the following would prove necessary.

1. Road pricing—equating social costs with price.
2. Parking policy—designed to reflect the economic costs of providing space for car parks, etc.

Criticism might be levelled at this article on the grounds that it uses 'economic' criteria only, on the basis that there is more to transport than commercial viability. It is important, however, to point out that when an 'economic' approach is put forward it does not imply that profit is the only criterion to be used. What an economic policy demands is that if some existing system is regarded as socially desirable, the subsidy paid to maintain it should be at a minimum to attain this objective and that it should be clearly identified.

An economic approach attempts to achieve the most from given resources, or to minimize the resources needed to fulfil a particular aim, or combines these two aims to the best advantage. It is concerned, therefore, with a limited aspect of social aspirations: for the rest, for the setting of ultimate objectives, for promoting the values

[26] J. M. Thompson, 'An Evaluation of Two Proposals for Traffic Restraint in Central London', *Journal of the Royal Statistical Society*, vol. 130, Part 3 (1967).
[27] See above, n. 13.

of a society and so forth, the economist can claim no special right of sanction or of veto.

The implementation of road pricing would cause considerable inconvenience to many road users, but there is no doubt that any attempt to solve the problem of urban congestion would be welcomed by the community in general. Solutions previously suggested (for example in the Buchanan Report) have stressed the distinction between essential and non-essential traffic, but have failed to produce any objective method of assessing priorities.[28] In effect the only sure way of deciding how much a particular good or service is worth to consumers is through a pricing system, and there is no reason to suppose that road use is different from any other service.

There is thus a strong logical argument in favour of a pricing system for congested urban roads. A pricing system would ensure that the best use was made of such roads by liberating economic forces which have been held in check for so long that we are hardly aware they exist. For example, access to the centre of Dublin by private car is seriously under-priced. A proper pricing policy would help to rationalize motor traffic on an economic basis and could also be adapted to favour individuals whose journeys are regarded as socially desirable. It would also no doubt assist public transport to achieve a more 'realistic' market share in Dublin which is very low by foreign standards.

[28] J. M. W. Steward, *A Pricing System for Roads*, University of Glasgow Social and Economic Studies, Occasional Paper No. 4 (Edinburgh, 1965).

19

The Use of Standards and Prices for Protection of the Environment

by William J. Baumol and Wallace E. Oates

INTRODUCTION

In the Pigouvian tradition, economists have frequently proposed the adoption of a system of unit taxes (or subsidies) to control externalities, where the tax on a particular activity is equal to the marginal social damage it generates. In practice, however, such an approach has rarely proved feasible because of our inability to measure marginal social damage.

This paper proposes that we establish a set of admittedly somewhat arbitrary standards of environmental quality (e.g. the dissolved oxygen content of a waterway will be above x per cent at least 99 per cent of the time) and then impose a set of charges on waste emissions sufficient to attain these standards. Whilst such *resource-use prices* clearly will not in general produce a Pareto-efficient allocation of resources, it is shown that they nevertheless do possess some important optimality properties and other practical advantages. In particular, it is proved that, for any given vector of final outputs, such prices can achieve a specified reduction in pollution levels at minimum cost to the economy, even in the presence of firms with objectives other than that of simple profit maximization.

In the technicalities of the theoretical discussion of the tax-subsidy approach to the regulation of externalities, one of the issues

From *The Economics of Environment*, ed. P. Bohm and A. V. Kneese (Macmillan, 1972), pp. 53–65. Reprinted by permission of Macmillan, London and St. Martin's Press, Inc.

most critical for its application tends to get the short end of the discussion. Virtually every author points out that we do not know how to calculate the ideal Pigouvian tax or subsidy levels in practice, but because the point is rather obvious rarely is much made of it.

This paper reviews the nature of the difficulties and then proposes a substitute approach to the externalities problem. This alternative, which we shall call the environmental pricing and standards procedure, represents what we consider to be as close an approximation as one can generally achieve in practice to the spirit of the Pigouvian tradition. Moreover, whilst this method does not aspire to anything like an optimal allocation of resources, it will be shown to possess some important optimality properties.

DIFFICULTIES IN DETERMINING THE OPTIMAL STRUCTURE OF TAXES AND SUBSIDIES

The proper level of the Pigouvian tax (subsidy) upon the activities of the generator of an externality is equal to the marginal net damage (benefit) produced by that activity.[1] The difficulty is that it is usually not easy to obtain a reasonable estimate of the money value of this marginal damage. Kneese and Bower[2] report some extremely promising work constituting a first step towards the estimation of the damage caused by pollution of waterways including even some quantitative evaluation of the loss in recreational benefits. However, it is hard to be sanguine about the availability in the foreseeable future of a comprehensive body of statistics reporting the marginal net damage of the various externality-generating activities in the economy. The number of activities involved and the number of persons affected by them are so great that on this score alone the task assumes Herculean proportions. Add to this the intangible nature of many of the most important consequences—the damage to health, the aesthetic costs—and the difficulty of determining a money equivalent for marginal net damage becomes even more apparent.

This, however, is not the end of the story. The optimal tax level on an externality-generating activity is not equal to the marginal

---

[1] We will use the term marginal *net* damage to mean the difference between marginal social and private damage (or cost).

[2] A. Kneese and B. Bower, *Managing Water Quality: Economics, Technology Institutions* (Baltimore, Md., 1968).

net damage it generates *initially*, but rather to the damage it would cause if the level of the activity had been adjusted to its *optimal* level. To make the point more specifically, suppose that each additional unit of output of a factory now causes 50 cents worth of damage, but that after the installation of the appropriate smoke-control devices and other optimal adjustments, the marginal social damage would be reduced to 20 cents. Then a little thought will confirm what the appropriate mathematics show: the correct value of the Pigouvian tax is 20 cents per unit of output, that is, the marginal cost of the smoke damage *corresponding to an optimal situation*. A tax of 50 cents per unit of output corresponding to the current smoke damage cost would lead to an excessive reduction in the smoke-producing activity, a reduction beyond the range over which the marginal benefit of decreasing smoke emission exceeds its marginal cost.

The relevance of this point for our present discussion is that it compounds enormously the difficulty of determining the optimal tax and benefit levels. If there is little hope of estimating the damage that is currently generated, how much less likely it is that we can evaluate the damage that would occur in an optimum world which we have never experienced or even described in quantitative terms.

There is an alternative possibility. Instead of trying to go directly to the optimal tax policy, one could instead, as a first approximation, base a set of taxes and subsidies on the current net damage (benefit) levels. Then as outputs and damage levels were modified in response to the present level of taxes, the taxes themselves would in turn be readjusted to correspond to the new damage levels. It can be hoped that this will constitute a convergent, iterative process with tax levels affecting outputs and damages, these in turn leading to modifications in taxes, and so on. It is not clear, however, even in theory, whether this sequence will in fact converge towards the optimal taxes and resource allocation patterns. An extension of the argument underlying some of Coase's illustrations[3] can be used to show that convergence cannot always be expected. But even if the iterative process were stable and were in principle capable of yielding an optimal result, its practicality is clearly limited. The notion that tax and subsidy rates can be readjusted quickly and easily on the basis of a fairly esoteric marginal net damage calculation does

[3] R. Coase, 'The Problem of Social Cost', *Journal of Law and Economics*, vol. 3 (1960), pp. 1–44.

not seem very plausible. The difficulty of these calculations has already been suggested, and it is not easy to look forward with equanimity to their periodic revision, as an iterative process would require.

In sum, the basic trouble with the Pigouvian cure for the externalities problem does not lie primarily in the technicalities that have been raised against it in the theoretical literature but in the fact that we do not know how to determine the dosages that it calls for. Though there may be some special cases in which one will be able to form reasonable estimates of the social damages, in general we simply do not know how to set the required levels of taxes and subsidies.

THE ENVIRONMENTAL PRICING AND STANDARDS APPROACH

The economist's predilection for the use of the price mechanism makes him reluctant to give up the Pigouvian solution without a struggle. The inefficiencies of a system of direct controls, including the high real enforcement costs that generally accompany it, have been discussed often enough; they require no repetition here.

There is a fairly obvious way, however, in which one can avoid recourse to direct controls and retain the use of the price system as a means to control externalities. Simply speaking, it involves the selection of a set of somewhat arbitrary standards for an acceptable environment. On the basis of evidence concerning the effects of unclean air on health or of polluted water on fish life, one may, for example, decide that the sulphur-dioxide content of the atmosphere in the city should not exceed x per cent, or that the oxygen demand of the foreign matter contained in a waterway should not exceed level y, or that the decibel (noise) level in residential neighbourhoods should not exceed z at least 99 per cent of the time. These acceptability standards, x, y and z, then amount to a set of constraints that society places on its activities. They represent the decision-maker's subjective evaluation of the minimum standards that must be met in order to achieve what may be described in persuasive terms as 'a reasonable quality of life'. The defects of the concept will immediately be clear to the reader, and, since we do not want to minimize them, we shall examine this problem explicitly in a later section of the paper.

For the moment, however, we want to emphasize the role of the price system in the implementation of these standards. The point here is simply that the public authority can levy a uniform set of taxes which would in effect constitute a set of prices for the private use of social resources such as air and water. The taxes (or prices) would be selected so as to achieve specific acceptability standards rather than attempting to base them on the unknown value of marginal net damages. Thus, one might tax all installations emitting wastes into a river at a rate of $t(b)$ pence per gallon, where the tax rate, t, paid by a particular polluter, would, for example, depend on b, the BOD value of the effluent, according to some fixed schedule.[4] Each polluter would then be given a financial incentive to reduce the amount of effluent he discharges and to improve the quality of the discharge (i.e. reduce its BOD value). By setting the tax rates sufficiently high, the community would presumably be able to achieve whatever level of purification of the river it desired. It might even be able to eliminate at least some types of industrial pollution altogether.[5]

Here, if necessary, the information needed for iterative adjustments in tax rates would be easy to obtain: if the initial taxes did not reduce the pollution of the river sufficiently to satisfy the present acceptability standards, one would simply raise the tax rates. Experience would soon permit the authorities to estimate the tax levels appropriate for the achievement of a target reduction in pollution.

One might even be able to extend such adjustments beyond the setting of the tax rates to the determination of the acceptability standards themselves. If, for example, attainment of the initial targets were to prove unexpectedly inexpensive, the community might well wish to consider making the standards stricter.[6] Of

[4] BOD, biochemical oxygen demand, is a measure of the organic waste load of an emission. It measures the amount of oxygen used during decomposition of the waste materials. BOD is used widely as an index of the quality of effluents. However, it is only an approximation at best. Discharges whose BOD value is low may nevertheless be considered serious pollutants because they contain inorganic chemical poisons whose oxygen requirement is nil because the poisons do not decompose. See Kneese and Bower (note 2 above) on this matter.

[5] Here it is appropriate to recall the words of Chief Justice Marshall, when he wrote that 'The power to tax involves the power to destroy' (McCulloch v. Maryland, 1819). In terms of reversing the process of environmental decay, we can see, however, that the power to tax can also be the power to restore.

[6] In this way the pricing and standards approach might be adapted to approximate the Pigouvian ideal. If the standards were revised upward whenever there

course, such an iterative process is not costless. It means that at least some of the polluting firms and municipalities will have to adapt their operations as tax rates are readjusted. At the very least they should be warned in advance of the likelihood of such changes so that they can build flexibility into their plant design, something which is not costless.[7] But, at any rate, it is clear that, through the adjustment of tax rates, the public authority can realize whatever standards of environmental quality it has selected.

OPTIMALITY PROPERTIES OF THE PRICING AND STANDARDS TECHNIQUE

Whilst the pricing and standards procedure will not, in general, lead to Pareto-efficient levels of the relevant activities, it is nevertheless true that the use of unit taxes (or subsidies) to achieve the specified quality standards does possess one important optimality property: it is the least-cost method to realize these targets.[8] A simple example may serve to clarify this point. Suppose that it is decided in some metropolitan area that the sulphur-dioxide content of the atmosphere should be reduced by 50 per cent. An obvious approach to this matter, and the one that often recommends itself to the regulator, is to require each smoke-producer in the area to reduce his emissions of sulphur dioxide by the same 50 per cent. However, a moment's thought suggests that this may constitute a very expensive way to achieve the desired result. If, at existing levels of output, the marginal cost of reducing sulphur-dioxide emissions for Factory A is only one-tenth of the marginal cost for Factory B, we would expect that it would be much cheaper for the economy as a whole to assign A a much greater decrease in smoke emissions than B. Just how the least-cost set of relative quotas could be arrived at in practice by the regulator is not clear, since this obviously would

was reason to believe that the marginal benefits exceeded the marginal costs, and if these judgements were reasonably accurate, the two would arrive at the same end product, at least if the optimal solution were unique.

[7] See A. Hart, 'Anticipations, Business Planning, and the Cycle', *Quarterly Journal of Economics*, vol. 51 (Feb. 1937), pp. 273–97.

[8] This proposition is not new. Whilst we have been unable to find an explicit statement of this result anywhere in the literature, it or a very similar proposition has been suggested in a number of places. See, for example, Kneese and Bower, Chapter 6, and Ruff, 'The Economic Common Sense of Pollution', *The Public Interest* (Spring 1970) (pp. 69–85).

require calculations involving simultaneous relationships and extensive information on each polluter's marginal-cost function.

It is easy to see, however, that the unit-tax approach can *automatically* produce the least-cost assignment of smoke-reduction quotas without the need for any complicated calculations by the enforcement authority. In terms of our preceding example, suppose that the public authority placed a unit tax on smoke emissions and raised the level of the tax until sulphur-dioxide emissions were in fact reduced by 50 per cent. In response to a tax on its smoke emissions, a cost-minimizing firm will cut back on such emissions until the marginal cost of further reductions in smoke output is equal to the tax. But, since all economic units in the area are subject to the same tax, it follows that the marginal cost of reducing smoke output will be equalized across all activities. This implies that it is impossible to reduce the aggregate cost of the specified decrease in smoke emissions by re-arranging smoke-reduction quotas: any alteration in this pattern of smoke emissions would involve an increase in smoke output by one firm the value of which to the firm would be less than the cost of the corresponding reduction in smoke emissions by some other firm. We might point out that the validity of this least-cost property of unit taxes does not require the assumption that firms are profit-maximizers. All that is necessary is that they minimize costs for whatever output levels they should select, as would be done, for example, by a firm that seeks to maximize its growth or its sales.

The cost saving that can be achieved through the use of taxes and subsidies in the attainment of acceptability standards may by no means be negligible. In one case for which comparable cost figures have been calculated, Kneese and Bower (p. 162) report that, with a system of uniform unit taxes, the cost of achieving a specified level of water quality would have been only about half as high as that resulting from a system of direct controls. If these figures are at all representative, then the potential waste of resources in the choice between tax measures and direct controls may obviously be of a large order. Unit taxes thus appear to represent a very attractive method for the realization of specified standards of environmental quality. Not only do they require relatively little in the way of detailed information on the cost structures of different industries, but they lead automatically to the least-cost pattern of modification of externality-generating activities.

WHERE THE PRICING AND STANDARDS APPROACH IS APPROPRIATE

As we have emphasized, the most disturbing aspect of the pricing and standards procedure is the somewhat arbitrary character of the criteria selected. There does presumably exist some optimal level of pollution (i.e. quality of the air or a waterway), but in the absence of a pricing mechanism to indicate the value of the damages generated by polluting activities, one knows no way to determine accurately the set of taxes necessary to induce the optimal activity levels.

Whilst this difficulty certainly should not be minimized, it is important at the outset to recognize that the problem is by no means unique to the selection of acceptability standards. In fact, as is well known, it is a difficulty common to the provision of nearly all public goods. In general, the market will not generate appropriate levels of outputs where market prices fail to reflect the social damages (or benefits) associated with particular activities. As a result, in the absence of the proper set of signals from the market, it is typically necessary to utilize a political process (i.e. a method of collective choice) to determine the level of the activity.[9] From this perspective, the selection of environmental standards can be viewed as a particular device utilized in a process of collective decision-making to determine the appropriate level of an activity involving external effects.

Since methods of collective choice, such as simple-majority rule or decisions by an elected representative, can at best be expected to provide only very rough approximations to optimal results, the general problem becomes one of deciding whether or not the malfunction of the market in a certain case is sufficiently serious to warrant public intervention. In particular, it would seem to us that such a blunt instrument as acceptability standards should be used only sparingly, because the very ignorance that serves as the rationale for the adoption of such standards implies that we can hardly be sure of their consequences.

[9] As Coase and others have argued, voluntary bargains struck among the the interested parties may in some instances yield an efficient set of activity levels in the presence of externalities. However, such co-ordinated, voluntary action is typically possible only in small groups. One can hardly imagine, for example, a voluntary bargaining process involving all the persons in a metropolitan area and resulting in a set of payments that would generate efficient levels of activities affecting the smog content of the atmosphere.

In general, it would seem that intervention in the form of acceptability standards can be utilized with any degree of confidence only where there is clear reason to believe that the existing situation imposes a high level of social costs *and* that these costs can be significantly reduced by feasible decreases in the levels of certain externality-generating activities. If, for example, we were to examine the functional relationship between the level of social welfare and

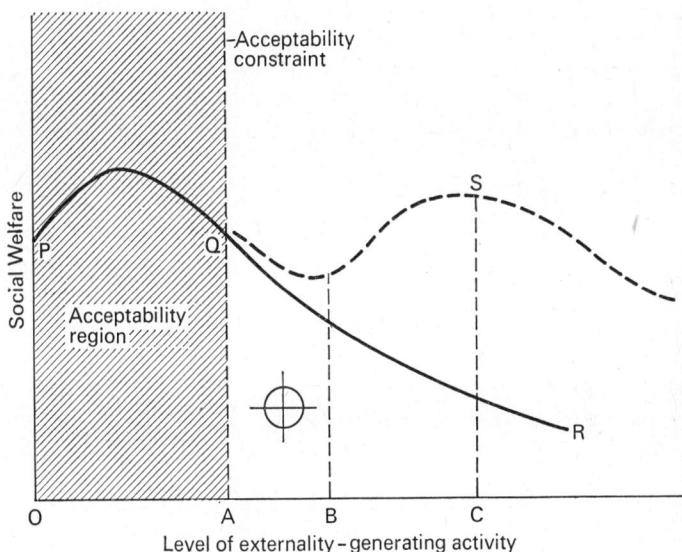

FIG. 1

the levels of particular activities which impose marginal net damages, the argument would be that the use of acceptability standards is justified only in those cases where the curve, over the bulk of the relevant range, is both decreasing and steep. Such a case is illustrated in Figure 1 by the curve *PQR*. In a case of this kind, although we obviously will not have an accurate knowledge of the relevant position of the curve, we can at least have some assurance that the selection of an acceptability standard and the imposition of a unit tax sufficient to realize that standard will lead to an increase in social welfare. For example, in terms of the curve *PQR* in Figure 1, the levying of a tax sufficient to reduce smoke outputs from level OC to OA to ensure that the quality of the air meets the specified environmental standards would obviously increase social welfare.[10]

On the other hand, if the relationship between social welfare and the level of the externality-generating activity is not monotonically decreasing, the changes resulting from the imposition of an acceptability standard (e.g. a move from S to Q in Figure 1) clearly may lead to a reduction in welfare. Moreover, even if the function were monotonic but fairly flat, the benefits achieved might not be worth the cost of additional intervention machinery that new legislation requires, and it would almost certainly not be worth the risk of acting with highly imperfect, inconclusive information.

In some cases, notably in the field of public utility regulation, some economists have criticized the employment of acceptability standards on both these grounds; they have asserted that the social costs of monopolistic misallocation of resources are probably not very high (i.e. the relevant portion of the social-welfare curve in Figure 1 is not steep) and that the regulation can itself introduce inefficiencies in the operations of the regulated industries.

Advocacy of environmental pricing and standards procedures for the control of externalities must therefore rest on the belief that in this area we do have a clear notion of the general shape of the social-welfare curve. This will presumably hold true where the

[10] The relationship depicted in Figure 1 is to be regarded as an intuitive device employed for pedagogical purposes, not in any sense as a rigorous analysis. However, some further explanation may be helpful. The curve itself is not a social-welfare function in the usual sense; rather it measures in terms of a numeraire (kronor or dollars) the value, summed over all individuals, of the benefits from the output of the activity minus the private *and* net social costs. Thus, for each level of the activity, the height of the curve indicates the *net* benefits (possibly negative) that the activity confers on society. The acceptability constraint indicates that level of the activity which is consistent with the specified minimum standard of environmental quality (e.g., that level of smoke emissions from factories which is sufficiently low to maintain the quality of the air in a particular metropolitan area). There is an ambiguity here in that the levels of several different activities may jointly determine a particular dimension of environmental quality, e.g. the smoke emissions of a number of different industries will determine the quality of the air. In this case, the acceptable level of pollutive emissions for the firm or industry will clearly depend on the levels of emissions of others. If, as we discussed earlier, unit taxes are used to realize the acceptability standards, there will result a least-cost pattern of levels of the relevant externality-generating activities. If we understand the constraint in Figure 1 to refer to the activity level indicated by this particular solution, then this ambiguity disappears.

evidence indicates, first, that a particular externality really does have a substantial and unambiguous effect on the quality of life, if, for example, it makes existence very unpleasant for everyone or constitutes a serious hazard to health; and second, that reductions in the levels of these activities do not themselves entail huge resource costs. On the first point, there is growing evidence that various types of pollutants do in fact have such unfortunate consequences, particularly in areas where they are highly concentrated. See, for instance, Lave and Seskin.[11] Second, what experience we have had with, for example, the reduction of waste discharges into waterways suggests that processes involving the recycling and re-use of waste materials can frequently be achieved at surprisingly modest cost.[12] In such cases the rationale for the imposition of environmental standards is clear, and it seems to us that the rejection of such crude measures on the grounds that they will probably violate the requirements of optimality may well be considered a kind of perverse perfectionism.

It is interesting in this connection that the pricing and standards approach is not too different in spirit from a number of economic policy measures that are already in operation in other areas. This is significant for our discussion, because it suggests that regulators know how to work with this sort of approach and have managed to live with it elsewhere. Probably the most noteworthy example is the use of fiscal and monetary policy for the realization of macroeconomic objectives. Here, the regulation of the stock of money and the availability of credit along with adjustments in public expenditures and tax rates are often aimed at the achievement of a selected target level of employment or rate of inflation. Wherever prices rise too rapidly or unemployment exceeds an 'acceptable' level, monetary and fiscal variables are readjusted in an attempt to 'correct' the difficulty. It is noteworthy that this procedure is also similar to the pricing and standards approach in its avoidance of direct controls.

Other examples of this general approach to policy are not hard to find. Policies for the regulation of public utilities, for instance,

---

[11] L. Lave and E. Seskin, 'Air Pollution and Human Health', *Science*, vol. 21 (Aug. 1970), pp. 723–33.

[12] Some interesting discussions of the feasibility of the control of waste emissions into waterways often at low cost are contained in Kneese and Bower. In particular, see their description of the control of water quality in the Ruhr River in Germany.

typically utilize a variety of standards such as profit-rate ceilings (i.e. 'fair rates of return') to judge the acceptability of the behaviour of the regulated firm. In the area of public education, one frequently encounters state-imposed standards (e.g. subjects to be taught) for local school districts which are often accompanied by grants of funds to the localities to help ensure that public-school programmes meet the designated standards. What this suggests is that public administrators are familiar with this general approach to policy and that the implementation of the pricing and standards technique should not involve insurmountable administrative difficulties. For these reasons, the achievement of specified environmental standards through the use of unit taxes (or subsidies) seems to us to possess great promise as a workable method for the control of the quality of the environment.

CONCLUDING REMARKS

It may be useful in concluding our discussion simply to review the ways in which the pricing and standards approach differs from the standard Pigouvian prescription for the control of externalities.

1. Under the Pigouvian technique, unit taxes (or subsidies) are placed on externality-generating activities, with the level of the tax on a particular activity being set equal to the marginal net damage it generates. Such taxes (if they could be determined) would, it is presumed, lead to Pareto-efficient levels of the activities.

2. In contrast, the pricing and standards approach begins with a predetermined set of standards for environmental quality and then imposes unit taxes (or subsidies) sufficient to achieve these standards. This will not, in general, result in an optimal allocation of resources, but the procedure does at least represent the least-cost method of realizing the specified standards.

3. The basic appeal of the pricing and standards approach relative to the Pigouvian prescription lies in its workability. We simply do not, in general, have the information needed to determine the appropriate set of Pigouvian taxes and subsidies. Such information is not, however, necessary for our suggested procedure.

4. Whilst it makes no pretence of promising anything like an optimal allocation of resources, the pricing and standards technique can, in cases where external effects impose high costs (or benefits), at least offer some assurance of reducing the level of these damages. Moreover, the administrative procedures—the selection of standards and the use of fiscal incentives to realize these standards—implied by this approach are in many ways quite similar to those used in a number of current public programmes. This, we think, offers some grounds for optimism as to the practicality of the pricing and standards technique for the control of the quality of the environment.

20

An Economic Comparison of Urban Railways and Express Bus Services
by Edward Smith

INTRODUCTION

Better urban public transport is widely recognized as essential to give every citizen a greater range of opportunities for employment, shopping and leisure activities, to sustain the economic vitality of the town centre, and to provide an attractive alternative to the private car that is less expensive to the community, less damaging to the environment, and more efficient in the use of land. More than a dozen cities in the past decade have built or begun work on new urban railway lines, whilst studies of Leeds,[1] Milwaukee[2] and Edinburgh[3] have concluded that future public transport needs in those cities would be better served by express buses. The purpose of this paper is to compare the total economic cost to the community, including the opportunity cost of all resources, of urban railways and express bus services along corridors with peak traffic sufficient to utilize the capacity of a railway.

It is necessary first to describe the urban railway and express bus

From *Journal of Transport Economics and Policy*, Jan. 1973, pp. 20–31. Reprinted by permission of the author and the editor of the journal.

[1] *Planning and Transport—the Leeds Approach* (London: H.M.S.O., 1969).

[2] Barton–Aschman Associates, Inc., *An Evaluation of Alternative Transit Equipment Systems for Milwaukee County* (Chicago, May 1969); idem, *Milwaukee Area Transit Plan* (Chicago, June 1971).

[3] Colin Buchanan and Partners; Freeman, Fox, Wilbur Smith and Associates, *Alternatives for Edinburgh*, Second Interim Report (Edinburgh, October 1971).

services to be compared. London Transport's Victoria Line, built in the 1960s, will be taken as representative of modern urban railways. The Victoria Line is a radial route, length 21·5 km, connecting central London with local centres and suburbs to the north and south. There are no branches on the line. The average passenger journey distance is about 8 km. This railway is constructed in deep tunnel, bored through London clay at an average depth of about 20 m. Here the Victoria Line differs from some of its contemporaries in other cities, which are often sub-surface cut-and-cover, and occasionally in part on viaduct or embankment.

The average station spacing is 1·4 km, but stations are closer together in the central area and further apart in the inner suburbs. All stations but one on the Victoria Line are sited to allow easy interchange with existing London Transport and British Railways lines. The suburban stations are typically in important local centres. They are reached by feeder bus, private car and walking.

The average train journey speed is 39 km per hour, every train stopping at every station. The Victoria Line in the peak hour carries 28 trains in each direction. Each train has 8 cars, both in the peak and in the off-peak. The railway cars are 17 m long with an average 38 seats and room for 90 passengers standing. These cars are typical; but cars for BARTD (San Francisco Bay Area Rapid Transit District) are designed for 72 passengers seated, with no standing.

It would be quite possible to run a convoy of buses stopping at Stations, A, B, C, D, etc. in the same way as an urban railway operates. Because buses move passengers in a larger number of smaller groups, and because one bus can overtake another, the service becomes more efficient if some buses go direct from A to C without stopping at B. This is an express service in its simplest form: rather than a single stopping service trying to satisfy every travel need along a corridor, several specialized services are tailored to fit the various travel patterns more closely. Many refinements on the fundamental express service are possible. Instead of collecting all passengers at Station A, the express bus is able to go wherever there are roads, and can be its own feeder so that fewer passengers have to change.

For the line-haul section of the journey it will be assumed that the express bus stops only at one or two important interchange points. In the town centre it will make several more stops, setting down

most passengers near their destinations but also simplifying interchange with other services.

An express bus can operate on any road; but if the service is to be
as fast and reliable as the urban railway service the bus must not be
hindered by traffic congestion. For city streets it will be assumed in
this paper that buses have reserved lanes wherever other restraint
measures are not adequate to protect buses from congestion. On a
motorway or other limited-access road any likely bus traffic occupies
only a fraction of the capacity of a reserved lane, wasting valuable
road capacity. Metering access is a more satisfactory means of
giving motorway buses priority. A traffic signal controlling the on-
ramp turns red when the speed on the motorway drops below the
desired minimum. Buses have a reserved lane to bypass the waiting
queue of vehicles, but once on the motorway the bus no longer
requires priority.

As it will be assumed that any new track built for the bus service
will achieve the same penetration of town centres as is expected of
urban railways, road on viaduct will be used in this paper to illustrate track cost. Underground road might be a more realistic
assumption for town centres, but costs are better documented and
more predictable for viaduct. Moreover, a route that is underground in the town centre and on embankment or in open cut in
the suburbs is likely to have the same average cost as a route that is
entirely on viaduct.

It will be assumed that the express bus service employs 12-m
double-deck buses wherever vertical clearance allows. These
vehicles will carry 100 passengers seated, or 150 passengers with
75 standing on the lower deck. A 17-m articulated bus will be
preferred where a double-deck bus is not possible, but a 12-m single-
deck bus must be used if, as in the United Kingdom, an articulated
bus is illegal.

The London Transport Executive publishes urban railway and
bus operating costs on a comparable basis. The data used in this
study are those for 1970.[4] The 3,513 cars required by London
Transport railways for service in the peak operate on 383 route-km
of electrified 1·435-m track with an average station spacing of 1·3 km.
Much of this network was built in the last century, but station
spacing, train length, loading gauge and other characteristics are on
average little different from those of the Victoria Line, which em-

[4] London Transport Executive, *Annual Report and Accounts 1970*, London.

bodies current thinking in urban railway design. Therefore London Transport railway operations may be presumed to reflect typical costs on a modern urban railway. London Transport bus operations —with a peak schedule of 5,550 cars operating on 2,740 km of road —are predominantly stopping services, often in congested traffic. Buses handling the passenger traffic appropriate for urban railways would be organized as a variety of express services, with bus priority to make high journey speeds attainable. However, by separating 'standing costs' (costs incurred with time) and 'running costs' (costs closely related to distance run), cost parameters can be developed that are applicable to very different services.

There are several reasons for choosing as the unit to compare railway and bus costs the car-km rather than, say, the seat-km or capacity-km. The most important costs, including track and driver costs, do not vary significantly with car size. The number of seats and the total capacity depend as much on the production of total floor space given to seating as on the car size; in a given vehicle reducing the number of seats increases the total passenger capacity. Finally, the floor area of the average Victoria Line car, 38 m², is the middle of the range for maximum bus sizes, being less than that of a 12-m double-deck bus, equal to that of a 17-m articulated bus and greater than that of a 12-m single-deck bus.

Taxes, duties, grants and subsidies are transfer payments within the community and should therefore be disregarded in a study concerned with costs to the community. Fuel tax is sometimes taken to represent the cost of building and maintaining the roads, but it is better to estimate the actual cost of roads and disregard payments of fuel tax. All calculations will assume a discount rate of 10 per cent, the figure generally used for the public sector in the United Kingdom. Major railway and road construction projects commonly take about ten years from inception to completion. As it is not possible to foresee social and technological change 35 years hence that might make these facilities obsolete, an amortization period of 25 years will be assumed. Foreign prices will be expressed in pounds sterling at the exchange rates current in 1970.

OPERATING COST ON EXISTING TRACK WITH NO OPPOR-
TUNITY COST

Rolling Stock and Escalators

Recent orders of railway rolling stock have cost HHA (Ham-
burger Hochbahn Aktiengesellschaft) £30,000 per car, London
Transport £40,000, Oosaka Underground Railway £53,000, Oslo
Metropolitan Railway £64,000, New York City Transit Authority
£89,000 and BARTD £111,000 per car. British buses generally
cost between £8,000 and £12,000 each, the dearer buses being
double-deck with a centre exit. These prices do not include the
elaborate and troublesome fare-collection equipment on trial on
some London Transport buses. In other countries single-deck
buses can cost up to £15,000 each.

The Victoria Line is a deep-tunnel railway and the capital cost of
escalators, 40 per cent of the capital cost of rolling stock, was
greater than would be expected for a surface or sub-surface railway.
Because some use was made of existing escalators this cost was not
as great as it might be for another deep-tunnel railway with the
same station spacing. The Victoria Line figure will be taken as
representative, but it should be understood that the possible range
for the capital cost of escalators is wide.

If the useful life of a modern railway car is 2 million km and the
current replacement cost is £40,000, the depreciation will be 2·0 p
per car-km. If the capital cost of escalators is 40 per cent of the
capital cost of rolling stock in peak service and if the escalators are
assumed to have a life of 25 years, the depreciation per car in peak
service will be £12·3 per week. If the life of a bus is 800,000 km and
the current replacement cost is £12,000 the depreciation will be
1·5 p per car-km.

If it is assumed that the rolling stock and escalators are on average
half life-expired, the value on which interest should be charged will
be about half the replacement cost. Allowing for 15 per cent spare
cars, the interest per car in peak service will be £44·1 per week for
railway cars costing £40,000 to replace, £15·3 per week for railway
escalators costing £16,000 to replace and £13·2 per week for buses
costing £12,000 to replace. The interest and depreciation calculated above would not be sufficient to amortize the capital cost
of all-new equipment, but in practice the difference would be

balanced by interest on the deferred maintenance cost of all-new equipment.

Staff

One-man train operation is technically feasible on any urban railway, with or without automatic train control, and is a feature of most new urban railways. One-man bus operation has been standard for many years in North America and is now preferred for all types of service by London Transport, National Bus Company and most other bus operators in Great Britain and Europe. The use of season tickets by commuters could ensure quick loading.

The labour intensity of operation and maintenance can be expressed as staff employed per car-km run in the peak hour. If the average vehicle journey speed is the same for urban trains and express buses, say 40 km per hour, the labour intensity of each will be proportional to the staff per car in peak service. No separate staffing figures are available for express buses apart from stopping buses, but it is reasonable to assume that the staff per car in peak service (but not the staff per car-km run in the peak hour) will be essentially the same for stopping and express bus services. London Transport employs 6·2 staff per car in peak service for the railways and 4·7 for the bus services, excluding guards and conductors. The median value for seven urban railways (Table 1) is 6·8 staff per car in peak service; the median value for eleven bus undertakings is 3·8. The least labour-intensive urban railway in the sample, HHA, employs 2·5 staff per car in peak service, whilst the least labour-intensive bus operation, Atlanta TS, employs 2·2 staff per car in peak service. Electricity-generating staff are included in Table 1 only if employed directly by the urban railway, and for railways other than London Transport the staff per car in peak service is therefore underestimated by about 0·1. The bus figures do not include track maintenance, but it will be seen later that the bus share of road and signal maintenance is a negligible fraction of bus running costs. As the staffing for both railways and bus services can be less than half the present London Transport figures, the labour element in the operating costs must be considered uncertain. But, in common with London Transport experience, urban railways generally tend to require more staff per car in peak service than do bus services. The popular belief that railways are inherently less

TABLE 1

Staff per Car in Peak Service

	Total Staff	Guards and Conductors	Cars in Peak Service	Staff (less Guards and Conductors) per Peak Car
Urban Railways				
HHA (Hamburg)	1,830	0	740	2·5
RATP (Paris)	19,399	2,644	2,926	5·7
London TE	23,700	1,900	3,513	6·2
Montreal UCTC	1,966	90	276	6·8
BVG (West Berlin)	4,440	0	650	6·8
TRTA (Tokyo)	9,215	0	1,189	7·8
FCM de Barcelona	2,026	125	163	11·7
Bus Undertakings				
Atlanta TS	1,058	0	474	2·2
AC Transit (Oakland, Cal.)	1,559	0	651	2·4
HHA (Hamburg)	1,876	0	723	2·6
City of Detroit	2,407	0	878	2·7
Southern California RTD	4,073	0	1,284	3·2
West Midlands PTE	7,945	1,851	1,606	3·8
Leicester CT	930	241	180	3·8
RATP (Paris)	19,237	3,085	3,481	4·6
London TE	36,500	10,600	5,550	4·7
Tyneside PTE	2,010	566	308	4·7
BVG (West Berlin)	8,524	1,765	1,312	5·2

Sources: information received from the undertakings.

labour-intensive arises from counting drivers rather than total staff.

The costs of drivers and traffic staff are more a function of time than of distance run, and will therefore be treated as standing costs. The average train length for London Transport is 7 cars, but driver and signalling costs will be adjusted on the assumption of 8-car trains, as on the Victoria Line.

Maintenance

In Great Britain the cost in 1970 of maintenance, cleansing and administration for motorways and trunk roads was £24·7 millions.[5] The average width of 1,060 km of motorways was 19·4 m and the average width of 15,000 km of other trunk roads was 8·2 m.[6] The equivalent cost of maintenance, cleansing and administration for a 3·6-m lane is £620 per lane-km-year. If the lane carries the equivalent of 2 million buses yearly, this cost for buses is 0·03 p per car-km. This figure properly applies to a heavy-duty road surface, as found on most urban roads.

The maintenance of traffic signals in Greater London cost £650,000 in 1970. It is reasonable to assign 10 per cent of this cost to London Transport buses. For other types of bus operation the cost of signal maintenance could be very different, but would remain a negligible portion of total costs.

Electricity and Fuel

The average electricity consumption for the London Transport railways is 2·2 kWh per car-km or 7·9 MJ per car-km, below average for urban railways with comparable station spacing (consumption being 2·0 kWh per car-km for HHA but 5·4 kWh per car-km for the Montreal Metro). If the electricity were generated by an efficient modern steam turbine the total energy consumed would be about 30 MJ per car-km. The average fuel consumption of London Transport buses is 0·34 litres per car-km, equivalent to a total energy consumption of 13 MJ per car-km. This is typical for a stopping service but is as high as would be expected of an express service employing 12-m double-deck buses with a high power to weight ratio. The high total energy consumption of an urban railway is explained by heavy rolling stock, generally about three times the weight of equivalent buses, having to stop and start at every station.

[5] British Road Federation, *Basic Road Statistics 1971*, London.
[6] S. C. Tanner, *Traffic Survey at 1300 Sites: Analysis of Carriageway Widths*, LR294 (Crowthorne: Road Research Laboratory, 1969).

TABLE 2

Operating Cost on Existing Track with No Opportunity Cost
(Based on London Transport Costs in 1970)*

Standing costs per car in peak service

£ per week	Railway	Bus
	£	£
Administration:		
Central	21·6	16·6
Operating	2·1	2·0
Maintenance	10·3	3·3
Rates, rents, etc.	3·7	3·1
Maintenance:		
Buildings	8·7	2·7
Signaling (8-car train)	9·5	0·2†
Lifts, escalators, pumps	4·0	—
Interest on rolling stock	44·1†	13·2†
Interest on escalators	15·3†	—
Depreciation of escalators	12·3†	—
Drivers (one-man operation, 8-car train)	17·5	78·0
Traffic staff	51·4	16·7
Signal operation (8-car train)	4·1	—
Staff training	2·2	2·8
	£207	£139

Running costs p per car-km	Railway	Bus
	p	p
Electricity or fuel (without tax)	1·8	0·3
Tires	—	0·1
Cleaning, lubricating, servicing	0·3	0·8
Station cleaning	0·3	—
Tickets and machines	0·1	0·1
Compensation for accidents	0·0	0·1
Vehicle repairs	1·7	2·2
Track and structure maintenance	1·2	0·0†
Depreciation of rolling stock	2·0†	1·5†
Miscellaneous	0·2	0·2
	7·6	5·3

* London Transport Executive, *Annual Report and Accounts 1970*, London.
† Estimates not from London Transport sources, but see text.

Comparison

Table 2 lists operating costs on existing track with no opportunity cost, applicable to London Transport railways and buses in 1970. These costs are expressed in Table 3 as a function of the distance

TABLE 3

Operating Cost on Existing Track with No Opportunity Cost—p per car-km

Car-km per week per car in peak service	Urban Railway	Bus
	p	p
1,200	25	17
1,800	19	13
2,400	16	11

run per week per car in peak service. This distance is about 1,800 km for London Transport railways and about 1,200 km for London Transport bus services. It will be assumed that a bus serving the same function as a railway car and having the same average journey speed will travel the same distance per week.

TRACK

Capacity

A modern urban railway with 8-car trains can reliably carry up to 240 cars per track-hour without a serious drop in the level of service. More trains than 30 per hour lead to operating instability if loading unduly delays a train at one station. Buses use motorway lanes only for running. Loading is off the motorway, either in bus-bays beside the motorway or in city streets. If one bus is delayed other buses are not affected. Experiments by the General Motors Corporation using 12-m buses proved that the possible capacity of a motorway is 1,400 buses per land-hour for a running speed of 70 km per hour.[7] An independent study by E. A. Hodgkins of the U.S. Bureau of Public Roads concluded that the possible capacity

[7] R. Rothery, R. Silver, and R. Herman, 'Analysis of Experiments on Single-Lane Bus Flow', *Operations Research*, vol. 12, No. 6 (Nov.–Dec. 1964), pp. 913–33.

of an exclusive bus lane is 1,300 to 1,450 buses per-hour.[8] Because buses do not work to a timetable as rigid as that for trains, the practical capacity would be perhaps 25 per cent lower than the possible capacity to allow for peaks within the peak hour. A practical capacity of 1,000 buses per lane-hour is about four times the capacity of a railway track.

Cost

The track capital cost per car-km run in the peak hour is a measure for comparing the track cost-effectiveness of different systems. The track cost-effectiveness, E, may be expressed as $E = \dfrac{C}{SQ}$, where C is the track capital cost, S is the track length (*not* the route length), and Q is the maximum traffic flow in cars per track-hour. An equivalent expression is $E = \dfrac{C}{NV}$, where N is the maximum number of cars in service in the peak and V is the average car journey speed.

For the Victoria Line the capital cost per car-km run in the peak hour was £10,600, excluding rolling stock, escalators, and lifts, but including capitalization of interest at 10 per cent during construction. Despite the difficulties in comparing prices in cities with different labour costs, property costs, soil conditions, design standards, and construction techniques, the costs of other urban railways built in the past decade have been very similar if expressed in terms of car-km run in the peak hour. An exception is BARTD, for which this cost is over four times as great as for the Victoria Line. The cost per track-km of BARTD is similar to that of the Victoria Line, but the expected traffic flow on BARTD is very much lower. Several urban railways in smaller cities have a cost per track-km lower than that of the Victoria Line but they also have a lower traffic flow. If allowance be made for inflation the Victoria Line cost represents the minimum for a future urban railway.

London's Westway, a route mostly on viaduct, cost £1·3 millions per lane-km, including capitalized interest, and may be typical for motorways in Inner London. Along the length of a route the cost of

[8] Edmund A. Hodgkins, 'Effect of Buses on Freeway Capacity', *Highway Research Record No. 59* (Washington, D.C.: Highway Research Board, 1965), pp. 66–82.

a motorway would vary greatly. In the suburbs it could be less than £0·3 millions per lane-km. In the town centre and any conservation areas expensive underground construction may be demanded. The Heathrow cargo tunnel, a deep tunnel in clay, was £1·1 millions per lane-km (including £0·27 millions per lane-km for ventilation),[9] but bus-bays, junctions, and more difficult soil conditions could raise the price of deep-tunnel road to £3 millions per lane-km. Experience abroad suggests that cut-and-cover would generally be dearer than viaduct but often cheaper than deep tunnel. Despite the possible variation the average cost for the whole route is not likely to be more than £1·3 millions per lane-km.

In practice there is no corridor in which the passenger traffic warrants as many as 1,000 buses per hour. Whereas unused capacity on a railway will magnify the track capital cost per car-km, spare capacity on a road can be utilized by other vehicles provided that some form of restraint, such as metering non-bus traffic at entry points, is available to ensure a high level of service for buses. Thus the bus need be charged only the cost of that proportion of the road capacity which it actually uses in the peak. For shared track assumed to be fully utilized in the peak Q will indicate the practical bus capacity rather than the actual bus flow in the peak. If $Q = 1,000$ buses per lane-hour the track capital cost per car-km run during the peak hour, E, for a bus on a road costing £1·3 millions per lane-km, $\frac{C}{S}$, will be $\frac{£1·3 \text{ millions}}{1,000} = £1,300$. If the vehicle journey speed, V, is 50 km per hour, a depot costing £2,000 per bus in peak service and bus-bays costing £5,000 per bus in peak service will add $\frac{£2,000 + £5,000}{50} = £140$, bringing the capital cost to £1,440 per car-km run during the peak hour.

The total capital cost of the Victoria Line, including rolling stock and escalators at 1970 prices, is £12,150 per car-km run in the peak hour. A bus service costing £21,000 per car in peak service for vehicles, bus-bays, and depot and with an average journey speed of 50 km per hour will have the same total capital cost per car-km run in the peak hour if for the whole route the average cost of the road shared by the bus service is $\left(£12,150 - \frac{£21,000}{50} \right) \times 1,000 =$

[9] G. Margason and R. G. Pocock, *A Preliminary Study of the Cost of Tunnel Construction*. LR 326 (Crowthorne: Road Research Laboratory, 1970).

£12 millions per lane-km, more than twice the cost of the new Blackwall Tunnel, which was the most expensive section of road ever built in the United Kingdom.

If the construction cost is amortized at 11 per cent yearly, liquidating a debt with interest at 10 per cent in 25 years, the yearly cost of track and depot per car-km run in the peak hour will be £10,600 × 0·11 = £1,165 for the Victoria Line and £1,440 × 0·11 = £158 for a bus service on a motorway costing £1·3 millions per lane-km, with assumptions as above. If the daily cost is apportioned at the ratio of Monday–Friday daily traffic to yearly traffic on the London Transport railways, $\frac{1}{305}$, the daily cost of track and depot capital will be $\frac{£1,165}{305} = £3·82$ per car-km run in the peak hour for the Victoria Line and $\frac{£158}{305} = £0·52$ per car-km run in the peak hour for the equivalent bus service.

The track cost per car-km run during the day will be the cost per car-km run during the peak hour multiplied by the ratio of peak-hour traffic to all-day traffic: the peak-hour factor. The costs for a range of peak-hour factors are given in Table 4. For costs as in Table 3 (1,800 km per week) and Table 4 the total operating cost to the community of urban railways and express bus services on new track is given in Table 5 as a function of the peak-hour factor. It will be seen that on new track, for the circumstances considered and

TABLE 4

Cost of New Track—p per car-km

Peak-hour factor	Urban Railway	Bus
0·10	38	5
0·15	57	8
0·20	76	10
0·25	96	13
0·30	115	16
0·35	134	18
0·40	153	21

Note: Railway cost as for Victoria Line. Bus cost as for London's Westway, with allowance for bus-bays and depot and assuming the cost of road capacity not required by buses in the peak is assigned to other vehicles.

ignoring passenger time cost, the cost of an urban railway is about three to five times that of an express bus service.

TABLE 5

Operating Cost on New Track—p per car-km

Peak-hour factor	Urban Railway	Express Bus
0·10	57	18
0·15	76	21
0·20	95	23
0·25	115	26
0·30	134	29
0·35	153	31
0·40	172	34

Note: Costs from Table 3 (1,800 km per week) and Table 4.

Existing Facilities

Consider an existing urban railway that is suitable for conversion to a road. If the present operating cost is 18 p per car-km (assuming no escalators), the operating cost of an express bus is 13 p per car-km, and the traffic is 600,000 cars per track-year, the savings on operating cost possible by substituting buses is 600,000 × (18 p − 13 p) = £30,000 per lane-km-year. If the cost of conversion is £24,000 per lane-km (the median total cost of 22 cases of railway conversion using the existing formation),[10] the reduction in operating cost will give a yearly return on investment of 125 per cent.

The lane capacity in the tunnels of a converted railway would be as much as 20 per cent below the capacity on sections without restricted lateral clearance.[11] The standard vertical clearance for roads is 5·1 m in Great Britain and Ireland but 4·0 m in most other countries. The height of double-deck buses is 4·1 to 4·4 m in Great Britain but 3·9 m in Germany. In most railway tunnels a vertical clearance of 4·0 m for the full width of 3·5-m lanes could be achieved at low cost and bus routes through those tunnels could employ double-

[10] Railway Conversion League, *The Conversion of Railways into Roads in the United Kingdom, 1970*, London.
[11] Highway Research Board, *Highway Capacity Manual*, Special Report 87 (Washington, D.C., 1965).

deck vehicles. Deep-tunnel urban railways—even those with a large bore—are not suitable for conversion to roads: the necessary ventilation, bus-bays, and other modifications would be too costly.

For track already built the construction cost is not relevant in a study concerned with economic costs. Instead any use should be charged the opportunity cost, the highest value of the facility for a different use. If a community is prepared to pay a cost of £1·3 millions per lane-km (Westway) for a new road, and if there is a railway along the same corridor that could be converted to a road at a cost of £24,000 per lane-km, then the opportunity cost of the railway is £1,300,000 − £24,000 = £1,276,000 per lane-km. To justify economically its continued monopoly of this resource the railway should pay the community the interest on the opportunity cost, £127,600 per lane-km-year if the discount rate is 10 per cent. This opportunity cost is equivalent to £127,600/420,000 = 30 p per car-km if the railways carries 420,000 cars per track-year, the average traffic on London Transport tracks. If the railway carries only 100,000 cars per track-year, typical of many British Railways tracks in London, the opportunity cost will be £1·28 per car-km. Clearly an existing railway route is not likely to be economic if even a fraction of it has a high opportunity cost.

The opportunity cost of a bus on existing roads is the cost to the community of diverting or restraining that traffic displaced by the bus. This will often be less than the cost of new road capacity, particularly if some commuters find the express bus service an attractive substitute for the private car and if the existing road capacity is sufficient to satisfy the off-peak demand.[12]

For a city street the bus capacity of a lane is lower than for a road with motorway characteristics. A bus-only lane on average 4·0 m wide (3·5 m widening to 6·5 m at bus stops) in a city street can typically carry 240 buses per lane-hour and is equal in capacity to an urban railway track. In London and many other cities most two-way roads are not wide enough for bus-only lanes plus lanes for other traffic, and in British and European cities the practicable opportunities for one-way streets are limited. However, a bus-only road to carry two-way flows at speeds up to 50 km per hour need be only 7 m between curbs, widening to 10 m for a bus stop on one side.

[12] Edward Smith, 'Design Capacity for Urban Roads', *Traffic Engineering and Control*, vol. 42, No. 4 (Aug. 1970), pp. 182–5.

PASSENGER TIME COST

For any comparison of public transport costs to be complete the relative cost of passenger time must be considered. Travel decisions are affected by the door-to-door journey time of each option, but passengers value time spent walking, waiting and interchanging two to three times as highly as in-vehicle time.[13] To compare the services attainable with urban railways and express buses it is helpful to divide the morning commuter journey into suburban collection, line-haul, and central-area distribution.

Because most passengers do not live near a station, railway suburban collection must be supplemented by feeder buses, private cars and the willingness of patrons in every sort of weather to walk long distances. On a busy urban railway with a single pair of tracks and no loops, each train must stop at every station. The station spacing must therefore be a compromise between the needs of suburban collection and line-haul. A spacing of 1·4 km on the Victoria Line gives an average vehicle journey speed of 39 km per hour. With a greatly variable station spacing averaging 3·7 km BARTD is expected to have an average vehicle journey speed of 75 km per hour; but nearly all passengers will have to change from feeder buses and private cars, and the time cost for interchanging will be considerable. On an urban railway, passengers with destinations outside the one or two central-area corridors served directly must change, bearing a high cost for the loss of time and convenience. On some existing railways the track does not cross the town centre, and most passengers must change for central-area distribution.

In a corridor where passenger traffic warrants 240 buses per hour in one direction, 20 different services can run at a 5-minute frequency, each service designed to suit best the needs of 5 per cent of the corridor's passengers. The express bus separates its suburban-collection and line-haul duties, allowing a comprehensive suburban collection followed with a minimum of interchange by line-haul at 60 to 90 km per hour on a motorway or converted railway. In the central area buses from most suburbs can serve many corridors, again minimizing the need for interchange, and either metered-access roads or bus-only lanes can ensure an average vehicle

---

[13] D. A. Quarmby, 'Choice of Travel Mode for the Journey to Work', Journal of Transport Economics and Policy, vol. 1, No. 3 (Sept. 1967), pp. 273–314.

journey speed in the central area comparable with that of the urban railway, 20 to 30 km per hour.

CONCLUSIONS

Compared with an urban railway, an express bus service can utilize costly track much more intensively, employs light-weight, inexpensive rolling stock, tends to be less labour-intensive, and by largely eliminating line-haul stops and minimizing interchange achieves faster and more convenient services. Whatever the discount rate, amortization period, or cost of labour, the construction of a new urban railway is not likely to be economically justified in typical circumstances. If there are valid non-economic reasons for preferring a new railway, these reasons ought to be clearly identified and weighed against the advantages of the best bus alternative.

Some existing railways could readily be converted to roads, with considerable benefit to the community. The much higher capacity attainable with a bus service would be welcome in the peak hour on routes now worked by overcrowded trains. For equal loading standards the bus service should have a lower operating cost, the savings quickly repaying the cost of converting the railway. The improvement in service would be particularly great in the case of existing suburban railway lines which do not cross the town centre; the replacement buses could run through the town centre in bus-only lanes, and fewer passengers would have to change. Economically the greater benefit, during the off-peak as well as during the peak, would generally be from the use of the converted railway by additional traffic. It is most important, however, that access by private vehicles be metered whenever congestion threatens to slow buses.

21

Disasters and Charity: Some Aspects of Co-operative Economic Behaviour
by Christopher M. Douty

Recent investigations by economists and other social scientists into events pursuant to natural disasters have revealed an unexpected pattern of behaviour. Economic theory suggests that the sudden, largely unanticipated destruction of wealth by an external force—the characteristics which define a disaster—will lead to a higher price level for necessities. It may also be expected that the cloak of the ensuing mass confusion and uncertainty will result in an increase in all forms of antisocial behaviour. Yet, empirical research has repeatedly shown that prices rarely rise enough to clear markets, that natural disasters are typically followed by an increase in charity by residents of the disaster zone, and that there is an increase in 'community feeling' generally. The fact of post-disaster charity, and of generally heightened concern for the well-being of others, is of greater theoretical interest than its quantitative importance. Apparently, for some time after a disaster, resources are typically used differently and with more generosity toward others.[1] This fact presents an anomaly for economic theory to explain. It is the task of this paper to offer such an explanation. It is hoped that the theory advanced also serves to shed light on the 'social cement' that normally exists within a community.

From *American Economic Review*, Oct. 1972, pp. 580–9. Reprinted by permission of the American Economic Association.

[1] However, an intellectually dissatisfied economist may still derive much emotional satisfaction from these unexpected benevolent actions of human beings under trying circumstances.

The behaviour pattern to be discussed has been observed not only after natural disasters, but after virtually all disasters of external origin.[2] Systematic empirical studies of the effects of the 1917 munitions ship explosion in Halifax harbour, of the social effects of World War II bombing, of the events following the 1953 tornadoes at Worcester, Massachusetts and at Waco and San Angelo, Texas, and a study of the 1961 disaster caused by Hurricane Carla have all revealed similar post-disaster behaviour.[3] More recently, the economic investigations by Dacy and Kunreuther into the 1964 Alaskan earthquake and a study by Douty[4] of the effects of the 1906 earthquake and fire in San Francisco have turned up essentially the same sequence of events.

This sequence, which Hirshleifer[5] calls the 'disaster syndrome', has been described in terms of sociological theory by Thompson and Hawkes.[6] The community is seen in 'normal' periods as a multipurpose system that is organized to enable it to utilize its resources for the achievement of many simultaneous objectives. A disaster is seen as an event that destroys not only wealth but also the allocative and 'integrative' (organizational) mechanisms. Initially, a disaster sharply reduces the interaction— exchange and otherwise—among primary units (i.e. families); this is soon followed by a resurgence of interaction among primary units in relief and rescue operations, but with much greater dependence upon non-market co-ordination than normal. Despite plentiful opportunities, there is virtually no looting or other antisocial behaviour; instead the community appears as a 'super-organization' with allocative decisions made by a centrally controlled bureaucracy

---

[2] Internally generated disasters, such as civil disorders, apparently result in a different behaviour pattern.

[3] See D. C. Dacy and H. Kunreuther, *The Economics of Natural Disasters: Implications for Federal Policy* (New York, 1969); H. E. Moore, *Tornadoes over Texas* (Austin, Tex., 1958), and *. . . and the Winds Blew* (Austin, Tex., 1964); and S. H. Prince, *Catastrophe and Social Change* (New York, 1920).

[4] C. M. Douty, 'The Economics of Localized Disasters: An Empirical Analysis of the 1906 Earthquake and Fire in San Francisco', unpublished doctoral dissertation, Stanford University, 1969.

[5] J. Hirshleifer, *Disaster and Recovery: An Historical Survey*, Rand Corporation RM-3079-PR (Santa Monica, Calif., 1963).

[6] J. D. Thompson and R. W. Hawkes, 'Disaster, Community Organization and Administrative Processes' in G. W. Baker and D. W. Chapman (eds.), *Man and Society in Disaster* (New York, 1962).

often headed by the pre-disaster civic leaders. Co-operation and generally selfless behaviour by the victims and others near the disaster zone is strikingly evident. However, with the beginning of long-run recovery, individuals resume their normal degree of egocentredness, with the centralized allocative mechanism either breaking down or withering away.

Discussions of the disaster syndrome have suffered from *ad hoc* theorizing and the difficulty of disentangling reports of events from theories about human behaviour under the specified conditions. Several writers anxious to improve on this state of affairs and convinced that economic theory ought to be able to say something about disaster phenomena, have produced the theoretical work that is critically summarized in Section I. Section II develops an alternative theory and its implications are examined.

I. SOME ECONOMIC INTERPRETATIONS OF POST-DISASTER BEHAVIOUR

An obvious peculiarity of observed post-disaster economic behaviour is the failure of prices to rise as rapidly as would be suggested by simple supply and demand analysis. The destruction of the stocks of 'necessity goods', of which food, clothing, and shelter are prime examples, might normally be expected to lead to sharply rising prices during the Marshallian market period (which lasts at least until outside aid is received), as competition for the remaining supplies of necessity goods intensifies.[7] However, social scientists who have studied disasters assert that prices rise less than would be predicted on the basis of pre-disaster economic relationships and the magnitude of the disaster involved.[8] Apparently, a disaster motivates persons within the disaster zone who have retained undestroyed stocks of necessities to increase their charity. Dacy and Kunreuther and Louis De Alessi have offered theoretical explanations for these phenomena which we shall discuss.

The empirical evidence on post-disaster price behaviour is sketchy

[7] This statement implicitly assumes a high survival rate of the population relative to that of non-human wealth and that the victims retain some means of making their offers of exchange for goods and services effective. The former assumption is empirically correct; the latter often is not.

[8] This should not be interpreted as meaning that there are never any price increases or that 'extortionate' prices are never observed. See the next section.

and impressionistic. Breakdown of communications and transportation obviously fragment markets and increase the expected price dispersion for a commodity within a given geographical area. Records of transactions are few and of certain representativeness. Consequently, we shall not attempt to argue that after a disaster prices go up 'much' or 'little'. What is clear is that transactions typically occur at prices that would seem far below what the market would bear. Collateral evidence that this is so, is the prevalence of queues for all sorts of goods with no appreciable tendency for supplies to disappear (to black markets) and queues to rapidly shorten.

In analysing the behaviour of suppliers (donors) in disaster zones, it is useful to divide them into the following groups: (1) households within the disaster zone with accessible undestroyed stocks of necessity goods; (2) large business firms operating wholly or substantially within the disaster zone; (3) private economic units located in 'support' zones; (4) the central and state (or provincial) governments having sovereignty over the stricken area. With the probable exception of category (1) above, the donor is unacquainted with the recipients of his charity; therefore most charity is given to a generalized group called 'victims'. The analysis of this section applies only to donor categories (1) and (2); in Section II all four categories are considered.

The observed failure of post-disaster prices to rise as sharply as might be expected, indicates to Dacy and Kunreuther, pp. 63–70, that there has been a structural shift in the utility functions of the stricken population. Their analysis assumes, conventionally, that (1) individuals maximize their utility; (2) that the utility enjoyed by each individual depends only on his own consumption of goods and services; (3) business firms seek maximum profits in order to maximize the consumption possibilities of their owners, and (4) philanthropic behaviour is inconsistent with profit maximization. These assumptions, commonplace in economic textbooks, imply that a disaster-caused leftward shift of market-period supply curves coupled with unchanged demand curves, should result in higher short-period equilibrium prices for necessity goods.[9] Though the

[9] The decrease in community wealth occasioned by a disaster could also lead to a leftward shift of demand curves, assuming that wealth (or income) elasticities of demand are positive. However, Dacy and Kunreuther believe, pp. 65–6, that in the wake of disaster, purely egoistic concerns would lead to an increase in hoarding,

extent of these price increases may be mitigated by expectation of outside aid, the failure of prices to rise at all following the disasters considered by Dacy and Kunreuther is seen (by them) as due to 'emergent altruism' among those disaster zone residents whose circumstances permit them to offer charity.[10] Thus their explanation of upward price stickiness is that tastes have changed to include more altruism. They allege that at some later date the taste for altruism disappears, thereby 'explaining' the fact that the observed increase in community feeling is only temporary.

De Alessi[11] points out that the explanation offered by Dacy and Kunreuther cannot be empirically refuted because no one has yet learned how to directly observe shifts in utility functions. However, he notes that if 'interdependence of utility functions' is admitted, then it is possible to retain the customary assumption that utility functions are unchanged, and yet to develop hypotheses that are, in principle, empirically testable. Interdependence is assumed to imply that individuals feel compassion for those who are less well off materially than themselves. This compassion manifests itself normally in a steady flow of charity from relatively wealthy to less wealthy individuals, with the utility of the donors being maximized when the marginal dollar used for the 'purchase' of charity yields an increment of utility equal to that yielded by the marginal dollar spent on any other commodity.

A disaster changes the relative asset positions of the donor and the recipient. Assuming that the pre-disaster recipient is so unfortunate as to be a disaster victim, the relative deterioration of his position will increase the marginal utility to the donor of a given amount of charity, subject only to the condition that the donor's indifference curves be convex. Therefore the donor will increase his flow of charity until he is again maximizing his utility.

---

causing the demand curves to shift to the right thereby accentuating upward pressure upon prices.

[10] Chapter 5 of their book contains a fairly extensive presentation of relevant data on the 1964 Alaskan experience and briefer descriptions of observed price behaviour following other disasters. However, evidence presented by Douty, ch. 4, on San Francisco's 1906 earthquake and fire indicates that completely stable post-disaster prices are not universal. Although some of the data are unreliable, it is unquestionable that room rents rose substantially.

[11] L. De Alessi, 'A Utility Analysis of Post-Disaster Cooperation', in Virginia University, *Papers in Non-Market Decision Making*, 3 (Fall 1967), 85–90.

The alleged interdependence of utility functions also provides a basis for an explanation of the post-disaster charity given by business firms (see De Alessi, 'The Utility of Disaster', *Kyklos*, vol. 21 (1968), pp. 525–32). If the utility functions of individuals who are managers contain non-pecuniary elements, business conduct inconsistent with the presumed goal of the maximization of the present value of the owners' equity will be generated. The tendency for such conduct to exist will be stronger if the owners and managers are different sets of people, than if there is owner management.[12]

The fact that many firms give some charity during non-disaster periods is taken by De Alessi to be evidence that firms may increase their philanthropic activity in post-disaster situations. Furthermore, if the firm counts goodwill among its assets, managerial utility maximization through post-disaster donations of some of the firms's wealth may be consistent with the wealth-maximizing interest of the stock-holders. The existence of goodwill implies that the market in which the firm sells its products is imperfect. Charity may be offered to help the firm maintain its goodwill. Therefore De Alessi concludes, '. . . other things being the same, the smaller the degree of competition, the more post-disaster charity a firm will give' (1968, p. 531).

This argument has considerable appeal because of its simplicity, its ingenious use of conventional economic theory and because it provides testable implications. However, it also has some disturbing implications and leaves unanswered a number of important questions. De Alessi's analysis says little about the characteristics of the donors and the recipients. Perhaps it can be reasonably assumed that

[12] This statement is true if the income of managers is only loosely correlated with their success at maximizing profits. Non-employee stockholders have the option of selling their stock in firms which from their point of view are managed poorly, a fact that enlarges the potential scope for 'non-economic' managerial behaviour still more. (It is presumed here that existing managements can be dislodged only with difficulty.) The managers of a regulated public utility have especially great scope for discretionary behaviour; the guaranteed profit rate that their firms typically enjoy means that non-economic managerial behaviour has relatively little adverse effect on the owners' equity position. Therefore the scope of such behaviour is limited only by the ability of the regulatory commission to enforce standards of managerial competence. However, any degree of monopoly in the seller's market permits some non-economic behaviour (see A. A. Alchian and R. Kessel, 'Competition, Monopoly and the Pursuit of Pecuniary Gain, in *Aspects of Labor Economics*, Universities–Nat. Bur. Econ. Res. Conference Series (Princeton, N.J., 1962)).

all 'needy' victims receive aid, from a 'spontaneously generated' post-disaster relief organization. Such organizations do in fact often arise, but what causes their emergence? Is it possible to predict who will lead these organizations? Is post-disaster charity given only by individuals who have been benefactors of the relatively poor prior to the disaster?

Let us see what can be said on these matters. In regard to business firms, is the degree of imperfection of competition a relevant factor in determining their post-disaster behaviour? Can anything be said about external aid, including that of governments?

II. A THEORY OF POST-DISASTER CO-OPERATION

The proposition that an individual makes those decisions that best serve his own interest, narrowly conceived, has been found to be highly useful in economic analysis. Therefore, it is incumbent upon us to develop a theory of post-disaster charity that shows that 'altruistic' behaviour may under some circumstances be consistent with enlightened self-interest.

At the risk of belabouring the obvious, we note that interdependence of economic units constitutes much of the subject matter of economic analysis, with market interdependence receiving the greatest emphasis. Theorizing about market behaviour has most often proceeded as though the institutional environment were a constant.[13] The institutional environment includes the network of rules and regulations by which a society lives. Some of these are formalized into law; others are self-enforcing customers. The institutional environment is a sort of collective good that can be regarded as the result of a consensual agreement.[14] The agreement need

---

[13] Neoclassical economists generally only enumerated the functions of government which they saw as consistent with a *laissez-faire* economic framework. The choice of an actual institutional framework was seen as something apart from economic analysis. In recent years theoretical work on the nature of social choice and collective goods and the related work by Alchian, Harold Demsetz and others on the theory of property rights has introduced a degree of integration of institutional choice and market behaviour into the mainstream of economics. Needless to say, the 'Institutionalists' (e.g. John R. Commons) did not take the institutional environment as a constant. The same applies for economic historians and economists working in many applied areas, especially in economic development.

[14] Hirshleifer, whose paper 'Disaster Behavior: Altruism or Alliance' (1967; unpublished) has been very helpful in the formulation of these ideas, calls the

not be universally accepted in all particulars, but it must be generally adhered to if the environment is to be viable. This agreement provides a set of guidelines that specifies the allowable scope of actions that an individual may take in his own interest. Such guidelines are required if there is to be substantial market interdependence and a high degree of specialization according to comparative advantage. The benefits of a stable institutional environment are shared in some degree by all members of the community. A major task of government is to see that these benefits are in fact widely diffused and are not captured entirely by a small minority of individuals within the community who undertake illegal or unethical actions.[15]

This discussion is relevant in this context because the rapid change in the physical environment that an unexpected disaster imposes causes the pre-disaster institutional arrangements to become largely inoperative. The degree of the breakdown of institutional arrangements is in large measure a reflection of the magnitude of the disaster and of the uncertainty that it creates. The existence of uncertainty causes individual behaviour to be governed by indefinite expectations concerning the future. Among the major factors that determine these expectations are the memory of the pre-disaster institutional environment and the individual's perception of his current situation in relation to that of the rest of the community. The former includes the individual's pre-disaster web of social and economic relationships. The latter, of course, will change as the individual gains a clearer perception of his and the over-all post-disaster situation. The analysis that follows emphasizes the effects of the continuing reassessment of the post-disaster situation by all of the affected individuals, showing in particular that the widely noted increase in community feeling is the expected outcome of individualistic rational behaviour.

However, the increase in community feeling is usually not the first collective post-disaster reaction. The initial reaction is the fragmentation of the stricken community into very small units that

---

consensual agreement an 'alliance'. This term, in turn, has been borrowed from Mancur Olson, *The Logic of Collective Action* (Cambridge, Mass., 1965).

[15] One of the characteristics of a viable institutional environment is that it must provide for an 'equitable' distribution of the benefits of the consensual agreement. If the distribution of benefits is seen by a substantial number of the members of a community (not necessarily a majority) as inequitable, the agreement is no longer sufficiently consensual and will be much more difficult to maintain.

have been called 'kinship groups'.[16] At this point the victims probably observe that a large part—perhaps most—of the pre-disaster population seems to have survived, although much of the capital stock has been destroyed.[17] However, the individual ignores the larger community until the survival and well-being of persons with whom he had maintained his closest personal ties has been determined. The determination of the survival status of family members can be regarded as the first step in the reduction of post-disaster uncertainty, without which rational decision-making is impossible. During this interim period of community fragmentation, market transactions, if any are consummated, are often at elevated prices.[18] However, when the survival status of close relatives is determined, usually through a reunion with them, the period of fragmentation ends. The problem as seen by the individual then becomes the survival of the larger community and the restoration of a viable institutional framework.

Assuming that a supply of 'necessity goods' survives the disaster in usable form, these must be distributed in such a manner as to allow the victims to subsist without being forced to evacuate the disaster zone. The charging of elevated prices, or even positive prices, for these goods is inconsistent with the maintenance of the population unless these prices are within the means of all of the victims.[19]

[16] On fragmentation, see Thompson and Hawkes and the references therein. On the concept of kinship groups, see the references in Olson, pp. 17–18.

[17] The behaviour of victims who become totally disoriented by the disaster is not considered here. Most disaster studies indicate that disoriented victims are the exception, rather than the rule.

[18] There were many dramatic reports of prices being increased to anywhere from ten to fifty times their pre-disaster levels following the 1906 San Francisco earthquake and fire. See Douty, ch. 4, for references. Recent disasters have produced few such reports, however. The generally smaller magnitude of recent disasters may be responsible.

[19] In an article on non-price rationing ('The Political Economy of Consumer's Rationing', *Rev. Econ. Statist.*, vol. 24 (Aug. 1942), pp. 114–24), Tibor Scitovsky defined a shortage as existing when the rise of the price of a commodity would cause it not to be distributed on an 'egalitarian basis', or if the charge of any commercially viable price would cause a great inequality of distribution of that commodity. Obviously, this definition can be reasonably applied only to necessities, such as staple foods and shelter. However, these are the types of commodities for which sharp advances in prices would be expected following a disaster if economic individualism was carried to an extreme. A disaster creates shortages in Scitovsky's sense of the term; since these shortages exist, there is a case for non-price rationing.

A means of non-price rationing is probably required, since many of the victims are likely to be without accessible liquid assets.[20] The desire to see a continuance of the community leads to the development of such a rationing system and causes social pressure to be brought to bear on possessors of 'necessity goods' who are attempting to 'extort' high prices from the victims. These phenomena deserve further attention.

Consider the social pressures that a small grocer with an undestroyed inventory stock faces. He has tomorrow as well as today to think about. His regular customers will be aware of his elevation of prices. The grocer will know that if other grocers are not raising prices, his short-sighted behaviour could cost him his clientele—if not immediately, then in the near future. This implies that the desire to maintain continuing economic, as well as personal, relationships will moderate any tendencies to attempt to extract all of the consumers' surplus from buyers. Furthermore, if many of the victims are unable to buy food and if none is donated to them, the grocer could soon find that he is unable to prevent the removal of his merchandise without the formality of payment. Hunger pangs are not to be denied. Therefore, if the grocer perceives that he will receive little revenue even if he attempts to charge sharply higher prices, he may then decide that the rational thing to do is to offer his merchandise free to the victims, on a first come, first served basis. No current revenue is realized by this act of charity, but it may be that there is no long-run sacrifice as the grocer's charity may gain him goodwill in the future. Thus it may be possible to rationalize behaviour that appears altruistic as reflecting a long-run view of self-interest. A similar rationale may apply to many other acts of kindness commonly observed after a disaster; for example, families taking in homeless friends and relatives (sharing housing) without compensation; donating or lending clothing without reward.

Reconciling this type of behaviour with the hypothesis of individual utility maximization—which is maintained—presents an interesting theoretical challenge with several different, though not

[20] It is conceivable that individuals in the disaster zone who possess accessible liquid assets could lend money to those in need of it. However, in this context, such loans are unlikely to be forthcoming even at very high interest rates because the overwhelming environmental uncertainty would create doubt as to the borrower's earning capacity and hence his ability to repay the loan. Finally there is the possibility that the banks will be closed, causing most of the liquid assets of *all* persons within the disaster zone to be inaccessible.

mutually exclusive answers. First, families, both primary and extended, and networks of friends are linked together in an unwritten mutual insurance plan against economic adversity. The implicit obligation to help others in need is especially strong when the utility loss is great and is manifestly unrelated to any failure on the part of the victim. Natural disasters clearly qualify as situations where 'insurance benefits' may be claimed. The obligation to render assistance, upon those able to do so, is enforced *de facto* by the (implied) threat of thereafter being denied insurance protection. As implicit contracts of this sort cannot be enforced through the courts, they tend to arise among people who can exert social pressure upon one another to honour commitments; for example, such implicit contracts are likely to arise among members of an ethnic, racial or religious group. Much altruism is this sort of honouring obligations to members of one's 'mutual insurance club.'[21]

But it is also necessary to account for charity towards total strangers, which is frequently observed in the aftermath of a disaster. Part of the explanation lies in the breakdown of communications and transportation so that the normal sources of aid from mutual insurers are temporarily cut off; also a clustering of members of an insurance network (not uncommon) may put great strain upon or overwhelm those located elsewhere; this increases the importance of aid from 'outsiders'. That is, a natural disaster tends to put pressure upon all members of a community to act as though there were an informal reinsurance society to backstop the informal (primary) insurance networks.

To specify the channels through which this pressure is exerted requires identifying a second spring of altruism: community leadership. Community leaders all have an important stake in maintaining a sense of community values. A sense of community values is manifested by participating in the production or purchase of public goods without being overtly covered; i.e., by not attempting to act as a free rider. Religious leaders benefit from a wide diffusion of a sense of community values in that it facilitates money raising and the contribution of free time. Military leaders benefit by getting more willing soldiers; political leaders by making it easier to collect taxes,

[21] Of course this is not an attempt to describe the psychic states of charity givers in a post-disaster situation. The argument contends only that the donors act 'as if' they were optimizing individual utility in the circumstances in which they find themselves.

enforce laws, get public support for costly public goods, etc. Business leaders obviously have an interest in promoting respect for law and order.

Failure to provide for needy members of the community in time of need engenders cynicism towards community values and resistance to demands made in their name. Conversely, manifestation of community values by provision of disaster insurance promotes belief in an unwritten social (insurance) contract respect for which enhances the utility of community leaders. The ability of leaders to reward those who co-operate with them and punish those who do not is obvious.

Yet a third rationale for post-disaster benevolence is the need for immediate community approval. Normally, the sanctity of life and property are protected by the courts and the armed force they can muster to enforce their decisions. In the aftermath of a disaster, courts cannot function and soldiers cannot be mobilized. An individual more fortunate or foresighted than others cannot expect safely to hold his property for what he thinks the market will bear, secure in the knowledge that his property is sacrosanct, regardless of the needs of those around him. On the contrary, his property may be seized and his person severely punished as an engrosser. Security of life and property may depend upon close conformity to community norms of behaviour, particularly as regards prices charged. A stricken community has little tolerance for entrepreneurial deviance.

In the terse language of the theory of choice, most individuals own one or more (unwritten) insurance policies which 'pay off' when their income falls below a certain minimum level for a socially acceptable cause (e.g. a natural disaster). Conversely, they have a contingent obligation to aid others in danger of falling below the implied minimum for an unacceptable reason. The enforcement of this obligation is by social pressure, subordination to which is necessary to avoid unacceptable risks to life, property and reputation (implicitly related to ability to buy and sell on the same terms as others). Nothing further need be said about the characteristics of anyone's utility function, though, 'true altruism' may be present in post-disaster situations.

It may be recalled that De Alessi (1968) concluded that any firm in the stricken area may give charity if its managers have a positive taste for charity. Firms in imperfect competition give more charity than atomistically competitive firms in order to protect their goodwill, as indicated above. However, the postulated taste for altruism is not required if the argument is reframed in terms of the degree of involvement of the firm with the stricken community and the firm's size. Our primary concern here is with large firms, as small firms (i.e. small grocers, etc.) have already been considered. However, it is a fact that the largest private benefactors of a stricken community are large firms that had enjoyed extensive operations in the disaster, with many of their assets intact.[22] The location of the surviving assets, whether inside or outside the disaster zone, is not relevant. Size is relevant, however, because it connotes identifiability (particularly if the firm deals with the general public rather than with a specialized group of customers), a significant financial capacity and a degree of goodwill in the markets in which it sells. The firm has an incentive to protect its goodwill if possible. This goodwill is threatened if the firm engages in behaviour that the disaster victims regard as unfair. Local executives, whether or not these be the firm's top management, sense this intuitively and therefore extend charity to the victims. Furthermore, they might press for charity from branches of the firm located outside the stricken area. Franchised monopolies are the most vulnerable if they fail to be charitable; 'profiteering' at the expense of the victims could cause the firm's franchise to be revoked. The executives can be regarded as part of a 'privileged group' whose welfare is tied in a very intimate way to that of the community as a whole. As a result we often observe post-disaster charity not only by large firms, but the executives are frequently prominent in leading the relief bureaucracy. Only if a firm had been suffering chronic losses and planned to go out of business would it have no self-interest in appearing charitable. In this case, the disaster, by causing an 'instant amortization' of the firm's local assets only hastens its departure from the stricken region. However, in most cases, large firms will give more charity than small because of their probable greater financial capacity, their greater identifiability and because they possess more goodwill, than smaller firms.[23] But in cases of both large and small firms, business

---

[22] Two examples will suffice. The Southern Pacific Company was San Francisco's largest benefactor following the 1906 disaster (Douty, ch. 4). In Alaska in 1964, the Safeway supermarket chain did not increase the prices charged for staple food items, and in a few cases lowered some of them, despite the existence of shortages (Dacy and Kunreuther, pp. 113–18).

[23] It might even be conjectured that large firms will give relatively more charity than small firms (as a percentage of their tangible assets); however, this is far from

philanthropy can be explained entirely without reference to altruistic motivations.

Firms that do not have a major commercial interest in the survival of the stricken area are not, in general, important post-disaster donors. Again, this proposition could be tested empirically. Also, the *typical* individual located outside the disaster zone cannot be expected to give charity. Yet disasters do frequently result in a flood of uncoordinated contributions of cash and goods in kinds from outside individuals. Some of this charity is undoubtedly given by persons who have relatives or good friends living within the disaster zone.[24] But it cannot be assumed that this accounts for all outside private charity. Some post-disaster philanthropy can be regarded as evidence of pure altruism, motivated by a vague feeling of cultural identification with the victims, and perhaps by the knowledge that their gifts will be put to a use that the donors believe is appropriate.[25] However, only a small portion of the persons residing outside the disaster area do give charity and the size of their individual gifts is usually quite small relative to the donor's assets. It is quite possible that individuals who give post-disaster charity give less than they otherwise would have to other eleemosynary institutions during the relevant time period; i.e. a disaster may have the effect of shaping the timing and form of philanthropy by nonresidents, but not its total amount. Regardless of the empirical validity of this last statement (which would be very difficult to test), the existence of outside charity is extremely important in enabling the stricken community to hold together during an emergency

---

certain. In the absence of perfect knowledge, 'unreasonable' demands could be made on relatively weak firms that happened to be readily identifiable to a large segment of the victims. The determination of the optimal amount of charity (defined here as the equating at the margin the benefit to the firm in the form of a higher level of goodwill than would otherwise be realized in the post-disaster period with the cost of the goods or revenue donated) is not totally within the donor's range of discretion. Under conditions of uncertainty, the optimal amount of charity could vary for firms of equal financial capacity, raising the possibility that small firms could be called on to give relatively more charity than large firms.

[24] Evidence that there are personal ties between outside residents and the victims is the existence of the 'convergence' problem, where communications and other links to the outside world become overloaded. This problem has been noted frequently in sociological investigations. See Charles Fritz and J. H. Mathewson, *Convergence Behavior* (Washington, D.C., 1957).

[25] The bulk of outside charity to victims comes from individuals sharing the same nationality, implying the importance of cultural identification.

period. Whilst individual outside donations are usually very small, in the aggregate they often bulk very large relative to the immediate needs of the victims.

Despite the regularity of the outpouring of private outside post-disaster charity, federal aid has become increasingly important in more recent disasters. Much of this aid is intended to facilitate private reconstruction, but some emergency aid is extended through the Office of Civil Defense and other agencies. Most of the emergency aid is designed to help maintain order, to assist in the administration of private charity, and in population evacuation if it is required. But the fundamental purpose appears to be improvement of the post-disaster environment. These efforts apparently have the approval and support of the federal government's constituency. There is no effective way that a private individual living outside the disaster zone can organize an order-keeping force; nor is there any incentive for him to try to do so, as he would share the 'benefits' of the order-keeping machinery whether or not he bears any of its costs. The federal government has order-keeping machinery at its disposal and can effectively carry out the wishes of its constituents in this regard.

Delayed federal aid which is aimed at facilitating private reconstruction is offered because the stricken community has suffered a net loss of wealth for which it is not fully compensated by private charity and insurance payments. If the loss of wealth exceeds the magnitude of private transfer payments (including insurance) from external sources, there may be concern that the pre-disaster institutional environment cannot be restored. Compassionate feelings for the victims may also have been stirred. As with emergency aid, the incentive for a private individual to extend reconstruction aid is very weak because of an absence of a connection between the cost outlays of the donor and the benefits received. Hence there is a rationale for federal aid.[26]

The argument of this paper refers only to disasters from 'external'

---

[26] Current [U.S.] federal policy towards disasters has been devastatingly criticized by Dacy and Kunreuther, ch. 9–12; also Kunreuther. The critique is restricted to the method of providing reconstruction aid, which is seen as leading to inequitable treatment of the victims. His point is only to show that some federal aid will be offered following any well-publicized disaster, regardless of the institutional framework for providing that aid. Admittedly, the offer of emergency aid is more certain than of reconstruction aid.

causes. It does not directly apply to disasters such as civil disorders. In principle, our analysis could be developed so as to apply to post-riot behaviour as well as post-earthquake. However, this development would require more conceptual apparatus than we have presented here.

III. A CONCLUDING NOTE

It perhaps is not too surprising that societies that experience a severe externally derived source of stress should exhibit an intensified degree of community feeling. Mere threats of destruction by an external agent, such as a threat of aggression by a foreign power, often appear to draw societies more closely together. The conditions for increased community or national solidarity as a result of a threat are that the threat be credible to the populace and that there be an effective consensual agreement concerning the preservation of pre-existing law and custom. If or when such a threat materializes, consensual agreement operates to generate superficially selfless actions. The interests of the community and the individual's own self interests are both served by individual philanthropy.

FURTHER READING

DEMSETZ, H., 'Toward a Theory of Property Rights', *Amer. Econ. Rev. Proc.*, vol. 57 (May 1967), pp. 347–59.

IKLE, F. C., *The Social Impact of Bomb Destruction* (Norman, Okla., 1958).

KUNREUTHER, H., 'The Case for Comprehensive Disaster Insurance', *J. Law Econ.*, vol. 11 (Apr. 1968), pp. 133–68.

LEIBENSTEIN, H., 'Bandwagon, Snob and Veblen Effects in the Theory of Consumer's Demand', *Quart. J. Econ.*, vol. 64 (May 1950), pp. 183–207.

WALLACE, A. F. C., *Tornado in Worcester* (Washington, D.C., 1954).

Indexes

Index of Subjects

Index of Authors